INSIDE REHAB

INSIDE REHAB

The Surprising Truth About Addiction Treatment—
and How to Get Help That Works

ANNE M. FLETCHER

VIKING

VIKING
Published by the Penguin Group
Penguin Group (USA) Inc., 375 Hudson Street,
New York, New York 10014, U.S.A. • Penguin Group (Canada), 90 Eglinton Avenue East, Suite 700, Toronto, Ontario, Canada M4P 2Y3 (a division of Pearson Penguin Canada Inc.) • Penguin Books Ltd, 80 Strand, London WC2R 0RL, England • Penguin Ireland, 25 St. Stephen's Green, Dublin 2, Ireland (a division of Penguin Books Ltd) • Penguin Group (Australia), 707 Collins Street, Melbourne, Victoria 3008, Australia (a division of Pearson Australia Group Pty Ltd) • Penguin Books India Pvt Ltd, 11 Community Centre, Panchsheel Park, New Delhi—110 017, India • Penguin Group (NZ), 67 Apollo Drive, Rosedale, Auckland 0632, New Zealand (a division of Pearson New Zealand Ltd) • Penguin Books, Rosebank Office Park, 181 Jan Smuts Avenue, Parktown North 2193, South Africa • Penguin China, B7 Jaiming Center, 27 East Third Ring Road North, Chaoyang District, Beijing 100020, China

Penguin Books Ltd, Registered Offices: 80 Strand, London WC2R 0RL, England

First published in 2013 by Viking Penguin, a member of Penguin Group (USA) Inc.

10   9   8   7   6   5   4   3   2   1

LIBRARY OF CONGRESS CATALOGING-IN-PUBLICATION DATA
Fletcher, Anne M.
  Inside rehab : the surprising truth about addiction treatment : and how to get help that works /
Anne M. Fletcher.
    pages   cm
  Includes bibliographical references and index.
  ISBN 978-0-670-02522-0
  1. Addicts—Rehabilitation.   2. Substance abuse—Treatment.   I. Title.
  RC564.F54 2013
  362.29—dc23
  2012037030

Printed in the United States of America

ALWAYS LEARNING   **PEARSON**

For all of the people who so selflessly contribute to my books

And in memory of Dr. Alan Marlatt, who encouraged and inspired me to write about addiction and recovery

Just because it is written in stone it does not mean it cannot change.

—*On a stone outside a rehab dormitory*

NOTE TO READERS

The ideas, procedures, and suggestions contained in *Inside Rehab* are not intended to be a substitute for consulting with a physician, mental health professional, and/or credentialed substance use disorder treatment professional in dealing with any kind of drug or alcohol problem or any underlying psychiatric conditions, such as depression or anxiety. Neither the publisher nor the author is engaged in rendering professional advice or services to the individual. Anyone who has been overusing alcohol or drugs consistently should consult a physician and/or consider going to a professional detoxification unit or a hospital emergency department before giving up drugs or alcohol completely. Neither the author nor the publisher shall be liable or responsible for any harm, loss, or damage allegedly arising from any information or suggestion in this book or omitted from this book.

The names and, in some cases, identifying details of people who shared their stories about their drug and alcohol problems have been changed. Some remarks that are in quotations were edited slightly for clarity. Most of the information in this book was gathered over the course of the years 2009–12, and some information, such as any particular facility's rehab policies and procedures, may have changed since that time. While an effort was made to provide a comprehensive picture of the nature of and possibilities for substance use disorder treatment, this book does not cover every aspect of treatment or every type of program.

Readers should bear in mind that some programs operate multiple sites and that statements about a particular facility may not apply to other facilities in the same program. The rehab stories collected for this book involve many more than those from programs the author visited. Information about programs other than those the author visited is largely taken from interviews with clients who attended those programs and/or staff members who are currently or were previously employed at such programs. The experiences of any one person may or may not be representative of the experiences of others who attended the same facility. Praise or criticism of one aspect of a program should not be construed as a representative view of the entire program.

Because of the possibility of post-publication developments in behavioral, mental health, or medical sciences, readers are encouraged to confirm the information in this book with other reliable sources. Neither the publisher nor the author vouches for the value, merit, or accuracy of any of the outside resources (books, articles, Web sites, etc.) mentioned in *Inside Rehab,* nor are they responsible for the use of any information or advice found in any of these outside resources. For the resources discussed in this book, the author has made every effort to provide accurate telephone numbers and Internet addresses at the time of publication, but neither the publisher nor the author assumes any responsibility for errors or for changes that occur after publication.

CONTENTS

INSIDE REHAB

WHAT'S WRONG WITH ADDICTION TREATMENT? WHAT WILL HELP?

AN INTRODUCTION TO *INSIDE REHAB*

nside Rehab is filled with disturbing accounts of seriously addicted people getting very limited care at exhaustive costs and with uncertain results—but in my experience, they are accurate accounts. Indeed, my research on addiction treatment programs suggests that this discouraging picture may even underestimate the conceptual and procedural problems in this very distressed but essential treatment system. But how did it get this bad?

There has never been a question that alcohol and other drug addictions are immense problems for society. The question instead was always, Just what kind of a problem is addiction—and who should manage it? Because the stereotypical "drunk" or "junkie" was often seen as violent, a liar, a thief, and in general disruptive of family and social life—problems that were viewed as moral or lifestyle failings—addiction was addressed by laws, social sanctions, and moral teachings. But when unparalleled numbers of America's veterans returned from service with drug and alcohol problems after the Vietnam War, it became politically untenable simply to punish these young addicts. In the early 1970s a national addiction treatment system was called for. Few physicians or nurses knew much about addiction medicine—there was very little to know. Almost no scientific research on the origins of alcohol or other drug addiction was available upon which to develop treatment. Instead, the treatments were derived from the earnest efforts and experiential wisdom of those who had overcome their *own* addictions and were willing to help others. The Minnesota model of residential care that had grown out of do-it-yourself treatments offered at "Hazel-den" (the name of the farm property on which Hazelden's main campus now stands) several decades earlier proliferated at rehabs across the country, and "therapeutic communities" employing ex-addict counselors grew in number.

Perhaps most significant, the addiction treatment system was purposely designed as a segregated system—separated financially (through funding largely with government block grant dollars, not medical insurance), culturally, and often physically from the rest of general health care. (The Veterans Administration was an important exception because its general health care, addiction treatment, and mental health care have long been integrated.) That segregated system grew into today's network of over thirteen thousand addiction "programs"—still largely isolated from the rest of medicine and health care; still largely financed by separate protected dollars; and still largely distinct in terms of the types of interventions applied and the professional providers involved. Like other segregated systems, it is loaded with stigma. Few addicted individuals (about 10 percent) are willing to enter care. Drop-out rates are high. And among treatment completers, one-year relapse rates are 40 to 60 percent. The public deserves more and our society desperately needs reliably effective care.

Addiction has not been the only segregated illness, however. Many "conditions," including depression, polio, and tuberculosis, were not recognized as medical illnesses and have only recently been taught in most medical schools and treated by physicians. They were seen as "lifestyle problems" and care was typically provided by concerned, committed individuals or institutions not well connected to mainstream health care. Tuberculosis provides an instructive case. While TB had long been considered a serious threat to the health and safety of most societies, science had not developed to the point where it could explain the causes or the course of the illness. Those with "consumption" were offered the treatments of fresh air, nutritious food, and relaxation in sanitaria under the view that this "lifestyle problem" would benefit from those healthy conditions. By 1935 there were more than fifteen thousand sanitaria in the United States. In fact, this type of care—though based upon inaccurate conceptions of the disease—often produced recovery, particularly among those who were otherwise healthy and in whom illness was detected early. Thus it was seventeen years before TB was recognized and treated by many traditional physicians and health-care facilities as a bacterial disease, and labeled as such in medical textbooks. The parallels with contemporary addiction treatment are hard to ignore.

Thanks to four decades of NIH-sponsored research there is a new foundation for the treatment of addiction. This science now suggests that addiction is best considered a chronic illness. As in other chronic illnesses, a still incompletely understood combination of genetic and environmental risk factors combined with risky personal behaviors—particularly repeated drug use itself—produce the chronic illness of addiction. Most scientists agree that the genetic, brain, and behavioral changes associated with addiction do not appear to be completely reversible—like other chronic illnesses, most cases of severe addiction can be managed, but not cured, with continuing care. But as revealed in Anne Fletcher's research in *Inside Rehab*, continuing care according to a chronic care model is very hard to find—and there are still few insurance plans that support such evidence-based treatment.

This divide between what we know about the genesis and development of addiction, and how we insure, treat, and evaluate it cannot last. As was the case in tuberculosis treatment, addiction science has advanced, and both the public and policy makers are becoming more informed and aware. Ultimately, the insurance and treatment systems will meet the new scientific understanding and the new public demand. Addiction treatments in the near future will build upon the emerging science and will borrow from advances in disease management practices, team treatment methods, tailored treatment planning, and continuous patient monitoring that are now common in the management of other chronic illnesses. Group counseling, individual counseling (hopefully, more of it than we see now), and recovery support groups will likely remain key elements of future addiction treatment because they are economical and effective methods for changing and maintaining a recovery lifestyle. But these good old-fashioned elements of addiction treatment are likely to merge with greater use of currently approved and to-be-developed medications, remote telemonitoring of blood drug and alcohol levels, continuous patient contact outside of clinic settings, and marital and family therapy, as well as team-based disease management to foster treatment adherence and forestall relapse. And thanks to health-care reform legislation, the great majority of addiction treatment—as well as prevention and early intervention for less severe substance use disorders—is expected to be reimbursed by health-care insurance. As in the case of treatments for polio, depression, and tuberculosis, addiction treatment will become integrated into conventional medical and nursing education and into mainstream health care.

In closing I admit that it was personally difficult for me to read about the problems within this distressed field that Anne Fletcher has documented so carefully in *Inside Rehab*. I have made my income and professional identity from work in the addiction treatment field. More important, I owe the lives of several of my family members to very fine addiction treatment. My deepest regrets to this day are that even as an expert in this field, I was not able to get my brother or son into the kind of treatment that could have saved their lives. But as you will see as you read *Inside Rehab,* addiction treatment must change and it *can* change. My hope is that the important information provided in this book promotes public demand for the kind of effective addiction treatment that now is well within reach.

A. Thomas McLellan, PhD, CEO and Cofounder,
Treatment Research Institute, Philadelphia

CHAPTER ONE

REHAB NATION

THE QUESTIONS AND THE ISSUES

Lindsay and Britney have been there, along with Robin Williams, Robert Downey Jr., Charlie Sheen, Eminem, a former Miss USA, Mel Gibson, Congressman Patrick Kennedy . . . and the list goes on. Rehab seems to be the place where celebrities and politicians go when they mess up, not only to "get clean" from whatever addiction ails them but, sometimes, in an attempt to change their public personas from ne'er-do-wells to helpless victims.

Media and public interest in addiction, drugs, and rehab is fervent, fueled by accounts of famous people yo-yoing in and out of celebrity programs, along with sensational stories of untimely deaths caused by prescription drug abuse, a number of which, sadly, took place during the writing of this book. That, and the popularity of reality shows on addiction interventions and "celebrity rehab" all indicate that a lot of people want to know what really goes on inside addiction treatment programs— sometimes in a voyeuristic way, but more often for compelling personal reasons.

It seems to be accepted as fact that when someone is struggling with addiction, we should simply send him or her away to a place to "get fixed" by a team of experts. But does the view of addiction treatment we get from TV shows and movies provide an accurate picture of what happens when most people go in for help? Is the rehab to which wealthy and famous people flock much like the rehab available to the general public? And are most people with serious addictions likely to "get fixed" from a month-long stint in rehab? As *Inside Rehab* will demonstrate, the answer to all three questions is a resounding No.

—————

Why *Inside Rehab*?

My desire to write a book on rehab was kindled by a shocking front-page story titled "The Treatment Myth" that ran in the *Minneapolis Star Tribune* shortly after I'd moved to Minnesota from the East Coast in 1993. As someone who had personally struggled with a drinking problem, I was immediately drawn to the subheadings of the four-page feature: "Chemical dependency programs exaggerate their success rates"; "Treatment has little scientific support"; "For many clients it's a revolving door"; "Even an elite treatment program has many failures." As I found in researching this book, the current treatment system continues to suffer from many of the issues that were documented in this article.

I recall thinking at the time that at some point I'd like to write a book about all of this, and I did go on to write a book that challenged many myths about overcoming addiction: *Sober for Good: New Solutions for Drinking Problems—Advice from Those Who Have Succeeded* (Houghton Mifflin, 2001). It is about the many different ways people achieve long-term sobriety and personal guidance for recovery rather than rehab for addiction.

After the publication of *Sober for Good*, my interest in drug and alcohol rehab grew as I got to know A. Thomas McLellan, PhD, cofounder of the Treatment Research Institute (TRI), a group dedicated to conducting studies to evaluate what works in addiction treatment, and why. I'd periodically call him to find out about developments in the field. Much of what he shared was appalling. "If you've seen one rehab, you've basically seen all of them. Yes, there are exceptions, but of the many thousands of treatment programs out there, most use exactly the same kind of treatment you would have received in 1950, not modern scientific approaches. Counselor training is impoverished, and staff and director turnover in these programs is higher than in fast-food restaurants." Of the rehab consumer, Dr. McLellan said, "When it comes to picking a rehab, most people ask more questions before buying a vacuum." In 2009, McLellan became deputy director of the Office of National Drug Control Policy, or what's commonly known as the "deputy drug czar" for the Obama administration, but has since returned to be president and CEO of TRI.

Early in this book's writing, I spoke with the late renowned Alan Marlatt, PhD, former director of the Addictive Behaviors Research Center at the University of Washington in Seattle. Our conversation made me realize that it's not unusual for addiction experts themselves to be in the dark about what happens inside the walls of treatment centers. Amid the media frenzy over one of Lindsay Lohan's early trips to rehab, *People* magazine interviewed Marlatt, who later told me, "This reporter called, and one of the first questions he asked me was, 'How can we find out what goes on inside these places?'" The truth is that even Dr. Marlatt didn't know.

When people I cared about were struggling with addictions, I'd also faced frustrations in seeking treatment that was effective, affordable, and timely. Most people simply know little or nothing about the extensive range of rehab and recovery options, the uneven quality across treatment programs, and the big-picture problems within the addiction treatment infrastructure in the United States.

Through visits to programs, stories of people who went to rehab, and interviews with experts, *Inside Rehab* explores the strengths, weaknesses, and current state of the addiction treatment industry in the United States. More specifically, the goals of the book are:

- To give consumers a realistic picture of what goes on when a person goes to residential or outpatient rehab
- To uncover myths and facts about addiction treatment in the United States
- To address problems and issues faced by people in rehab and by the treatment industry itself
- To provide a guide to different types of treatment and ways to recover
- To inform consumers about science-based practices that *should* form the basis of addiction treatment and to spotlight programs and professionals using those practices
- To provide guidance for finding quality treatment

GETTING THE INSIDE STORY

To get a firsthand picture of what really goes on inside rehab, I visited fifteen addiction programs—from so-called celebrity rehabs to the outpatient options available to most people—in different parts of the country. "Rehab" usually refers to residential programs in which the traditional stay is about a month (unlike outpatient treatment, where people typically go multiple times a week to group sessions lasting several hours during the day or evening). For the purposes of the book, I use the word "rehab" to describe all types of addiction programs. After all, the goal, regardless of where you go, is rehabilitation from drug and/or alcohol problems. (For more on the different types of rehabs, see chapter 2.)

At most of these programs, I was able to get a close-up view of what treatment is like by attending group counseling sessions, sitting in on individual client* appointments with counselors, and/or participating in activities such as relaxation exercises. In so doing, I promised to protect the privacy of clients. My visits focused on primary or "phase one" care, which refers to the first stage of treatment, typically about a month at a residential rehab and variable but often longer at an outpatient program. (Extended and continuing care refer to subsequent phases of treatment, and are discussed in chapter 9.) My goal from the visits was to get an overall, day in, day out picture of what went on in each setting—to see for myself what different types of programs are like, to find out if things I'd heard were true, and to answer my many questions.

I also spent countless hours reading questionnaires completed by and interviewing more than one hundred current or past program administrators, staff members, and other clinicians from various programs and practices across the country, many at the places I visited. I read scientific studies on what works best for recovery and frequently queried leading experts in the field, particularly those who study addiction treatment to determine what's effective and what's not.

I realized, however, that the best way to get an accurate picture of what

---

* Some rehabs refer to their participants as patients, while others call them clients. In this book, I simply use *clients*.

goes on inside rehab was to interview people who had recently gone through treatment themselves or were currently going through it, again making it clear that any information they gave me would be rendered anonymous. Hence, my decision to collect more than one hundred stories* from clients and/or their family members, many of whom I met at the programs I visited, and include a subset of individuals who recovered from drug and alcohol problems without going to rehab. Some people came my way by word of mouth or through recruitment notices I sent to addiction professionals or posted on e-mail lists. I had the opportunity to follow quite a few individuals over time, sometimes for several years and also periodically as they struggled through relapses and went to multiple programs. Knowing that it's hard to admit a setback, I give them credit here both for staying in touch with me and working so hard on their sobriety.

Some of their rehab stories are disturbing while others are inspiring. All provide an honest and critical look at addiction treatment in the United States. Their accounts illustrate serious issues facing individuals in rehab *and* the treatment industry today, yet they also highlight some of the innovative approaches used by selected programs across the country. Perhaps most important, *Inside Rehab* gives a voice to people who have been there, whether their treatment experiences were good or bad. Those who had a positive outcome eagerly showed that they wanted to reach out and share the great news, often in the hope that others would benefit from their experiences. Those who had a negative time of it often felt beaten down and as though they had nowhere to turn; as a form of catharsis, and to spare others from a similar misfortune, they welcomed the chance to divulge what had happened to them.

WHO OPENED THEIR DOORS

In selecting rehabs I went coast to coast, making an effort to visit a wide range of programs, some famous for the celebrities who've walked through

---

* Because programs change over time, I made an effort to recruit participants whose most recent treatment experiences occurred within the past three to five years. The majority of the research for the book was conducted in 2009 and 2010.

their doors and others better known for working with individuals on public assistance. It turns out that my home state of Minnesota is renowned for its multiplicity of addiction facilities—from traditional twelve-step-based residential and outpatient programs representative of those across the country to unique programs that serve certain subgroups of people. So I rounded out my visits by also visiting a number of places close to home.

I wondered if at high-end rehabs I'd find posh, indulgent vacation-like settings where clients were having massages and getting their nails done. I also was curious about whether I'd observe what had been described to me as harsh, in-your-face approaches designed to break down addicts and alcoholics. In reality, I came across neither one. Contrary to the notion that high-end rehabs are more like resorts than places that heal, even at the most expensive ones I witnessed no kid-glove handling, no fancy "spa" cuisine (and I ate plenty of patient fare), and saw no luxurious bedrooms—in fact, some of them were quite basic, even dormitory-like. Two high-end places only provided chair massages, and at one that's been called a celebrity rehab, I saw young men getting haircuts while sitting in a straight-backed chair—which reminded me of when I used to trim my kids' hair in my own kitchen.

And although I sometimes questioned the approaches used in treatment, I saw almost none of the old-school, confrontational strategies common in the past. However, I was told about some more recent, rather demeaning experiences people had had at certain programs I didn't visit.

What astounded me most in my travels was the number of places that opened their doors to me and how open they were, some having prepared elaborate schedules for my stay. Following my visits, many helped me contact clients for anonymous interviews for the book. For a complete list of programs I visited, please see The *Inside Rehab* Tour on pages 31–42.

WHAT'S AN ALCOHOLIC OR AN ADDICT?

In rehab parlance, if I were in a traditional residential program, I'd no doubt introduce myself this way many times each day: "I'm Anne, and

I'm an alcoholic" (or "an addict"). So would my fellow group members at the opening of every group session. One day, at one of the residential rehabs, I heard women in the same unit, all of whom knew one another, introduce themselves this way many times. Someone forgot to do this at one point, and a fellow client who was leading the group said, in a rather confrontational way, "What *are* you?" as if everyone needed to be reminded, and that the label somehow defined the person.

Personally, I don't care for the words "alcoholic" and "addict" because, in my opinion, both labels come with a lot of stigmatizing baggage. (For more on this, see "What's in a Name?" in chapter 7.) I'd rather ask, "What does it mean to be a person who's addicted to alcohol and/or drugs?" (In this book, alcohol and illicitly used drugs are sometimes collectively referred to as "chemicals" or "substances"; and alcohol is a drug, too.) The word "addiction" comes from a Roman law having to do with "surrender to a master." When she first contacted me, Shari P. shared what it was like to lose control to her "master" as follows: "I come from a good family and even managed to attend a university, although I wasn't able to graduate because the drugs became too important. My life has been a never-ending cycle of chaos in which heroin is the central cause. The sheer amount of time spent finding, getting, and using the drug is exhausting. You feel like the biggest loser on earth but you just do it over and over and over again. I am desperate for change."

The definitions that professionals typically use to diagnose someone with alcohol and drug use disorders are determined by a guidebook called the *Diagnostic and Statistical Manual of Mental Disorders (DSM)*. The DSM edition that was in use for many years and was just about to be retired as *Inside Rehab* was being written used the term "dependence" to describe what most people think of as addiction. ("Abuse" is another category, often used to describe less serious drug and alcohol problems.) However, it is expected that the new edition—the DSM-5, due for release in May of 2013—will do away with the terms "dependence" and "abuse" and instead use the term "substance use disorder" and employ subcategories such as "alcohol use disorder," "cocaine use disorder," and so on. The list of eleven possible defining characteristics of a substance use disorder includes failure to meet work, social, or family obligations because of substance use; continued use despite persistent negative consequences; tolerance (needing more chemical to get the desired effect); regularly taking a substance in larger amounts or over a longer time than intended; devoting a lot of time to getting, using, or recovering from the effects of a substance; withdrawal (physical or mental symptoms if the drug is abruptly stopped); craving; and a number of others. People with two to three of the characteristics would be considered to have a mild substance use disorder, while those with four to five of them would be in the moderate category. Neither of these categories would be considered to be addiction. A person who meets six of the criteria, however, would be considered to have a severe substance use disorder or what most people would term an addiction.*

It's important to note, however, that tolerance to and withdrawal from some medications—such as certain painkillers, antidepressants, and antianxiety medications—can occur even when these medications are taken at appropriately prescribed doses, without a user having a substance use disorder. Many individuals use these drugs without any evidence of abuse or aberrant behavior.

Alcohol and drugs produce their pleasurable, euphoric effects by directly or indirectly targeting what's known as the brain's reward system, flooding it with a neurotransmitter or chemical messenger called dopamine and motivating use again and again. With repeated use, dopamine's impact on the reward system in the brain can become abnormally lowered, so that even heavier and more frequent use results in less pleasure or "high." Other brain systems such as the stress response system become overactive and result in unpleasant feelings such as anxiety and "the blahs." As addiction worsens, afflicted people are driven to repeated use more in order to relieve these unpleasant feelings than to seek pleasure. In other words, they use to feel "normal" or "not sick" more than to get high. Addictive use eventually leads to profound changes in the brain and its memory systems such that reminders of

---

* As *Inside Rehab* went to press, the DSM-5 was not completely finalized.

drug or alcohol use—for instance, seeing a needle or a martini glass—can trigger cravings, even after many years of abstinence. In short, chronic heavy drug and alcohol use can alter the brain's structure and function, resulting in changes that last long after someone stops using, and may explain why relapses can occur after prolonged periods of abstinence.

Certainly, some people are more prone to addiction than others, depending on their genetic background. Genetic factors are believed to account for between 40 and 60 percent of a person's vulnerability to addiction. Use of drugs and alcohol at an early age also increases the odds of addiction, as does having a history of childhood trauma, including physical or sexual abuse and serious neglect. Plus, living, working, or going to school in places where alcohol and drug use is common increases the likelihood of addiction. The bottom line is that there's a biological as well as an environmental component to becoming addicted to drugs and alcohol, and the role that each plays varies from person to person.

THE QUESTIONS

The stories of clients and interviews with treatment professionals, as well as visits to treatment facilities, helped me find the answers to questions like these:

- What determines whether someone should go to rehab in the first place?
- How do most people choose a rehab? Is there much variation from one rehab to the next?
- How much money do people spend on rehab? What percentage is typically covered by health insurance—and what if you don't have health insurance?
- Does more expensive treatment mean better treatment?
- Who are the professionals who work with patients in rehab, and how are they trained?

- What do people actually do in rehab? How do they fill their time, and what do they do on weekends?
- If someone is struggling with another psychological problem, such as depression, can he or she expect to get help with that at rehab? Should one problem be tackled before the other is treated?
- Are family members usually included in treatment? What does that entail?
- How much of a say do clients have in what goes on in their rehab experience?
- What happens if someone has a slip with drugs or alcohol while in rehab?
- What happens after you get out of rehab? What occurs next for both the client and his or her family members?
- How do you know if a program is effective?

A QUESTION OF HONESTY

Have you ever heard this joke?

Q: How do you know when an addict is lying?

A: When his lips are moving.

Quite frankly, I find it offensive. It stems from the widespread notion, often promulgated in addiction treatment itself, that virtually all people with alcohol or drug problems are dishonest. Even a nationally known expert in the field included "they're all liars" in his definition of an addict when talking with me. Emily E. said that at a halfway house she attended, "They told us we're addicts and we lie and can't be trusted. It made you feel like crap." And at one outpatient group I visited, where the counselor seemed to have a good overall rapport with her clients, she said to them with a smirk, "The one thing we know about alcoholics and addicts is that you're always one hundred percent honest." It's hard to imagine that this is therapeutic, but is her implication accurate?

I had to think this through, realizing that some people might question the veracity of the stories I heard, particularly those from people who shared negative treatment experiences. There's no question that in most cases I was only getting one side of the story. For a variety of reasons, it would have been very difficult to try to confirm the client's version by going to the treatment programs for their views of what had happened. Not only would this have violated the confidentiality of the clients who shared personal information with me, but there's no way of knowing if the rehabs would have given me a balanced view either. Indeed, psychologist Tom Horvath, PhD, director of Practical Recovery, a California program I visited, said, "Self-deception is a process any of us can develop. It can occur in providers just as easily as in clients."

What does the research reveal about whether you can trust the reports of people with addictions? In response to this question, respected addiction experts Mark Sobell, PhD, and Linda Sobell, PhD, psychologists at Nova Southeastern University in Florida, summed up their findings from extensive research on this topic: "The bottom line is that if people believe what they are telling you will be confidential—particularly that it will not incur adverse consequences—and they are asked in a clinical or research context, then what they say tends to be reliable and valid. (This all holds if the person has no substances in their system at the time of the inquiry.) But people are not stupid—if telling the truth about using drugs or drinking to a significant other, probation officer, schoolteacher, or work supervisor is going to bring trouble, why not lie and avoid the negative consequences? In short, if people have no reason to lie to you, the evidence suggests they will be truthful."

Certainly, the people I interviewed had no reason to be threatened by participating in my book anonymously. Still, when tackling a subject like this, there's bound to be some distortion from the client's perspective, at least part of the time, even if it's just the result of faded memories. To get another perspective on some of the stories, I did ask certain individuals to sign a release form that allowed me to talk with their counselors, therapists, and/or family members. In some other cases, I talked with other people who'd been to the same treatment program around the same time period.

However, so many of the same issues were raised—both by clients and professionals—so often and with so much similarity, that it's difficult not to believe them. And many of the negative impressions shared with me were representative of problems consistently reported by experts who have studied the field.

MYTHS UNCOVERED IN *INSIDE REHAB*

As I interviewed person after person who'd been through treatment, talked with staff members, queried experts, and read studies on addiction treatment, the following myths became apparent. These will be explored in greater depth throughout the book:

MYTH: To recover from addictions, most people need to go to rehab.

FACTS: While the knee-jerk reaction when someone has a drug or alcohol problem is "Get thee to rehab!" the truth is that most people recover (1) completely on their own, (2) by attending self-help groups, and/or (3) by seeing a counselor or therapist individually. (Chapter 5 takes a look at who belongs in rehab and who doesn't.)

MYTH: Most people who go to addiction treatment programs go to overnight residential rehabs.

FACT: Of the more than two and a half million people who go to a treatment program each year, the vast majority do not "go away to rehab." After numerous studies showed no difference in how people fared after going to residential versus outpatient programs, insurers and other funding sources drastically cut back on paying for residential rehab. Today, various forms of outpatient help comprise more addiction treatment experiences in the United States than residential stays.

MYTH: Thirty days is long enough to "fix" most people with addictions.

FACTS: The idea that someone goes away to a thirty-day rehab and comes home a new person is naïve. Rather, there's a growing view that people with serious substance use disorders commonly require care for months or even years, just as they would for other chronic medical conditions, such as diabetes. Unfortunately, the length of treatment often depends less on a person's needs and more on financial coverage limits imposed by health insurers, and/or the patient's ability to pay. The short-term-fix mentality partially explains why so many people go back to their old habits. The majority who complete treatment start using alcohol or drugs again within a year, and at least half do so within thirty days after leaving rehab.

MYTH: Group counseling is the best way to treat addictions.

FACT: While group counseling is the staple approach in the vast majority of programs, there's little evidence that the type of group counseling used at most of them is the best way to treat addictions. On the other hand, individual counseling, which has been found to be helpful, is used infrequently at most programs and may not even exist at others. Zack S., who first went to an outpatient program where there was no individual counseling, told me, "I'm fairly introverted and didn't participate much at all in groups." When I interviewed him, he was still struggling with alcohol and attending a unique program that primarily provides individual counseling. (Chapter 6 has a discussion of group versus individual counseling.)

MYTH: Highly trained professionals provide most of the treatment in addiction programs.

FACTS: Addiction counselors provide most of the treatment at rehabs, and states have widely varying requirements in both educational level and training for a person to become a drug and alcohol counselor. Some states don't require any degree for becoming a credentialed addiction counselor and many require just a high school diploma, general equivalency diploma (GED), or associate's degree, according to a groundbreaking 2012 National Center on Addiction and Substance Abuse at Columbia (CASA Columbia) report on the state of addiction treatment titled "Addiction Medicine: Closing the Gap

Between Science and Practice." Although there's been a movement to professionalize treatment, much counseling still is provided by minimally trained addiction survivors-turned-counselors whose own rehabilitation forms much of the basis for their expertise. And sometimes, when standards are raised for new counselors, old-timers are "grandfathered in" with their existing credentials (or are given a certain amount of time to obtain the new ones), and they may or may not be well qualified. Most of the people I interviewed for *Inside Rehab* were oblivious about the credentials of the people who provided their care. When I asked Ann B. about the counselors at the outpatient program she attended, she responded, "You just assume you're seeing a doctor or that they know what they're talking about." In the state in which she was treated, a licensed addiction counselor was not required to have a college degree. These facts are particularly disturbing given the complexity of substance use disorders and the fact that more than half of people in the general population with addictions suffer from at least one other mental disorder such as depression, anxiety, or bipolar disorder, which also must be treated to optimize their chances of recovery. One woman I interviewed went to a famous celebrity rehab, where she never received any professional psychological counseling for her troubled past. While I was writing the book, she died from a cocaine overdose when dealing with a possible reunion with someone who'd sexually abused her throughout her childhood. (For a discussion about the rehab work force, see "Who's Minding the Store?" on pages 164–65.)

MYTH: The twelve steps of Alcoholics Anonymous (AA) or a similar program, such as Narcotics Anonymous (NA), are essential for recovery.

FACTS: When I wrote *Sober for Good*, more than 90 percent of rehabs in the United States were based on the twelve steps. While the ratio appears to have dropped somewhat, most programs still base their approach on the twelve steps, include a twelve-step component, require twelve-step meeting attendance, and/or hold twelve-step meetings on-site. As was well documented in *Sober for Good*, however, the twelve-step approach isn't for everyone, and many people overcome addictions using other methods. Yet it's hard to find a program that doesn't include the twelve steps, and most people I interviewed were offered no alternatives. When I asked Elizabeth F., who went to a renowned high-end residential rehab, about this, she said, "The only thing they'll talk about is the twelve steps. When I brought up Women for Sobriety [an alternative group to AA], I was met with a blank stare. When I asked about when we'd be getting into other modes, the counselor said, 'We are a twelve-step program.' There was no other literature, discussion, etc. They were fairly adamant that 'this is what we have to offer, and if you want what we have, this is how you get it.'" (See chapter 6 for more about twelve-step programming and information about alternative routes to recovery.)

MYTH: Most addiction programs offer state-of-the-art approaches shown in scientific studies to be effective.

FACTS: Although many say they use them, rehabs commonly fall short on implementing practices that studies show lead to the best outcomes for clients. The 2012 CASA Columbia report mentioned earlier concluded that "the vast majority of people in need of addiction treatment do not receive anything that approximates evidence-based care" and that "only a small fraction of individuals receive interventions or treatment consistent with scientific knowledge about what works." To bring practice in line with the evidence and with the standard of care for other medical conditions, it said, "Nothing short of a significant overhaul in current approaches is required." The report went so far as to raise the question of "whether the insufficient care that patients with addiction usually do receive constitutes a form of medical malpractice," given the prevalence of substance problems, the extensive evidence available on how to identify and address them, and continued failure to do so. When it comes to providing services that address the whole person and thereby improve the chance of success, a 2010 report from the University of Georgia's National Treatment Center Study suggests that fewer than a third of 345 representative private rehabs offered any kind of vocational services, housing or shelter assistance, legal assistance, educational services, or financial counseling. (The full five-hundred-plus-page CASA Columbia report can be found at http://www.casacolumbia.org/templates/NewsRoom.aspx?articleid =678&zoneid=51. For more on the gap between what goes on and what should go on in addiction treatment, see pages 28–31 in this chapter and chapter 4.)

MYTH: If you relapse and go back to rehab, they'll try something new.

FACTS: Rather than being offered a new approach, clients who return to using alcohol or drugs are commonly blamed for "not getting with the program" or not trying hard enough, and often have to "start all over again," even though they've experienced very similar programming many times before. Sometimes, they just were not ready to tackle their addiction and could benefit from more of the same; other times, they need a completely different approach upon returning. Emily E. went to multiple twelve-step-based programs in an effort to get off prescription painkillers (initially prescribed for severe migraines) and heroin. She finally met a counselor-intern who said, "You don't need more treatment, you need to go on methadone." When I interviewed her, Emily had a year of sobriety with the help of a methadone program and its non-twelve-step outpatient program. She concluded, "So many addicts just go to rehab again and again, and the same basic kind of treatment never changes. It's ridiculous." (Chapter 8 addresses the topic of relapse.)

MYTH: Addiction treatment programs have high success rates.

FACTS: "Treatment works" has long been a mantra of the rehab industry, but reliable statistics supporting it are hard to come by. There's a great deal of inconsistency in the quality of care provided across programs and in how success is measured, if it's measured at all. In a *Los Angeles Times* article, University of Texas researcher Scott Walters, PhD, coauthor of a landmark study on treatment success rates, said, "Anybody can make any claim they want and get away with it. . . . It's essentially an unregulated industry." Yale University School of Medicine's Kathleen Carroll, PhD, one of the foremost experts on addiction treatment in the United States, asks, "In what other area of medicine can you go to a place for treatment and not have them be able to give you any idea of their outcome rates or point to the scientific basis for the treatments you might receive? I think if consumers started pushing for information on outcomes, a lot of these places would dramatically change how they deliver and measure treatment." (For more on success rates, see chapter 9.)

MYTH: You shouldn't use drugs to treat a drug addict.

FACTS: Research clearly shows that certain prescription medications help people addicted to drugs and alcohol get sober and stay sober. Yet many rehabs are unfamiliar with them or refuse to use them because of the old-fashioned notion that drugs should not be used to treat an addict—or that they should be used *very* sparingly. In the course of writing *Inside Rehab*, I got to know addiction psychiatrist Mark Willenbring, MD, who had just stepped down from his position as director of the Division of Treatment and Recovery Research at the National Institute on Alcohol Abuse and Alcoholism. In practice as an addiction psychiatrist in Minnesota, he told me, "I've been particularly disturbed by several patients of mine who recently went to a treatment program for opioid addiction, and none of them received maintenance Suboxone. All of them relapsed. This is unconscionable." Sometimes rehabs will use drugs like Suboxone just to "detox" a patient during treatment, but research suggests that most people addicted to opioids* or heroin need to be discharged on "maintenance" doses of such medications or they are

---

* Opioids are natural opiates, which are drugs derived from the opium poppy, and also their synthetic and semisynthetic relatives, including many prescription painkillers.

very likely to relapse. Shari P. told me that one of the rehabs she went to actually gave patients Suboxone and took it away depending on whether their behavior was "good or bad." (See chapter 9 for a discussion of medications for people with drug and alcohol problems.)

MYTH: More money gets you better treatment.

FACT: Not necessarily. Sometimes, programs that treat clients who rely mostly on public funds have counselors with more qualifications and use more state-of-the-science approaches than expensive rehabs. Margaret F., who went twice to both an expensive high-end rehab and a community outpatient program said, "I thought the outpatient program was at least as good as the residential one."

MYTH: Treatment approaches used for adults work for teens, too.

FACTS: According to the nonprofit research institute Drug Strategies, "Treatment experts agree that adolescent programs can't just be adult programs modified for kids"—which is often what happens. And sometimes, kids are put in programs with adults, a practice definitely against professional recommendations. Also, despite minimal research support, the majority of teen programs incorporate AA's twelve steps. What works best for adolescents, according to a plethora of studies, is family-based treatment, something rehabs seldom offer, instead favoring teen group counseling, twelve-step approaches, and family education groups, none of which have been found to be as effective as interventions involving the entire family. (Chapter 7 is devoted to adolescent rehab.)

THE FACTS OF THE MATTER

How many drug and alcohol rehabs are out there and how many people use them? The grand total for 2010 was 13,339 according to the

National Survey of Substance Abuse Treatment Services (N-SSATS), a figure based on a yearly inventory of all known specialty facilities that treat drug and alcohol problems maintained by the federal government's Substance Abuse and Mental Health Services Administration (SAMHSA). (An unknown number of other rehabs exist, probably fewer than a thousand, but they either didn't respond to the survey or were ineligible for participation.) Of the types of care offered at these programs, 81 percent were outpatient, accounting for nine out of ten of all clients in treatment. About a quarter of the programs offered residential (nonhospital) treatment, which accounted for about one out of ten clients in rehab. Hospital inpatient treatment was offered by 6 percent of facilities and only accounted for 1 percent of clients in treatment. (See chapter 2 for the differences in these types of programs.)

Another way that SAMHSA tracks how many people go to addiction treatment programs and where they go for help is through the National Survey on Drug Use and Health (NSDUH), which queries a large nationally representative group of noninstitutionalized U.S. civilians (about 67,500 people), age twelve and older, about drug and alcohol use, problems, and treatment in the past year. Of the 22.1 million individuals (almost 9 percent of the population age twelve or older) who were estimated to have a substance use disorder in the past year, according to the 2010 NSDUH, 2.6 million received help at a specialty facility. Another 2.3 million people went to a self-help group, such as AA, but this is not considered formal treatment. That same year, just over 7 percent of teens (about 1.8 million) age twelve to seventeen were reported to have a substance use disorder but only 138,000 of them went to an addiction treatment program.

The message is that with more than thirteen thousand residential and outpatient rehabs out there and more than twenty-two million adults and teens estimated to have a drug or alcohol problem, only a small minority receive professional help each year. Of those who do, far more go to outpatient programs than to residential programs.

DRUG OF CHOICE

What kinds of substance problems brought the *Inside Rehab* participants to treatment programs? "Drug of choice"—meaning the drug (or drugs) that a person prefers—ran the gamut. For many it was "just alcohol" that took its toll. In fact, alcohol can be a dangerous drug—heavy drinking is the third leading preventable cause of death in the United States. Marijuana was the primary drug problem for others. Some administrators told me things like, "Alcohol is a given" and "alcohol and marijuana are always mainstays," suggesting that most clients had a problem with *at least* those two.

For many people, a combination of drugs wreaks havoc. Steve R. began abusing drugs and alcohol at the age of fourteen and told me, "I've used almost every drug, ending with an addiction to meth. I couldn't get through a day without being high or drunk or both. I was thirty-nine when I was finally busted with a meth lab." When I interviewed him, he had had a successful experience at a Christian rehab, followed by a drug court program.

At high-end programs, the preferred drugs of abuse were alcohol, opioids such as Vicodin, OxyContin, and Percocet, and benzodiazepines, commonly known as "benzos" and included brand-name drugs such as Valium, Klonopin, and Xanax. At one of the programs that serves a low-income population, the most commonly abused drugs were less likely to be pills and benzos and more likely to be crack cocaine, alcohol, and PCP (phencyclidine, which has hallucinogenic effects). Programs that treat teens told me they were seeing abuse of painkillers (often taken from parents), heroin, Adderall (a stimulant drug commonly used to treat attention-deficit/hyperactivity disorder), and inhalants—all in addition to alcohol and marijuana. Rural programs were seeing a resurgence of methamphetamine problems.

At the national level, according to the 2010 National Survey on Drug Use and Health, of those who received help from a facility, about 37 percent said they did so for alcohol use only; 34 percent for illicit drug use only; and 24 percent for both alcohol and illicit drug use. (The numbers don't add up to 100 percent because some people didn't specify whether their treatment was for a drug or an alcohol problem.)

ONE PROGRAM, CONTRASTING EXPERIENCES

As I visited rehabs, I told administrators, "I will no doubt find people who say that your program saved their lives. But others may tell me that your program was wrong or even destructive for them." Indeed, that's what I found. Chantal R. says of one of the most prominent residential treatment programs in the country, "It was one of the best experiences I have ever had. I can't think of one thing that didn't help me. They lectured AA and the importance of it—the tools are so simple to use. I would recommend every person I meet to go there in a heartbeat. It changed my life."

Another woman who went to the same place told me, "While there were some valuable lessons there, I was very unimpressed with most of the counseling and the facilitating of group discussions. What I really got was that the most important thing was AA, reading the Big Book [*Alcoholics Anonymous*, the so-called bible of AA], doing the twelve steps, living your life every day a day at a time, and all the other '-isms' that were thrown around. From day one, it didn't resonate with me, and the day I left I knew that it was not how I was going to live in recovery and be happy about it. I was humbled by the people that I met and the places their addiction had taken them, but there was a lot that I just hated. I can't believe they have the reputation that they do."

One explanation for such contrasting experiences at the same program is that, sometimes, people are simply at different life stages when they enter treatment: one may be more ready to get sober; or a person may have a different or more severe addiction than others. People may go into a facility with dissimilar expectations or levels of experience—perhaps one person has had years of psychotherapy while others have not. Also, one's reaction to a certain program may compare unfavorably to previous treatment. The variable reactions may also stem from differences in personality, religiosity, or education. Sometimes, it's a matter of the counselor the client is assigned or the unit he or she is placed in that colors their experience. And although most of the people I spoke to had been in treatment within a few years of one another, programs can change within a very short period of time, depending on owners, directors, and funding sources. One woman whose son had been to seven different rehabs told me, "The director changes, and the whole place changes."

I found that some of the rehabs I visited became more progressive in the course of the three to four years that I was in contact with them. For instance, a mental health professional called one of the programs "a dinosaur" because she felt it used antiquated approaches. One year later, however, after a change in leadership, she was making referrals to the place.

WHEN TREATMENT ISN'T RIGHT

In some cases, people were hurt by what they'd experienced in treatment. I heard sad tales of repeated visits to rehab with the implication that the client had somehow failed, when it seemed apparent that something about the treatment had very likely failed the individual. Other stories came from people who didn't belong in rehab at all, but were coerced to go. The following is just a sampling of what I heard:

• Will R.'s alcohol abuse was secondary to serious psychological issues left unaddressed by his first rehab, where no individual counseling was provided over the course of residential treatment. When I interviewed him, Will had found a second rehab with highly individualized care that recognized the complexities in his case and realized that his psychological needs should be the primary focus of his treatment rather than substance use itself. This is counter to the philosophy of many treatment programs.

• Carrie G. went to two famous residential rehabs, one of which, she said, "had no medical staff at all for $40,000 a month." (She qualified that by stating that a psychiatrist came in once a week and that "we'd be called out for five minutes for random assessment, no conversation.") When she was in their "detox," she felt her medical needs were not managed appropriately, and she wound up in a hospital emergency room. (For this amount of money, it would be logical to expect that a rehab would provide adequate medical supervision of someone in detox, but she got the impression that they were not "equipped for a hard-core physical addiction.") As far as counseling was concerned, she said, "I never saw a psychologist or social worker. All the therapists were recovered addicts." The only one-on-one counseling she received for her money was a once-a-week session with a woman she believes was a drug and alcohol counselor. The rest of the time, it was group counseling.

• Sam D. overcame his addiction to painkillers through individual counseling despite the fact that a physician he asked for help in tapering off the drugs admonished him, "You'll never do this without rehab." The doctor actually refused to assist him unless he went to a program, even though the young man was already regularly seeing someone who was licensed as both a mental health and addiction counselor. After going through a very painful withdrawal, Sam broke free of the painkillers with the help of weekly sessions with his counselor and had been off them for three years when I interviewed him for this book.

• Wyatt D. said his years-long addiction to heroin took him to thirty-day treatment "probably at least twelve times." He added, "I always went right back to using drugs, sometimes within hours after getting out." Although he never connected with the twelve-step philosophy, he wasn't offered an alternative until he went to the non-twelve-step rehab, where we met. When I asked why he kept going back to the same kinds of places, he said, "I didn't think there was anything else. If I'd bring up any alternatives to the twelve steps, they'd be frowned upon, and I'd be told they wouldn't work."

Dr. Willenbring affirmed what I heard so often: "I keep coming across patient after patient who has been through rehab with either no benefit or [with] negative effects. It's sad. Since coming back and really diving into clinical practice in the private sector, my tolerance for the existing way of doing business is gone. It's atrocious that this is allowed to continue. And the treatment system systematically blames people for not responding. It's as if you want to buy a car and there is only one model available, so you're forced to buy it, often literally forced. Then when the car you're sold doesn't work, you get the blame because you drove it incorrectly."

Dr. Willenbring wasn't alone in his concerns about rehab. Deni Carise, a psychologist PhD who conducted studies in more than two hundred treatment programs as part of her research at the Treatment Research Institute, said as I was planning my visits to outpatient programs, "I've been in programs that show movies like *Die Hard 3* instead of conducting group counseling sessions and they may do urine drug screens. *That's* what they call 'treatment.'" She's also been at programs that make people wait two weeks for their first appointment, essentially to make sure they are "committed," even though they know the research shows that it's important "to strike when people are ready."

THE GAP BETWEEN WHAT GOES ON
AND WHAT SHOULD GO ON

Following her fourth arrest for drunk driving, Beth O. was court-ordered to attend rehab in order to keep her young child. When the judge told her about a new state-licensed program that would allow her to bring her child with her to treatment, she enrolled for four months, and the fee was fully paid for with public funds. She described her experience there as follows: "We listened to people glorify their using, watched movies like *I, Robot*, and did some 'inspiration cards.' We sat downstairs and did nothing a lot. There just wasn't anything there." When I asked about twelve-step treatment work, she said, "*I* asked for stuff to work on" and "*I* started a twelve-step meeting." (Having been in both residential and outpatient treatment before, she had some sense of what treatment normally is like.) She continued, "When they finally gave us things to work on, like for self-esteem, it was basically for kids. They didn't go over any relapse stuff, and that's why I was there. Every now and then we'd have a lesson about something—sometimes, an outside lady would come in and she was good."

Most upsetting to Beth, her assigned addiction counselor was a woman who had married into Beth's family. Not only was it inappropriate for a relative to be counseling a family member, but Beth told me that the counselor disclosed personal information about Beth to her fellow clients. Beth recalled, "She said things about me in group that I felt weren't appropriate and (without my permission) also told one of my relatives things that were going on in treatment." Beth said she complained to an administrator at the facility, but she said nothing was ever done about the situation.

When I asked Beth whether she got anything out of the treatment, she said, "No, but I stayed because I didn't want to lose my daughter." The last month she was there, she was allowed to go home for one day, and when she did, she drank. "They didn't even test me when I came back," she said. (According to the National Institute on Drug Abuse, drug use during treatment should be monitored continuously—this is often done through urine testing.) When treatment ended, Beth said, "They didn't have anything set up, or help you do anything." (As mentioned throughout the book, helping clients negotiate what happens after rehab is critical to their success.) Beth's story is a rather glaring example of the gap between what *should* go on in addiction treatment programs and what *does* go on in some settings.

There's no question that, in recent years, addiction treatment and health care in general have shifted toward providing what's known as evidence-based treatment. Evidence-based practices have undergone scientific evaluation and stand in contrast to approaches that are based on tradition, convention, intuition, belief, or anecdotal evidence. (See chapter 4 for a discussion of what those evidence-based practices are and do to help people with addictions.) There's a gap between what research shows to be effective and what's actually practiced in every area of health care, but as Dr. McLellan pointed out in a recent interview in *Counselor* magazine, "The gap is bigger and wider in the substance use field." Although the rehab industry often boasts that "treatment works," McLellan feels that "treatment—as it is presently practiced and funded—is way oversold." He adds that while we have many evidence-based therapies that can be effective for people with addictions, most treatment programs do not have the resources to implement them. The reality, as rehab expert and historian

William White, MA, points out, is that "addiction treatment in the United States is a smorgasbord of diverse settings, philosophies, and techniques that also vary significantly in their effectiveness." The result? Many people with substance problems fail to receive the care they need. This conclusion was supported in the Institute of Medicine's 2006 publication *Improving the Quality of Health Care for Mental and Substance-use Conditions*, which cited evidence that people with alcohol addiction receive care "consistent with scientific knowledge" only about 10 percent of the time. More recently, the CASA Columbia report mentioned earlier concluded, "In many ways, America's approach to addiction treatment today is similar to the state of medicine in the early 1900s" and referred to the many programs that offer "unproven therapies and little medical supervision." Throughout *Inside Rehab*, recent findings and client experiences will illustrate the large gaps between science and practice in this field. Dr. Willenbring added, "No one wants to say, 'Treatment as we've been doing it probably isn't as effective as we thought, and we need more basic research to really come up with new tools. In the meantime let's do what we can to help suffering people in the most cost effective way and strive to not harm them.' It's a discouraging message and undermines the prevailing push, not to mention the whole structure and funding of the treatment system. But I think we're going to eventually have to face up to this fact and the longer we go on saying that the emperor has elegant clothes on, the worse it will be."

On the bright side, I came across many individuals who had positive rehab experiences. Dorothy D. says of her time at a prominent twelve-step residential program, "It was amazing and I really think that it saved my life. They helped me deal with the grief that I was experiencing as well as controlling my anxiety and ADD [attention deficit disorder]." A man in his early twenties, who was an "older" patient in the adolescent program at another famous twelve-step residential rehab told me, "The staff saved my ass. They have great continuity between addiction treatment and mental health. The psychologist there was a Godsend and one of the kindest people I ever met."

As it explores the gap between "best practice" and reality in addiction treatment, *Inside Rehab* will also provide readers with thoughtful guidance about how to find quality care when it's needed. Through both positive and negative stories of people who have been there, future chapters will examine the issues people face as they search for help with addictions, offer practical solutions, and assist in finding the right fit for those seeking care.

THE *INSIDE REHAB* TOUR

Following are the facilities I went to in order of my visits and my personal impressions of these places:

PRACTICAL RECOVERY. Unique because it doesn't rely on group treatment or the twelve steps of Alcoholics Anonymous, this nontraditional practice in La Jolla, California, allowed me to spend a week at its upscale intensive outpatient program (IOP). Clients who want more of a residential experience can stay in a nearby, supervised sober house from which daily transportation is provided, or they may stay in hotels. In summer 2011 Practical Recovery also opened a residential treatment program, Reunion San Diego, and in 2012, it opened a less expensive men's residential rehab. Housed in a complex of office suites, Practical Recovery's facilities felt more like medical offices than a stereotypical rehab. But that feeling quickly dissipated once I spent time in their nicely furnished offices with the staff, predominantly doctoral-level psychologists whose focus is providing one-on-one therapy. Clients also had the option of participating in some groups, as well as holistic services, most of which were offered in the same building.

Over the course of the week, I spent quite a bit of time with the founder and director of the program, who set up individual interviews for me with staff, as well as with a number of current and past clients. I also attended several group treatment sessions and portions of staff meetings, and I had my own private sessions for acupuncture, meditation, massage, and "energy healing." Since most of the care at Practical Recovery involves individual therapy, client privacy precluded my observing those sessions. But the director's assistance in my follow-up with individual clients after I left gave me a good sense of how this unique program operates.

HAZELDEN FOUNDATION. Seen as the grandparent of twelve-step treatment programs, Hazelden allowed me to visit two of its multiple campuses. I spent nearly a week at its famous Center City, Minnesota, location, observing treatment on an adult women's primary unit. I also went to an aftercare meeting for women who had completed primary treatment, and participated in Hazelden's Professionals in Residence program, which educates professionals about Hazelden's model for providing help to people with addictions. Even though I went there in March, which is still very much gray-winter in Minnesota, I could appreciate the beauty of this rural campus, which sits on a small lake and features leaf-covered walking trails. The facility has much more of a college dormlike feeling than the "celebrity rehab" image that some ascribe to a place of this reputation. The women stayed three to a bedroom and bath—nice, but rather modest. Clients seemed comfortable lounging in the unit's shared kitchen and common room. Long hallways took us to the cafeteria, where we ate in dining rooms that separated women from men, as well as to a large classroom and auditoriums for group lectures.

Although I was closely shadowed by a public-relations person, I was surprised at how close I was allowed to get to the treatment process, most of which was done in groups. On the women's unit, for instance, I loosely followed the clients' schedule right along with them—sitting in on group counseling, large lectures (some of them coed), a few individual sessions with addiction counselors, and eat-all-you-want meals (showcasing a variety of "comfort" foods) right at the tables with clients.

I also observed some multidisciplinary staff meetings (typically called "staffings") at which treatment plans for individual clients were discussed. The only activities I was not allowed to observe were, understandably, individual counseling with a psychologist and specialty counseling groups for such issues as psychological trauma. Hazelden also made the notice about my interest in interviewing clients available to the women on the unit I observed—without preselecting clients I'd be allowed to interview according to how successful their treatment had been.

Hazelden then invited me to come back for another week at their facility for adolescents and young adults in Plymouth, Minnesota. This facility was in a more suburban neighborhood, also near a lake, and had the same "college" feel that the Center City program had. Here, I observed their four-day family program for parents and siblings of young people in treatment. I also spent time in some primary and extended-care treatment groups and interviewed counselors and a few patients. I was allowed to interview two young men without a staff person present and was again impressed that these patients were not chosen as ones who would necessarily give me a "rah-rah" view of the program.

CARON. Another long-standing twelve-step-based treatment program, listed at Forbestraveler.com as a "celebrity rehab retreat" and one of the "top detox destinations," Caron allowed me to visit its main campus in a beautiful area of southeastern Pennsylvania, where a packed week had been planned for me by their public-relations director, who accompanied me most of the time. I found this description at Forbestraveler.com to be accurate: "Located in a pinprick of a town . . . this former resort hotel features 110 acres of grounds, state-of-the-art fitness facilities, and an indoor challenge course for adventure therapy." The lovely stone-and-brick buildings enclose more modest interiors with more of a hybrid college-hospital feel than that of a place that would attract stars and starlets.

Here, I got to see a smattering of different programs but mingled less with clients than at Hazelden. Over the course of six days, I observed part of Caron's five-day adult family education program, then spent two days on an adult women's primary treatment unit. Since Caron is one of the few rehabs with exclusive programming for young adults, I was fortunate to spend time observing its young adult male program over the course of two days. I concluded my visit with time in the adolescent female program.

While on the units, I attended some group therapy sessions, large group lectures, and staffings. I had the opportunity to interview a number of staff members—sometimes while having lunch in Caron's cafeteria, where clients and staff all ate together and could choose from a wide variety of healthful foods. I met with the medical director of Caron, directors and coordinators of several programs, and counselors from the units I spent time on.

A highlight of the visit was attending Caron's Sunday chapel service—a source of pride for Caron and led by their beloved (and sometimes provocative) "Father Bill." As described on their Web site, the service "integrates 12-Step traditions, elements of Christian worship, and material from other spiritual sources. Persons of all spiritual traditions are welcome. There are tears and testimonials, and music with messages for the hungry heart." Despite the Bible readings, Lord's Prayer recitation, and Christian communion ceremony, at least some of the non-Christians present seemed to feel comfortable participating. (One young woman seemed dismayed when she told me after she'd been there, "We even had to sit in a church some of the time." The service is actually held in a large auditorium.)

THREE OUTPATIENT PROGRAM VISITS IN THE PHILADELPHIA AREA

Drs. Thomas McLellan and Deni Carise have studied countless outpatient programs in Philadelphia and surrounding communities. They were gracious enough to set up the following three outpatient program visits for me.

SOBRIETY THROUGH OUT PATIENT, OR STOP. At the other end of the spectrum from the high-end rehabs, the STOP program in Philadelphia was the first of nine outpatient programs I visited. I grew up in the Philly suburbs and the neighborhood that houses STOP was one that, for safety reasons, we didn't approach when we were kids. But behind the walls of the bare-bones building in a low-income neighborhood, I was greeted by a tall cage with chirping cockatiels and then led into a warm-feeling, nicely furnished waiting area with a large fish tank and a big TV.

Designed to serve the needs of the minority community, STOP has served the Philadelphia area for more than twenty years. Its clients are predominantly low income and have minimal education. But when it comes to services, you name it, and it seems STOP provides it. (In fact, when I saw their list of services at their Web site, I thought, "How can they possibly do all of this?!") However, they offer and obviously are proud to show off not only their counseling services but their barbershop, food service program, massage therapy facilities, computer lab, small gym, and more. Over the course of two days, I met with the executive director, spent time with the CEO/founder, interviewed counselors and therapists, attended a client lecture, observed a music and art therapy group, had lunch with the clients and staff, attended a general group therapy session, and was even interviewed by clients on STOP's own radio station.

SODAT OF NEW JERSEY. On another two days of the same week, I spent time with the SODAT outpatient programs, whose CEO was kind enough to transport me to two of their six treatment facilities in New Jersey. (SODAT stands for Services to Overcome Drug Abuse Among Teenagers, but their programs serve adults, too.) Before coming to Philly, I had been told that SODAT "treats the poorest of the poor" and, indeed, 75 percent of their clientele are in the lower-income strata. I started out by attending a meeting with program administrators, who shared the woes of being an agency largely dependent on public funds and grants for survival. One relatively new supervisor talked about how overwhelmed she was when she assumed her position: "They threw me the ball and didn't give me the playbook. It's been good-challenging. When I leave here, there will be nothing I won't be able to do."

I also attended several group treatment sessions with adults and with adolescents, sat in on a staffing, and interviewed some staff members. At one facility, where I observed some of an adult outpatient group session, I could see how a positive relationship with a counselor can override financial or physical constraints a program might have. Clients said things like, "We're like a family. . . . Here, it's at your own pace, your own choice, everyone gets to share." Another SODAT facility in Camden, New Jersey, had trouble finding a location when it wanted to relocate. I was told, "No one wanted drug addicts in their neighborhood." But they found a space—minimalist, but with room for child care while parents are in treatment. All the staff members seemed overworked. The supervisor, who was filling in for three absent counselors the day I visited, mentioned that she typically works ten-hour days.

REHAB AFTER WORK/REHAB AFTER SCHOOL. My week of visiting outpatient programs in the greater Philadelphia area was rounded out by spending a day at a Rehab After Work program, which is part of a large multistate chain of outpatient programs designed, as the name implies, to allow clients to continue to work at their jobs while attending outpatient treatment. I went to the Paoli program, which serves working-class to higher socioeconomic status clientele in a suburb of Philadelphia and spent some time interviewing several staff members and attending part of a regional staff meeting. This office is one of many that also hosts an outpatient Rehab After School program for teens having problems resulting from their alcohol and/or drug use, and I sat through an hours-long group treatment session with about ten teens present. My day ended with a group adult outpatient program session, half of which was an AA meeting.

PROMISES TREATMENT CENTERS. I was welcomed for a two-day visit at Promises, which skyrocketed to the top of the celebrity rehab chart when it was reported that both Britney Spears and Lindsay Lohan were treated there in 2007. But the staff would rather not be labeled that way, preferring to emphasize the quality of their treatment. (In fact, I was told that celebrities compose less than 10 percent of Promises' client caseload.) Although important at all the programs I visited, privacy and confidentiality were given the greatest emphasis at Promises, and it was the only program that did not allow me to meet any clients who were in treatment. In fact, my visit seemed to be arranged for a time when no clients were around. Should I see a celebrity, it was suggested, I should look the other way. I was also told that they rarely grant requests for visits like mine, and that they'd carefully vetted me beforehand.

Promises has two residential facilities, one at its original site in a quiet neighborhood in West Los Angeles and the other in Malibu, California. (Treatment at the two places is totally separate, and unlike Hazelden and

Caron, which treat men and women separately, Promises treats them in the same program.) But before going to either one, I spent time at Promises' outpatient facility, which was in a restored building in L.A. whose interior I'd describe as warehouse-chic, nothing posh, with exposed brick walls and concrete floors. Promises brought me there to interview some rehab alumni as well as families whose relatives had been through their programs.

The next day, I visited both residential facilities. The main building of the more modest West L.A. facility is a lovely older craftsman-style home on a tree-lined street. With its large, welcoming porch and dark wood-paneled rooms, it was reminiscent of a nice bed-and-breakfast. Across the street were offices and additional client accommodations housed in plainer buildings. From there, I was driven along an ocean route and then up a long, winding hillside road to the more luxurious—but not what I'd call ostentatious—Malibu facility, with mountains on one side and an ocean view on the other. I was told that access is purposely difficult, to discourage paparazzi. Gardens and crannies for quiet meditation are tucked around four buildings, tennis courts, and three pools. The main house has the feel of a mini-mansion and is filled with warm, terra-cotta tones. Surprised at how unpretentious both the bedroom and bath I saw were, I was told by my escort that many of their clients "live in far more opulence" at home. Clients at both Promises residential programs were transported and accompanied by staff to separate exercise facilities and twelve-step meetings in the community. And all clients were expected to do some community service, such as serving meals to the homeless.

My Promises tour wasn't just show. In addition to my meetings with some program "graduates" and family members, interviews had been arranged with various staff members, including their CEO (an addiction psychiatrist), clinical and executive directors (both psychologists), and a staff psychologist. I got to eat a healthy buffet-style meal prepared by the chef at Promises, Malibu (the same fare that clients would get)—fresh, summery, and healthful but nothing different than I'd serve in my own home. When I asked about criticisms leveled at celebrity rehabs for their ocean views and high-thread-count sheets, I was told, "If you want people to stay long enough to benefit from treatment, you have to create a relationship with them in the context of their ambivalence about changing. One of the ways we accomplish that is through a physical environment that's beautiful, comforting, and familiar so that clients can focus on their core problems." And unlike programs that preach "all addicts are the same," Promises' philosophy has long been that people tend to have better outcomes when treated with others who are similar to them socially, educationally, and economically.

CELEBRATE A NEW LIFE AT HOPE BY THE SEA. Aware that there are quite a few rehabs with a strong Christian component, I decided to visit one during one of my research trips to California. I chose the Celebrate a New Life program, which had been started eight months earlier as a Christian track within an established treatment program called Hope by the Sea in San Juan Capistrano. (Hope by the Sea has been featured regularly on A&E's series *Intervention*.)

My contact was Celebrate a New Life's director of admissions, a former Hope by the Sea employee who personally had difficulty getting sober with AA, then did so with the help of Christianity. He came back and approached Hope by the Sea's owner and administrator about starting a Christian track. In our initial phone conversations, he told me that he wanted it to be a program that was more Bible-based, with an emphasis on Christianity, and that relied on God instead of the rather undefined "higher power" concept common at most treatment programs and twelve-step meetings. (For more about AA and the twelve steps, see chapter 2.)

Hope by the Sea provided most of the services that other residential twelve-step-based programs I visited provide, but their setup was quite different. Technically, the program was certified to provide outpatient care, but clients who came for a residential treatment experience were housed in regular homes in the area and then driven to the main administrative and counseling offices for treatment each day. I visited several of the homes; the ones I saw were more than comfortable and in nice residential neighborhoods.

Clients were also transported to other outside services such as licensed detox centers (if they needed detox when they first arrived) and an outside gym for exercise most days of the week. My host said that he felt this model prepares clients for life after treatment because "it's more like the real world—they can go to outside twelve-step meetings with a sponsor, a gym club in the community." The clients also had chores and took responsibility for preparing meals.

During my long day there, in addition to visiting the homes, I interviewed staff members, attended a group counseling session led by a minister, and took a side trip to see the famous Saddleback Church, where Rick Warren (author of the huge bestseller, *The Purpose Driven Life*) ministers, and where Celebrate a New Life clients attend Sunday services and Christian recovery meetings. I got back in time to attend a rather moving Christian AA meeting, which opened with religious folksinging accompanied by a guitarist, with some people standing, rocking to the music, and raising their hands in the air. The meeting then followed a typical AA format with a speaker telling his "before and after" addiction story and celebration of sober anniversaries. The difference was that people openly talked about their relationship with God and Jesus, which is not customary at AA meetings.

MUSCALA CHEMICAL HEALTH CLINIC. Knowing that one-on-one treatment is an important and underused route to recovery, I spent a day at this unique Minnesota-licensed drug and alcohol treatment clinic in the suburbs of Minneapolis, where Bob Muscala, RN (registered nurse), has been bucking the tide of the Minnesota model for more than thirty years. (See pages 70–71 for a description of the Minnesota model, the treatment approach that's still used, in some shape or form, in most rehabs across the country.) Muscala operates a one-person shop in which he provides one-on-one non-twelve-step counseling—plus a few weekly groups—to people with drug and alcohol problems. Because most of his work with clients is done in individual sessions, I wasn't able to observe treatment, so I spent most of my time there interviewing clients, as well as learning about Muscala's philosophy and some of the challenges of running this kind of program. (For more about this program, see page 66.)

FOUNTAIN CENTERS. To get a feel for treatment in a rural setting, I visited two Fountain Centers programs, which are part of the Mayo Health

System in southern Minnesota. I spent a week driving back and forth between the tiny town of Fairmont, where I attended their adult outpatient program, and the larger town of Albert Lea, visiting their adolescent residential program. I went to these facilities expecting rather old-fashioned twelve-step rehabs but instead found programs in transition—ones that had recently come under the clinical direction of a psychologist who was in the process of helping the staff implement more state-of-the-art counseling approaches.

Fairmont, a lakeside town with a population of ten thousand, feels about as rural as it gets in Minnesota. The Fountain Centers outpatient program was housed in a rather austere little building that looked more likely to be home to a Moose Lodge or an American Legion hall than an addiction rehab. The small staff of three counselors and a receptionist did its best to make the place feel homey. In addition to the waiting area and two bathrooms, there were just four rooms, several serving as both counselors' offices and group counseling rooms.

The counselors were multipurpose, too, in their way. Once, when I mentioned that there was something unpleasant that needed to be cleaned up in a bathroom, a counselor said, "Oh, I'll take care of it." (They had no dedicated cleaning help.) Another counselor told me that she served not only as counselor for up to sixteen clients at a time (usually it's eight to twelve) but also acted as their case manager—a job that higher-end rehabs delegate to a separate practitioner. She told me she coordinated services with health and mental health providers, monitored clients' medications, and dealt with social services. Here, over different days, I observed several consecutive three-hour sessions of morning and evening adult outpatient adult groups, which gave me a good taste of what transpires over the course of a week in outpatient treatment.

The Fountain Centers adolescent program is in Albert Lea, a community of just over eighteen thousand and located, along with other addiction programs, in a medical complex. On the outside, the building looks like a modern hospital, but inside, it has that old-fashioned "medical" feel to it and seemed somewhat run-down. (The clinical supervisor who was my contact told me that plans were in the works for a new facility.)

At the coed teen program (one girl and about six boys), I attended some group counseling sessions, "community groups" in which staff and kids talked and aired concerns, and the school classroom—where young people who are still in school worked with a licensed teacher during their stay. Between visiting the adult and adolescent facilities, I also got to sit in on several intakes with clients who were new to the programs.

HEALING JOURNEY PROGRAM AT MINNESOTA INDIAN WOMEN'S RESOURCE CENTER (MIWRC). An addiction professional I met at a conference suggested that I visit some programs tailored for minority groups, whose chemical-health issues are not always met in traditional treatment programs. One of these is the Healing Journey Program at the MIWRC. Healing Journey is the only program I went to that's not a drug and alcohol treatment program—rather, it calls itself a "harm reduction" program for Native American women. (A licensed treatment program was in the works there as I wrote this book.) While their ultimate goal is to help clients recover from drug and alcohol problems, clients may remain in the program if they continue to struggle with use. They're asked, however, to be sober when they come to sessions. When I arrived for my day there, the women had just participated in a Native American sage-smudging ceremony, followed by a meditation reading and a check-in session that gave each woman the opportunity to report to the others how she was doing. The women sat and did crafts such as beading during all of this. We then went to a local community facility that provided lunch for low-income people and, next, took a trip to a craft store to restock the shelves that keep the women's hands busy. This gave me a chance to talk with some of the women about their current and past treatment experiences. (For more about this program, see page 353.)

AFRICAN AMERICAN FAMILY SERVICES (AAFS). Tucked in among ethnic restaurants on a street the locals call "Eat Street" sits AAFS, in a colorful, diverse Minneapolis neighborhood. The mission of this long-standing program, which also has offices in St. Paul, Minnesota, is to provide "community-based, culturally-specific chemical health, mental health, and family preservation services to the African American Community." I spent a day there, learning how a program pays special attention to the particular needs of African Americans, by visiting with staff members, sitting in on an out-patient group, and having lunch with its chief operations officer and another staff member. According to its Web site, "The atmosphere of AAFS is one where not only African Americans can feel supported, but also bi-racial and/or multicultural families can feel that their needs will be met."

The group I attended was a three-hour "Tier I" outpatient group, which was for people just beginning treatment. (Other tiers were for those further along in the treatment process.) This took place in a warmly colored cinderblock classroom set up lecture-style. Following a lesson presented by an intern addiction counselor, chairs were moved into a circle and the format became more of a check-in and discussion of personal issues such as feelings about the death of a parent and dating people who drink.

SPECIALIZED TREATMENT SERVICES. I didn't want to write this book without visiting an opioid maintenance program, so I visited what I was told is the largest such facility in the state of Minnesota, Specialized Treatment Services (STS), in Minneapolis. STS prescribes both methadone and Suboxone—replacement medications for people recovering from addiction to opioid drugs including heroin and certain painkillers. I spent time learning how patients receive their medications, met with its director and its physician, and attended a three-hour session of their outpatient treatment program, which uses a non-twelve-step approach. I also sat in on an intake session with a client who was addicted to painkiller medications. (For more on STS, see pages 363–64. A discussion of replacement medications can be found on pages 357–58.)

CHAPTER TWO

GOING INSIDE

WHAT IT'S LIKE TO BE IN REHAB

While millions of Americans walk through the doors of residential and outpatient rehabs each year—many of them as repeat guests—few of us really know what they experience inside. What do people do when they're in treatment? How do the programs differ? How do you even know if you should go to rehab and who belongs in what kind of program? Based on my visits, interviews, and consultations with professionals, this chapter takes a look at the basics of what goes on in traditional rehab settings. By traditional treatment, I'm referring to the majority of residential and outpatient programs that incorporate the twelve steps of Alcoholics Anonymous and provide most of their intervention via group counseling along with varying degrees of individual counseling. As the book continues, these approaches will be examined in greater depth. (I also visited some nontraditional rehabs, which will be discussed throughout the book.)

DIMITRI R.'S STORY OF "BEING INSIDE"

By the time he was in his early twenties, Dimitri R. had made the rounds in the world of rehab. He'd spent three months at an adolescent program, followed by an entire year of supervised living at an adult sober house combined with outpatient treatment. Next came more than four months at two traditional twelve-step residential facilities that also have reputations as celebrity rehabs.

Dimitri's drug use began before the age of fifteen, when he started abusing cough medicine, smoking pot, using inhalants, and drinking. His eventual involvement in wild parties with older kids led to easy access to drugs and heavy weekend use of cocaine, meth, and ecstasy. "Before I was out of high school," he said, "I ended up hospitalized after someone found me practically in a coma from a combination of four different drugs." That incident led to Dimitri's first rehab experience. "After being hospitalized, I thought I was going home. But my parents drove me straight to a teen treatment program and told me I was just going to look at it." Dimitri wound up staying there for three months despite his best efforts to leave earlier. When I asked about his experience, he said, "I wasn't ready to be sober or commit to anything. Looking back on it, it's a waste of time if someone's not wanting to be sober.

"There were groups every single day—twelve-step. Everyone would share, [with] role playing, and doing stuff with scarves and saying things like 'that's the color of your addiction.'" He added, "The staff were all recovering addicts and alcoholics themselves. Everybody had an individual counselor, and I saw that person once a week for forty-five minutes." When I asked if he also saw a psychologist during his long stay at this high-end program, he said, "I don't remember calling anyone doctor."

After three months, the program staff decided that Dimitri could move on and referred him to what he described as a "highly structured" sober house for adults, where he lived for a year. During the day, Dimitri went back to the adolescent rehab for its intensive outpatient and school program, which enabled him to get his high school diploma. He had some trouble remembering what he did during his outpatient treatment and said, "All the groups of every program feel the same to me. Lots of AA stuff and stuff about feeling hopeful about being sober and how to change everyone in your life so you stay sober. I just started agreeing with everything they said because it didn't really make sense to me, but I knew I needed to agree so I could move on."

Of his experience at the sober house, Dimitri said, "I was in there with some crazy characters. There were people who were on their seventh treatment. I was really uncomfortable for a long time, but I tried to act a lot older than I was. That's where I really learned a lot of stuff I shouldn't have learned—like I became friends with a guy who told me if I hadn't done heroin, I hadn't had the best high there was, and he told me ways to get around drug testing."

Nevertheless, at the end of a year, Dimitri "graduated" from the sober house, got an apartment with a young man he'd met at the teen rehab, went to daily AA meetings, and got an AA sponsor—just as he'd been instructed to do. Within a short time, however, he reconnected with old friends and the guy from the sober house who'd talked about the great heroin high. "He introduced me to painkillers, which I immediately started using in an addictive way. But I couldn't support that expensive habit and very hesitantly decided to try heroin, [eventually] becoming addicted." (It's not uncommon for people to switch from abusing pain medications to heroin, which can be gotten more cheaply.)

Not long thereafter, Dimitri said his parents made him go back to rehab, even though he didn't feel ready. So he went to detox for two weeks at a prominent residential program. "It was my favorite place," Dimitri said. "The staff had their hearts in the right place and really cared about people. My counselor was like an angel, and he was fighting like the death for me to stay."

Despite his counselor's best efforts, however, after two weeks, Dimitri was transferred to a second high-end residential program in another part of the country because it was decided it would be best for him to be located far away from where his drug use had occurred. (All of his treatment thus far had taken place near his home.) His first impressions of the new place were, "I felt extremely deceived by their brochure—they made it out to sound like a wonderful place. It felt like a hospital psych ward. They immediately cut me off from calling my parents, and I had to wait until the next day to talk to a therapist. They just saw me as a whining addict who wanted to do drugs. It was one of the most traumatizing thirty days in my life because I was stripped of everything. We couldn't even look at the women in the program."

Describing rehab activities, Dimitri said, "We were in groups all day. They took us to groups every night. It was twelve-step, twenty-four hours a day. Compared to other treatment programs, it felt cold. When people shared, it seemed like they were put on the spot. My primary counselor felt like the principal of a boys' school." However, Dimitri continued in the extended-care program at that rehab and wound up being at the place for a total of four months altogether. Compared with primary care, he said, "Extended care didn't feel different in terms of what we talked about. We just had more freedom. After that, the program wanted me to go to a sober-living house, just like I did after the teen rehab. I was freaking out that my life was just going to be in these programs, trying to get out. I did not see the point."

Toward the end of this last experience, however, Dimitri told me that a family member began reading about alternatives to twelve-step programs, which prompted them to seek something different for him. Dimitri said, "They wanted me to go to a place where I could start being honest" instead of doing and saying what he thought was expected. Dimitri started twice-weekly individual therapy, with as-needed phone or e-mail check-ins, in a non-twelve-step outpatient program where doctoral-level psychologists provided almost all of the treatment. In addition, he began learning some new life skills. For the first five months, he said, "I also went to the program's groups. My favorite one wasn't about addiction—it was about planning what you need to get a job, get enrolled in college. There was also a communication group, where you can act out things you need to discuss with people in life. And there was an interpersonal skills group, a mindfulness group, and a DBT group." (Dialectical behavior therapy has been found to be effective for a number of psychiatric problems—it includes cognitive-behavioral therapy, problem solving, help with learning how to regulate emotions, and meditation practices.)

Dimitri gave me permission to talk with his clinical psychologist, who confirmed his story and added that, along with a substance use disorder, he had some mental health problems that she felt had not been adequately addressed during his many previous rehab experiences. She said, "I think he's been self-medicating since he had a chance to." At the time I interviewed Dimitri, which was nearly four years following his first rehab experience, he was still seeing this psychologist for individual sessions twice a week and going to one weekly group session. Dimitri told me, "The hardest part for me, even after all these places I've been and all these different people I've seen, is that I still need a lot of help. And I'm just starting to get the help that I need. I have had several slips since being where I am now but remain determined to reach some sort of serenity and healthy lifestyle."

THE MANY SHAPES OF REHAB

Dimitri R.'s family did what most people assume you should do when someone you love has an addiction. You send them to rehab, and, if you have the money, you send them to "the best." I heard stories like Dimitri's over and over again—told by people who, from the time they were teens or young adults, had bounced in and out of treatment programs of different kinds and sizes over the course of many years. The stories came from all over the socioeconomic spectrum. Most people who experience addiction treatment go to residential or outpatient programs, the main types discussed in this book. However, rehab can take place in other settings. Here's a run-down of the different types of programs for drug and alcohol problems, most of which treat both issues:

RESIDENTIAL*—Care that's provided most often in a freestanding facility where clients stay, day and night, for weeks or months, typically receiving traditional addiction treatment along with some medical and psychological care—what most of us think of as rehab. As mentioned previously, residential places that offer primary care—which for most people is a period of initial stabilization during early recovery—may be separate from those offering extended-care treatment, a second phase of treatment commonly lasting several months.

OUTPATIENT—Clients live at home while attending treatment programs at various kinds of facilities—freestanding clinics, those affiliated with residential programs, and hospitals—usually up to nine hours a week and lasting thirty to a hundred twenty days. Services are often provided in the

---

* Because the distinction was not always clear between residential and inpatient treatment nor between outpatient and intensive outpatient care—and it was not always possible for me to tell from interviewees which level of care they received—for simplicity's sake I generally just made the distinction between *residential* and *outpatient* treatment.

evening so people can still hold their jobs. Outpatient treatment is typically significantly less expensive than residential and is often the only form of care someone receives, but it may also be used as transitional or "step-down" care after residential rehab. However, people commonly start out by going to outpatient but are "stepped up" to residential care if they keep struggling. (Dimitri R. thinks his parents chose a residential rehab as his first program because they felt his problem was too serious for outpatient.)

INTENSIVE OUTPATIENT (IOP) AND DAY TREATMENT—Similar to outpatient, IOP and day treatment typically involve more hours of the same type of treatment. Clients commonly attend at least nine hours per week. Such programs often step people down to regular outpatient hours as their treatment progresses.

INPATIENT—Round-the-clock addiction treatment is provided in specialty units of regular or psychiatric hospitals or medical clinics. Some inpatient programs offer both detoxification and customary addiction treatment services, while others offer detox alone with addiction treatment provided elsewhere. (See pages 52–58 for details on detox.) Inpatient treatment is typically used for people with serious medical conditions or mental disorders.

OPIOID TREATMENT PROGRAMS (OTPS)—People addicted to opioids, such as heroin and prescription painkillers like oxycodone (OxyContin is the well-known brand name), attend these specialized outpatient facilities to receive replacement medications including methadone and Suboxone. The most effective programs also provide counseling and other services. (For more on OTPs and these medications, see chapter 9.)

THERAPEUTIC COMMUNITIES (TCS)—With a residential stay usually lasting six to twelve months, therapeutic communities often treat people with long histories of drug addiction, involvement in crime, and psychological problems. The focus in TCs is on resocializing, and the program's entire community becomes part of the therapeutic process, with peers in recovery serving as role models and staff members acting as authorities and guides. By providing a lot of structure, TCs help clients become accountable, productive, and responsible. Some TCs are designed to meet the needs of pregnant women and women with children.

SOBER-LIVING FACILITIES—After addiction treatment, people some-times make the transition to drug- and alcohol-free living facilities, such as halfway houses and "sober homes," where they live in a supervised en-vironment with others in recovery. Usually sober living is not a form of treatment in and of itself, but clients may go to outside outpatient pro-grams, as Dimitri R. did. He said that the main difference from his resi-dential experience was that, at a certain point "you start to earn more privileges—you can leave in between groups with your [AA] sponsor, and you get a later curfew." As is often the case, he was also required to attend daily twelve-step meetings (such as AA or NA). (For more on such facili-ties, see chapter 10.)

INDIVIDUAL TREATMENT—One-on-one treatment can take place with licensed mental health professionals, such as psychologists or psychiatrists who specialize in helping people with substance use disorders, or from addiction counselors in private practice. While an addiction counselor might help someone recognize and understand the nature of his or her sub-stance problem and promote strategies of personal recovery, most are not qualified to conduct in-depth psychotherapy unless they have additional specialized training. Mental health professionals with addiction expertise can also assist with underlying psychological issues such as depression or post-traumatic stress disorder, which are frequently associated with addic-tion. Unfortunately, many mental health professionals are not knowledge-able about addiction; finding one who can treat both problems is ideal.

———

All of the residential adult programs I visited had multiple offerings, in-cluding residential, outpatient, sober living, and extended-care facilities—often referred to as "levels of care." And all of their outpatient programs accepted clients directly, without having to go to the residential facility first. But their outpatient programs consisted primarily of people who'd already been through residential treatment. With the exception of African American Family Services in Minnesota, which grouped people according to stage of treatment, all the programs I visited had clients of various stages mixed together on units and in the same treatment group—for ex-ample, people who'd just arrived were in the same group as those who were about to "graduate." Most programs in the United States use this model. I only came across one residential program—Chatsworth Pavilion in Montreal, Canada—that uses a "closed group" model wherein a small number of clients start and finish their residential treatment at the same time. Chatsworth believes this model is preferable to the "revolving door" system that sacrifices group cohesion and flow for ease of admission.

UPON ARRIVAL

At residential rehabs, I didn't get to observe anyone when they first walked through the door, but I asked the programs I visited, and some of the people who'd been through the drill, what happens when you first get there. Everyone's initial experience is a bit different, depending on what they're addicted to, how advanced the addiction is, the condition in which they arrive, other problems they might have, and the program's policies and philosophy. But there's typically a lengthy intake and admissions process in which forms are completed, the client's belongings are searched, psychological tests are taken, and professionals ask a lot of questions about the client's background and history of substance use. A physical exam is usually conducted at some point, too. (The order of events varies.)

Jackie H., who was addicted to benzos and alcohol, said of her stay at a high-end residential program, "When I first got there, there were mountains of paperwork. I spent an hour and a half with a psychologist, who asked about past trauma in my life and past treatment experiences [at eating-disorder programs]." Dorothy D. said she checked into a similar rehab at about eleven p.m. and was asked "a million questions—about my drinking history, depression, anxiety, and other issues I might need to deal with when there." She added, "They explained everything to me. My family was there with me, and they gave me a chance to say good-bye to them. It put me at ease." The whole check-in process took several hours.

Although I'd heard about strip searches and body-cavity searches for hidden drugs, none of the programs I visited engage in these practices. All of them did dignified searches of clients and what they brought with them—one program said a same-sex staff member searches' clothed clients, and others ask people to empty their pockets. Luggage and other belongings were typically scoured for drugs, and any medications were confiscated. At one program I was told, "We take away anything that could be self-injurious. All medications have to be approved by our physician. With the exception of self-administered medications, like inhalers, we lock up and administer everything." Aerosol containers and toiletries with a high alcohol content may be prohibited or kept in a secure place and only brought out for use in the presence of a staff member.

Somewhere in all of this, depending on the type of substance use disorder and its severity, detox is likely to take place in a hospital-like part of the rehab. Dorothy D. spent only twelve hours in detox because her alcohol addiction wasn't so advanced that she had withdrawal symptoms. While there, she said, "I slept, the nurses checked on me, and they asked if I wanted to go outside and smoke. They woke me up early to do blood work, and they let me go back to sleep. Then I saw the doctor." While the alcohol withdrawal process typically takes place within a week, other drugs such as benzos and opioids can take longer—so much so that the client is still having withdrawal symptoms after leaving the detox and taking part in activities at the regular treatment unit. (For more on withdrawal, see pages 52–58.)

I did get to observe several intakes at outpatient facilities in which clients were asked countless questions—sometimes the same ones more than once—about their past drug use, other treatment experiences, their psychological history, and their family situations. At one of them, a woman who had relapsed and was returning to the program for a second time met with a drug and alcohol counselor who administered a psychological questionnaire consisting largely of yes-and-no type questions followed by a "vulnerability assessment." Then the counselor did an addiction assessment, asking questions about how the client learned best, about her involvement in religion and her understanding of a higher power, about her family, and many questions about her drug and alcohol history. Later, there would be another lengthy assessment of the client's "bio-pyscho-social history" and substance-related issues. As in residential treatment, the goal was to assess the client's background and come up with an individualized plan for treatment.

None of the outpatient programs I visited had detox capabilities, and all of the clients I met at these facilities were past that stage. At the rural outpatient program I went to, I was told that clients rarely need detox and that if they do, they may get referred to the program's medical center in another community that had a special detox unit. I also spoke with Norman Briggs, an administrator at ARC Community Services, a women's outpatient program in Madison, Wisconsin, who explained that a number of different screening tests are available to assess the need for detox. If a patient has a high score on the alcohol assessment the center uses, he said, "we get them to a detox facility, usually by cab."

DETOX BASICS

As a teenager, Kelli O. went through detox, which is more appropriately called "medically supervised withdrawal" or "medical withdrawal management," about seven times in one year, thinking it would be different each time. But with detox alone, she went right back to heavy drinking. Detox is the process of providing medical supervision and managing the symptoms of withdrawal as the body rids itself of alcohol and/or drugs. Withdrawal is what the body goes through after long-term use of a drug is reduced or stopped abruptly. Detoxification may take place at a residential or outpatient rehab or at a special detox facility. Some people who need medical supervision of withdrawal show up at an emergency room, and, if warranted, they may get admitted to the hospital. Others just go to their physicians or psychiatrists, who prescribe medications to help them get through withdrawal on an outpatient basis.

Detox alone is not considered adequate treatment because it doesn't address the psychological and social problems that commonly go along with addiction, nor does it provide the skills for staying sober. According to the 2010 Treatment Episode Data Set, which includes admissions to the vast majority of treatment programs in the United States, 20 percent of admissions were just for detoxification services. This number can be deceiving, Dr. Willenbring said, because it's inflated by the small number of people who go through detox again and again. While some of them may be resistant to getting help, he explained, "many have severe substance use disorders and most have been through traditional rehab over and over, so what's the point in going again? Would you accept a referral for treatment that had been tried repeatedly and was not effective?"

The length of time withdrawal takes, and its symptoms, vary with the type of drug and, if not medically monitored, can be particularly unpleasant and even dangerous. Guidelines from the Center for Substance Abuse Treatment (CSAT), which is part of SAMHSA, state that "supervised detoxification may prevent potentially life-threatening complications that might appear if the patient were left untreated." The types of substance use disorders that may warrant medical supervision, and the need for withdrawal medications as people go off them include addictions to alcohol, sedative-hypnotics (such as benzodiazepines and barbiturates), and opioids. While withdrawal from alcohol, benzos, and barbiturates can be lethal, withdrawal from opioids and stimulants including cocaine, amphetamine, and methamphetamine generally does not directly result in life-threatening symptoms. However, going cold turkey from opioids is miserable—something like having a severe case of the flu—and doing so without an alleviation of discomfort can cause needless suffering and act as a major barrier to getting sober. Administering medications like buprenorphine (trade-named Suboxone or Subutex) or methadone during detox can prevent people from dropping out of treatment and strengthen the bond with their treatment providers. (For more on these medications, see chapter 9.)

Former liter-a-day vodka drinker Eddie F. went through detox twice prior to his two stints at the same outpatient program. He told me, "My first detox was done on my own—white-knuckled and puking in the basement for three days and nights. It was total hell, and I was totally ignorant about coming down off of alcohol. It was pretty much like a scene from a seventies movie about a heroin addict—seeing things, hearing things. My heart was about to jump out of my chest. I had no idea how dangerous it is to do this without medical help." He tried contacting a number of treatment facilities but none had an open bed—the closest one took people on a first-come, first-served basis. On his third day of self-detox, Eddie contacted his psychiatrist to ask for help and, within four hours, was in a hospital-based rehab. His second time around, he knew how things worked, took himself to the ER of the same hospital, and told them he needed treatment for a drinking problem. He said, "It took a couple of hours to get admitted but compared to the three days of hell, it was well worth it. The treatment facility had the staff and the knowledge to make detox tolerable. After a few days on the detox unit, I immediately started my outpatient program."

It pays to ask questions about what the detox experience will be like, especially if you or a loved one in need of rehab has special concerns. Elizabeth F., who arrived drunk at a prominent twelve-step program, said she had a "horrific" time of it in detox. "Medicated men were on the other side of the hall, and they could walk in on you at night. It triggered my own issues with men. When I complained about it, nothing was done. So I sat at the nurses' station until five a.m." Elizabeth was also upset that her high blood pressure medications were taken away from her, and then a new prescription for the same drugs was billed to her insurance company. She thought it was a way for the rehab to make money. It turned out, however, that by law that facility couldn't administer medications they hadn't prescribed.

Selecting a detox facility with health-care practitioners who have expertise in detoxification is critical. An intake coordinator at an outpatient program I visited who stressed how important it is for detox to be safe said, "I know of people who have had strokes during detox." She added that it's wise to look for a detox facility with a low staff-to-client ratio and that doesn't mix detox patients with general psychiatric patients. Alexis J. learned this the hard way when she went to a detox program where they did mix them; she found it to be "a free-for-all." She said, "There was a man who put my clothes on and was peeing in my garbage can. And the mental health patients were talking about using and getting drugs all the time—it was terrible for the substance abuse patients." Another staff person said that he often hears about unpleasant detox experiences occurring on the weekend, "when there's a skeleton staff." Elizabeth F. raised the point that it pays to ask about exactly where detox will take place before going to a residential rehab. She sent her son to a high-end extended-care program and found out that they used a detox place that was off the premises—"and it wasn't a very nice one."

According to the 2010 National Survey of Substance Abuse Treatment Services, medications were routinely used during detoxification in just 77 percent of the facilities providing these services. The same survey showed that only 9 percent of outpatient, 7 percent of residential, and 5 percent of hospital inpatient addiction treatment facilities provided detox care. As mentioned earlier, however, detox often occurs in hospitals, and some physicians can manage withdrawal. In short, it's best to seek out detox facilities that are part of addiction treatment programs offering a wide range of services, including the ability to prescribe medications (and the knowledge to withhold them, if necessary). For alcohol withdrawal, a facility that uses state-of-the-art approaches will use medications, usually benzodiazepines, both to treat withdrawal symptoms and prevent physiological complications. For opioid withdrawal, they'll use buprenorphine or methadone—if they don't, the experience can be very uncomfortable.

DETOX WHETHER OR NOT YOU NEED IT?

When I began writing this book, several experts told me that most people don't need detox. So I was confused when one prominent rehab informed me that "most clients need detox," and, according to their Web site, before assigning them to a treatment unit, all new clients spend their first twenty-four to forty-eight hours on a medical unit to make sure they're medically stable. At another residential rehab, an administrator said that 85 to 90 percent of their primary women's treatment clients went to detox—some just for a day, but for others, the time was longer.

One of the experts who made a comment about detox being unnecessary in most cases added, "It's a huge moneymaker." A day in detox at a residential program can easily cost more than double the rate of a day in residential primary care. Daily rates at one high-end program, for instance, were about $2,100 per day for detoxification services versus $860 for primary residential treatment. Another authority made the point that many places use a multiday detox, stabilization, and evaluation period that isn't always needed from a physiological perspective, but, he noted, "Clients often do need to get some sleep, some food, and to be evaluated prior to starting real treatment. While this doesn't necessarily justify detox, the motivation isn't all mercenary." Social situations can also necessitate going to a detox facility—for instance, when a person who wants to quit using can't because of interference from others in his or her life.

Richard Saitz, MD, MPH, director of the Clinical Addiction Research and Education Unit at Boston University School of Medicine, said that the answer to the question of whether people often undergo detox unnecessarily is complex and pointed out that "detox often serves as the entry to treatment," which can be a good thing. However, detox often winds up being one of the multiple ways in which the addiction treatment system tends to treat all clients the same way. As Saitz said, "Patients are the nails and the treatment system has a hammer and uses it; if you go to a treatment program, you get what they offer. At a lot of programs, that means you wind up in detox—not because you need it, but because that's the only way to get into treatment. Some places aren't comfortable letting clients in without detox." Dr. Saitz has seen people addicted to drugs such as cocaine, that don't require detox, who lied and said they were alcoholics just so they could get detox and then get into the treatment system.

Of course, people who wind up in residential rehab are more likely to have severe drug and alcohol problems than those in outpatient settings, placing them at greater risk during withdrawal, so you'd expect a higher proportion of them to need the extra care a detox unit can provide prior to starting primary treatment. However, I heard a number of stories that reinforced the view that people are sometimes sent to detox unnecessarily, several of them from people with alcohol use disorders who were sent to detox even though they hadn't had a drink for a week or two.

The most unsettling detox story was that of Holly Y., who had a drinking problem and went to an outpatient program, where she wound up being sent to a separate detox practitioner and prescribed four different drugs, including one for possible seizures, even though she had not had a drink in "a good two weeks." When Holly asked why she'd need all these drugs and told them she'd had no problems, she said she was told that they put everyone on them. Not only was she concerned about the cost and the questionable need for detox, but also about taking medications that she didn't feel were necessary and that caused what she described as potentially dangerous side effects, some that caused her to hurt herself.

When I asked Dr. Saitz at what point after giving up alcohol detox should be unnecessary, he responded, "If you haven't had a drink in twenty-four hours or more and you aren't having symptoms of withdrawal, it's unlikely you'd need detox medications or medically supervised withdrawal—assuming you're not using other drugs and previously have not had severe withdrawal symptoms (such as seizures, convulsions, or hallucinations). It's conceivable that you could have a seizure or hallucination after that, but this usually happens in people who've had those symptoms before—when they've cut back—so they know what to anticipate. Three or more days without a drink and symptoms, and there's absolutely no question that withdrawal medications and detox would be unnecessary." Saitz added that common non-life-threatening symptoms when someone quits drinking include shakiness, anxiety, nausea, and agitation, and that even for a period into sobriety people may still have trouble sleeping. But these are not problems that require detox. He stressed that the decision to send people to detox should not be one size fits all and should be based on the chances of medically complicated withdrawal and a person's social situation. A rehab should be able to explain if and why you need detox as well as what it is about you and your situation that determines the detox procedures they intend for you.

For people who do need medically supervised withdrawal, only a minority need to be in an inpatient or residential facility, and few know that the process can be accomplished on an outpatient basis. Outpatient detox is most appropriate for individuals who have mild to moderate withdrawal symptoms, no major coexisting problems, a support person willing to monitor their progress closely, and a living situation supportive of sobriety. Although outpatient detox requires daily contact for several days to monitor progress and adjust doses of any prescribed medication, it's certainly cheaper than a residential detox facility.

To save money, Saitz said, there's no reason why someone who's about to attend a residential rehab can't ask ahead of time if it's possible to be evaluated on an outpatient basis to see if detox is necessary and, if so, to go through the process as an outpatient. He added, "It would surprise me that this would be declined if you have a letter of referral and the medical records from an outpatient detox specialty place giving a stamp of approval that you've been assessed and detoxed." If the residential rehab had concerns about the client using alcohol or other drugs between detox and entry into treatment, it could be agreed that the client would be transferred directly and tested upon arrival.

DETERMINING WHO GETS IN AND WHO GOES WHERE

If you or someone you care about needs help, how do you know the extent of the problem, what kind of help is needed, and whether rehab is appropriate? What should a good assessment look like—who should do it and what tools should they use? How do you know if the client should start out in an outpatient, intensive outpatient, or residential program? Or would a one-on-one approach be more appropriate than a program relying primarily on groups? Many experts will say that successful treatment of substance use disorders begins with and depends on a careful, accurate assessment of the person with the problem.

Assessment isn't the same as *screening* for substance problems. Screening is used to identify people who *might* have substance problems and to determine how bad those problems possibly are, often by having them complete questionnaires, answering such questions as "Have you ever felt you should cut down on your drinking?" and "Have you ever felt bad or guilty about your drinking?" If the score suggests the person has a problem, the next step might be to have an in-depth professional assessment. The purpose of an assessment is to determine whether a person has a bona fide substance use disorder and, if so, how severe it is; to find out if any additional medical or psychiatric problems exist; to begin taking appropriate steps to deal with the problems, which may include determining the level of treatment a person needs (for instance, outpatient versus residential); and sometimes to enhance motivation for change. (To confuse matters further, the term "intake" typically refers to first contact with a treatment program, when either a screening or full assessment is conducted.)

A good assessment combines what the client has to say with additional sources—such as information from other family members—to identify client needs, which should then become the basis for an individualized plan for treatment and for monitoring progress throughout treatment. But in the case of addiction, as with almost all psychiatric diagnoses, unless the substance problem is severe, there are usually few (if any) anatomical or physiological "symptoms" that unequivocally define the problem, or the extent of it. So the process is more subjective than assessment and diagnosis of a medical condition for which one might have more definitive lab work, X-rays, and/or an MRI.

At several of the more traditional residential rehabs, when I asked administrators how alcohol and drug problems are evaluated before and after people arrive there—as well as what assessment tools they use to determine the severity of the substance problem, whether addiction treatment is appropriate, and, if so, where clients should be placed—I was told they used "the DSM and ASAM criteria." As mentioned in chapter 1, the *Diagnostic and Statistical Manual of Mental Disorders* is the guidebook for diagnosing psychiatric disorders—it's not a comprehensive tool for assessing the many aspects of a person's life that play a role in addiction and recovery and doesn't determine how to proceed with treatment.

The "ASAM criteria" mentioned by a number of programs refers to the widely accepted American Society of Addiction Medicine's "Patient Placement Criteria," which outlines six treatment-planning "dimensions"—addressing such areas as relapse potential, readiness to change, and medical needs. Two different sets of criteria exist, one for teens and the other for adults, and some states mandate their use. These criteria were designed to provide a common language to describe the severity of clients' substance problems and to guide their placement in the most cost-effective level of care.

In reality, according to John Cacciola, PhD, an expert in the assessment of substance use disorders and co-occurring problems at the Treatment Research Institute in Philadelphia, "The ASAM placement criteria are very complicated to implement, with potentially hundreds of decisions to make. So what usually happens is that the program does an interview, looks broadly at the ASAM assessment *dimensions* (which are pretty straightforward)—not the specific *placement criteria* as they were designed to be used—and says the client is appropriate for whatever level of care they want. It's not hard to justify a level of care. Places say they use the ASAM placement criteria, but they are not adhered to in any rigorous or systematic manner." Also, in their 2011 book, *Treating Addiction: A Guide for Professionals*, Drs. William Miller, Alyssa A. Forcehimes, and Allen Zweben, PhD, include a review of studies designed to determine whether placing clients in levels of care according to the ASAM criteria results in better outcomes for those clients and conclude that, thus far, the scientific support for the criteria is "weak." The truth, according to Dr. McLellan, is that "there is no assessment tool or test that definitively determines who should go where."

I had expected to find more programs using what are known as "validated" and "reliable" assessment tools designed by researchers to assess multiple needs of clients and to help treatment staff design interventions to meet their many needs. (Some states require the use of their own assessment forms for people trying to access public funds for treatment.) In *Treating Addiction*, the authors offer a long list of such tools and state, "It is unwise to develop homemade assessment instruments when evidence-based options are available." In my travels, I heard little about the "gold standard" assessment tools, such as the Addiction Severity Index (ASI) and the Global Appraisal of Individual Needs (GAIN) that I'd read about in research studies, magazines for addiction counselors, and textbooks. The ASI, for instance, examines severity of problems in five different aspects of life, from medical to family relations, that may be affected by substance problems. The ASI can then be used to develop a treatment plan targeting those areas, which can improve outcomes for clients. The GAIN is a series of instruments, and the most widely used version assesses clients on a wide array of issues, including substance use patterns and treatment history, physical and mental health, and social issues. It helps clinicians make decisions related to diagnoses, place clients in the appropriate level of care, prioritize needs, and, with client involvement, plan evidence-based treatment and help to manage addiction as a chronic condition. As it turned out, the only programs on my tour that were using such gold-standard tools were four outpatient programs: African American Family Services, the STOP Program, SODAT, and Hope by the Sea. And in 2011, after my visit, Promises Treatment Centers started using ASI.

LaVerne Hanes Stevens, PhD, a national trainer on assessment, then at Chestnut Health Systems in Bloomington, Illinois, said, "The clinical unstructured interview, where a counselor sits and talks with the client in an informal way has been the standard in our field. Clinicians tend to feel more comfortable when they can purely dialogue and don't have to be guided by an evidence-based, structured protocol. They understand the value of building rapport, and the latter may feel too rigid." But a concern with unstructured assessments is that the clinician may miss important information if he or she doesn't ask the right questions.

TWO ASSESSMENT STORIES
WITH VERY DIFFERENT OUTCOMES

Carl D.'s story was one of the few I came across in which a person who had a pretty serious substance problem went for an assessment at a treatment program and *wasn't* told that he needed rehab. Years ago, his family went for counseling, and at one point in a session his wife shared her conclusion that their issues were caused by Carl's drinking. She said, "I think you're an alcoholic." At that point, Carl was regularly drinking a twelve-pack of beer on weeknights; on weekends he'd "start drinking at about noon on Saturday and wouldn't stop until 11:00 Sunday night." So Carl agreed to go for an assessment at a drug and alcohol program.

The hour-long assessment—a verbal interview—was done by a licensed addiction counselor, who told Carl he thought Carl had a drinking problem but didn't know if he was an alcoholic. He recommended a six-month period without drinking. At the end of six months Carl told himself, "I don't think that was long enough, I'll go another six months." When that six-month period was over, he decided to go another year. He never went back to the addiction counselor or to AA but "became very spiritual, asked God to help me a lot, reflected heavily on scripture, and got a lot of support from my wife." Over time, he realized that he had no desire to drink, and he hasn't had a drink since 1996. When he quit drinking he found that "things were going well in my life. My relationship with my kids was better, and I was feeling physically better, sleeping better. Frankly, I was getting more sex, too!"

From what I was told, George W.'s assessment experience at a famous rehab is more typical—that is, you go for an assessment for a substance problem and are then advised to have treatment at the very rehab that does the assessment. Following a period of serious and heavy drug use for several years when he was in his twenties, George subsequently went through a ten-year period during which he married, became a father, and had a few slips with drug use that were nothing like his past experience. When I met him at an outpatient program, he'd had several years with minimal drug use, but after going through a stressful time, had recently been caught stealing Vicodin from a relative. Pressured by his wife and other family members to get an assessment of his substance problems and how they might best be handled, George turned to a renowned residential rehab, expecting that they might recommend counseling once a week. He was blown away when the conclusion of the rehab psychologist's assessment was that George should go to residential treatment. George told me that the psychologist said, "One of the best treatment facilities in the country is right here; why not go here?"

George explained that there had been a misunderstanding about completing his forms and that although he wrote down that most of his serious drug use had occurred about ten years earlier, he felt that the assessment was done as if "everything had happened within the last year." (During his time with the psychologist, they didn't talk about the past year, when his drug use had been minimal.) The next day, when George called to straighten things out, the psychologist agreed that "other factors may render his recommendation not the most appropriate or practical course of action." But in the end, he stood by residential treatment as the preferred course of action, a recommendation that neither George's personal therapist nor his family thought was appropriate. George told me, "I think the psychologist already knew what his diagnosis and recommendation were going to be before I walked into the room." George decided instead to attend a non-twelve-step outpatient program and was also treated for ADHD, which played a role in his drug problems. About a year later, when I checked in with him, George was continuing to do well.

PUTTING THE CART BEFORE THE HORSE

When I asked administrators at several high-end residential programs about their assessment practices, they said that there's usually first a phone conversation, considered screening, between the client and an intake person at the rehab. One place stressed that the screeners are not formally diagnosing, but are "making the determination clinically as to whether the problems presented directly related to alcohol and substance use warrant an admission" to the program. (Here, I was also told that the initial conversation is conducted by "intake/admissions specialists" who are not necessarily licensed counselors.) Based on the data collected, the person is recommended to either continue the admission process or is referred to another type of facility, although the majority of callers did end up being admitted to the initial facilities contacted.

Another administrator told me, "We try to get as much information as possible before they come. We ask about what past treatment they had—if they never tried anything else before, we might suggest an outpatient program. We want to make sure they are psychiatrically stable because we do so much work in group." A woman who went to that program said, "I had a sense that the person on the other end of the line was not a professional—it seemed more like someone answering the phones. I think it took thirty to forty-five minutes. The next person they refer you to is the finance person. After you're there, the assumption is made that you're staying in residential rehab." A representative at another program told me that their phone screening takes about ninety minutes and is conducted by a certified addiction counselor before someone arrives at their residential facilities.

Once the client comes to the program, they usually undergo what several administrators described as their "bio-psycho-social assessment," which involves a team of professionals such as counselors, psychologists, nurses, and physicians. The process usually takes place over the course of at least several days—more or fewer, depending on the client's detox status. A representative at one place described their typical course of events during this time as follows: "The first assessment deals with medical stability; then we look for psychiatric stability [if the client is "cleared," admissions paperwork is completed at this point]; then we begin doing the social-chemical assessment to determine degree and severity of their addiction; then there is additional psychological assessing to determine emotional/behavioral co-occurring issues and personality characteristics, as well as family and spiritual considerations that all end up being integrated into a master treatment plan." (An administrator at this facility mentioned that three psychological tests are used and that if results "show they are intellectual, we may need to stretch them in sharing with their peers.") A physical exam also takes place early in the process. These programs consider assessment to be ongoing. Treatment plans are adjusted in regular team meetings at which they discuss client progress. (I was allowed to observe some of these.)

I was somewhat confused when residential rehabs told me that so much of the assessment process really takes place *after clients are admitted to the residential facilities.* I thought that assessment would largely occur *before* admission, on the basis of a professional assessment and not on the basis of a phone screening. However, according to Dr. Stevens, "Rarely is a comprehensive assessment done *before* people get placed in treatment—it's usually made in the facility. This practice is the rule rather than the exception, and it's like trying to use a remedy before the problem is identified."

Dr. Cacciola concurred. "If they're doing your assessment and determining your level of care while you're in residential treatment, then they're doing it backwards. What determines where people are placed depends on what phone call they make and what door they wind up going through. If you're a person in the public health care system and you call your local outpatient program and you walk through that door, you will get treatment in that clinic unless it is wildly contraindicated. If you call a high-end residential program, they're not likely to say no. A residential place that has a paying customer who's generally appropriate usually won't turn someone away." Some places do occasionally refer people elsewhere after admission if they're not the right fit, but it seems rare. Dr. Cacciola said that even when you go to an individual practitioner for an assessment, you can easily wind up with that person as your treatment provider. In my visits, though, I found that places relying on one-on-one counseling did regularly make referrals to treatment programs.

I got a sense that the programs I visited truly believed that what they have to offer is, in fact, the best level of care for their clients—and it may often be. However, one could question the practice of evaluating a person and then advising that he or she attend *your* program, particularly when he or she came to you for an independent evaluation, and you haven't given the person other treatment options. George said of his experience, "I went for an independent assessment and was not interested at all in the treatment the facility offered. I thought that they would know about and recommend other types of programs that would be a better fit. I went there only because I thought they would have the most up-to-date information, resources, methods of testing, and qualified evaluators." In fact, the U.S. Department of Transportation, which helps to ensure that transportation providers employ "drug- and alcohol-free" operators, explicitly states in its Substance Abuse Professional Guidelines that "to prevent the appearance of a conflict of interest," those who evaluate employees for a problem cannot refer them to the evaluators' private practices or any other entity with which they are financially associated, including "in-patient, out-patient, and education organizations or practices."

GETTING AN OBJECTIVE, INDEPENDENT ASSESSMENT

If you're looking for an objective, independent assessment of a substance problem, Bob Muscala, RN, owner of Muscala Chemical Health Clinic in Edina, Minnesota, suggests considering the following about the assessor and the process:

- Is the focus clearly on your *current* problems?
- Are you offered thoughtful *options* for treatment or do you feel that you're being evaluated as a potential candidate for the assessor's program only?
- If you were referred to an assessor by another professional, are you sent back to the referent with a report containing recommendations that you can then sort through together to decide how to proceed—or do you sense that you're being pressured to make a quick decision?

The non-twelve-step outpatient programs providing more one-on-one treatment over the course of many months rather than weeks had quite different ways of doing things. Tom Horvath, PhD, director of Practical Recovery, where most of the care is provided by doctoral-level clinicians, said, "In our case, assessment is ongoing. The most important things you need to know about a person you won't get in an assessment because clients don't trust you yet. So assessment that occurs only at the beginning usually misses the most critical information. A pre-set program of treatment based on initial assessment only will be of limited value."

QUESTIONABLE ASSESSMENT PRACTICES

A psychologist who had left the employ of a high-end residential rehab shortly before I started visiting programs expressed frustration with the program's assessment practices when he told me, "Once clients arrived on campus, they were almost never given a diagnosis that would signal that they didn't need residential care. If I gave them a diagnosis for a less serious substance problem, it would be questioned very severely." He was also troubled that psychological testing was used as part of what he saw as a form of marketing. At one point, the rehab had psychologists give new clients who had just entered treatment or were considering a month-long treatment undergo a battery of psychological tests "to show them how terrible their functioning was." He said, "It would be used as a tool to get them to do thirty days of treatment, and there was a coercive element in eliciting the patient's participation. They were told that this testing was part of the package of services they were receiving and would yield important information about their functioning."

Noting that early in treatment people may perform poorly on a number of psychological tasks because some are still under the influence of alcohol or drugs, he added, "It seemed disingenuous to test a patient whose cooperation and full consent were somewhat compromised and who likely did not fully understand the reason and purpose for testing. It was not a model that allowed people to think about whether and why they need residential treatment and felt like a ruse." (He thought it might have been more appropriate to propose testing at the start of treatment and then again at the end to gather information about progress.) Although he pressed for a more scientific protocol for the program's overall assessment procedures, he found "The administrators were resistant to it."

THE PICTURE OF A GOOD ASSESSMENT

Knowing that treatment programs more often than not don't use gold standard assessment tools, what should consumers look for to make sure that a program is gathering all the information that they need to come up with a good evaluation of a drug and/or alcohol problem, which in turn should determine the course of treatment? Dr. Cacciola said, "The issue is one of getting a *multidimensional* assessment. In other words, if the questions are all about drugs and alcohol (how much you used and what you're going to do to stop using) and that's it—but you're not asked about your family, work, and psychiatric problems—that's a bad assessment." He went on, "To be good, it has to cover many areas of your life. How are they going to be able to help you if they don't know if you're diabetic or depressed? Do you have family support? Are you working or not, and how does that affect your use?" On the other hand, Cacciola emphasized that if the questions about drug and alcohol use are only cursory, that's a bad assessment, too.

Who should be doing the assessment? Ideally, the assessor should be an experienced person with at least a master's degree in a mental health field, and, if possible, someone who's not affiliated with a treatment program under consideration. (One would need to check with his or her insurance company to find out if that aspect would be covered.) If a program under consideration has both outpatient and residential units, one should consider going to the outpatient unit for an assessment instead of contacting the residential unit first. This might save money and also give the prospective client time to think about the results of the assessment as well as options for getting help before actually being admitted to rehab.

I also wondered about *timing*—if a person is in a lot of distress or still under the influence, is that the time for an assessment? Dr. Cacciola responded, "Assessment should not be a one-time deal. You need a good baseline but then to be continuously reassessed throughout treatment. It shouldn't just be lip service—if you get assessed and then thrown into a group and never asked questions again, then it's not good care." He added that if a client has psychological problems and the rehab doesn't arrange for a mental health professional to assess them, that's a problem. He explained that the initial assessment should be used to develop an individualized plan for treatment and that ongoing assessment of progress during treatment should provide a feedback mechanism to clinicians who may need to modify their approaches. In reality, however, according to a 2011 article in *The Bridge*, a publication of the Addiction Treatment Technology Centers, "ongoing assessment infrequently occurs."

An ideal assessment takes into consideration the following about the client:

- Substance use history, noting whether the problem is occurring right now or took place in the recent or distant past and including the date of last use, as well as how much was regularly used. The history should determine whether the client is currently intoxicated, withdrawing, or abstinent.
- Age, gender, marital or partner status, and educational status
- Occupation and financial status
- Culture and ethnicity
- Medical history (some programs also include laboratory tests and a physical exam conducted by a medical professional)
- Psychiatric/psychological history and assessment for current problems
- Degree of a client's insight into the substance problem
- Treatment history
- Collateral information from previous treatment experiences and other care. If the client grants permission, it's also helpful to get information from his or her spouse or partner, relatives, or friends.
- Readiness and motivation for dealing with the problem
- Need for various kinds of support—medical, financial, legal, housing, marital, and other family support
- Religious affiliation
- Identification of the client's strengths, supports, and resources. While problems are often the focus of assessment and treatment, it's important to identify the assets a person might draw upon in recovery.

Finally, Cacciola maintains that "the process of having an assessment and then getting a recommendation should end up in a way that feels informative and collaborative with the prospective client. The person doing the assessment should inform and solicit feedback from the prospective client—for instance, saying, 'This is what I think would be helpful for you and this is why. What are your thoughts, and how can we continue to move forward in getting you the help you need?'"

ON THE MINNESOTA MODEL, TWELVE-STEP GROUPS, AND TWELVE-STEP TREATMENT

At Hazelden Foundation's Web site, it is claimed that "Hazelden invented modern addiction treatment." While some might have difficulty seeing an approach developed more than four decades ago as "modern," the most common form of residential treatment in the United States—the so-called Minnesota model—did in fact have its origins in work carried out at several Minnesota treatment facilities, including Hazelden, in the 1950s. The cornerstone of successful treatment with this model is abstinence from all drugs of abuse, including alcohol—even if alcohol was never a problem for the client. The model is based on a disease theory of addiction (for more on this, see pages 80–83) and uses as care providers addiction counselors as well as physicians, social workers, psychologists, and nurses. Employees are often recovered themselves—most of the residential programs I visited reported that about 50 to 60 percent of their staff were "in recovery," although none of them had hard numbers, and at one place the estimate was considerably higher. Major goals of treatment under the model include introducing patients to the twelve steps of AA and establishing continued involvement in twelve-step groups such as AA and NA following discharge.

An essential part of this traditional approach is "milieu" treatment, that is, living with others who have had similar experiences and difficulties and who can offer insight and advice on the recovery process. Its traditional twenty-eight- to thirty-day stay has become more flexible of late with acceptance of the notion that serious addiction problems warrant longer treatment periods. And indeed, every residential program I visited expressed a need for more time with clients.

After most clients initially go through detox, they typically attend educational lectures on various aspects of addiction, the twelve steps, and the effects of substance problems on family members. Most of their counseling is provided in the form of multiple daily group sessions with occasional individual counseling—all to help build motivation, resist substance use and find new activities to replace it, enhance problem-solving skills, and improve relationships.

It's important to note that AA, NA, and other twelve-step groups that commonly hold meetings in community settings such as churches, town halls, and libraries are self-help groups (or what experts often call "mutual-help groups") and are *not* considered a form of treatment, even though the majority of rehabs in the United States have incorporated the twelve steps into their programming to varying degrees and in combination with other kinds of treatment strategies. (And many rehabs hold formal twelve-step meetings on-site.) A rehab that offers AA alone would not be considered one that offers appropriate treatment. In his book *A Clinician's Guide to 12-Step Recovery*, psychologist Mark Schenker, PhD, notes that "the pervasive application of 12-step concepts in treatment settings is not an official extension of AA or NA" and that there's a clear distinction between the activities of AA and rehabs using its concepts as their foundation. He adds, "This is a subtle distinction that is often lost in the public mind and, at times, in practice."

As chapter 6 illustrates, most U.S. addiction treatment programs rely on the twelve steps in some fashion. Those that gear their treatment around the steps are often said to offer twelve-step-based treatment. Others offer more of an eclectic mix of approaches, of which the twelve steps are but one component. Most rehabs encourage their discharged clients to become involved in twelve-step self-help groups in the community. Only a minority of rehabs don't use the twelve steps at all.

JUST ANOTHER DAY IN REHAB

So what's a typical day like inside a traditional residential rehab, after you go through the admissions, detox, and assessment processes and begin a month or so of primary treatment? Here's a composite schedule I put together, along with a description of some daily activities, based primarily on my observations at the high-end rehabs I visited, but also on client interviews. This schedule is similar to schedules of rehabs I found online.

Wakeup—6 to 6:45 a.m. The residential rehab day typically starts early with some chores, which can vary from routine bed making and room straightening to vacuuming and more. One woman said, "We dusted, cleaned the kitchen, and mopped the floor. Our rooms had to be immaculate, with nothing on the floor or desk. I got docked a dollar because two inches of a sheet were showing, literally." She presumed that the thinking behind the chores was to provide structure to the lives of people who had had little and to encourage camaraderie. However, at the time she said she found herself thinking, "You're kidding me. I'm paying $1,000 a day and I'm cleaning toilets?!" She was annoyed because it was time that she would have liked to spend finishing her homework.

Meditation—7 to 7:30 a.m. Elizabeth F. seemed disappointed that, while each day began with meditation, it was not mindfulness meditation, in the Buddhist tradition, that some research suggests may help with relapse prevention. She explained that during this time "they took attendance and then we said the serenity prayer, sat quietly, did some daily readings or got a thought for the day—usually from twelve-step literature." Dimitri R. had a similar experience: "At rehab, I'd get really excited when they said we were going to do meditation, and then they'd whip out a book. But it would be reading from twelve-step material."

Breakfast—7:30 to 8:15 a.m.

Medication time—8:15 to 8:30 a.m. While on the regular primary treatment unit, some people are still receiving medications that help with the detox process. Others are getting meds that make it easier for them to stay off drugs, alcohol, or tobacco. Those who have co-occurring mental disorders are prescribed medications such as antidepressants.

Large group lecture—8:30 to 9:00 a.m. Most of the large group lectures I attended were given by addiction counselors and had to do with the twelve steps. Two of the residential rehabs I visited had separate treatment for men and women, but they brought them together for some of these large lectures. As an example, one lecture I attended covered step 7, which reads, "Humbly asked Him to remove our shortcomings. . . . The attainment of greater humility is the foundation principle of each of AA's 12 steps. For without some degree of humility, no alcoholic can stay sober at all." Afterward, as seemed to be common, the women went back to their unit to discuss the lecture, without a counselor present. Sometimes, processing the lecture simply meant going around the room and mentioning one thing you got out of it.

Group treatment or activity—9:00 to 9:45 a.m. Large groups at residential rehabs often split into smaller groups for group therapy or "process groups," which are counseling sessions wherein clients explore personal issues and get feedback from addiction counselors and peers. Some of the groups deal with learning about AA's twelve steps. Others have to do with practical skills for such issues as sleep problems, relationships, stress management, leisure activities, and dealing with situations that might trigger a relapse. I sat in on a group that dealt with defense mechanisms that the counselor defined as rationalizing, blaming, denial, minimalizing, and intellectualizing. (The example of intellectualizing that was used by the counselor was "when someone asks what the program's dropout rate is." I believe this is a question everyone should be able to ask of a treatment program.) Some rehabs have small groups that only people with certain mental health issues attend—for example, groups for people who have experienced trauma, grief, anger management issues, or eating disorders—and these were co-led by psychologists at places I visited.

Group treatment or activity—9:45 to 10:45 a.m. One group session I observed discussed assertiveness training; another took the form of a fascinating interactive lecture, led by a counselor specializing in spirituality, designed to help women explore different meanings of religion and spirituality. I also went to a women's large group nutrition lecture by a dietitian who addressed eating disorders, which a number of women on the unit were struggling with or had dealt with in the past.

Treatment work time—11:00 to 11:30 a.m. Treatment work consists of written assignments that clients complete during their stay, often workbooks or worksheets on the twelve steps or on skills that will help them stay sober or stay off drugs. There may be activities such as writing a "good-bye letter" to their drug of choice. Some of Margaret F's assignments had to do with "selfishness, reasons I turned my back on my family for my drug of choice, the alcoholic mind, and passive-aggressive behavior being transformed into assertive behavior." She said, "The assignments pretty much filled a binder and seeing it in writing made it all too clear how I got where I was."

Lunch—11:30 a.m. to 12:15 p.m.

Medication time—12:15 to 12:30 p.m.

Group treatment or activity—12:45 to 2:00 p.m. A group therapy session I observed was dominated by a client's presentation of a detailed written history of her alcohol abuse and its consequences, followed by group members' reactions. (This is often called a "first step" because it has to do with the substance of AA's Step 1: "We admitted we were powerless over alcohol—that our lives had become unmanageable.")

Group treatment or activity—2:00 to 3:00 p.m. One day, I participated in a "mental health group" that dealt with the consequences of drinking and drug use. First, the counselor elicited responses from the group and then I got to take part as the clients did small-group skits having to do with the topic. I also had several opportunities to participate in large classes in which clients were taught relaxation exercises. (I was so relaxed that I even fell asleep during one of them.) Another program did this as a small group therapy session with a psychologist.

Recreation—3:00 to 4:30 p.m. Recreation commonly includes physical exercise, and two of the rehabs I visited have complete fitness centers. Other activities might include arts and crafts, yoga, and drumming.

Free time, treatment work time—4:30 to 5:00 p.m. Margaret F. said, "It was during the free time I chose to do my power walking to clear my mind. It also allowed time for doing homework."

Dinner—5:00 to 6:00 p.m.

Medication time—6:00 to 6:15 p.m.

Group treatment or activity—6:15 to 7:00 p.m. During this time at one program, I sat through two lengthy "usage histories"—timelines that clients shared before fellow clients, without a counselor present—using big posters they'd made to document their earliest history of substance use (with related consequences) through to the present time. Afterward, the presenters asked for others' reactions and got feedback about possible trouble points and personal assets that might be anticipated in sobriety. I was told that the histories are prepared with a counselor's guidance and that the idea is for clients to take a critical look at the pattern and progression of their chemical use.

Lecture—7:15 to 8:30 p.m. (or later). The residential programs I visited either had outside guests (laypeople) come in to share their recovery stories or large group lectures on twelve-step-related topics. The outside speakers I heard were perceived by clients to be of mixed quality—one was a rambling elderly man who closed his testimonial with the Lord's Prayer. Another place regularly took clients off-campus to twelve-step meetings in the community, a practice that some people criticize because clients can attend meetings free of charge at home. But the argument for doing so is to expose clients to meetings in the "real world." (Some residential rehabs hold AA meetings on-site, while others don't. Betsy H. went to a rehab at which clients were required to attend as many as three on-site AA meetings a day.)

Step 10 group—9:00 to 9:30 p.m. Clients in residential programs often close their day with an activity related to AA's tenth step, which reads, "Continued to take a personal inventory and when we were wrong, promptly admitted it." According to one rehab's handbook, the goal in having clients reflect on this step is also to help them identify what they're thinking and feeling each day, to figure out if they're engaging in any behavior likely to trigger a relapse, to encourage them to look at the positive aspects of recovery, and to note things for which they're grateful.

Free time—9:30 to 11:00 p.m. This is a time when treatment homework can be done, short phone calls can be made on the unit phone with a calling card, and limited television watching may be allowed.

11:00 p.m. Lights out.

———

At some of the residential rehabs there was almost a "kumbaya" feeling in the air. On one women's unit, where clients were referred to as "sisters," clients were assigned rotating roles from a storybook tale, and group recitations took place. For departing clients, tearful and rather moving ceremonies involved passing their graduation medallions around the room for fellow clients to silently hold, followed by a group hug. At another place that held "commencement" ceremonies, everyone at the rehab formed a circle, placing their arms around one another. Graduates got to ring a bell, the staff played a song, and the Serenity Prayer was recited in unison.

————

Weekend schedules at residential rehabs are similar to those of the rest of the week, but some places allow clients to sleep a little later and to have a "fun night" or group recreational activity. Also, family visits and special programming involving family members often take place on weekends. While one program held its own Sunday service, others said they accommodate attendance at places of worship.

THE SERENITY PRAYER

Group recitation of the Serenity Prayer is a mainstay sometimes occurring more frequently than meals at residential rehab and is often recited at AA meetings as well. It goes:

> God grant me the serenity to accept the things I cannot change, courage to change the things I can, and wisdom to know the difference.

At some of the programs I visited, I was asked to participate in the ritual of saying the prayer at the end of group sessions, as we all stood in a circle, arms around one another or holding hands—and at one program, all looked upward.

When I asked Margaret F. about the frequency of reciting the prayer, she said, "Actually, as I progressed from residential treatment through outpatient and continuing care to AA meetings, people who were in recovery said that saying the Serenity Prayer hundreds of times kept them focused on a better life and staying sober."

ALL ABOUT AA AND THE TWELVE-STEP PHILOSOPHY

Whether the problem is alcohol or drugs, Alcoholics Anonymous has long been the center point of addiction treatment in the United States. As the "mother" of all twelve-step and other "anonymous" programs—from Narcotics Anonymous to Overeaters Anonymous—AA's twelve steps have been adapted to form the basis of all of them. Best described as a fellowship, AA is a nationwide network of some 57,900 groups (close to 108,000 worldwide) with U.S. membership of more than 1.25 million. Alcoholics Anonymous officially started in 1935 when cofounders Bill W. (Bill Wilson) and "Dr. Bob" (Dr. Robert Smith) formed a relationship with each other as fellow alcoholics trying to stay sober. They met through an evangelical Christian movement known as the Oxford Group, whose practices in part laid the foundation for AA. From the start, Bill W. viewed alcoholism as a spiritual, physical, and mental malady, and he carried that view into his AA writings and teachings. AA's central proposed mechanism of recovery is through a "psychic change" or "spiritual awakening" achieved through completion of the twelve steps, which, in turn, leads to changes in attitudes and behavior.

The twelve steps, meant to be worked through sequentially, begin with admitting powerlessness over alcohol (or your drug of choice). The belief is that one must accept this notion for progress to take place. It's not that you have to admit you're an alcoholic or addict; the only requirement for AA membership is a desire to stop drinking. (Yet almost all clients I met at traditional rehabs defined themselves this way upon introducing themselves in groups.) What's viewed as critical to recovery is seeing that, once a person starts using such chemicals, he or she cannot consistently predict and control how much they'll use—and the same goes for their actions while using. Abstinence is seen as essential to achieving and maintaining recovery.

The next two steps are about believing in a power greater than oneself and turning one's will and life over to the care of "God as we understood Him." Although AA scholars have noted that AA's founders intended a personal relationship with a transcendent presence, today it's accepted that a higher power can pretty much be whatever you want it to be—some use the power of the group, a belief in nature, or a force of some kind that is greater than oneself. (In my book *Sober for Good*, I even mention one man who chose his dog as his higher power.)

Steps 4 through 10 have to do with taking a "moral inventory" and then admitting things you did that were wrong while drinking or drugging; asking your higher power to remove your "defects of character"; seeking humility; making restitution to those you've harmed; and continuing to self-examine. Step 11 is about making contact with your higher power through prayer and meditation. Finally, step 12 has to do with reaching out to others who still struggle with alcohol. Although outsiders may assume this is purely altruistic, step 12 is at least partly in the spirit of "helping you helps me stay sober."

While the twelve steps are guidelines for personal change, AA's traditions are the foundation by which AA groups operate. The traditions specify the membership requirement and stress the importance of anonymity, as well as the autonomy of each AA group. Thus, there can be great variation from one AA meeting to the next. Other traditions are that each group's primary purpose is to carry its message to "the still-suffering alcoholic" and that "there is but one ultimate authority—a loving God as He may express Himself in our group conscience."

Another AA cornerstone is sponsorship, exemplified by an AA member who has made progress in the program working one-on-one in an ongoing relationship with a newer member to help him or her feel more comfortable in and learn about the program. Sponsors generally are not people with formal training. According to AA materials, "A sponsor is simply a sober alcoholic who helps the newcomer solve one problem: how to stay sober." Sponsors are, however, supposed to be of the same sex as their charges and to have had some time in the program and in recovery.

For many, AA becomes a way of life involving a commitment to a changed lifestyle, seen as essential for maintaining sobriety. Their actions and changes include regular attendance at AA meetings (newcomers are often encouraged to do "ninety in ninety," which means going to a meeting every day for ninety days), actively taking part in meetings, reading twelve-step literature, getting a sponsor, making friends in the fellowship, and giving up the "people, places, and things" they associate with drinking and that may pose a threat to sobriety.

Although the exact date is not known, Narcotics Anonymous (NA) was founded around 1950 to help people addicted to drugs other than alcohol. It has its own guidebook, *Narcotics Anonymous*, often called the "Basic Text," and other literature, but its steps and traditions are those of AA, with minor word changes. Most of NA's other characteristics are similar to those of AA. However, in NA's first step, rather than an admission of powerlessness over a drug or drugs, the stated powerlessness is over *addiction*, which opens the door to include any and all drugs, including alcohol.

Despite AA's view of itself as a spiritual rather than a religious program and the fact that the steps state that you may make AA your higher power, they go on to suggest that "the doubter" who does this will "presently love God and call Him by name." A number of people shared with me their difficulties with this aspect of treatment. When Jackie H. was at a high-end residential rehab, she applied herself to making the twelve steps work because she wanted to feel better. However, when I interviewed her after she left rehab, she said, "It feels too much like a religion for me. There's a higher power, commandments (the twelve steps), a prophet (Bill Wilson), a Bible (the Big Book), weekly meetings you must attend, and if you relapse, you'll die. And in the beginning, there's a process where you have to be converted from the alcoholic to the 'saved' AA member. It's a religion that claims to not be religion, and that scares me."

Nevertheless, I've interviewed agnostics and atheists who are comfortable in AA, and AA groups specifically for agnostics and atheists can be found in some communities. All kinds of other "specialty" twelve-step meetings and groups exist, too—for instance, for men, women, nonsmokers, gays and lesbians, medical professionals, people with co-occurring mental health problems, and those who prefer a more Christian atmosphere. (For more about how the twelve steps are used in treatment programs, see "Twelve-Step Facilitation Therapy" in chapter 4.)

THE TWELVE STEPS OF ALCOHOLICS ANONYMOUS

1. We admitted we were powerless over alcohol—that our lives had become unmanageable.
2. Came to believe that a Power greater than ourselves could restore us to sanity.
3. Made a decision to turn our will and our lives over to the care of God *as we understood Him.*
4. Made a searching and fearless moral inventory of ourselves.
5. Admitted to God, to ourselves, and to another human being the exact nature of our wrongs.
6. Were entirely ready to have God remove all these defects of character.
7. Humbly asked Him to remove our shortcomings.
8. Made a list of all persons we had harmed, and became willing to make amends to them all.
9. Made direct amends to such people wherever possible, except when to do so would injure them or others.
10. Continued to take personal inventory and when we were wrong promptly admitted it.
11. Sought through prayer and meditation to improve our conscious contact with God *as we understood Him,* praying only for knowledge of His will for us and the power to carry that out.
12. Having had a spiritual awakening as a result of these Steps, we tried to carry this message to alcoholics, and to practice these principles in all our affairs.

THE "DISEASE" OF ADDICTION?

In visiting traditional rehabs, particularly residential programs, I found that great emphasis was placed on getting clients to accept that their addiction to alcohol and/or drugs was a disease. Margaret F., who'd been to a high-end rehab twice, said something that seemed to capture a core belief at such programs: "I truly believe no treatment will work on a person with an addiction if the patient hasn't fully given themselves over to the fact that they have a disease that does not heal itself." The Web site for another program stated that its goal, "first and foremost," was to teach clients that addiction is a disease.

As the historical foundation of the U.S. treatment system, the "disease" model is viewed by most as inseparable from AA and the twelve steps. (It should be noted that AA cofounder Bill W. shied away from the notion that alcoholism is a disease.) In its written philosophy, another facility I visited summarized succinctly what the disease model is about with its description of addiction to alcohol and other drugs as an illness that has "a predictable and progressive" course, which, if left untreated, "inevitably results in premature death." It stated, "Alcohol and drug dependency interferes with every aspect of the dependent person's life, inhibiting his/her freedom to function." The disease model views addiction as a primary disorder—not a symptom of some other underlying problem—that is treatable, resulting in sustained remission, but not curable. The Minnesota model is typically viewed as the most effective form of treatment, and lifelong affiliation with a twelve-step program is often recommended, as one program put it, "in order to effectively recover for life." Many who subscribe to the disease model and twelve-step philosophy believe that people can only be "in recovery" or "recovering" but not actually recovered, although the past tense is used often in AA literature.

Numerous experts and professional organizations continue to view alcohol and drug addiction as a brain disease. Over time, for instance, the American Medical Association, American Psychiatric Association, and World Health Organization all came to endorse the notion that addiction is a disease. But most of them conceive of it in a more sophisticated way than that described by the traditional disease model. (While an in-depth discussion is beyond the scope of this book, not everyone agrees that addiction is a disease. For instance, McLean Hospital research psychologist

Gene Heyman, PhD, argues to the contrary in his 2009 Harvard University Press book, *Addiction: A Disorder of Choice*.)

Because of the shame and guilt that come with addiction, calling it a disease can bring tremendous relief and a sense of being absolved of personal blame. When Chanteil J. first arrived at a prominent residential rehab, she said, "Nobody judged me or looked down on me. I will always remember the lady that checked me in, who sat on the floor in front of me and my parents. She did not call me an alcoholic, a loser, or a horrible person. She comforted me and told me they just wanted to help me. She said that I had a disease and millions of people struggle with this disease and they were there to help me and give me tools to help me live a sober life. I felt okay at that moment and knew that I needed to change my life."

However, as one man I interviewed put it, some people find the conventional disease model to be an unwanted "life sentence." Eddie F. said that what helped him least in the outpatient program he attended was "hearing the concept that you were born a drunk and you will always be a drunk. I don't believe that to be true. I believe there is something bigger and broader going on in an addictive person's life." Similarly, Emily E. found that at the several programs she attended as a young adult, the most unhelpful message was "the idea I can't get better—it is a disease." (For other perspectives on this, see "Young People Speak Out About the Twelve Steps and the Disease Model" and "What's in a Name? The Addict Label" in chapter 7.)

The tenets of the conventional disease model, in the words of William White, "have a poor scientific foundation and a narrowly defined clinical profile that does not reflect the diversity of individuals seeking help for alcohol- and other drug-related problems." Still, they're commonly presented as fact, as demonstrated by a training program for professionals I attended at a rehab at which the audience was told that "alcoholism is a disease that's chronic, progressive, and potentially fatal" and that personal and family denial are "hallmarks of the disease." While some disease model tenets hold true for some people with addictions, future chapters will discuss how outcomes vary from one person to the next and how many people overcome substance use disorders (even serious ones) on

their own, "mature" out of them, and/or stay sober without the help of recovery groups. And contrary to the notion that addictions always progress
and that people who relapse will just pick up "where they left off" if they
start using again, research has shown that this is not necessarily the case—
alcohol and drug problems do not have a predictable course and commonly wax and wane depending on the individual. Many addicted people
are well aware of their problems long before they seek treatment and are
not in denial.

GROUP, GROUP, AND MORE GROUP

As the schedule suggests, if a client is a "group" person, traditional residential rehab probably will agree with him or her; if not, too bad, because
there's some type of group counseling, education, lecture, or other group
activity about eight hours a day—not including meals. It may, in fact, be
surprising to learn how little individual counseling can go on when spending upward of $25,000 for a month at a high-end rehab. Said an adminis-
trator at one prestigious program, somewhat boastfully, "The hallmark of
our treatment is the community—group counseling."

For people just coming off drugs and alcohol and who may have lacked
structure in their lives, it's a lot of "seat time"—although one place I visited told me they intentionally schedule groups and classes to last no longer than thirty to sixty minutes. At another program, groups lasted sixty to
ninety minutes. I occasionally saw women nodding off, even in short
groups, some presumably because they were still in the drug withdrawal
process or perhaps having sleep problems that are common in early recovery. But for others, I have little doubt it was at least partly the somnolence-
inducing seat time.

Throughout the day, clients were pulled from the group schedule for
occasional individual appointments with addiction counselors, psychologists, psychiatrists, and "spiritual care" personnel. At some high-end
twelve-step residential programs, where the units held twenty to twenty-
four clients and the ratio was five to seven clients per addiction counselor,
clients typically had an individual session with that (usually bachelor's or

master's degree level at the programs I attended) counselor a few times a week and for brief interludes in between sessions. (Two sessions that I observed lasted about thirty minutes.) Also, clients saw a psychologist when they first came to the program but didn't necessarily see one again unless they were diagnosed with another psychological problem in addition to addiction, in which case they typically had a session with the psychologist for an additional hour each week. Dimitri R. affirmed that at one of the prominent rehabs he attended after his teen program, "I met with a psychologist to get my diagnosis and then saw him once a week." In sum, individual counseling at a high-end residential rehab can work out to just five hours a week or even less. At a smaller, more expensive program, you may get more individual sessions each week, but at most places the treatment is still predominantly carried out in groups.

In observing quite a few hours of group time, particularly at the high-end twelve-step-based residential rehabs, I often found myself wondering, "Where's the counseling?"—I felt like the woman from the old Wendy's campaign, asking "Where's the beef?" I'd expected to see a more active therapeutic role on the part of the counselors. As a case in point, in one group, clients offered more specific tools for a problem than did the counselor, whose solution was to stay away from drugs and to use the support of the group. My notes from my time at another residential program read, "The clients did most of the therapy."

It's not unusual to have "community group" or peer-group meetings on units. But at some residential rehabs, clients were more involved in running groups or in leadership roles than I anticipated. A woman who went to one place that had frequent counselor-free community groups said, "I was very surprised that several times a day we were led by a peer. I thought each group would be led by someone trained in that area and that if a peer was leading it, it would be a person with more sobriety. It put a lot of responsibility on someone who had their last drink three weeks ago. I could see it happening once a day, but I'd say that several times a day we were led by a peer." A few clients I interviewed gave me conflicting reports from those I got from staff, with clients saying peer-led groups were more frequent than staff acknowledged. At this particular program, just about all of the evening activities appeared to go on without a counselor present, but they seemed to be orderly and functional. Jackie H. said, "A few times in peer groups, I felt a counselor should be there, but we stopped the group and went and got one." At another facility, I observed a staff meeting that included a client who had been given a leadership role, where counselors shared information as a new shift came on duty. With this client present, other clients were discussed by name.

Finally, residential rehabs also have counselor assistants (CAs), whose duties include getting clients to appointments on time, providing day-to-day emotional support, giving twelve-step lectures, doing night duty, and helping with assignments. A high school diploma may be all that's required to be a CA.

THE NUTS AND BOLTS OF OUTPATIENT PROGRAMMING

Unlike the residential programs I visited, which primarily treat people with more serious drug and alcohol disorders, at several traditional twelve-step-based outpatient programs I went to, people with problems of mixed degrees of severity were all in the same treatment groups. Sitting at the same table at one facility, for instance, was a woman with a long-term meth addiction who'd been in and out of jail much of her life and a woman who said she occasionally smoked marijuana to deal with her mental health issues. (Some places have separate groups for people with less serious substance problems.) Most of the clients at these programs were from a low-income group, and quite a few were required to be there by the criminal justice system because they had committed a drug or alcohol-related offense.

The length of outpatient programs varies, but those I visited usually lasted at least several months. One counselor told me she felt that being able to work with people over such an extended period of time—eight to eleven weeks as opposed to four weeks in a residential rehab—is a major advantage of outpatient treatment over residential. All but one outpatient program treated men and women in the same group, and sessions ran about three hours, several times a week.

Most outpatient groups open with some sort of "check in." At one program I visited, they called this a "tenth step daily inventory," in accord with one of AA's steps. This consisted of going around the room and having each client respond to a checklist indicating whether they needed to apologize to or thank anyone, what their positive or negative actions the day before were, who they contacted the day before regarding their program, and what their goals and positive affirmations for the present day were.

Betsy H., who went to two different outpatient programs I didn't visit, said of one experience, "Each session was one hour lecture, two hours discussion. Most of [the discussion] was going around the room and talking about the lecture we had just heard. I didn't get much out of it." Once again, this model of care—with so much seat time for people who might be dealing with aftereffects of their drug and alcohol misuse—didn't make sense to me. (About once an hour, short breaks are usually scheduled—often used for cigarette smoking.) William White, MA, author of *Slaying the Dragon: The History of Addiction Treatment and Recovery in America*, said, "Given what we know about the cognitive impairments that can extend into early recovery and what we know about principles of adult learning, it is surprising that so many programs continue to have their patients in passive, information-receiving roles in the earliest stages of treatment."

Overall, in the outpatient programs I visited, clients seemed to feel less compelled to identify themselves as alcoholics or addicts than they did in residential rehabs. In fact, when an adolescent in an adult outpatient group was clearly ambivalent about introducing himself as "an addict," the counselor asked him if he meant it. When he said, "No," her response was, "Then don't say it." And although the amount of emphasis depended on the program, generally there seemed to be less time devoted to the twelve steps. Anna J. spent five months attending one of the outpatient programs I visited, going three days a week, three hours each day. She said, "The program wasn't all about the twelve steps—that wasn't a big focus of day-to-day treatment. It was more about how to deal with your feelings and how to cope with everyday life. It's when you go to [outside] meetings that you learn about the steps."

The expectation for clients to attend outside twelve-step meetings could be demanding. Anna's counselor expected her clients to go to three AA or NA meetings each week, get an AA or NA sponsor, meet with the sponsor once a week, and to sign a release form so that she could speak with the sponsor. This was on top of the three weekly three-hour group program sessions. Clients were also supposed to make an appointment "to complete a fifth step" with a chaplain. (Step 5 of AA is "Admitted to God, to ourselves, and to another human being the exact nature of our wrongs.")

MORE GROUP TIME

At most of the outpatient programs I visited, even more activity was group based than in residential rehabs. An exception was the STOP program in Philadelphia, where clients were given an individual counseling session each week. In fact, in my state, when I was doing research for the book, there was no requirement for a minimum amount of individual counseling in licensed drug and alcohol treatment programs, only that some individual counseling must be provided. I interviewed people who told me they received no one-on-one counseling in their outpatient treatment. Betsy H. said of one of her outpatient experiences in another state, "There was no individual counseling. The only individualization was that the homework I did was different from that of the guys. The whole program was educational, which was fine for me because I was seeing a therapist on the side, but I'd think that would be hard for someone who didn't have that."

Part of the problem is that outpatient counselors often carry a heavy caseload—it ranged from about ten to thirty-five clients per staff member at the programs I visited. However, several counselors said that they were able to accommodate an occasional client whose special needs warranted individual rather than group treatment. Anna J. said that, at her program, if you wanted to talk with the counselor individually, you could, and hers would sometimes ask Anna if she'd like to come in for an hour—"but it wasn't a regular, scheduled thing."

What was discussed during the long group sessions in outpatient rehab? Usually, a topic was planned for each session, such as "having a weekend plan" or "internal motivators" (e.g., wanting to regain custody of your children) versus "external motivators" (e.g., being required to be in treatment because of a drunk-driving citation) for being in treatment. At other sessions, outside speakers from AA meetings gave a presentation, and a chaplain gave a lesson about trust.

A fair amount of group time was spent having clients share their assignments while others just sat and listened. Assignments addressed topics such as triggers for relapse, people to avoid, and fun things to do in sobriety. While some programs used published workbooks for homework assignments, most seemed to allow counselors a fair amount of flexibility in the content of their group sessions. One of them showed me what he referred to as his "own concoction" of assignments, which resembled those of residential programs and included writing a "good-bye letter" to your addiction; asking a family member or loved one to write a "cost letter" explaining how your addiction adversely affected him; listing ten consequences of addiction; and completing a first-step guide (e.g., "the price I have paid"). Betsy H. sent me her notebook of assignments from one outpatient program that consisted of readings from AA's Big Book with accompanying questions about how the chapters applied to the reader.

In both the groups I observed, and from the stories I heard, there seemed to be an expectation that people would share personal details of their lives with the group. One counselor gave clients a written expectation to "discuss problem areas in your life." As an observer, I sometimes felt like personal therapy was being done in front of others and that an inordinate amount of time was often spent on a single person's issues and problems. For example, a large portion of one group was devoted to one client's concerns about ending a relationship, and the counselor gave personal advice in front of the group.

Anna J. said that it didn't bother her to spend a lot of time on an individual's needs, nor was it difficult for her to share her problems with everyone. "Some days, it might take forty-five minutes to regroup a person," she explained. "That was a good thing because they could talk about it and get feedback from others. If you didn't want to talk about things, the counselor didn't push you, and you could do it with her alone." But she could see how sharing with others might be difficult for some. (See chapter 8 for more on "sharing secrets.")

Although almost all of what went on was group based, just about all programs say they individualize treatment. When I asked a clinical supervisor to explain the apparent contradiction, he responded, "When observing a group as an outsider, you wouldn't necessarily see individualization because part of the unique plan for each person is what the counselor is helping the client work on outside the program—such as legal, financial, psychological, or educational issues. It's what a counselor does to help people put out all the fires and to start growing some trees in their lives. Outside the group, a guy might be reconnecting with his wife, reengaging with work, or going back to school." Such issues are processed with the group and counselor, some related homework may be assigned, and then the client faces the real world, hopefully with new skills and ideas.

The supervisor added that another way in which approaches are individualized is in communicating with clients—the counselor might communicate differently with someone who's more ready to quit using drugs or drinking than someone who doesn't think he has a problem and is mandated to be there by a judge. All of this would be part of a comprehensive treatment plan that the counselor carries out with input from the client and based on the client's initial assessment. (As mentioned earlier, treatment plans ideally get modified over time.) Anna J. affirmed that, after she completed her "twenty harmful consequences of addiction assignment," her treatment at this program was personalized. In fact, she felt it was the only rehab of several she'd been to previously where the help was individualized. She said, "The counselor pinpointed on the nose what you needed to work on—for me, it was coping skills. And different people were working on different things." As other stories in the book will illustrate, however, this is not the case at all rehabs—at some places, there's little individualization.

THE RULES OF REHAB

I learned that when going to a treatment program, the client should be prepared for a number of rules that some will find restrictive, even demeaning. Warren T. said he voluntarily went to a "lock-down place" where clients could have no cell phones or non-twelve-step reading materials. He added, "You couldn't leave the premises without an escort, and you had to sign in and out for meals. I thought the next thing they would do is shave my head and de-louse me! It was an awful feeling of confinement and debasement." Although the rules varied from place to place, it wasn't uncommon at residential programs for reading to be limited to recovery or "spiritual" materials, for cell phone and computer use to be restricted, and for visual media to be limited or "filtered" by the staff.

I was most taken aback in my travels when I saw a notice on the wall of a famous rehab's bathroom that read, "Not to embarrass you, but to protect the integrity of the program, it is necessary to have a staff person observe you produce a urine sample." While there's good reason for this in some cases—for instance, when people are being deceptive about drug testing—I thought how offended I personally would feel in this situation.

At one place, young men were told that reading classic novels wasn't allowed because "some guys might read *Harry Potter*" and wouldn't be able to wait to get back to that instead of doing program work. And they weren't allowed to watch movies with "triggers" for substance use or to listen to music in vehicles while being transported to AA meetings because that might serve as a trigger, something that I thought rehab is supposed to help you learn how to negotiate. At a women's program, no music was allowed, but I was told that this was more about preventing "defocusing on treatment" than removing triggers. At the same place, watching TV was not allowed and the only reading material, aside from that having to do with recovery and spirituality, was newspapers.

At another facility, the rationale for taking cell phones away upon arrival was also to help clients "focus on treatment." (Another problem with cell phones is that their built-in cameras might compromise clients' privacy and confidentiality.) Computer access was allowed for about one hour a week, with a staff person present. This particular rehab had buildings on opposite sides of a street that appeared to have little traffic, so I was somewhat baffled that one of their rules was that clients weren't allowed to cross unaccompanied. Partly this involved liability concerns, but I was also told, "If you can't follow our simple suggestions, how are you going to follow other important suggestions?" This struck me as paternalistic and part of the classic rehab model that says, "We're in charge and you're not." Adding to a general feeling of distrust were the rules that clients were accompanied by staff everywhere they went and that taking clients back to the same twelve-step meeting within a certain time period was a no-no because they wanted to "avoid bad influences." This seemed to me to be inconsistent with helping people understand the fellowship aspect of AA.

At Practical Recovery's new residential facilities, the policy is to start from a greater position of client trust. For instance, the use of cell phones and laptops is allowed unless the staff sees reason to remove them. Director Dr. Tom Horvath explained that there are practical reasons for some of the rules of rehab but that they shouldn't be used in a one-size-fits-all way. He said, "For a few, complete transition into a new world—to include no TV, computers, or cell phones—is necessary." In some cases, restricting cell phone and computer use is needed to reduce the likelihood that communicating through them will result in drugs being delivered to the facility. And some people need help with what Dr. Horvath described as "developing a higher level of self-regulation." He elaborated: "Often, clients don't have regular schedules for sleeping, waking up in the morning, eating regular meals, getting exercise, and participating in activities. A degree of imposed external discipline can be helpful, particularly in a younger person. That's why TV may need to be limited, too. The general improvement in self-regulation allows for the pursuit of goals, which in turn protect against relapse." Horvath hopes eventually to have a range of facilities with different rules in each one. Since some places are more flexible than others, it pays a client to ask ahead of time about things like access to computers and cell phones, if such are important.

———

To sum up, traditional rehab in the United States, whether residential or outpatient, predominantly involves group treatment, introducing clients to the twelve steps of AA, encouragement to get involved with a twelve-step program, counseling to help people learn how to deal with life more effectively, and various rules about what is and isn't allowed. For some, this traditional model absolutely does work; for others, like Dimitri, it becomes a merry-go-round of rehab admissions, long stays, and relapses—all at a tremendous financial and emotional cost. The next chapter examines this cost.

CHAPTER THREE

THE COST OF REHAB

FROM THE WALLET TO THE HEART

Multiple trips through detox, rehab, and sober houses can take a financial toll that's almost beyond belief. Steep costs were paid directly out of the pockets of many I interviewed, while others went for treatment time and time again at the expense of private health insurance companies or by benefit of public funding—all adding up to a heavy burden for individuals, families, third-party payers, and taxpayers through government assistance programs. This chapter explores the "investment" in rehab—a look at how the financial costs add up and who pays them—as well as the emotional price of addiction treatment.

ALEXANDRIA B.'S STORY ABOUT THE COSTS OF HER DAUGHTER'S REHAB EXPERIENCES

Alexandria B. shared the story of her thirty-three-year-old daughter, Krista, whose fifteen-year heroin addiction was so severe that "she ate out of garbage cans, was raped countless times, slept in alleys, and saw friends get stabbed and killed right in front of her eyes." Krista's drug problems—abuse of pot, cocaine, alcohol, and eventually heroin—started in her early teens. As responsible, well-educated parents, Alexandria and her husband initially sent Krista to a number of psychologists, all of whom said she was acting like a "normal" adolescent. It wasn't until she was nineteen that Krista had the first of multiple rehab experiences that, in the end, cost her parents "hundreds of thousands of dollars." After Krista was arrested for writing bad checks from her mother's account, a judge agreed that Krista could avoid going to jail if she went to a rehab. Alexandria told me, "We wound up choosing a residential program that a lot of people said was good. I called there, and everyone sounded nice. What did I know about what a good program was?" (Although not among the most famous, the rehab they chose is quite prominent.)

Alexandria said, "We got in the car and dropped her off. It was good-bye at the door, and our daughter wasn't very happy. We were cut off at that point because the program didn't communicate much with us, and Krista wouldn't talk with us at all during her sixty days there. It was painful and confusing." Alexandria added that family meetings were available every couple of weeks but that Krista refused to allow her parents to visit. "The staff didn't explain anything to us or help us in any way," Alexandria recalled. "When treatment was over and we went to pick Krista up, they said there was no hope for her. They pretty much just said 'good-bye' after connecting us with a therapist where we lived." (The therapist turned out to be unprofessional; Alexandria said he discussed payment in the waiting room in front of other clients. They left for good after one visit.)

As Alexandria recalls, this first rehab stay, which took place more than ten years ago, cost her and her husband about $35,000. When I asked if, given the lack of communication and the price they were paying, she and her husband considered pulling Krista out of the program, she responded, "No, because it was a condition of her 'incarceration.' If she weren't there, she would have been in jail. And it was our very first rehab experience— we were newbies. We didn't understand what rehab was, and the place didn't educate us on what to expect. They just happily cashed our checks. And our daughter happily avoided treatment while she was there, fighting them all the way. She was counting the days until she could go back on the streets. The day she left the program, she was using again."

For the next dozen or so years, Krista went through multiple detoxes— at about $10,000 each—and she was in and out of several more rehabs. Most of it came out of her parents' pockets because Krista rarely had health insurance, and, although she would have been eligible for pubic assistance for addiction treatment, her mother said, "At first, we didn't feel right getting her on it—we felt like we should pay, not realizing how much money we were going to have to shell out as time went on."

Eventually, Krista went to a small faith-based rehab that helped people at different stages of recovery and where fees were geared to the client's ability to pay. She lived there for two years. Alexandria said, "For a long time, they were a big support for her and for us. At least I knew she was safe. But they weren't very strict and didn't have a real program." Unfortunately, Krista kept using drugs during her stay, and the rehab finally dismissed her.

Although she went "right back to the streets" and used for years afterward, Krista did attempt a few periods of sobriety, and her mother went through some horrendous detox experiences with her, complete with hallucinations, diarrhea, and the like. With time, Krista decided to give rehab another shot and went to a "highly recommended" rehab. Alexandria described this short-lived experience as follows: "We initially gave them a check for $13,000 and were supposed to give them the rest later. But Krista only stayed for twenty-four hours because she had an infected abscess [from needle injections]. They had physicians, so I thought they had medical care. But they kept sending her back to us, and she kept using when home." In the rehab, Krista was given Suboxone to help her come off the heroin, but when she was sent home, her mother said, "they refused to give her a prescription for Suboxone, so she was not weaned from it and went right back to heroin." At some point, the rehab asked for another $13,000. In the space of two weeks, they received $26,000 from the family. "She never actually received any real treatment there," Alexandria recalled. "I was very pissed at them because they collected a full month's fee and did not return any of it. There were many times like this, when treatment or detoxes were not completed, yet we got no money back."

After another short-lived experience at the small rehab, which again ended when Krista used drugs, she began staying with friends who were drug addicts. The turning point came when she overdosed, became extremely ill, and was hospitalized for two months. Alexandria stayed at her daughter's bedside fifteen to twenty-four hours a day. Although it was touch and go about whether she would live or die, Krista survived, and when she was well enough to leave the hospital, she said, "I want to go to rehab."

This time, they took the recommendation of a former counselor who suggested a different small program with a highly regarded director. Alexandria described it this way: "The place was strict. Krista got a great therapist, and the groups were wonderful. None of the other places she went to had prepared people for life. But this place took clients to supermarkets, had cooking classes, took them to the gym every morning, and did yoga with them." Both Alexandria and her husband also felt that a major difference between this place and others Krista had attended was the emphasis on individual counseling. Alexandria said, "She had daily private sessions with her therapist as well as groups. All other treatment programs were only groups." It was a sixty-day program but Krista chose to stay an extra month. The entire stay cost about $35,000, half the normal price as a courtesy because of all the family had been through.

After she left the rehab, Krista was connected with a "fabulous" therapist (one she saw for almost five years and who also did some counseling with the whole family), went to live in a sober house, worked at several rehabs, and remains actively involved in a twelve-step program and with her sponsor. Alexandria said, "This is my kid, who the doctors said, 'She's not going to live. If she does, she'll never live on her own. She'll need constant care the rest of her life.'" She added, "Krista went from strength to strength and recently celebrated her fifth year of sobriety. She never says, 'Oh, I wasted so much of my life.' She feels like everything she did prepared her for what she's doing now."

THE FINANCIAL TOLL OF REHAB

Altogether, Alexandria figures they spent $300,000 out of pocket for Krista's treatment-related expenses, much of it from her and her husband's retirement savings. She added, "There were also many psychologists after the rehabs." When I asked her how she felt about the whole ordeal and all they spent, Alexandria replied, "My husband and I are in our sixties, we have no money, need a new roof, and have a thirty-year-old carpet. We'll be working until we die. We gave it all for Krista, and it was absolutely worth it." Although some of their experiences took place a while back, the total picture captures well both the financial and emotional issues people face today with treatment as we know it in the United States.

Others I interviewed agreed that the money for rehab was, in the end, well spent. But some were less sanguine about the investment, whether it came out of their own pockets, from private health insurance, or through public funding. Here's how the costs stacked up for some of them:

- When I last talked with Emily K., her cocaine-addicted son had been to a youth wilderness program, six residential rehabs, and several sober houses. Plus, she and her husband had paid for an expensive alternative regime including prescription medications and nutrition supplements. Initially, some of the expenses were covered by health insurance: about $30,000, as she recalled. But another $200,000 came from their own funds.
- Nancy B. paid $26,000 out of her own funds *just for a residential detox program*—it lasted a month and provided no counseling.
- Wyatt D. estimates that "over a million dollars" was spent on his more than twelve residential rehab stays. At one point, he spent four months at a famous psychiatric center that has a separate division for people with substance problems. He said, "My diagnosis was that I had enough money to pay for being there."

Shari P.'s mother told me of her daughter's experiences at more than twenty residential programs. "Some of the facilities Shari went to took partial insurance, but many in our state did not. At the 'better' or more 'well-known' rehabs, you must either be a rock star or celebrity to go, as they run about $35,000 to $50,000 a month. Over the years, we personally spent, including all the extra costs, around $200,000 or more." And this woman did her homework, having researched places all over the United States, Canada, even in Tibet. (She talked with someone from the TV show *Intervention*, but even with a reduced fee, their treatment suggestion was unaffordable.) She said, "Affordability is the main obstacle. I've begged, cried, even offered to come to the facility to cook, clean, work in the office, or whatever. But it was always 'No, No and No. . . . If you cannot pay, you do not go.' Simple as that." (Halfway through writing this book, Shari and her family had become so frustrated with the U.S. treatment system that she went to a rehab in Argentina and had been there for nearly two years as the book was coming to a close. This rehab was costing the family about $2,000 a month.)

Bear in mind in all of this that numerous studies have shown that outcomes are about the same with residential and outpatient treatment, the latter generally being far less expensive. An expert who stressed this point is Oregon Health & Science University's Dennis McCarty, PhD, a leading authority on organization, quality, and funding of addiction services. He said, "Parents are especially vulnerable because they'll do anything to help their child. It's good when people are able to find the care they want and it's effective. Should it cost hundreds of thousands of dollars? is another issue."

In the space of two days, I met with two physicians with extensive addiction treatment experience who expressed concern about the high cost of residential rehab. One of them pointed out that you could book a room at a nice hotel for a month (let's say at $150 per night), have all your meals there ($100 per day), see a psychiatrist twice a week ($300 per visit) and a psychologist three times a week ($275 per visit), get a membership at a fitness club for the month ($100), go to a massage therapist once a week ($100), and you still wouldn't come close to the $30,000 that a typical rehab costs for twenty-eight days. If you add it all up, plus throw in seeing an addiction counselor three times a week at a rate of $130 per hour, the grand total for the month comes to not quite $15,000, or about half the price of many a residential rehab. Another physician, an addiction psychiatrist who provides one-on-one therapy and medical care to people with drug and alcohol problems, said, "You could buy a heck of a lot of my time for $30,000." If he got $300 per hour, you could see him twenty-five hours per week for an entire month for that $30,000. But health insurance would never cover that. This is not to say that residential treatment is never in order or that some people don't require a level of care with close supervision, but it illustrates how much individualized care you could get for far less money than many people pay for rehab.

In the end, financial obstacles are a major reason why people don't get the help they need. According to the National Survey on Drug Use and

Health (NSDUH), the most common reason for not receiving treatment reported by people who felt they needed treatment but didn't receive it was that they had no health coverage and could not afford the cost. The recent changes in legislation discussed in this chapter may make addiction treatment more affordable and accessible for many people.

HOW MOST TREATMENT GETS FINANCED

People who go to upscale facilities like the residential programs I visited and that celebrities frequent are in the slim minority. According to NSDUH, about 27 percent of individuals who went to rehab in 2010 said they used Medicare as a source of payment for their most recent treatment, while 65 percent used Medicaid or public assistance other than Medicaid, making government the most common source of addiction treatment financing in the United States. (State and local governments also finance much of addiction treatment.) About four out of ten used their own savings or earnings, while just over a third of them said they used private health insurance to pay for treatment. Approximately 23 percent said they got financial help from family members. (People could report more than one way of paying for treatment.)

Medicaid is a health insurance program for low-income families and children, pregnant women, the elderly, and people with disabilities. While the federal government provides a portion of the funding for Medicaid and sets broad guidelines for the program, each state operates its own Medicaid program and has choices in its eligibility requirements and benefits packages. Thus, Medicaid varies by state, as may its name and the use of its funds for substance use disorder coverage. *Medicare* is a federal health insurance program that serves people age sixty-five or older and those under age sixty-five with certain disabilities. Only some facilities accept Medicaid or Medicare, whose rates of reimbursement tend to be lower than those of private insurance plans. The most recent N-SSATS showed that just over half of rehabs in the United States accepted Medicaid while only about a third of them accepted Medicare or federal military insurance as forms of payment. In contrast, just under two-thirds of them accepted private health insurance. For a comprehensive overview, see "Health Services and Financing of Treatment" at pubs.niaaa.nih.gov/publications/arh334/389-394 .pdf.

When it comes to how rehabs fund themselves, the largest proportion of programs are freestanding, nonprofit corporations. In 2010, about 58 percent of rehabs were organized as private nonprofit corporations, while just under a third were private for-profit facilities. (The "profit" versus "nonprofit" distinction has to do with the tax status of the facility.) The others (about 12 percent) were public programs run by local, state, federal, or tribal governments. However, many private programs receive some public funds—for instance, from state and local governments and/or from grants. All of the rehabs I visited were private, but they represented a mix of for-profit and nonprofit status. Some took clients with public funding, to varying degrees, while others did not. When people refer to "public funding," they're talking about Medicaid, Medicare, federal military insurance, state-financed health insurance plans, and separate funding or grants from county, state, or federal governments.

HOW THE BILLS GOT PAID

In Krista's case, Alexandria said, "She was on our health insurance until a doc reported to the insurance company that he treated her for an abscess secondary to heroin addiction. They then refused to cover her for any addiction-related issues. After that, we paid for all the rehabs. Had she tried to get into the ones covered by Medicaid, she'd probably still be waiting because the waiting lists were impossible. I once called to find out how long the wait was, and they asked if she was pregnant. They take pregnant women first. When I told them she wasn't, they said to try to find another way to get her off drugs. At that point, I sent a nasty letter to my congressman. She should get pregnant to get help getting off drugs?! I understand why a pregnant woman would have priority, but if someone is not pregnant, then there are no services?" Dr. McCarty confirmed that programs with federal grant funding prioritize admission for pregnant women and that waiting lists still exist for publicly funded programs. However, I interviewed others who had better experiences than Krista in accessing such treatment, including some whose treatment was state- and county-funded.

For some people with private health insurance, personal rehab costs were comparatively minimal. Lee Ann B. went to a high-end, twelve-step residential rehab that was almost totally covered because her insurance company had an agreement with them. She said, "I was pre-approved by my insurance company, so I didn't have to pay anything up front. I think I had a $150 deductible. However, there were 'extra' charges that a patient would have to pay out of pocket, if deemed necessary, such as extra therapy sessions and meds for detox or depression. They were considered to be personal expenses."

Even with good insurance coverage, however, things can add up. Over the course of eight years, Bruce O.'s twenty-three-year-old daughter had gone to rehab at least a dozen times and through multiple detoxes and hospitalizations for her substance use disorder. Here are his estimates for just some of the expenses:

Six months at an adolescent residential program = $15,000
Five months at a high-end residential adult rehab at $25,000 = $125,000
Medications: 100 x $20 = $2,000
Twelve or more hospitalizations at $10,000 = $120,000*
Twelve ER visits at $6,000 = $72,000

The grand total came to $334,000. Even though 95 percent of this was covered by insurance, Bruce's 5 percent co-pay still amounted to almost $17,000. Add to that another $4,000 for eight years of insurance deductibles, plus co-pays for a number of other rehabs she attended and the $1,000 a month he paid to keep his daughter (and her sister) on his insur-

* Costs because of medical problems related to addiction and co-occurring psychological issues.

ance policy after she was no longer eligible as a dependent. (Bruce managed to have her deemed disabled so he could continue her coverage.) Now, unless the Affordable Care Act (or what some refer to as Obama Care) changes or is repealed, most health plans that cover children must make coverage available to young people until they are twenty-six.)

Sometimes, people chose to pay for rehab out of their own funds because they preferred not to have an addiction diagnosis or history of treatment in their medical or insurance records. According to the most recent NSDUH, two of the most common reasons why people who knew they needed help for a drug or alcohol problem didn't receive help were that they were concerned about the possible negative effect on their job or the opinion of people in the community. When Frank D. decided to get off prescription painkillers, he first paid for his methadone program himself to avoid a paper trail. After telling his employee assistance program counselor about his addiction, he was told, "Believe me, you're not the only one." Frank said, "From what I know, they can't tell my employer. It was a good thing to get off my chest." He then decided to use his health insurance to pay for treatment. When I asked if he was worried about having the addiction on his insurance record, he replied, "I'm more worried about being clean than anything. It doesn't bother me now, but I hope it doesn't affect me in the future."

For others, treatment coverage was more of a mixture of personal and private insurance funding while loved ones went on and off insurance plans. This was the case with Heather P.'s adult daughters, both of whom have struggled with alcohol problems since adolescence. As a single mom, Heather guesses that, even with some private health insurance coverage here and there, she spent about $20,000 on each daughter out of her own funds. As someone in a profession deeply affected by the economic recession, Heather told me, "I have real anxieties about my financial condition; I have no more money. I've had rehabs tell me, 'You're just going to have to sell your house.' The message feels like, 'You're going to have to give up your whole life.' But if you've destroyed yourself, then you're not there for your kids. Some treatment centers may not be realistic. I think some of them take advantage of people who are desperate."

Although I got a sense that most programs make their recommendations with good intentions for clients, it seemed there was validity to Heather's questioning of some rehabs' expectations about sinking so much money into treatment. At one of the high-end rehabs I visited, when I asked an extended-care coordinator how people pay for the extra care—often several months long and seldom covered by insurance—she matter-of-factly stated that some parents are using their retirement funds. It was as if to say, "That's just what people do." And at a residential program for adolescents, many of whom came from low-income backgrounds, a counselor told me that, in the interest of their best care, she wished she could send all of her clients to halfway houses or group homes after primary treatment—a recommendation she appeared to make frequently. Yet when questioned, she seemed to have no idea how much such care would cost. When I commented at one place that I might not be able to afford their $10,000 option if I had to pay out of pocket, the intake coordinator looked incredulous. Feeling a bit chagrined, I continued, "Well, if my kid had what I perceived as a life-threatening addiction, I guess I'd find a way to pay for treatment." And this is what many families do—over and over again.

A staff person at one rehab went so far as to say about other programs at which she worked, "I didn't feel like they stood behind what they said. They misrepresented what goes on, what you'll get, and how payment works. You go in thinking one thing, and it's all stripped away from you. That's not okay."

NATIONAL SPENDING ON ADDICTION TREATMENT

According to a 2011 study in the journal *Health Affairs*, the estimated amount spent on treating alcohol and drug use disorders in the United States in 2005 was about $22 billion, and analyses estimate that the figure will increase to $35 billion by 2014. Despite the high number of people with substance problems, this represents "an almost trivial" 1 percent of the nation's $1.9 trillion in total 2005 health-care expenditures, according to Tami Mark, PhD, lead author of the study. Bruce O., whose two daughters and wife struggled with substance problems, said, "When given a choice of employee-provided medical coverage, I have always based my selection on mental health and addiction treatment benefits. Too few insurance programs have robust coverage for this."

According to the *Health Affairs* study, "Spending on substance abuse services during the past three decades can be characterized by a period of boom and bust." Insurance benefits and access to treatment broadened through the early part of the 1980s, but by the end of the decade, escalating health-care costs—in substance treatment, in particular—became a concern enhanced by the growing private rehab industry. As a result, managed care began to place limitations on twenty-eight-day residential and inpatient rehab stays, overall spending on treatment fell, and treatment shifted more to outpatient settings. In more recent years, spending has increased again and Dr. McCarty and others are observing something of a shift back to more funding for residential treatment.

Tom Horvath, PhD, director and founder of Practical Recovery in San Diego, California, has found that health insurance companies are more likely to pay for expensive residential rehab stays than their less costly outpatient option. He said, "A one-month stay at a high-end residential rehab in this area of the country can easily cost $45,000 to $60,000 or more, and it's not uncommon for health insurance to cover at least part of that." On the other hand, if someone were to attend Practical Recovery's upscale intensive outpatient program five days a week, including three hours of individual therapy per day—far more individual sessions than almost any rehab offers—with treatment provided primarily by doctoral-level psychologists, and to also stay at their supervised sober house (single room, shared bath), the cost for a month of care would be about $20,000. However, insurance coverage for this is rare. Dr. McCarty pointed out that coverage varies in different parts of the country, adding, "Overall, my guess is that the direction will continue to be reduced reliance on residential care and increased reliance

on outpatient services. I could be wrong. . . . Never underestimate the public and the market for traditional drug and alcohol treatment."

Coverage for mental health and substance use disorder treatment may improve now that the Mental Health Parity and Addiction Equity Act is in effect. The 2008 federal law requires that group health plans with more than fifty employees and health insurance issuers (such as private companies like Blue Cross/Blue Shield) ensure that mental health and substance use disorder benefits, if offered, are covered on par with medical and surgical benefits. While this law does not apply to groups with less than fifty employees or to individual health insurance plans, some states have their own parity laws that may apply in such cases.

The bad news is that health insurance companies are not required to cover mental health or addiction treatment expenses at all. However, the Kaiser Family Foundation's Employer Health Benefits survey indicated that in 2010 only a small number of companies eliminated such coverage for employees. (This can be a way of getting around the parity law in an effort to save money.) According to Dr. McCarty, "While some of the issues related to this law will probably be litigated and impacts won't be apparent for a while, estimated health-care expenses associated with the introduction of parity do not appear to cause a significant increase in the total cost of care." At this writing, the future of the Affordable Care Act (which expands parity) and, therefore, of funding for addiction treatment is uncertain. McCarty said, "In a perfect world with full implementation of the Affordable Care Act, most U.S. citizens will have health insurance from a plan that covers addiction treatment, and Medicaid will cover more people than in the past. However, Republicans will certainly campaign against ObamaCare and it will become history if they control the House, Senate, and White House. If the Democrats remain in the White House and control the House or Senate, then we'll probably maintain the status quo. Anything in between those two options leads to more uncertainty." If the act stays in place as is, not only will more individuals with addictions likely be covered than previously, but benefits will be available for those with less serious drug and alcohol problems.

THE "ADD-ON" COSTS OF ADDICTION TREATMENT

When I started writing this book, I was unaware of the "add-on" direct and indirect costs of going to rehab—cumulative costs that can take a toll when someone seeks help, such as the following:

- Wynn O. said that in addition to steep treatment expenses that her family paid out of pocket for her daughter's multiple residential rehab experiences, there was the cost of travel expenses to and from programs for parent and child on top of forfeited college tuition.
- Margaret F. pointed out that although the cost of her two stays within the space of a year at a residential rehab were covered by her health insurance, she was off work and without pay for two months.
- Heather P. said, in talking about expenses related to her two daughters' numerous residential rehab stays, "It's not just the treatment— it's their medications at the rehab that have been shocking to me. One month, one of the girls' prescriptions was $800." She added that because she didn't want her daughters to lose their cars or ruin their credit ratings while away, she made their car and insurance payments. (She said, "It's been devastating to me financially. I'm almost sixty, and I can't afford my own meds.")
- Emily E.'s severe addiction and time in treatment programs kept her from working, which was making it hard for her to find a job when I interviewed her. She said, "All anyone sees is I have been out of work for sixteen months now and that I have a misdemeanor on my record, which will thankfully be off in a few months. No one seems to want to look at my education, my professional awards, or my years in prestigious work positions."
- Elizabeth F. applied for long-term disability insurance but when it was noted that she had been to a rehab for an addiction, she was told that in order to be eligible, she would first have to "keep a clean

slate" for seven to ten years. (Dr. Horvath said, "Once an insurer has a record of alcohol or drug addiction, it stays with the insured's record and is available throughout the insurance industry, such as when you apply for life or disability insurance. Therefore, I tell clients that if the record of substance problems is not established, they may wish not to use insurance.")

- Claire L. was denied health insurance coverage because of her past history of alcoholism and depression. She said, "That was a blow because you do all the right things to get your life back on track and the insurance world is all about money, not people."

With passage of the Affordable Care Act, denial of health insurance because of preexisting conditions will no longer be allowed beginning in 2014. (This rule is already in effect for people under the age of nineteen.) In the meantime, private insurers can still deny adults coverage because of a preexisting condition. However, until 2014, health insurance is available to such individuals through what's called the Pre-Existing Condition Insurance Plan (PCIP), which can vary by state. The government's easy-to-navigate, comprehensive Web site (http://healthcare.gov) that explains the Affordable Care Act helps you explore insurance options and has a place for checking PCIPs state by state.

JACKING UP THE COST OF REHAB: BRAIN SPECT (SINGLE-PHOTON EMISSION COMPUTED TOMOGRAPHY) IMAGING OR SCANNING

You've probably seen those "this-is-your-brain-on-drugs" images in TV shows on addiction. SPECT imaging, which involves injection of a radioactive tracer, is a brain imaging tool used by researchers to study how drug use affects areas of the brain and how addicts' brains "light up" in situations associated with drug use. Several high-end rehabs I had contact with that were using SPECT imaging suggested that it could help with treatment planning. One indicated that the use of

SPECT images could be used for patient evaluations and allowed for use of more targeted therapies and enhanced patient motivation for treatment. When I asked the National Institute on Drug Abuse (NIDA) about such uses of SPECT imaging, I was told, "There is insufficient empirical data available at this time to support the proposed clinical diagnostic use of any brain imaging method. NIDA is interested in well-designed studies that can advance the science on this approach, but there is not enough data yet to show its clinical effectiveness." Practically speaking, Dr. Henry Kranzler of the Treatment Research Center at the University of Pennsylvania said, "This promises to be an expensive way to convince people that they need help and, given the present state of the science, will probably not contribute meaningfully to treatment." And SPECT imaging is expensive—$1,500 according to one residential rehab—plus it exposes people to radioactivity, albeit a low dose.

THE MIDDLE-CLASS SQUEEZE

As I was writing this chapter, I heard a show on Minnesota Public Radio about mental health issues in young people in which psychiatrist and president of New York City's Child Mind Institute, Harold Koplewicz, MD, said, "If you are poor or you are rich, you are covered." He further explained that if you're poor and you have Medicaid, you probably have better mental health coverage than a working-class or middle-class family. He added, "Or if you are very rich and you can pay out of pocket, you're kind of okay. But if you're stuck in the middle . . . , you are really at tremendous risk because the services are expensive; they're scarce." An addiction counselor at an outpatient program affirmed that "you're almost better off having no money than being in the middle." My own son once was going through a rough time and tried to access public health care, only to find that he made too much money as a part-time pizza delivery man to qualify.

Jacqueline Duda is a journalist who knows this issue well. I corresponded with her after reading a heart-wrenching 2008 *Washington Post* story she wrote titled "Why We Couldn't Save Nicole." It was about how—after repeated attempts by her middle-class family to navigate the addiction treatment system—her twenty-two-year-old daughter died from an accidental drug overdose. In the article, Duda wrote, "Surely, we thought, college-educated suburbanites like us could locate professional help: drug counselors, doctors, therapists specializing in addiction. Surely detoxification centers would treat desperate addicts and work out a payment plan. Surely we could check her into some kind of residential treatment program with a minimum of delay. We were wrong. The next several months of trying to get her affordable treatment were like entering some unknown circle of hell."

Expecting that after Nicole's first emergency room experience for heroin withdrawal symptoms she'd be admitted directly to a rehab—only to be given a medication patch to ease drug cravings, handed a listing of dozens of local treatment programs, and discharged—the family began its "initial foray into the drug-treatment world." Duda wrote, "When private clinics learned that Nicole had no insurance and had been determined ineligible for Medicaid, most simply said 'sorry' and hung up; and at $15,000 to $25,000 for a 28-day residential stay, they were out of middle-class reach. The public, government-funded centers were stuffed to the gills, often with patients from prison-related programs. As one counselor told us, an addict can get in faster if he commits a crime than if he just asks for help."

After three weeks, Nicole was finally admitted to an outpatient program that charged $20 for each of its sessions, which were conducted two to three times a week. However, she continued the battle of trying to quit, and kept relapsing, often winding up in the local hospital's emergency room (which was not equipped for drug detox). Finally, after months on a waiting list for a spot in a residential county program, Nicole was admitted and stayed for thirty days. But she refused to live in the halfway house that had been arranged for her afterward. Six months later, while Duda was making dinner one evening, she got "the visit"—two county police officers showed up and "told us the words no parent ever wants to hear."

Duda, who has since served as an advocate for better health coverage and written a number of stories on the topic, said in an e-mail, "Thirty days of treatment isn't enough. It's not enough time to treat cancer, or obesity, or any chronic, relapsing disease. The same goes when treating addiction or mental illness. But even families with impressive insurance plans find their coverage is limited to 5-day, 10-day, or 14-day stints for mental illness and/or addiction treatment. Facilities that have the funding and support to individualize addiction treatment plans and the opportunity to employ a vast selection of integrative health care, meeting all needs under one roof, and implementing evidence-proven practices over a longer period of time are experiencing more success. Our public treatment system is vastly overwhelmed. Yet there are many dedicated and hardworking treatment professionals in the public system who are doing everything they can, despite being affronted by enormous budgetary and time restrictive challenges."

People in the public system sometimes have better access to comprehensive care than those who have financial means or those "in the middle." After receiving her first drug charge and going to jail at the age of eighteen, Shelly T. was in and out of outpatient addiction treatment (and jail) several times before going to a program for women that first offered ninety days of residential treatment, which she said "was the best experience for me to have while trying to get off drugs." After that, the program provided transitional services for an entire year, including housing, outpatient addiction treatment, medical and mental health care, plus help with job skills, employment, and education. She also got her GED and her driver's license while in treatment. Medicaid covered all of her treatment. (See also the story about Jaden M., who went to the ARC program, in chapter 4.)

COVERED OR NOT COVERED?

Rules for coverage of substance use disorder problems can be nonsensical. Milwaukee psychologist Ned Rubin, PsyD, who specializes in helping people with substance use disorders, said, "Sometimes it seems arbitrary and capricious the way access decisions are made. For instance, I have two offices and a client's insurance may pay for him to see me at one office but not another, even if one is easier for someone to get to. And the biggest obstacle for people facing treatment is that they don't know where to go or how to easily access treatment, much of which is dictated by insurance companies and provider panels." While a discussion of all the ins and outs of private insurance payment is beyond the scope of this book, here are some of the scenarios people faced in getting coverage:

Sadie A. found that it was important to insist that financial assistance personnel at treatment programs she was considering speak directly to her insurance company about whether or not she was covered for treatment at their facility. She particularly wanted to go to a prominent twelve-step rehab, and at first the program told her that she was not covered. However, she discovered that "after my deductible, I *was* covered 100 percent. Persistence paid off." When her month-long stay was up, subsequently staying at a sober house was not covered. She said: "So you need to ask about that or you might wind up with a big fat bill at the end that you weren't prepared for." After attending the residential program, she went to their outpatient program, which resulted in new deductibles and co-pays.

Elizabeth F. went to the same rehab as Sadie A. and her insurance "paid for 100 percent" of her three weeks of treatment. She said, "I never paid them a dime." However, she went there not knowing how long of a stay would be covered. She explained, "Before you check in, they run your insurance and ball-park what they will and will not cover. I was told that my insurance company would approve me a week at a time, but wouldn't commit to covering me at all until I got there." She added, "Before I went, there was a hint given to me by the intake staff that it would help my case with the insurance company if I showed up unable to drive safely. Of course I took it literally and drank heavily at the airport right before arriving at the rehab." (She found, in doing her homework ahead of time, that some insurance companies have a checklist of prerequisite conditions for coverage for residential addiction treatment.) After a relapse, however, the hospital where she went for detox didn't accept her insurance. But they didn't inform her of this while she was there and she wound up with a $20,000 bill. Because she was unemployed, she couldn't pay the fee, and she wound up with a legal judgment against her. Eventually, the insurance company settled with the hospital, but the insurance company admonished her that coverage should be verified when being admitted to a hospital, even through the emergency room. Of course, someone in need of detox isn't necessarily in a condition to do this.

Eddie F. found that his insurance company would cover his attendance at an outpatient addiction program for twelve weeks. However, he said, "People there on the county would go for six months to a year. I got the feeling that the length of time was dependent on how you got there and who was paying for it, not that it was based on want or need or evaluation. The staff made sure they knew how you got to the program: court, human resources, on your own, etc. In my case I was told, well the whole group was told, I would be 'graduating' from the place because that was all my insurance policy would pay for. They were that blunt. In fact, my counselor went on to talk about the shortcomings of the insurance industry."

––––––––

A number of staff people told me about their difficulties in helping clients secure funding. Dave Sherman, an addiction counselor to adolescents at Rehab After Work in Paoli, Pennsylvania, said he spends fifteen to twenty hours a week on the phone seeking authorization from insurance companies for coverage for his clients. He said, "If I could change the treatment system in any way, it would be to make benefits easier to access."

Ned Rubin said, "The hardest part of my job is getting treatment paid for. We have had these two silos of money—for substance abuse treatment and for mental health treatment. Of course, many people suffer with co-occurring disorders, but depending upon which diagnosis is first, the billing, rules, treatment providers, etc., are all different. So much is determined by what insurance individuals have rather than their own choice. But it's far worse for those with no insurance." He also finds that "the most difficult treatment approach to get paid for, at least where I live, is residential addiction treatment. Even if someone meets all of the professional criteria suggesting the need for it, it's rare that any insurance company will pay for it or pay for it long enough to actually have a clinical impact on the person's life." Along these same lines, some clients said that insurance companies told them they had to "fail" at outpatient treatment before they would be covered for residential care.

Tony Rizzo, PhD, a psychologist with addictions expertise who works in the managed care field as part of a large health plan, pointed out that "with health care reform and federal parity the issue of failing at lower levels of care is no longer acceptable as a reason to deny coverage. Now we can make that recommendation based on the patient's actual needs—for instance, if someone needs sober support, help restoring activities of daily living, a protective living environment, or care for co-occurring psychiatric problems, residential treatment can be approved for the first treatment attempt." He added, however, that in a denial, a third-party payer can argue that "a less restrictive level of care can be reasonably expected to yield the same outcome." (That's because of research suggesting residential is not more effective than outpatient treatment.) Dr. Rubin affirmed that he had begun to see some benefits of the parity law, with fewer "hoops" to jump through and better access to coverage with some insurers.

PROGRAM-BY-PROGRAM COSTS

Costs for primary care treatment (the initial phase) at the adult residential programs I visited ranged from $27,000 to about $55,000 for a twenty-eight- to thirty-day stay. In an effort to get people to stay longer, one program that cost about $38,000 charged the same amount whether you were there for thirty or ninety days. I was told, "Those who stay for ninety days have a 50 percent greater likelihood of being sober at the end of one year than clients who leave after thirty days." At some of them, there were extra charges for such costs as psychiatrist and psychologist visits and prescriptions. Residential extended-care costs following primary treatment at these programs ran from about $13,000 to $25,000 a month. The most expensive program I came across but did not visit was an exclusive outpatient program that provided one-on-one care and charged $5,000 per day. Hazelden was the only one of the high-end residential rehabs I visited that directly billed insurance companies, but all of these programs helped clients in getting reimbursement (if any was to be had) from their insurance companies. (Hazelden is actually an in-network provider for a number of insurance companies.)

Both Hazelden and Caron have large financial-assistance funds to help a limited number of individuals who need help paying for treatment. As confirmation, one person who went to Hazelden sent me a copy of her final bill, which suggested that they nearly halved her fees—insurance paid about $12,000, she was billed $2,000, and the remaining amount was a "contract adjustment" that the person didn't have to pay. Promises Treatment Centers occasionally offers "scholarships" for clients in need, alumni, and family members of alumni. (The 2010 National Survey of Substance Abuse Treatment Services [N-SSATS] found that 62 percent of facilities reported using a sliding fee scale, while 50 percent said they offered treatment at no charge for people who can't afford to pay.)

Next in cost came programs that were technically outpatient but that provided sober housing, running about $18,000 to $20,000 a month, depending on the number and amount of services a client chose. As suggested previously, outpatient treatment without a residential stay is generally far less expensive, and health insurance is much more likely to pay for it. For instance, outpatient treatment at one of the high-end rehabs costs $5,000 for an entire eight weeks of treatment consisting of three three-and-a-half-hour groups per week, compared to the approximately $28,000 it charged for a month of residential care. For comparison, I asked the administrator of a publicly funded program what the cost would be for that same amount of outpatient care if I wanted to come to his facility and pay cash. It added up to about $2,000. Another exclusive rehab that offers expensive residential care charged about $9,000 for eight weeks of outpatient treatment consisting of fifteen days of six-hour-a-day outpatient care followed by another five weeks of treatment, several hours per night, five nights a week.

A number of the outpatient programs I visited had a client base that relied heavily on public funding sources. Ninety-five percent of the clients at the STOP program in Philadelphia are Medicaid recipients and payment is based on the published Medicaid fee-for-service payment. The SODAT program is funded by various state and public agencies, as well as grants, and its director told me about some of the problems it runs into. "Our funding sources often go by having clients meet goals, not time in the program. But people might need more time in treatment, so we keep them even though their funding has run out." When I was there, their adolescent-funding source was frozen, which the director said happens every year. She added, "So I have to fight with our board to keep treating teens anyway."

MEETING PEOPLE WHERE THEY ARE FINANCIALLY

Michael M. feels that one of the most important questions for people to ask when seeking a rehab is this: "If my medical insurance ran out, would you kick me out or give me time to pay for my care until my coverage kicked back in?" It can, indeed, be extremely unsettling for someone who's ready to be sober to suddenly be left in the lurch by a rehab. But there are heartening examples of rehabs that don't just drop people when their finances run out, such as the Center for Motivation and Change, which has offices in New York City and White Plains, New York. When I interviewed codirector Jeffrey Foote, PhD, in his office in Manhattan, he told me that although most clients pay out of pocket at this unique non-twelve-step practice where doctoral-level psychologists provide the care, almost half of their clients are charged a reduced fee according to economic need. One college-age woman affirmed that she'd been paying a token fee since her health insurance ran out. Dr. Foote's partner, Carrie Wilkens, PhD, told me that in another situation, if a parent were to stop paying for treatment of a young adult, she was so committed to the case that she would have been willing to see the client gratis. Dr. Foote added, "We are hoping to start a new nonprofit arm to provide lower-cost treatment and take insurance, using psychologists working on their post-docs, under our clinical supervision, while they get really good training."

WHEN MONEY AND POWER
BRING PREFERENTIAL TREATMENT

Dimitri R. had a positive experience at a famous rehab but he also found that "wealthier people get preferential treatment." He added, "When a celebrity came in, they had us all change our rooms. At first, we didn't know what was going on, but we found out they were giving the celebrity the whole front of the house we were staying in." Usually rehabs have strict rules about participation, but Dimitri said the celeb wouldn't go to the morning groups or gym and got to sleep in. When the person did go to group, he didn't join the discussion. And although rehabs commonly have a policy of taking away or prohibiting cell phones, Dimitri said, "One day, the celebrity had a freak-out and wanted to get his phone back. When he complained, 'I can't do this anymore, get me a room someplace,' he got his phone back. Never have I seen anyone get their phone back!"

I also had the opportunity to interview a physician who had recently worked at a prominent high-end residential facility during a period when new administrators came on board and the emphasis seemed to shift toward making money. He said that during that time, a local man with a chronic, severe drinking problem was "dumped" at the detox unit's door, showing all signs that he was ready to change. After securing one of the program's scholarships for the man and admitting him to detox, the physician discovered after a few days that the man was gone. The physician said, "I was told that the scholarship spot was needed for someone on the board of the rehab. Not long after that, I resigned." In his opinion, "Once you start charging people lots of money and getting large financial donations, it's hard to have quality treatment because you don't want to make people mad." He added, "The best therapy can make the patient angry. If you're a patient with a lot of money, you can pay to keep everyone at arm's length. Rules get broken, too. For instance, there was a rule that no one could go for treatment there more than twice because that wouldn't necessarily be good for the patient. But I knew of big contributors to the program coming for treatment five times."

THE EMOTIONAL COST OF REHAB

While most people are familiar with the emotional cost of addiction—loss of self-esteem, wear and tear on relationships, guilt, depression, and the like—the emotional cost of going to rehab is often unforeseen and seldom discussed. Emmie P., who had been to treatment six times between the ages of seventeen and twenty-four, said, "It scares me that I'm so comfortable in treatment." Seemingly, she had become more at home in the world of rehab than in the outside world.

Susan B., who had month-long stays at two high-end residential rehabs, said, "My husband was angry when I went to the first program. He never let me forget for a day that I was getting treatment. When I returned home, he expected I would be 'fixed.' So when I relapsed, he felt I had failed my children. He resented me going away a second time and didn't let me forget I'd let everyone down. But he was entitled to his feelings, too. We had marriage counseling afterwards and did beat the odds in that we stayed together."

For Preston M., the cost was worry about what people at work were thinking while he was at residential rehab. He explained, "I went away for a holiday weekend and all of a sudden I wasn't there. No one at the office knew where I was and I started to think I'd better get back at work. I was wondering what everyone was saying and worried about the possible professional cost." He only stayed at the rehab for two weeks, although he wanted to stay longer.

Betsy H. struggled for years to quit drinking. Finally, family pressure led her to seek treatment, but she relapsed and wound up going to rehab several times. Of her last experience, she said, "Unfortunately, the *very day* I got home, my husband of twenty years told me it was over, didn't even say hello . . . no second chances now that I was sober. He had told me a day or two before I went that there was a chance we could work this out, so I went off with a lot of hope in my heart. Of course, it hit me like a ton of bricks. My whole world was turned upside down." Of the rest of her family, she said, "I came home with all this energy and they didn't care. All they knew was that I was an addict. I wanted to tell them all about rehab, and they looked at it like 'What the fuck do I care?' You have to be continuously sober for X amount of time for them to listen to you. That's really hard for the person who went away. You come home with all this hope and energy—you're way ahead of where they are. But you have to prove to them over time, well, you have to live it. And they may never come around. One of my daughters may never speak to me."

HOW IT FEELS WHEN YOUR KID'S IN REHAB

Then there are the painful feelings of having a child in rehab, as expressed by these parents:

• Alexandria said of their daughter Krista's many treatment episodes, "My husband and I both felt like failures as parents. We rotated between good cop/bad cop. Sometimes I was the one who wanted to do tough love and he just felt sorry for her. Other times I was the one who said, 'She's sick and needs our help,' and he just wanted to throw her out. We were embarrassed—certain that everyone was judging us, and in fact they were. We eventually sort of disappeared from social events. I cried a lot. I was so scared she would die before we could find a way to help her. I just wanted her to live long enough to get sober. All of my energies went to trying to find ways to help her."

• Emily K. said that when her oldest son went to rehab, she and her husband "decided early on not to hide it, be ashamed, be selective about who we told, or deny it. We were filled with a zillion emotions. When someone would see us and ask, 'Oh, what are the boys doing this summer?' we'd say, 'Scott has had some trouble and he's in addiction treatment.' You don't have to shout it to the world. But it helps to be honest about it." She added that this helped her younger son, "who was filled with shame, in dealing with going back to school and with his friends."

• Carla B., whose two sons went through residential rehab many years apart, said that the hardest part, emotionally, was going to visit one of them at rehab and having him treat them badly. "He'd always been a pretty loving kid. However, when he was using, it was like someone had taken over his body. We were so excited to see him, but the eye contact was lacking—he was grunting, indifferent. I thought maybe he'd be smiling a little bit, say 'Nice to see you.' It felt bad. You have to tell yourself that it's not about you. You can't take it personally. It doesn't mean they don't love you. But it's hard. I can see how some parents would want to give up." She also noted, "Having been through it before, to find out that another child had a problem made us feel like failures, like we'd done something wrong. But when our second son went to treatment, we at first felt relieved to know that there were experts who could say, 'Here's what you need to do.' It was certainly a very emotional time, but we felt blessed that he was there because we were so worried that he wasn't going to make it."

• Bruce O. found that one of his daughters' years of struggling "impacted every facet of our lives and was heart-wrenching. It was easier to explain her 'bipolar' diagnosis (more socially acceptable) rather than 'addict.'" But as time went on, he said, the feelings went from "ashamed, embarrassed, a failed parent, demoralized to a positive 'get better' state of mind—eventually to being proud of standing up for addressing this disease instead of hiding from it."

PAYING FOR TREATMENT, STEP BY STEP

What follows are the major ways to finance addiction rehab, from paying out of your own pocket to seeking public funding. At the outset, take notes from conversations with rehab personnel or insurance companies, write down names of people you talk to, be sure to get things in writing, and have a support person in on conversations when possible.

SCENARIO I: PAYING FOR ALL OR PART OF TREATMENT OUT OF YOUR OWN FUNDS

- Find out about sliding fee scales and how you might qualify for one.
- Get an itemized list of *all* fees and services up front and for the full length of time of your treatment. (While you're in treatment, Elizabeth F. advised that it's wise to stop by the billing office once a week to ask about your balance and to find out about elective aspects of treatment that you may choose to forgo.)
- Determine the refund policy. If you pay any up-front costs, ask if you'll be reimbursed for unused treatment if you leave early. Ideally, you should only be charged for services used and reimbursed for unused services if you paid in advance and leave treatment prema-

turely. However, money may be taken out for administrative charges. (One place told me they officially have a "no refund" policy but that, unofficially, they settle reimbursement requests case by case and typically use any remaining money as credit toward future treatment.)

- Some rehabs will arrange for loans to pay for treatment. Be certain to understand the exact terms of the loan.

SCENARIO 2: USING COMMERCIAL INSURANCE

- Determine your policy's substance use disorder coverage benefits and limitations, looking into the following:
  — Residential versus outpatient treatment
  — Detoxification
  — Group counseling
  — Individual counseling
  — Treatment duration
  — Medications prescribed during treatment
  — Extended care or sober housing after primary care treatment
  — Ancillary services, including laboratory tests and visits to the program's psychologist, psychiatrist, and other personnel (e.g., dietitians, fitness professionals, and massage therapists)
  — Coverage for treatment of underlying medical conditions (such as high blood pressure) if the rehab treats people for those
- Find out which treatment programs accept your insurance. The Web sites of some programs may mention specific carriers they work with, particularly if they are preferred providers for national insurance companies. Check your benefits to see if you have in-network and out-of-network rehab benefits, which cover different programs to varying extents, depending on the insurance company's agreements with facilities.
- Find out about any up-front referrals, authorizations, or precertifications required by your policy to attend a program. Get copies of any related correspondence.
- See if the program you want to attend has a financial assistance spe-

cialist who can help determine your insurance coverage. However, you may want to follow up with the insurance company yourself if you're not satisfied with the information you receive. (Sadie A. found that "insurance 'specialists' at the treatment facilities usually do not understand the insurance enough to know how much it's going to cost you.")

• Even if you have insurance coverage, some facilities don't handle insurance billing, requiring direct payment from you and leaving it up to you to seek reimbursement from the insurer. Find out if such programs will help you with any related paperwork and/or appeals.

SCENARIO 3: USING PUBLIC ASSISTANCE

• If you're eligible for Medicare or Medicaid, it's recommended that you contact your specific Medicare or Medicaid contractor and/or your county or state public assistance agency to discuss your benefits. Then determine which treatment programs accept your coverage and its limitations. (See previous section.)

• For help in determining which programs are publicly funded, consult the Directory of Single State Agencies (SSA) for Substance Abuse Services found at http://www.samhsa.gov/Grants/ssadirectory.pdf. Each state has an SSA that oversees treatment centers, counselors, and use of alcohol treatment and prevention funds. (It may take some exploring to find the right page.)

• Another useful resource is the Substance Abuse Treatment Facility Locator operated by the SAMHSA at http://findtreatment.samhsa .gov/. The entry for each program lists the type of funding it accepts. You can also call SAMHSA's twenty-four-hour treatment referral service at (800) 662-HELP (4357), which connects to a state-by-state information service.

CHAPTER FOUR

GETTING THE BEST FOR YOUR BUCK

WHAT ADDICTION TREATMENT *SHOULD* LOOK LIKE

Whether we're talking financial, emotional, or time investment, everyone wants a positive return when they or someone they care about goes to rehab. But in searching for a good fit, how do you begin to know what to ask? What would be on *your* list of questions to get the best bang for the buck in rehab? It turns out that most people don't know what to ask and frequently fail to get straight or satisfying answers. As stated earlier, there's often quite a gap between what goes on in treatment programs and what should go on to yield the best outcomes for clients. This chapter examines what rehab should look like according to the best scientific evidence and reviews the aspects of treatment that really matter.

SADIE A.'S STORY—HOW ONE WOMAN WENT "TREATMENT SHOPPING"

To choose a rehab, Sadie A. said she went "treatment shopping," approaching it as if she were writing a feature article for *Consumer Reports* magazine—quite remarkable, given her stressful circumstances. Perhaps more extraordinary as a true study in contrasts, Sadie wound up going to—at the very same time—a traditional twelve-step program *and* a program that openly challenges the concepts of traditional rehabs as outdated.

Before hitting a crisis point, Sadie was well aware that she had a "big problem with alcohol"—she was drinking as much as a quart of vodka a day. She talked about it with her pastor, who gave her some resources and referred her to an AA group at her church. She'd also started checking out local treatment programs, but in the midst of it all, was arrested for driving under the influence with her elementary-school-age son in the car. The arrest shifted the rehab search from optional to mandatory because it wasn't her first drunk-driving offense and there was a chance that she'd be sent to jail. Sadie then made her way through the complicated legal and rehab labyrinth, and by the time she was finished "shopping" she had researched twelve different programs in her geographic area.

Using her professional background in customer service, Sadie developed a list of questions to try to get what she wanted. Sometimes, she found she obtained more reliable information when she pretended to act on behalf of a client. Among her questions were "Can I see your facility? Can I meet your counselors? What are their credentials?" While outpatient programs were not receptive, most of the residential places were, but guardedly. The residential programs would allow a tour "but were not effusive," and one of them required her to have an assessment beforehand. Just a few would allow her to meet counselors before starting treatment.

Because she was separated from her husband, Sadie's greatest concern, as the primary caregiver for her child, was whether she'd be allowed to leave the program should there be an emergency, then come back to rehab after an alcohol test proved her sobriety. Some places were quite rigid, while others were flexible. If she were told there were no guarantees of returning, she "ditched that program." Also important to her were the facilities' visitation rules, which some rehabs would not clarify in advance. At certain ones, "it seemed to be the jail mentality, like you're incarcerated."

Whether or not a place was a state-licensed drug and alcohol facility was important to Sadie, too, as was the length of the program. She explained, "Most had twenty-eight days and then you're done. Some had three to six weeks; that flexibility was important to me. And I was also looking for a good aftercare program—some just lasted six to twelve weeks and if you wanted more care, you'd have to check yourself back into treatment." Another question on her list for residential programs close to home was whether they would allow her to leave to attend her regular, established support meetings such as AA. (The answer was invariably no.)

Few people would have thought to ask, as Sadie did, about a program's length of time in the industry and the staff turnover rate. She explained, "At small places, if they had a lot of turnover, it would be a sign that it wasn't a solid program." When she asked about turnover, she was typically told, "I can't answer that." Sometimes, however, she gained insights through asking the person on the phone how he or she liked working at the place.

Group versus individual treatment was on Sadie's list, too. She found that "the outpatient programs had very little ability to do one-on-one counseling. I suspected that they only offered that 'as needed' or if there was a problem." Some places said they did small groups but couldn't tell her how they divided people for them.

She also thought to ask about how treatment was individualized for clients at various stages mixed together on units and in the same group. Most couldn't answer, but a few had a way to work with people at different stages of treatment.

Finally, Sadie asked about whether the programs offered psychological evaluations. She found that some programs "wanted you to be in their program for thirty days before they did one, while others did one right away." She thoughtfully added, "If they do a psych assessment when you first get there and you're still under the influence, you might be suicidal but that could change later on. Why wouldn't you do a psych evaluation both times?"

What did Sadie finally choose? First, she elected to go to a non-twelve-step outpatient facility where clients were primarily seen individually. (Her insurance covered it once she paid her high deductible.) After attending three times a week for several months and doing well, she had her court hearing, during which the prosecuting attorney tried to get her to leave the program for a publicly funded program that incorporated the twelve steps. But Sadie felt that the program the attorney wanted her to attend "offered a one-size-fits-all approach." The director of the facility she was already attending (whom we'll call "Steve") appealed to the judge on Sadie's behalf, which made her feel that "we won the battle."

She remained in the program for almost a year and was able to remain sober for thirty to sixty days at a time with occasional one- to two-day lapses during which she'd drink for part of a day, and then stop. She had gotten good at identifying her drinking triggers, one of which was marital problems, and she became legally separated from her husband at this time.

While she continued to make progress, her slips violated the terms of her probation, which required abstinence from alcohol, and also made her feel the need for residential treatment. So she checked in for a twenty-eight-day stay at a prominent, traditional twelve-step rehab that not only was fully covered by her insurance but had answered all her "shopping" questions. Her overall experience at this rehab—one with a very different philosophy than the "AA alternatives" program she'd been going to—was quite positive. After her twenty-eight-day stay, she decided to live in a sober house and attend the intensive twelve-step-based outpatient program run by the residential rehab she'd attended. At the same time, she regularly called Steve at the non-AA program, saw him once a week, and attended a weekly group session at his facility. (Because she'd met her deductible and out-of-pocket maximum, as well as the clinical requirements, her health insurance covered both programs.)

Of the hundreds of people with addictions I've interviewed, there are a number who attended both twelve-step and non-twelve-step self-help groups; but never have I met someone attending two programs with such diverse ideologies at the same time. Sadie found herself educating each program about the other's materials and philosophies. I had the honor of following her for more than another year. Sadie's continued progress through the treatment system is documented in chapter 9.

HOW MOST PEOPLE CHOOSE A REHAB

Sadie A. wasn't like most people in the way she went about choosing a place for help with her addiction, which is to say, she did so in a thoughtful, methodical way. For many, it's just the opposite—a decision made quickly, in panic mode. Alexandria (profiled in chapter 3) told me that, the first time around, she and her husband made their choice for their daughter "in desperation." She said, "We had about two weeks to find a place, so I had to scramble, not even knowing what rehab is, what a good program would entail, or how much it would cost. I got on the phone, called everyone I knew, got names of places, and chose one that a number of people said was good." She and her husband grew more sophisticated in making decisions as time went on and their daughter had repeat stays, but not until after a great deal of financial and emotional hardship. The result, in Alexandria's words, was that "we had two pretty bad experiences, one okay experience, and one really great experience."

When I asked others how they chose rehabs, their responses were a mixed bag. For some, it was what they'd heard about programs' reputations; others chose places their relatives had attended. One person told me he went to a certain rehab because a famous athlete had gone there. Quite a few made their choices out of cost or convenience. Dirk B., who initially attended a traditional outpatient program, said, "I chose an affordable center that was located between my office and home. But after about three weeks, I began to grow concerned over what I was hearing and being told. So I did my research and discovered the whole wide and varied world of addiction treatment. I found my current counselor's Web site, gave her a call, and felt she was a good fit." When I interviewed him, he was seeing the same addiction counselor, who worked with clients individually.

People told me that usually they chose their rehabs after getting professional advice. While turning to professionals can sometimes be a good source of information, many of them don't really know what goes on inside specific programs. For instance, Dorothy D.'s short-lived stay at her first rehab came after a recommendation from her family physician, but the experience was so negative that she lasted there for less than a day. (One thing she particularly disliked was that during the twice-a-day cigarette breaks, all the clients had to go outdoors—whether or not they smoked and even in the winter—line up against a fence, and were "screamed at" if they moved from their spots.) Dorothy said, "Oftentimes, family physicians just don't have the knowledge to really help make a good decision for the patient."

The next most common way that people made a rehab choice was via the Internet. Aurora S.'s psychiatrist of many years had no suggestions when she asked for advice about where to go. After going to three different programs she chose from the Internet, she said, "Unfortunately I don't think you can get an authentic idea of a place from the Internet because they make themselves look better [than they are], like an advertisement for a Big Mac." She flew a great distance to attend a prominent program selected this way and wound up leaving before she even got started because a number of things that happened there did not seem appropriate.

Brock W. used the Internet to narrow down his choices, but then went to visit some rehabs with his father. One program he found to be "very clinical, sterile." Another gave the impression of being "like a bad sixth-grade camp up in the mountains—it didn't seem like you were getting what you paid for, although it looked good on paper." At the rehab he chose, he first did an on-site "consultation" and liked the place so much he stayed a month past his initial one-month commitment.

WHEN THERE IS NO CHOICE

Many times, individuals have little or no say in where they go to rehab. Ann B. told me, "My insurance company picked the program. I had no options." Likewise, Anna J., who went to multiple programs that were fully paid for by public assistance, said, "They were all chosen for me." Homer L.'s programs were state- or county-funded and he believes they were chosen according to "where I was living, how available my transportation was, whether there was space for a new person, and how bad my use was." But it never hurts to ask questions and assert your preferences. Sadie A. found that, at least in her state, people on public assistance *can* have a voice in where they go for treatment, but many don't realize this. She said, "The authorities have a list of programs that they know already meet their criteria. But it's an old list, and there may now be other ones that meet the criteria. People don't know you can ask for the criteria and then shop around yourself for other programs that are acceptable."

Sadie also recommended avoiding programs that have a substantial number of clients who didn't choose to be there. She explained, "If the program is extremely open to court-ordered clients, there are too many who don't want to be there versus the ones who really want help. That can be very distracting, disheartening, and makes the program less solid." She advised asking questions such as "Do you accept court-ordered clients? What is that ratio to self-admitted clients? Do you make a distinction between the two groups in any way?" (Bear in mind that even though Sadie was mandated to be in treatment because of her drunk-driving arrest, she had already been seeking help.) She also discovered while she was in a county detox that even though she wouldn't be relying on public funding for her treatment, the professionals who do assessments for such assistance can be good resources for where to go for treatment because it's their job to be familiar with programs throughout the state. One thing she learned, however, is that you can't necessarily rely on referrals based on information that's several years old; rehabs' staffs, policies, and treatment approaches often change.

I met Bruce O. at a residential program where his daughter was having at least her twelfth rehab experience. Often, where she wound up in treatment had been dictated by "the system." He told me, "In many cases, she'd start out in an emergency room, meet with a crisis team, and then be transferred to the first rehab in the vicinity that had an available bed. It's often luck of the draw based on where you're at. Many times, she was placed in a program in a less desirable [geographic] area, where volume of cases was greater, there was a higher poverty and crime rate, and the standard of care was not of the highest caliber."

As time went on, however, Bruce learned that there were ways to influence the system, and he became an advocate for his daughter. He explained, "Having experienced so many short- and long-term programs, we became 'expert' in which ones were effective—often, the more expensive and, therefore, harder ones to qualify for. I started to step in after learning how to make the case to insurance carriers that she needed mental health services. Once we figured it out—by illustrating family predisposition, plus number of previous detoxes and rehab experiences—we persevered every time." (As discussed on page 22, more money doesn't necessarily buy better treatment.) Bruce also began personally meeting with crisis evaluation teams in the ERs and providing them with written summaries of his daughter's past treatment, names of current psychiatrists, preferred residential rehabs, and his recommendation for long-term treatment. He said, "Sometimes, I'd dress in a professional suit, pass out my business card—anything to curry preferential treatment and extra effort from evaluators who are responsible for locating a 'bed' in a treatment facility."

HOW REHABS SAY "PICK ME"

Do an Internet tour of high-end residential rehabs—and even of some that aren't so high-end—and along with words like "holistic," "mind-body," "evidence-based," "individualized," "cutting-edge," and "bio-psycho-social-spiritual," you'll likely see the following potpourri of more specific offerings:

- Twelve-step meetings
- Group therapy
- Individual therapy
- Psychoeducational groups/lectures
- Motivational interviewing
- Music therapy
- Spiritual coaching
- Family program/family therapy
- Cognitive-behavioral therapy
- Adventure/recreation therapy
- Acupuncture
- Breath work
- Hypnotherapy
- Psychodrama
- Treatment of co-occurring disorders
- Relapse prevention

- Somatic experiencing
- Equine-assisted therapy
- Yoga/tai chi
- EMDR (eye movement desensitization reprocessing)
- Drumming
- DBT (dialectical behavior therapy)
- Trauma therapy
- Meditation/mindfulness
- Medication
- Chiropractic therapy
- Reiki
- Fitness/exercise opportunities
- Massage therapy
- Nutritional counseling/supplements
- Zero balancing
- Qigong
- Challenge, rocks, and ropes classes/courses

No one place that I came across touted all of these approaches, but many of them popped up with enough frequency to suggest they are the competitive buzzwords of today's addiction treatment world, meant to invite the choice of one rehab over another. In contrast to conventional approaches such as twelve-step lectures and group counseling, some rehabs promote alternative approaches such as equine-assisted therapy and Reiki as "integrative" and "experiential" therapies. I even found a rehab that offered hair nutrient and toxin analysis, once-a-week hyperbaric oxygen therapy, colon hydrotherapy, and eleven kinds of massage therapy.

Aside from providing a feel-good experience, do so-called alternative approaches improve the odds that someone will get sober and stay sober, as suggested by claims such as one at a famous rehab's Web site that holistic treatments have "proven" to be highly effective in improving recovery rates and preventing relapse? To find out, I turned to Yale University psychologist Dr. Kathleen Carroll, whose career field is the study and understanding of approaches most likely to help people with substance use problems. I asked her to take a look at some of the testimonials I'd read, as well as the "experiential/integrative" offerings of some high-end rehabs, including some of the therapies listed above. Her reaction was, "There is no evidence base for experiential therapy—no randomized clinical trial, no evidence of help with addictions."

Wynn O., whose daughter went to several high-end residential programs, was somewhat skeptical about the motivation behind offering "alternative-type" interventions. Her business background leads her to view this as a marketing strategy more than anything else for treatment facilities competing for attention. "When there are more than ten thousand treatment centers out there, you need something that makes you stand out," she said. "Having things that make you look trendy and differentiate you from the other places might make someone think, 'Maybe that's the one thing that will make a difference for my loved one this time.' It's about how you sell yourself when some desperate family needs help."

Mark Willenbring, MD, formerly director of the Treatment and Recovery Research Division at the National Institute on Alcohol Abuse and Alcoholism, described the status quo well when he said, "Treatment centers are able to offer just about whatever they want, regardless of whether there's scientific research or expert consensus concerning effectiveness. It's almost certain that the treatment recommendation will be whatever that program offers, and there seems to be no felt ethical obligation to educate consumers about treatments that may have better efficacy. Thus, consumers are often confused about how to decide about where to go and what treatment is effective. And consumers don't have any meaningful choice in the type of treatment available (except for the flaky stuff). Most importantly, there is very little access to newer treatments that are based on solid scientific studies."

A MENU OF EFFECTIVE THERAPIES

What *do* the scientific studies show? While there's no surefire way to guarantee a successful result for someone who goes to rehab, studies consistently point to the following menu of therapies as those associated with positive outcomes for people with drug and alcohol problems. (A number of medications fall into this category, too, but they're addressed in chapter 9.)

Cognitive-behavioral therapy (CBT) helps people understand the connections between their thoughts, emotions, and use of drugs and alcohol. It then offers them skills for changing their thoughts and reactions to "cues" for substance use—that is, situations, emotions, and people—in their everyday lives, along with teaching strategies for coping with life's ups and downs more effectively. (Other lingo referring to variations of CBT includes "rational emotive behavior therapy" [REBT] and "cognitive therapy.") Among the three programs Eddie F. attended was a non-twelve-step program about which he said, "We did worksheets identifying situations that we thought to be 'trigger' points. We then dismantled the situations and broke them into smaller parts to determine the exact nature of the trigger. I continue to use this in my everyday approach to my sobriety and try to journal daily. I go back and read my journal every week or so, trying to identify the situations where I felt most threatened and to determine the source of my discomfort so I'm less likely to drink." Strategies to prevent slips from becoming major relapses are also part of CBT, along with ways to get back on track if a relapse does occur. (Chapter 9 provides closer examination of relapse prevention practices and also examines new thoughts about this terminology.)

Observations: All programs I visited were using CBT to some extent, but the non-twelve-step programs that used more individualized approaches used CBT as more of a foundational approach, while the more traditional residential rehabs used the twelve steps as their cornerstone. Other places fell in between. Tom Horvath, director of the non-twelve-step-based Practical Recovery, told me, "We use several cognitive-behavioral workbooks and our six foundations of recovery are motivation, coping with craving, managing emotions, nurturing relationships, lifestyle balance, and finding purpose in life." In contrast, CBT approaches at traditional residential rehabs seemed to be used more intermittently, as occasional groups and in some lectures, interwoven with the twelve steps, and, as stated at one place, "in individual sessions—as counselors and psychologists see fit and according to their training." At that same program I was told, "The key element is the spiritual aspect of the treatment that you get the power from a power greater than yourself. With CBT [alone] you're not going to have that."

Motivational Interviewing (MI) is a counseling approach that helps people resolve their ambivalence about stopping drug or alcohol use and taking part in treatment. One technique is to encourage people to explore the benefits and costs of quitting drugs and alcohol. (For instance, "If I stop drinking, I'll have fewer hangovers and argue less with my wife, but I'll miss hanging out with my drinking buddies.") Recognizing that confrontation and trying to persuade someone about the urgency of the problem are likely to increase resistance and decrease the probability of change, a counselor using an MI approach elicits motivation from the client without imposing it from outside. Sarah J. said of the last treatment program she attended, and at which she achieved sobriety, "I knew I should stop but didn't want to. Each time I relapsed (about five or six times), there was no guilt or shame, they welcomed me with open arms, and I wasn't kicked out. We looked at 'Why did you start using?' and did a lot of cost-benefit analyses. The relapses became shorter and farther in between."

Observations: Although MI has been touted for many years as an effective practice, the staffs at the residential programs at the time of my visits did not seem to have received any sort of consistent training in this approach. One program had just launched campuswide training and at another, a clinical supervisor who personally had been trained in MI told me, "Training is voluntary—it's more a spirit of buying into it—rolling with resistance." A former client at this particular traditional program felt the philosophy of MI was present, saying, "When one woman said she wasn't sure she was an alcoholic, they asked her if she wanted to stay and check the program out. She wasn't confronted or pushed." At one of the outpatient programs that had been making a concerted effort to implement MI, a counselor told me, "Everyone has a choice. If someone doesn't seem to want to be here, I reframe it and might say, 'What would you like to work on?' Ultimately, it's meeting the client where he's at and seeing where we can be helpful." Inconsistent with MI philosophy, however, this counselor also told me that if a client resists twelve-step meeting attendance, he might be suspended from the program for a week or the counselor might say, "Try another program."

Twelve-Step Facilitation Therapy (TSF) is a structured approach that actively promotes spirituality as a key to lasting recovery and helps clients begin the process of bonding to the twelve-step community by understanding AA's main concepts and learning how to use its resources for support and advice. (Recall that twelve-step-based treatment is separate from and not the same as free-of-charge twelve-step groups in the community.) TSF commonly entails linking clients with current twelve-step members, getting them connected to a community group outside of treatment, monitoring their participation, and helping them overcome the barriers and challenges they encounter. Usually, the counselor discusses readings from twelve-step literature with the client and encourages the use of twelve-step resources in times of crisis. Eddie F. said, "At two programs I went to, twelve-step facilitation was used as the primary form of therapy. Both locations used a very similar approach of worksheets and group counseling. The worksheets would have you examine your own life—coming up with examples of harms caused by your addictive behavior—who it harmed, what were the consequences, how you felt. These real-life examples were then used to show how out of control the behavior was when we tried to control it on our own. I was then counseled into realizing how I would benefit from working the twelve steps."

Observations: As far as I could tell, none of the programs I visited used twelve-step facilitation as it was tested in the research studies demonstrating its efficacy. At traditional twelve-step-based residential programs where I spent blocks of time, what I observed were full days of treatment that felt like they revolved around getting patients to buy into the twelve steps and the disease concept of addiction, so much so that it seemed to get in the way of other things the programs were trying to accomplish. (As mentioned in chapter 2, other programs were less twelve-step-focused, and a few didn't use the twelve steps at all.) For example, at the opening of one group session, the counselor talked about having a "recovery toolbox and coping skills" (a CBT-type activity). But rather than delve into alternative tools for dealing with a desire to drink in response to a personal loss, the counselor talked about "the disease making the decisions for you," and also spoke about hope. But no "tools or coping skills" were offered. At another rehab where I sat in on a final session of a client and counselor at the end of a month of treatment, I'd expected the counselor to share concrete skills when the client expressed fears about dealing with alcohol cravings upon returning home. Instead, the counselor handed the woman her business card and indicated she could call her. When I asked the counselor about this afterward, I was told that the woman hadn't adequately worked on AA's first few steps. It troubled me that the implication was that she was, therefore, blocked from progressing enough to take part in their relapse prevention group. (I was told that all clients were taught about relapse prevention, but that the rehab also offered a group with an opportunity for more focus on the topic.) In fact, there is no need to master AA's steps to be able to master relapse prevention skills. After observing numerous sessions at such programs, my overriding sense was that multiple teachable moments were missed because of a pervasive focus on the twelve steps. (See chapter 6 for more on the twelve steps in treatment.)

Contingency Management encourages positive behavior change by providing incentives for being abstinent (as shown by negative urine test results), attending counseling sessions, or meeting goals. Incentives may be low-cost prizes (such as movie passes or food), money, or vouchers that can be exchanged for retail items. Sarah J., who went to an upscale nontraditional outpatient program, was the only person who mentioned use of this approach. She described how it helped her overcome her heroin and meth addictions: "The program paid me to have clean urines. The amount went up with more clean urines—but if I relapsed, it went back down. At the time, I needed money to live. That's motivating when you just need to buy deodorant, toothpaste, and basic necessities." (Her father gave the money to the program, and they, in turn, meted it out according to the goals of therapy.)

Observations: A few programs on my itinerary used contingency management but I didn't get the impression that it was used to any great extent in routine treatment. The Fairmont Fountain Centers outpatient program employed the approach for its drug court participants, while Rehab After

Work used it with adolescents. Practical Recovery's Tom Horvath said, "We typically use contingency management when a third party (e.g., parent, employer, licensing agency, or board) is involved. In the case of a younger person, we may use financial rewards for having 'clean' drug testing, with the rewards being paid for by the parents."

Community Reinforcement Approach (CRA) is really a package of approaches that's been determined in multiple research reviews to be among the most effective methods for treating substance problems. Ever hear of it? Neither have many rehab staffers. According to Robert J. Meyers, PhD, one of the leading experts and trainers for this approach, "CRA has been shown to be effective for people who have problems with alcohol, cocaine, opioids, and poly drug abuse." The overall goal of CRA is to help clients adopt a lifestyle that is more rewarding than one filled with alcohol and drugs. CRA includes modules for exploring the positive and negative consequences of substance use; a technique called "sobriety sampling," which, rather than recommending lifelong abstinence at the outset, gently moves clients there; behavioral skills, which include problem-solving and substance refusal training; job skills training; social and recreational counseling; relapse prevention; and relationship counseling. Unfortunately, according to renowned addiction researcher William Miller, PhD, Emeritus Distinguished Professor of Psychology and Psychiatry, University of New Mexico, "Very few U.S. programs try to deliver CRA, let alone have proper training and competence in it. There are probably more programs offering CRA in Ireland than in the whole of the U.S." To find a program that uses CRA, Dr. Meyers's advice is to call around and ask facilities (almost always outpatient) if they use CRA and have received formal training to do so. More information can be found at his Web site: www.robertjmeyersphd.com. (See pages 293–94 for information about the adolescent version of CRA.)

Behavioral Couples and Family Therapies help significant others and relatives evaluate factors that contribute to substance problems and work on changes to improve the situation. In couples therapy, partners work on better communication, problem solving, and finding activities that don't involve substance use. The person with the drug or alcohol problem might make a daily contract with the partner stating his or her intention not to drink or use drugs, and the other person would learn how to provide support for those efforts—sometimes monitoring the partner's taking of prescribed medication to enhance sobriety. Overall, including a client's significant other in treatment using science-based approaches can increase the chances of recovery, and, according to the National Institute on Drug Abuse's "Principles of Drug Addiction Treatment," "Family and friends can play critical roles in motivating individuals with drug problems to enter and stay in treatment." (Research suggests that family involvement is particularly important for young people with substance problems. See chapter 7 for more on this.)·

Observations: Residential rehabs commonly offer "psychoeducational" family weeks wherein relatives attend lectures and have peer-group discussions to learn about the disease of addiction, the twelve steps, and Al-Anon support groups for family members of people with addictions. I got to observe such activities at two rehabs. Outpatient programs often hold periodic family nights that have similar activities. Rehabs usually view addiction as a "family disease" that requires relatives of the addicted person to go through their own recovery process, most often through Al-Anon or a similar twelve-step self-help group like Nar-Anon (for families of drug-addicted people) or Families Anonymous. A related term that rehabs often use is "codependence," originally coined to describe the behavior of family members who inadvertently made it easier for addicts or alcoholics to continue using drugs or drinking. Now the term is often used more broadly to describe the characteristics of people with all sorts of behaviors but, overall, who obtain a sense of identity through unhealthy interactions with others. Some rehabs even have separate programs for treating codependence. However, according to Dr. Miller and colleagues writing in the 2011 book *Treating Addiction*, there's no scientific evidence that "something is wrong" with family members of people with addiction. They also note that the American Psychiatric Association rejected, on lack of evidence, an attempt to add a category of "codependence" to its diagnostic manual.

Of the rehabs I visited, the only residential program that consistently provided true family therapy—as opposed to a family week or evenings consisting primarily of group classes and activities to educate families about addiction—was Promises. For local clients, every Saturday was devoted to families and clients, starting with psychoeducational workshops and followed by joint family/client process groups facilitated by family therapists. Individual family therapy sessions were then offered to all clients and their families. When possible, arrangements were made for families of out-of-state clients to come to Promises several times for family work. For current and alumni families, Promises also provided an open-ended weekly support group facilitated by a psychologist and addiction counselor. The Sobriety Through Out Patient (STOP) program in Philadelphia, which serves very-low-income clientele, had a marriage and family therapist on staff for appointments as needed, while some high-end rehabs did not. One of the latter told me, "That doesn't mean that we don't make referrals for couples counseling." Some of Practical Recovery's psychologists had training in marital and family therapy, and some also were skilled in the Community Reinforcement and Family Training, or CRAFT approach, which was developed by Robert Meyers, PhD, and is explained in his book, coauthored with Brenda Wolfe, PhD, *Get Your Loved One Sober*, published by Hazelden.

Given its more than two decades of scientific backing, I was surprised that none of the other programs I visited even mentioned CRAFT. When I asked about the use of CRAFT at one residential program, I was told they hadn't heard of it. "We're all twelve-step based." At another rehab, a family program administrator who *was* familiar with CRAFT said, "It conflicts with Al-Anon, and I don't buy that family members can get an alcoholic or addict into treatment." Dr. Meyers said these are not uncommon views and practices in traditional treatment programs. CRAFT was designed for family members of loved ones who refuse to seek help, and it's been shown in research studies to be far more effective at getting people into treatment than strategies like those used on TV shows like *Intervention*. In fact, studies have consistently demonstrated that CRAFT is two to three times more successful than traditional interventions and Al-Anon. Rehabs may argue that CRAFT was designed to get people into treatment and therefore isn't relevant to those who are already there, but I couldn't help but think about how helpful it would be if family members knew about strategies to use if loved ones backslide, which they often do. Instead, the overriding message was to seek support from Al-Anon, which has as its fundamental underpinning the notion that "we cannot change another human being—only ourselves." Al-Anon suggests that family members "detach with love" from their addicted loved one and instead take care of themselves. At one point, when a participant in one of the rehab family programs I attended asked, "Isn't doing nothing what got us here?" the leader responded, "What you can do is work on you."

While there's evidence that family members involved in Al-Anon do reduce their own distress and improve their coping skills, rehabs' nearly singular focus on this approach prevents families from learning about scientifically based strategies that *can* favor recovery in their loved ones. In other words, in addition to what families commonly hear at rehabs about not doing things to "enable" someone's use of drugs and alcohol (such as making excuses for them when they're hungover), family members who go through CRAFT also learn steps they can take to reinforce a person's sobriety, encourage alternatives to drug and alcohol use, and enhance their own happiness.

Failure to use CRAFT is unfortunate because not only is it effective at engaging people in treatment, but family members have reported a sizeable reduction in their own physical symptoms, depression, anger, and anxiety after participating in CRAFT training. To locate a program that uses the CRAFT approach, Dr. Meyers suggests doing an Internet search using the terms "community reinforcement and family training." He also advises asking programs, "What types of therapies do you use for families?" to see if they say they use CRAFT or have any certified CRAFT therapists.

When high success rates are touted for interventions, bear in mind that you're probably not hearing about families who decided not to follow through once they got started on the process. In the three well-done studies on interventions, researchers found that more than two-thirds of families dropped out before the final stage.

TO LET GO OR NOT TO LET GO?

Although treatment usually focuses on the person who has the problem, there's no question that "the problem" often impacts families in a big way. A study reported in 2011 in the *American Journal on Addictions* suggests that four "significant others" are directly affected by any one individual's addiction-related problems. A big question that family members often struggle with is whether to let go or not to let go when a loved one is in the throes of addiction.

Grace G. said, "Al-Anon talks about detaching with love, and one of the major principles is 'you didn't cause it, you can't control it, and you can't cure it.'" She told me that she'd emotionally prepared herself for "turning her son out" if he refused to go to rehab, adding, "a friend had changed the locks on her house because of her son's behavior as an addict, and I was prepared to do that. I was at the point where if my son wasn't going to go to rehab and his addiction was going to ruin my life, I had to face the fact that I'd have to detach." When she revealed this to Luke for the first time during their family week at rehab, she said, "His eyes welled up and tears rolled down his cheeks. At first he wiped them away, but, overwhelmed, he began to sob. I think his hearing those words from me, the mother who had never not been there for him, was the shocker of his life."

Grace's comments, which reflect the struggle of knowing what is the right thing to do—whether to detach with love and let the addict hit bottom, as often seems to be the thinking in the twelve-step community, or to continue to "be there" for a child with a drug or alcohol problem—made me recall former senator George McGovern's book *Terry: My Daughter's Life-and-Death Struggle with Alcoholism*, which I'd read many years ago. After decades of repeatedly admitting Terry to expensive rehabs, only to watch her spiral downward soon after, McGovern and his wife followed the advice of a counselor to limit contact with her during what turned out to be the final six months of her life. After spending much of the previous month in and out of a detox center,

Terry was found frozen in a snowbank. He wrote very affectingly about the regret he felt for following that advice.

When I asked if there were scientific studies to guide the decision of whether it's better to detach with love and let loved ones hit bottom or to continue to be there for them, the University of Washington's Daniel Kivlahan, PhD, with his great command of the scientific literature on addiction and rehab, said, "There is good evidence that being abandoned by loved ones in fact hurts one's chances of getting clean. But despite the countless compelling and too often tragic anecdotes, I know of no research that would inform 'the right thing to do' at the level of the individual. All family members and loved ones have their limits and I consider it important to respect them."

Just as I was finishing writing *Inside Rehab*, I received a heartbreaking e-mail informing me of thirty-seven-year-old Wyatt D.'s drug-related death. In a conference call, I subsequently spoke with his mother and two sisters, who shared mixed feelings about Wyatt's many struggles with addiction and his rehab experiences. But in the end, they all agreed when one of the sisters said, "Sometimes, I got mad at him, but we were lucky we were on good terms. The last thing he said to our father was, 'Dad, I love you more than you'll ever know.' The tough love approach is not always the right way to go, and the judgment placed on those who don't go that route bothers me. If we had done that, Wyatt would have been dead a long time ago."

A REGISTRY OF PROGRAMS AND PRACTICES

Consumers and professionals can find more information about programs and practices that have some research support by accessing SAMHSA's National Registry of Evidence-based Programs and Practices (NREPP), a searchable online registry of substance problem and mental health interventions that have been reviewed and rated by independent reviewers. But bear in mind that because NREPP is a voluntary, self-nominating system intervention developers elect to participate in, the listed interventions are essentially self-selected and some science-based approaches are not included. Nevertheless, it's a place to read about various approaches for substance use disorder treatment and provides some sense of their efficacy.

DOES SCIENCE MATTER?

I find it fascinating that Sadie A. started out making good progress at an "AA alternatives program"—one that bases its treatment on CBT and is openly critical of Minnesota model-based programs at its Web site—then wound up going to and doing well at a twelve-step-based facility, and at various points used the two differing programs at the same time. It wasn't a question of which approach was right and which one was wrong. Sadie seemed to be able to take the best of each philosophy and put it all to work for her. She said, "I consider Steve to be my primary counselor and the other approach is secondary, to strengthen what's going on. I believe enough in what I'm learning about the twelve-step philosophy that it's helpful to me. I'm very open-minded and don't have to do all or nothing."

Research studies show that when different science-based approaches are tested head-to-head—for instance, comparing clients treated with a CBT therapy with those receiving twelve-step facilitation—the outcome is pretty much the same. That is, groups of people in studies do equally well regardless of the approach. (More on this in chapter 6.) But quite a shocker to academic circles that deal with substance use disorders—and quite honestly, to me while writing this book—is that a number of studies have shown *little or no* difference between programs implementing such "evidence-based approaches" and those that do standard "treatment as usual." (According to John Kelly, PhD, of Harvard Medical School's Center for Addiction Medicine at Massachusetts General Hospital, the term "treatment as usual" typically refers to what goes on in addiction programs when "counselors choose what they implement, as they see fit, without following a manual or sticking to established clinical guidelines. It often includes a combination of activities like twelve-step-related discussions, unstructured group counseling, role playing exercises, general 'sharing' of personal problems and situations, educational lectures, and CBT-ish things such as talking about 'triggers' or 'coping strategies.'") As part of a 2011 research project, Dr. Miller took a critical look at studies coming out of the Clinical Trials Network (CTN), a group of community addiction treatment programs across the country chosen to test science-based therapies versus "treatment as usual" and concluded, "So far, the CTN has published fifteen or so studies done at multiple sites, and what's striking is the absence in most of them of finding substantial differences between evidence-based practices and what clinicians were doing routinely at the same agencies."

I spoke with numerous experts to try to understand how programs that implement approaches shown in and of themselves to lead to good outcomes in scientific studies don't seem to have much of an edge over programs "doing their own thing," and got some interesting explanations. For instance, as I observed in programs I visited, "treatment as usual" varies tremendously from one program to the next, with some programs providing much better care than others. If a new scientifically sound treatment is tested in a program that already is working well, the new approach is probably less likely to come out ahead than if it were tested in a program that shows entertaining movies having little or nothing to do with addiction but considers that to be treatment. Adam Brooks, PhD, a researcher at Treatment Research Institute, added, "When science-based practices are tested in everyday programs, they're often assigned to counselors who have years of experience doing their work a certain way. And the new practices are introduced in the context of many other things the client is doing, like attending nine hours of group a week, that have nothing to do with the new practice. If the whole program doesn't shift to a new way of doing things, it's hard to see an effect of one relatively small change." Also, it's hard to imagine a new science-based therapy making a big difference in a program unless most staff members are invested in it. In studies such as those involving the CTN, for instance, certain counselors may be trained in a new approach while the rest of the program or staff is invested in another model or way of thinking.

When it comes to science-based treatment, it's important to note, too, that studies tend to disqualify many of the people typically seen in rehabs. In an analysis published in the journal *Addiction* in 2005, Keith Humphreys, PhD, a well-known researcher with the Veterans Affairs and Stanford University Medical Centers, and colleagues found that researchers tended to rule people ineligible for participation in addiction treatment research if they had a history of treatment, were judged "difficult" or "unmotivated," or had other medical problems or psychiatric problems in addition to addiction. Thus it's difficult to know if and how research findings from "hand-picked" higher-functioning groups of people apply to real-world clients.

So is science not important when it comes to choosing a rehab? Should so-called evidence-based approaches be abandoned? Every expert I talked with gave me an unequivocal *no*. Moreover, federal government agencies such as SAMHSA have invested and continue to invest huge amounts of money in developing, testing, and disseminating interventions from the previously described "menu" of therapies. The important message, according to Dr. Miller, is that "while there is no one superior treatment that works for all or even most people, we have a rich array of different approaches with reasonable evidence of efficacy. And we really should be using what research tells us is most effective." Also, because of the high variability of training of people working in this field, assuring use of science-based treatment strategies exerts an element of "quality control" rather than having counselors "do their own thing."

WHAT'S SAID AND WHAT'S DONE

So if you wanted to find out if a rehab you're considering uses approaches from the menu of effective options, how would you go about it? Why not just ask? I found that it wasn't always easy to get a straight answer when I did, and a number of experts pointed out that there may be a discrepancy between what programs say and what they do. John Kelly said, "What we don't know is whether programs are actually implementing scientifically sound approaches when they say they are. In my experience, programs may say they're implementing this or that evidence-based practice, but in nearly all cases it only vaguely resembles the real thing." While many states and funding agencies now require that science-based approaches be employed in licensed programs, Dr. Miller added that the criteria for selecting the "approved" approaches is often political and not necessarily based on the strongest evidence. (My own state had no such requirement when I was writing *Inside Rehab*. I was told by a state official that there's nothing in the licensing rules for treatment programs that "speaks specifically to a certain technique or style.")

On a national basis, the federal government's National Survey on Substance Abuse Treatment Services collects information (from a paper and pencil questionnaire) each year on the frequency with which treatment programs report using various therapeutic approaches, including most of the ones listed in the menu of effective therapies. In 2010, the most recent data year available, of the 13,339 facilities reporting, nearly two thirds indicated that they used CBT "always" or "often" and just over half said they used twelve-step facilitation and motivational interviewing that frequently. Far fewer used contingency management regularly. Six out of ten rehabs said they offered marital or couples counseling, while about eight out of ten of them said they did family counseling, but the term was undefined, so some may have been referring to family education programs. And only about a quarter of them provided such counseling to more than half of their clients, which is interesting given the common view that addiction is a "family disease." Moreover, since no time frame had to be given, one session could have been counted as marital or family counseling.

To find out what actually transpires when counselors are alone with clients, Dr. Kathleen Carroll and colleagues listened to more than 350 audiotapes of "standard" individual sessions from clinicians in community outpatient settings who professed to be using a range of science-based approaches. They published their findings in the *Journal of Substance Abuse Treatment* in 2008. Perhaps the most alarming finding was that what the researchers termed "chat" occurred much more frequently than science-based interventions. Often, the counselors revealed personal things irrelevant to the client's issues. (As an illustration, Allison E. went to a rehab where "the counselor would tell me a lot about her story. I had been to counseling and knew about treatment, and I thought that was odd.") Counselors consistently overestimated the amount of science-based care they were providing, and the researchers found that interventions related to therapies like CBT and twelve-step facilitation "were so rare as to be almost undetectable."

More recent, in a 2012 study, researchers from the Treatment Research Institute in Philadelphia observed and scientifically tracked what went on in group sessions of nineteen counselors at three typical outpatient programs over the course of twelve weeks. Ahead of time, counselors were told to use their very best relapse prevention and CBT interventions on preselected topics; they were then asked to report on the content and activities in all of their groups. Some groups were directly observed and rated by researchers. Consistent with my experience at a number of programs, a large amount of time was spent on "discussion" with almost no time given to strategies to elicit change in clients' lives. While counselors reported that over the twelve weeks they most frequently ran CBT groups, they also honestly admitted that they rarely spent time on activities for practicing CBT skills. And the counselors' scores for implementing relapse prevention strategies were very low. Adam Brooks, one of the psychologists involved in the study, said, "There was a lot of checking in with clients to see how they were doing, very little content in the areas of relapse prevention and CBT, and a lot of winging it. It wasn't unusual to see counselors get on a computer to 'Google' and download a worksheet before a group session."

It's important to keep in mind that, when new therapies are used in research settings, counselors have to follow carefully monitored protocols and that they usually have more training than at typical rehabs. And facilities frequently lack the financial and human resources needed to implement such therapies as they're intended to be used.

So while I encourage consumers to ask programs whether they employ science-based practices, it can be difficult to get a handle on what's really going on in any one rehab, and, if it is, whether it's being done well. (For details on what a state-of-the-art rehab should look like, see the write-up about the Center for Motivation and Change on pages 389–93 in chapter 10.)

CLINICALTRIALS.GOV

If you or someone you know might be interested in participating in a study on addiction, http://clinicaltrials.gov is a registry of federally and privately supported clinical trials conducted in the United States and around the world. This registry provides information about a study's purpose, who may participate (if participants are still being recruited), locations, and phone numbers to call for more details. You can search for studies by entering a word or phrase—such as the name of a medical condition (for instance, alcoholism or addiction) or intervention (contingency management, Suboxone, cognitive behavioral therapy) and a location (such as the nearest city).

OTHER MATTERS THAT MATTER

Effective substance use disorder treatment is more than a set of specific strategies and how they're implemented. While I wrote this book, the following additional important matters came to my attention over and over again:

ADDRESSING THE WHOLE PERSON MATTERS: *"Effective treatment attends to multiple needs of the individual, not just his or her drug abuse. To be effective, treatment must address the individual's drug abuse and any associated medical, psychological, social, vocational, and legal problems."* From "Principles of Drug Addiction Treatment," National Institute on Drug Abuse.

For instance, at the program Allison E. attended, she said they had clinical case managers to help clients "with outside issues like health insurance, court issues, and banking problems, so when you're prepared to leave there, things are set in place. They help you do a budget." And Jack S. saw a licensed drug and alcohol counselor for individual counseling who, he said, "addressed all of the needs a person may have to get better—this may be treatment for depression, lifestyle changes such as eating better or finding better living conditions, and managing finances properly." The Sobriety Through Out Patient program that I visited in Philadelphia had the following services built into the overall cost of the program: vision exams (including free reading glasses and vouchers for prescription glasses), parenting classes, on- and off-site legal assistance (such as for court appearances), vocational training in food service, barber, and cosmetology services and training, plus computer and multimedia training.

Research shows that outcomes can be improved when clients are provided with such recovery support services, which might also include medical care, housing, employment, education, and social services. As mentioned in chapter 1, many rehabs don't provide these services. When they do, they're often not covered by insurance companies. Although such services are not always available on-site, it's worth asking if programs can refer you to resources in the community. They may have clinical case managers serving in that capacity.

PERSISTENCE MATTERS: *"Remaining in treatment for an adequate period of time is critical."* "Principles of Drug Addiction Treatment," NIDA.

Although I found people for whom a month in rehab did the trick, over and over again the message I heard concerning most people with serious drug and alcohol problems was captured by Shari P.'s mother when she said, "The main issue with our rehabs here is that twenty-eight days just isn't long enough to recover or totally change in any way, shape, or form." Sadie A.'s counselor recognized her need for "time in sobriety," so he was willing to support whatever it took—even if it was counter to his personal philosophy. He told me, "If that meant going to a twelve-step program, then so be it. I was willing to buy her time by looking for structure and to hold her there for a while—to help her calm down her addiction so we could again treat it on an outpatient basis."

Although some of the residential programs I visited were still working from a four- to six-week primary care model, severe addiction is increasingly seen by treatment providers and researchers as a chronic illness rather than an acute condition, and most of the treatment staffers I met acknowledged this. A psychologist at one of the programs I visited said,

"Until the notion changes that thirty days is enough, people can still go to treatment and think that they'll work their magic." Mark Willenbring posed the question, "Do you know of any other chronic illness where we give people three to four weeks of therapy? That would be like sending diabetics to a spa for a month and teaching them diet and exercise—then saying, 'Go to your support groups.' It's 1950s treatment. Would we settle for that for any other condition?"

So where did the idea originate for a twenty-eight-day or month-long rehab stay? Several experienced treatment professionals said that they were personally told by the founder and primary architect of the Minnesota model, the late Daniel Anderson, PhD, that when they put together their lectures and lessons, the number just happened to be twenty-eight." Others have said that four weeks was the early limit some government funders and insurance companies chose for reimbursement. When one psychologist who worked at a rehab pointed to the lack of evidence justifying the standard four-week residential stay, he was told, "Well, from our experience, the magic happens in the fourth week—that's really when the change happens."

How long should treatment last? The party line, according to the National Institute on Drug Abuse, is that "research indicates that most addicted individuals need at least three months in treatment to significantly reduce or stop their drug use and that the best outcomes occur with longer durations of treatment." William Miller said, "The longer people stay with something, the better the outcome. That's true of residential treatment, outpatient treatment, therapeutic communities, medication, AA, and even placebo pills." A number of experts pointed out that although there's a correlation between length of time in treatment and "doing better," it's not necessarily being "in treatment"—particularly in residential rehab—that accounts for success. It's just as plausible that people who are more motivated tend to stay in treatment longer and that "sticking with any form of treatment may be a marker of motivation for change, not proof that longer programs are more effective by virtue of being longer."

The other reality is that clients are often resistant to a long view of treatment. Thinking her initial month-long rehab stay "would be the beginning and the end" of her treatment, Thayer A. was "blown away" when her counselor gave her an aftercare recommendation to go to another rehab that the counselor thought would continue to help with both her alcohol problem and an eating disorder that reemerged when she quit drinking. Her advice after going to five places for help was "Stick with it, and by that I don't mean just stay at a program. Engage with the issues. It's a process. I packed my bag for thirty days when I left for my first rehab and thought, 'Oh, I'll have a sober life,' and it's just not like that at all. You need to have a longer perspective. When you're younger, you don't have that longer perspective. Shit happens. But you just have to keep going and not give up."

HOW MANY PEOPLE COMPLETE TREATMENT?

While many professionals think that the notion of completing treatment within a fixed time period is obsolete, programs commonly run this way. Sadie A.'s prescribed stay at one of the country's best-known programs was four weeks at its residential facility, then six weeks at its outpatient program. Yet her treatment with Steve at the nontraditional facility had no prescribed end point and she preferred it that way because she recognized that the severity of her alcohol problem meant she might need professional support for years to come.

How many people actually "complete" treatment, which in government surveys of treatment facilities is considered as "all parts of the treatment plan or program were completed"? According to SAMHSA's latest Treatment Episode Data Set (TEDS) discharge summary, which primarily includes information from state-licensed drug and alcohol programs in the year 2008, 47 percent of discharges age twelve and over occurred because treatment had been completed. In other words, considering all types of addiction programs—from detox facilities to primary care to extended-care establishments—not quite half of clients stayed until the end. Looking at specific types of treatment, 55 percent of those admitted to short-term residential facilities—typically thirty days or less—stayed until the end compared with 42 percent in outpatient treatment and 36 percent in intensive outpatient. (TEDS tracks annual "admissions," not individuals who go to treatment each year, and, as such, a person admitted to and discharged from a rehab twice within a calendar year would be counted as two admissions and two discharges.)

CHOICE AND FLEXIBILITY MATTER: *"Motivation for participating in treatment is heightened by giving clients choices regarding treatment goals and types of services needed. Offering a menu of options . . . increases overall treatment effectiveness."* From Treatment Improvement Protocol (TIP) Series 35, Substance Abuse and Mental Health Services Administration.

When Salina S. voiced that the many assignments from an outpatient program focusing on her past and the negative aspects of her drug use were not helpful, she was admonished that she was "in denial" and not "in tune with her feelings." She told me, "They seemed to feel I was rejecting their program and they wouldn't listen. But I was just trying to tell them what works for me and what doesn't. I know myself. I don't feel like I was treated with equality and respect." Salina's experience illustrates the long-standing practice in the treatment world of letting clients know that they're not in the driver's seat.

Mike Panico, MS, LPC, director of the Seven Challenges adolescent program in Tucson, Arizona, said, "It's never been the role of counselors to prescribe 'behavior' as 'treatment'—except in drug treatment, where it's common to *tell* people what to do. Ideally, the heart and soul of what a counselor does is to give people the motivation and skills to satisfy the needs they're meeting through their drug use, in healthy ways. The 'prescription' needs to be taken out of it." Studies show, too, that therapists don't necessarily know what's best for clients, and there's no scientific way to predict which treatment will work best for any one person.

A 2009 review of psychological studies published in the *Journal of Clinical Psychology* indicated that clients matched to their preferred treatment were about half as likely to drop out of treatment and had close to a 60 percent chance of showing greater improvement when compared with clients not given a choice. Dr. Miller said, "People do have hunches about what will work best for them. And those who choose from among options tend to 'own' what they've chosen and stay with it. So why would you *not* let clients choose? If one thing isn't working, you can try something else."

Unfortunately, however, most programs are not well set up to provide a menu of options and informed choices. And most people going into treatment don't know enough about how or what to choose—or even that choices exist—at least until they're well into it and perhaps their funding has run out. As was the case with Salina, clients are often given the message that they don't know what's in their best interest, even when they do. After a previous experience in a program where he felt the message was to accept "AA or you will die," Jack S. talked about what a difference it made when he found a counselor who listened to what he had to say and made him part of the treatment planning process.

THE COUNSELOR (OR THERAPIST) MATTERS: *"The therapy relationship accounts for why clients improve—or fail to improve—as much as the particular treatment method."* From SAMHSA's "Evidence-Based Therapy Relationships" in the National Registry of Evidence-based Programs and Practices.

Having a counselor you connect with is probably at least as important as having one who's schooled in the latest science-based skills. Homer L. said that what helped the most at numerous programs he attended was "having a great counselor, meaning somebody you trust and are able to speak with and not worry about what he/she thinks of you after you say or do something . . . also someone who's not going to let you B.S. them." I met him at an outpatient program that helped him deal with his meth addiction and, indeed, found his counselor to fit this bill from both my observations and comments from other group members. His was an example of how the relationship with the counselor made all the difference in a program that had been described to me before I went as "beleaguered" because of its struggles for funding. I spoke with him again several years after he went there and he said that he was doing well—off hard drugs and reconnected with his young daughter.

A number of studies show that clients with addictions do better with counselors whose style is empathic, accepting, flexible, and open than with those whose style is less that way. Dorothy D., who I met at one of the high-end residential rehabs I visited, talked about how her treatment was defined by empathic, caring interactions that helped her get well. "While at the program," she said, "I received counseling from my assigned counselor, grief managers, a multitude of counselor assistants, the other women in my group, and psychiatrists. I received support for every aspect of my treatment plan and to combat every problem. The fact that I was treated like an individual and not a criminal made me feel comfortable and more willing to work toward my recovery. I felt like I was there as a sick person trying to get well and not a bad person trying to be good. This was *huge* in my recovery because it made me feel less ashamed."

But many people don't have such experiences with their counselors. Margaret F. made it clear that her relationship with a counselor was a great source of distress. She said, "I didn't feel I could trust her. She took counseling to the next level, and it felt like she was trying to play God." When I asked Margaret if she thought switching counselors would have been allowed if she'd asked, she said, "It didn't appear that I would get another counselor since they were all in agreement with her decisions. They thought I needed a 'no shit' counselor and she was it."

Several addictions experts explicitly stated that if you don't feel respected, listened to, and understood by your therapist, doctor, or counselor, find another one and seek help elsewhere. Not all programs honor such requests. At one that does, an administrator said, "We value the input of the client, and they're not always wrong. It doesn't help clients if I keep them in a cocoon and make all the decisions for them."

KEY QUESTIONS FOR RELATIONSHIPS WITH HELPING PROFESSIONALS

Here are some questions to ask yourself about your relationship with any counselor, therapist, or helping professional:

- Do I feel respected, accepted, and understood?
- Does my counselor provide me with options and choices?
- Does my counselor listen to how I would like to do things, and do I have a say in what happens in treatment?
- Am I able to be open with my counselor?
- Am I able to share my feelings?
- Does my counselor convey confidence in my ability to make changes?
- Do I trust my counselor?
- Does my counselor encourage me to ask questions and then answer them fully, or help me find the answers?
- Do I feel my counselor cares about me as a person?
- Do my counselor and I have common goals?
- Does my counselor work with me to take steps toward reaching my goals?

Adapted with permission from the "Health-Care Climate Questionnaire" developed by G. C. Williams, R. M. Ryan, and E. L. Deci at www.selfdeterminationtheory.org.

WHY THE GAP BETWEEN WHAT GOES ON AND WHAT SHOULD GO ON?

How did the gap between the goings-on in typical treatment and what's known to be most effective become so great? According to John Kelly, "Dissemination from research to front-line practice takes about ten years, on average, and that's only if it becomes fashionable." Other experts say it's because a system entirely separate from the rest of health care emerged to treat people with addictions—in part because of long-standing discrimination against them. In fact, until the middle of the twentieth century, there was little or no professional help for people with addictions. They were seen as social outcasts and refused treatment by most practitioners and hospitals. (William White said that when he entered the field in the 1960s, some hospitals still had morality clauses in their bylaws that prohibited them from admitting alcoholics and addicts.) This gave rise to both AA in the 1930s and a "rehab" care system that was apart from mainstream medical and mental health services and provided primarily by peers who were in recovery themselves.

According to William Miller and colleagues writing in the *Journal of Substance Abuse Treatment*, "a polarization of science versus practice" developed because treatment practices had been "guided by the folk wisdom of recovering people, particularly through the perspectives of Alcoholics Anonymous and related twelve-step programs." Thus, addiction counselors and facilities developed strong allegiance to particular treatment models—"often regardless of scientific evidence for efficacy or lack thereof."

In a recent trend, some private firms have begun to purchase treatment programs across the country and to consolidate their clinical and administrative management. While some experts think this may lead to innovation and improvements in quality and efficiency of addiction treatment, how it will impact quality of care remains to be seen. Several programs I came across that were part of larger consolidated firms were using a number of approaches that would not be considered science based.

THREE ORGANIZATIONS THAT BRING SCIENCE TO THE PEOPLE

- National Institute on Alcoholism and Alcohol Abuse—As part of the National Institutes of Health (NIH) and the largest funder of alcohol research in the world, NIAAA supports and conducts research on the impact of alcohol use on human health and disseminates research findings to health-care providers, researchers, policy makers, and the public: http://www.niaa.nih.gov/.
- National Institute on Drug Abuse—also part of the NIH, NIDA's focus is supporting and conducting research on drug abuse and addiction, as well as disseminating the results of that research to improve prevention and treatment and to inform policy as it relates to drug abuse and addiction: http://www.drugabuse.gov/.

> • Substance Abuse and Mental Health Administration—SAMHSA
> works to improve the quality and availability of substance use disor-
> der prevention and treatment, as well as mental health services, and
> helps apply research in these areas in the general health-care system.
> SAMHSA also administers a number of important grant programs
> and data collection activities: http://www.samhsa.gov/.

DOES PAYING MORE MATTER?

Experts generally agree that spending more money doesn't get you more effective addiction treatment, although there are always exceptions. "Some
so-called leading edge residential centers are in fact charging exorbitant
sums for treatment that is not more effective than your local community
treatment program or working individually with a physician or therapist
who has addictions expertise," according to Dr. Willenbring. He added, "It's
ironic that the wealthiest people are often getting no better than standard treatment approaches with a few embellishments, while equally or
more effective treatment is available at much lower prices and often locally."
Similarly, the 2012 CASA Columbia report on addiction treatment referred
to "posh residential treatment at astronomical prices with little evidence justifying the cost." Dr. Dennis McCarty, an expert on quality and funding of
addiction services at Oregon Health & Science University, said, "Money
can buy you a nicer building and better meals. But research continues to
show that residential care, which is more expensive, has the same rate of
abstinence at follow-up as less-expensive outpatient care. The findings
are consistent across type of addiction, time, geography, and private and
public sectors." He added, "Practically speaking, however, when you get
someone who needs treatment to say, 'Yes, I'll go but it's got to have a
swimming pool,' and that is her 'out' . . . if she thinks it's important, it's
important. It has to be considered. Maybe you need to give her what
she wants."

As suggested previously, some of the programs I visited (and others described by people I interviewed) that serve lower-income populations

seemed to provide treatment that was more comprehensive and more consistent with the aforementioned menu of effective therapies than that provided by some higher-end rehabs. I gathered that one reason for this was that facilities serving lower-income clients were reliant on grants requiring evidence-based approaches and documentation of follow-through, which is not necessarily the case at higher-end programs. External grants may also provide additional resources covering the added costs of implementing newer science-based treatments, according to McCarty. He agreed with my observation that these less costly comprehensive programs may be uncomfortable or inaccessible for middle-income and upper-class people because the clients come from different backgrounds and are generally struggling with different kinds of issues. He said, "This is an unresolved tension in the field (and society). Some programs try to serve both patient populations by offering attractive facilities. Others create separate services and market them to different payers. But for the most part, they do one or the other, not both."

PROGRAM SPOTLIGHT:
ARC COMMUNITY SERVICES IN MADISON, WISCONSIN

One of the people who made me aware of just how comprehensive programs serving lower-income groups can be was Jaden M., a young mother who sought me out after coming across the flyer for my book at ARC Center for Women and Children, part of ARC Community Services in Madison, Wisconsin. While attending ARC's intensive outpatient program and living with her baby in their halfway house, Jaden said, "We have cognitive intervention, anger management, and parenting classes. We have a nutrition counselor, trauma counselors, and we each have our individual substance abuse counselor. I also see a psychiatrist once a month." She added, "The treatment is awesome. They cover every aspect of what you need, and it's all women. We have health and wellness groups, living skills, spirituality classes, yoga classes, and art therapy. Ninety-five percent of your using has nothing to do with putting the drug in your body." All of her treatment is paid for by the state.

Linda Norton, MS, a clinical supervisor and addiction counselor at ARC, described their program as "a recovery-oriented, family-based treatment program for women, children, and their families." She said, "The women identify who their 'family' is, and they don't have to be blood relatives. We have a family therapist on staff who works with children, adults, and whole family systems, as desired. We also connect our clients with community resources, helping them with housing, legal issues, debt, and vocational and educational pursuits. One of our programs, Healthy Beginnings, specializes in the treatment of pregnant and postpartum women. And childcare is provided on-site." (The program does not incorporate the twelve steps, although women are free to attend meetings if they so choose.) Norton has worked in the field for nearly forty years and maintains, "Of the many places I've worked, this one truly is committed to getting to the root of the problem and not just addressing symptoms. This agency is dedicated to addressing all needs of clients who come here."

ARC's director of addiction services, Norman Briggs, EdM, told me that they must use evidence-based practices because of their funding sources and that all of their substance abuse counselors have master's degrees. He said, "All of our clinicians are also licensed in some behavioral health area—for instance, they're social workers, professional counselors, or family counselors in addition to being addiction counselors." Consistent with the finding that "persistence matters," Briggs added, "A few women are able to successfully complete our services in as little as three months, but most are in the four-plus month range, with some women here for up to a year." Completion of the program is determined not by time, but by meeting certain criteria—such as having at least thirty days of abstinence from all mood-altering drugs and a stable living environment—as well as achievement of at least 60 percent of a client's treatment goals. And clients set their own goals.

DOES ACCREDITATION MATTER?

When considering rehabs, you may come across such "seals of approval" as accreditation from Joint Commission (formerly JCAHO, or Joint Commission on Accreditation of Healthcare Organizations); CARF International (formerly Commission on Accreditation of Rehabilitation Facilities); NCQA (National Committee for Quality Assurance); and COA (Council on Accreditation). A number of programs I visited had accreditation from CARF International and/or Joint Commission, the two largest accrediting bodies for addiction rehabs. Do these national qualifications or state licensing matter when it comes to seeking treatment?

Mary Cesare-Murphy, PhD, executive director of behavioral health care (the division that accredits addiction facilities) at the Joint Commission said, "Joint Commission behavioral health accreditation means that an organization has participated in an in-person review conducted by experienced behavioral health professionals and experts in Joint Commission standards that focus on the quality and safety of behavioral health services. The standards do not specify what treatment is to be provided, rather the standards call for an assessment process to identify an individual's needs, strengths, preferences, and goals and use this information to plan treatment and to monitor outcomes."

But does accreditation translate into better client outcomes? In a report titled "Key Elements of Addiction Treatment Effectiveness for Adult Populations," an expert panel convened by the Treatment Research Institute in 2010 concluded that although there is some research indicating that this may be the case, panel members cautioned against using accreditation as an indicator of quality. They noted that in many instances, programs with more resources might take the extra steps to be accredited and that in many states, accreditation is mandatory. Thus, these apparent accolades don't necessarily inform people about nuanced differences between programs that in fact have varying levels of quality. And according to the comprehensive 2012 National Center on Addiction and Substance Abuse at Columbia (CASA Columbia) report on addiction treatment, CARF leaves qualifications of practitioners to state laws and professional associations, while Joint Commission requires staff credentialed "in accordance with the law"—both organizations accordingly allowing for great variation in education and training requirements.

Some people told me that it was important for them to seek out a state-licensed program. However, CASA Columbia's review of licensing and certification requirements for addiction treatment facilities revealed that regulations vary significantly from state to state and that certain programs (for instance many state-run and religious programs) are exempt from state regulation. Of the twenty-one states that specify minimum educational requirements for program or clinical directors of rehabs, only eight require a master's degree and just six require credentialing as an addiction counselor. The report concluded, "In facilities that are subject to state regulation, the staffing requirements do not consistently mandate the involvement of professionals who are capable of providing a full range of effective interventions (including pharmaceutical and psychosocial therapies), services rarely are required to reflect best practices and quality assurance requirements seldom stipulate that patient outcome data be collected, analyzed or made available to the public. For no other health condition are such exemptions from routine governmental oversight considered acceptable practice."

Director of Practical Recovery Tom Horvath advised, "Since state licensing standards may be minimal, individuals seeking a high-quality recovery program need to investigate in detail, asking questions about staff backgrounds and approaches to treatment. In some states, treatment approaches can be almost anything, whether or not they're evidence-based. Even credentialed or accredited programs may look better on paper than they operate in practice because, to a significant extent, the accreditation process may look more at consistency (did you do what you said you would do) than at the quality of what they're doing."

I know that in writing this book, I was told about state-licensed programs to which I wouldn't send a family member. Maia Szalavitz, author of *Help at Any Cost: How the Troubled-Teen Industry Cons Parents and Hurts Kids*—a critical and disturbing analysis of teen boot camps, "emotional growth" boarding schools, wilderness programs, and other tough-love centers, which often wind up caring for kids with substance problems—told me, "I found JCAHO- and CARF-accredited programs that used unethical and extremely abusive practices, such as public humiliation, brutal emotional confrontation, and punitive use of isolation and restraint." (For more on teen boot camps, see chapter 7.) She added, "The addiction field has been about as effectively regulated as banking before the economic crisis in many states. If we want better addiction treatment, consumers have got to stop fighting for funding for 'treatment' without being explicit about what that means. They can't just support no-strings-attached funding for whatever providers want to provide."

The CASA Columbia report recommended the establishment of national accreditation standards reflecting evidence-based care for all addiction treatment facilities and that federal, state, and local governments should subject all addiction rehabs to the same mandatory licensing processes as other health-care facilities.

WHAT DOESN'T WORK

Certain practices repeatedly struck down in studies as having no benefit are still in widespread use at rehabs. Some just seem to be a waste of time, while others are unhelpful or even detrimental. Here are some of them:

EDUCATIONAL LECTURES. Despite dozens of studies showing they have no impact, educational lectures and films continue to be used as a mainstay of treatment. In a review of 381 research studies, such methods were found to be the least effective of forty-eight approaches for treating alcohol problems. As already mentioned, the high-end residential rehabs I visited held lectures throughout the day and into the evening. Even at the outpatient program run by the prestigious rehab that Sadie A. attended, she said, "After we all checked in, they typically showed a video of something and talked about it. It might be a video on step one of AA or the hijacked brain on drugs."

DWELLING ON THE PAST. The groups I observed dwelled far more on substance use and its consequences than on moving on or the bonuses of quitting. Eddie F. affirmed that a message he received at one program was

"You were born a drunk and will always be a drunk. Look at your life and the consequences of your actions. Very little time was spent on creating a future once you cleared an area in your life." I sat in on a group exercise that waxed into a discussion of "war stories" with clients sharing sometimes humorous anecdotes about how they tucked booze bottles away so others wouldn't find them. Throughout the day and evening, more lectures—even one that was supposed to be on spirituality—continued on the harms of use. I'm not an addiction counselor, but I couldn't help but think about how much more helpful it would have been to hear some of the clients who had had periods of sobriety before relapsing share what their lives were like when they were sober rather than when they were drinking.

Some people talked about how bad the pessimistic tone made them feel. In trying to overcome her addiction to painkillers, Salina S. said of her counseling at several traditional treatment programs, "Normally, I'm not an insecure person, but they made me concentrate so much on all the negatives that I was starting to get insecure and wanted to use more. They were not focusing on our strengths at all; they were just magnifying our weaknesses." In fact, there's evidence that giving recommendations focusing on the advantages of stopping a health-damaging behavior are more effective in encouraging people to discontinue or curtail such habits than are those that dwell on the disadvantages of continuing.

In contrast to all the negative messages, at a group I attended at the Six Dimensions non-twelve-step program in Minneapolis, the counselor shifted the conversation away from the downside of drug use and the past by asking members, "What's changed for you?" I heard things like, "I feel good about myself. . . . You look inside and you find it. [At other places] you never get told to look."

GETTING IN YOUR FACE, SHOWING YOU WHO'S BOSS, AND WEARING YOU DOWN. Old-school confrontational approaches are among the least effective ways to help someone get sober, and, as stated previously, I witnessed very few overt incidents at programs I visited. However, in subtle ways, vestiges remain of the mentality that addicts need to be "broken down and then built back up." And at certain facilities I didn't visit, reports indicated that degrading tactics still exist.

Tracing the history of in-your-face approaches, which used to be standard in rehabs, William White and Dr. William Miller note in a 2007 *Counselor* magazine article on confrontation that it was believed that addicts have a faulty personality characterized by such terms as "narcissistic," "grandiose," "dishonest," "in denial," and "defiant individualist." One needs only to spend a little time with addiction counselors and recovered people alike to know that these descriptors are still commonly used to characterize drug- and alcohol-addicted people. The aggressive counseling style that emerged in American addiction treatment in the latter half of the twentieth century was authoritarian and quite the opposite of the nonconfrontational therapeutic relationship that more and more studies show is effective. White and Miller note that there's no scientific basis for believing that there's a unique "addict personality"—research shows that people with substance problems are an extremely diverse group.

The remnants of this old-school approach that came across at some twelve-step-oriented programs I visited were apparent more in words than in actions. For instance, I heard clients characterized as dishonest, narcissistic, and selfish. (Sometimes clients described themselves this way.) One staff person told me the resistance he encounters most is "terminal uniqueness," which was described as the attitude of "I'm different; no one understands me; that might work for them, but it isn't going to work for me." More than vestiges of confrontation remain in the world of rehab, as these cases at programs I didn't visit illustrate:

- Staff at one program that treats its low-income clientele with great dignity and respect informed me that it was just the opposite at some of the sober homes where clients stay at night—if they did something wrong, clients were made to wear punitive signs around their necks or sit on crates.
- Salina S. went to an outpatient program that also provided sober housing, where the staff used the old-fashioned practice of "pull-ups," which entail having one client give another immediate feedback regarding inappropriate behavior. She explained, "If I said 'shit,' another girl would say, 'Pull up, Salina. You said, "Shit."' And I'd have to say, 'Thank you.' If you had two pull-ups in one sentence, it got reported to your counselor."

(You could get a pull-up for something as inconsequential as forgetting to turn a light off in a room.)

- A young man who came from a dysfunctional family was told by his counselor, "You're a pathetic liar" when he shared details of his past. His grandmother told me, "The counselor said it again when he told her where his anger was coming from."

Citing study after study showing that confrontational approaches don't work and may even be harmful, White and Miller make the point that accusing, confronting, labeling, and demeaning people may in turn cause defensiveness and appear to confirm the "diagnosis" of their being "in denial," dishonest, and oppositional. When I sat in on a discussion at an outpatient program where clients were sharing their unfortunate experiences at various other rehabs, one person said, "To get recovery, you shouldn't have to be in fear." Then they talked about how, at their current program, they were not coerced to do anything and had choices. One of them said the upshot was, "You're more comfortable, more likely to tell the truth if you make a mistake."

WHO'S MINDING THE STORE?

Each tragic addiction-related celebrity death brings "the experts" out of the woodwork. True to form, after actor Corey Haim's death,* Larry King brought forth his panel of "experts," including actress Mackenzie Phillips and CNN host Jane Velez-Mitchell, both outspoken about their history of substance problems. With Dr. Drew Pinsky sitting beside them, it was Phillips and Velez-Mitchell who were asked what to do when someone has a problem and whether addiction leads to depression. While we watched, my husband facetiously remarked, "Addiction is the only disease for which having it makes you an expert. It would be like having kidney disease makes you an expert on kidney disease."

Consistent with historical reports that more than 50 percent of people

---

* According to the *Los Angeles Times*, Haim's death was officially attributed to pneumonia, but he was reported to have had a long history of drug abuse and rehab visits.

providing treatment are in recovery themselves, a number of programs I visited indicated that at least half of the professional staff was in recovery. At one program, just about every professional person I met over the course of a week was in post-addiction status. At another rehab, an administrator guessed that, overall, about six out of ten staff were in recovery—and eight out of ten were in some sort of twelve-step program if you included Al-Anon and Adult Children of Alcoholics (ACOA).

Despite the fact that some clients I interviewed said it was important to them to have a counselor who had shared their experience, it's a myth that "you have to be one to help another." Studies of addiction counselors have not found that those in recovery are more or less effective than those who are not. Addiction treatment is a field that historically "grew up" with recovering addicts and alcoholics treating others still afflicted, fostering the idea that "this is what worked for me, so it will work for you, too." And since most people working in the field recovered by using the twelve steps, this philosophy was transferred to their clients—a practice still the status quo at many rehabs. As addiction treatment historian William White has documented, however, in the 1970s a movement began to professionalize the role of addiction counselors via credentialing, certification, and licensure, and since that time the percentage of addiction counselors in recovery has reportedly declined to less than half nationwide.

ON BECOMING AN ADDICTION TREATMENT COUNSELOR

So what qualifies someone to treat people with drug and alcohol problems? Most individuals I interviewed who went to treatment programs had no clue. I can't say that knowing would have helped much. In the first place, rehab staffing covers a diverse world in which you may encounter physicians, social workers, nurses, psychologists, marriage and family therapists, and clergy. But the people who do the lion's share of treatment work are titled with variations on "counselor" and include addiction treatment counselor, alcohol and drug counselor, chemical dependency counselor, behavioral health counselor, and substance abuse counselor.

As mentioned previously, qualifications for becoming a credentialed addiction treatment counselor vary greatly from one state to the next. Carrie G. captured the state of this profession when she said, "It's a vague boundary-less field." A 2007 report commissioned by SAMHSA on the substance abuse and mental health workforce stated, "There is no agreement as to program standards, curricula, and how much, if any, supervised field work is required before the graduate is eligible for employment in a prevention or treatment position." According to the 2012 National Center on Addiction and Substance Abuse at Columbia (CASA Columbia) report on the state of addiction treatment, fourteen states required only a high school degree or general equivalency diploma (GED) as minimum educational requirements for becoming a certified or licensed addiction counselor, while an associate's degree was the minimum in ten states, and six states had no degree requirements. Only one state required a master's degree. The report concluded that most of the workforce in this field is not equipped with "the knowledge, skills, or credentials" to provide the full range of science-based services to treat addiction. Frederick Rotgers, PsyD, the 2011 president of the Society of Addiction Psychology, said, "The laxity of requirements for such a critical health problem is sad."

Often, the training of addiction counselors is via an apprenticeship model, with far fewer hours of education required than mandated hours working under another more experienced counselor. Consider New York, a state with one of the largest numbers of drug and alcohol treatment facilities and clients in the country, where the current credential for addiction counselors is "Credentialed Alcoholism and Substance Abuse Counselor" or "CASAC." (Note that certification is not required—in other words, you can practice as an addiction counselor in New York without certification or a license.) To become a CASAC, a high school degree or GED is required along with a minimum of 6,000 hours (approximately three years) of supervised experience in an approved work setting, plus 350 hours of education related to addiction counseling. But no psychology courses are needed.

With my master's degree in nutrition, however, if I wanted the CASAC credential, most of those 6,000 hours would be waived and I'd need just one year (2,000 hours) of supervised work experience in an appropriate setting. (My degree could also have been in speech pathology, education, theology, physical therapy—certainly not professions expected to prepare a person to help those with substance use disorders—among a number of other human-services fields.) I'd also have to pass an exam. If I wanted to work with adolescents, no special training or certification would be required. And if I had worked in the field previously, regardless of how long ago it was and despite the fact that many recommended approaches to treatment have changed radically over the years, my previous education and work experience would count toward my CASAC credential.

A concern with the apprenticeship-type model requiring little formal education is that it doesn't foster understanding of new research findings in the field, or critical thinking. While writing *Inside Rehab*, I subscribed to one of the leading magazines for addiction counselors to get a sense of what they might be reading and found that, while some of the articles were authoritative and written by experts in the field, others lacked substance and a scientific basis. Someone without much academic background might have difficulty making the distinction. One expert in the field commented that he "shudders" when he reads some of the articles in the two leading trade magazines for addiction counselors.

Another concern is whether addiction counselors in training receive adequate clinical supervision. A researcher who studies treatment programs told me, "They're often left alone with clients. Programs sometimes view interns as inexpensive labor and allow them to do clinical work at lower rates of pay than licensed counselors. Programs don't really have the time and resources to do training, and the supervision that is provided is to make sure things are consistent with state standards; it's often clerical supervision, not clinical supervision."

Finding the standards for becoming either a certified or licensed addiction counselor in your state can be a challenge because there's not a consistent way to locate them. I found that the easiest way to accomplish this was to do an Internet search using the following terms: "credentialing," "addiction counselor" (state name). Or you can contact your state substance abuse agency at http://findtreatment.samhsa.gov/TreatmentLocator/faces/abuseAgencies.jspx.

SETTING THEIR OWN BAR

This is not to say that individual rehabs can't and don't have their own more rigorous standards for hiring employees. The primary counseling staff at programs I visited had a wide range of educational credentials—almost all doctoral degrees at Practical Recovery, a mix of doctoral and master's degrees at Promises, and a mix of bachelor's and master's degrees at Hazelden Center City, Caron, Fountain Centers, and most of the outpatient programs I visited. (At one outpatient program, a college degree was not required.) As for addiction counselor certification, some programs required it of their primary counselors (or at least they had to be working on it) while others didn't. At one program, I was told that most staff were not certified because they paid so little that once people became certified, "they tend to move on to bigger-paying jobs."

On a national level, a 2007–8 survey of 345 representative private treatment centers conducted as part of the National Treatment Center Study (NTCS) at the University of Georgia revealed that, as their highest degrees, about half of the counseling staff had a master's, nearly a quarter of them had a bachelor's, and the remainder had associate's degrees or less. (Note that for Medicaid reimbursement for addiction treatment, regulations in many states require counselors with graduate degrees.) Six out of ten of them were certified addictions professionals, and about a quarter were certified mental health professionals.

Some programs for young people require special training pertaining to youth. At Hazelden's Center for Youth and Families, for instance, all clinicians must complete a course in adolescent and young adult development (and all counselors are state-licensed drug and alcohol counselors and have at least a bachelor's degree in a related field). At another adolescent program, I was told that about 70 percent of the counselors had master's degrees, but I met one who told me she had a degree in "rehab counseling," not addiction counseling or psychology, and had learned by working at the rehab.

When I asked one of the residential adolescent-program administrators about whether parents can ask questions about which counselor their child will have and make requests—say, about experience or personality style—she said, "We have done that sometimes, through our admissions staff, but it's not the way that we always do it. If it's a mother who wants someone with fifty-two degrees who's been in the field for a long time, it's not going to happen. [The decision] is going to be clinically driven." In other words, apparently it's up to the staff to make the decision. As a parent, the response to that question is something I'd take into consideration when choosing a teen rehab.

Parents should also ask about the role of treatment technicians or counselor assistants (CAs) and how much time their child might be spending with them, because it can be substantial—and these staffers generally don't have sophisticated training. At a residential teen rehab, I was told, "Counselor assistants are with kids twenty-four-seven. They take them through their daily activities, facilitate psychoeducational lectures, and share their stories. They are certified addiction counselors but don't necessarily have a bachelor's degree, and they have to be in recovery for at least two years." Another adolescent residential program had technicians who were required to have a high school degree or its equivalent, were expected to be free of chemical problems for two years, and largely received on-the-job training.

ALPHABET SOUP

Unlike professions defined by a single acronym such as MD for medical doctor, RN for registered nurse, or RD for registered dietitian, a confusing alphabet soup of credentials trails many an addiction professional's name. In addition to the certification and/or licensing standards for addiction counselors in each state that bear their own varied acronyms, such as CASAC in New York or LADC for "licensed alcohol and drug counselor" in Minnesota, are such national designations as NCAC I or II for national certified addiction counselor; MAC for master addiction counselor; and ASE for adolescent specialist endorsement—all credentials with standards set by the National Certification Commission

(NCC) of NAADAC, the Association for Addiction Professionals. (Note that "NAADAC, the Association for Addiction Professionals," is how they list their name, but NAADAC stands for National Association for Alcoholism and Drug Abuse Counselors.) NAADAC-NCC is one of two major national credentialing bodies. NAADAC claims it is the largest membership organization serving addiction counselors and other professionals in the field. You can check out the qualifications of a counselor holding any of these credentials by going to NAADAC's Web site and clicking under "certification." For instance, to become an NCAC I or ASE, a college degree is not required but for an NCAC II, a bachelor's degree is required; and to become a MAC, you must have a master's degree.

The other large organization that establishes standards for credentialing addiction professionals is the International Certification & Reciprocity Consortium, or IC&RC. They offer seven different credentials including Alcohol and Drug Counselor (ADC) and Advanced Alcohol and Drug Counselor (AADC), and Clinical Supervisor (CS). Standards for each credential can be found at www.internationalcredentialing.org.

The process for earning the certifications offered by both the NCC and the IC&RC requires various amounts of clinical experience, education, supervision, and testing, and combinations of these. In addition, most state boards that certify addiction professionals are members of IC&RC, which means that they use IC&RC's standards for certification. As of 2012, IC&RC, considering itself the largest international addiction-related organization, represented forty-seven states and territories, as well as the military services, and maintained that more than 45,000 professionals held its credentials. (In May 2011, 76,600 substance abuse and behavioral disorder counselors were employed in this country, according to the U.S. Bureau of Labor Statistics.) When I was writing the book, states were still using their own terminology for addiction professionals, but the IC&RC had recently voted to standardize the use of names and acronyms for its member boards, using the designations above, by the beginning of 2016.

In short, it's all pretty confusing and can be difficult to sort out what acronyms really mean in terms of qualifications. Personally, if someone were my primary care counselor, I'd want to know the following:

- What are your educational credentials—for instance, what is your highest attained degree, where was it received, and what was your major field of study?
- How did you receive clinical training and supervision?
- What professional licensing and/or certifications do you hold—and what do they mean?
- How long have you been working in the field?

OTHER PROFESSIONS THAT FALL SHORT

Many people mistakenly assume that other health and mental health professionals have expertise with substance use disorders, which typically isn't the case unless they have special training. In trying to get help for her son, who struggled for years with a cocaine addiction, Emily K. said they took him to numerous psychiatrists, most of whom were very expensive and came with high recommendations but turned out to have little or no expertise with addictions. She said, "If you have cancer, you get yourself to an oncologist. When you have an addiction, sometimes it feels like you have cancer but you're seeing a dentist or a podiatrist." The 2012 CASA Columbia report extensively reviewed education and training having to do with substance use disorders for a wide variety of health and mental health professionals and concluded that most are not sufficiently trained to diagnose and treat addiction. For instance, they found that in most states, addiction is not a required part of psychologists' training, and that, in general, physicians and other medical professionals receive little education in addiction science, prevention, and treatment. The report says, "Physicians, therefore, lack the basic education and training in addiction medicine that is needed to understand the science of addiction, translate research evidence into practice, screen for risky use, diagnose and provide treatment for addiction and the broad range of co-occurring health problems, or refer patients to other specialists as needed."

Beginning in 2001, general psychiatry residency programs were required to provide just one month of full-time equivalent training to residents in addiction—although in reality, at least part of this training often winds up being exposure to addicted patients, not substance use disorder treatment. Thomas McLellan pointed out that the limited training physicians sometimes receive can actually make matters worse because most get exposed to addiction in the emergency room, "where patients are at their absolute worst. What they get is a very prejudicial and distorted view." Another expert said that medical residents are often exposed to a narrow, old-school, one-size-fits-all approach to addiction treatment.

The CASA report cites evidence that we have some distance to go to get primary health-care providers to even recognize substance use disorders in everyday clients—for instance, one national survey of patients who had seen a general medical provider in the past year found that only about three out of ten were asked about alcohol and drug use. Of those who were asked about use and then identified as risky drinkers, less than half received any advice. Vince T. told me that although it was his choice to do something when he felt his alcohol consumption was getting out of hand, his doctor seemed surprised and wasn't convinced when Vince wrote him a letter, saying he wanted treatment—so he'd be "locked in." His doctor's response was, "Why are you asking for this?" Although the treatment referral went through, Vince felt that "physicians do such a terrible job of screening for substance abuse and talking to patients about it."

It behooves consumers to seek out helpers with special training in the field. The following professions have their own credentialing for members with addictions expertise:

- The American Board of Addiction Medicine (ABAM) offers certification to licensed medical doctors or osteopathic physicians who, post-residency, participate in a certain amount of continuing education in this subject area; have a minimum of one year of full-time involvement in the field of substance use disorders; and within five years of that, pass an exam. In mid-2011, the first group of medical residents began training in ten newly ABAM-accredited addiction medicine residencies around the country, with more expected to follow soon. To find a physician with ABAM certification: http://www.abam.net/find-a-doctor.

- The American Board of Psychiatry and Neurology offers specialty certification in addiction psychiatry for board-certified psychiatrists who pass an exam after completing one full-time-equivalent year of post-residency training in addiction psychiatry at a program accredited by the Accreditation Council for Graduate Medical Education. To locate a psychiatrist with this certification: https://application.abpn.com/verifycert/verifyCert.asp?a=4.

- The American Osteopathic Association offers a "Certification of Added Qualifications in Addiction Medicine" to osteopathic physicians who hold a specialty certification in anesthesiology, internal medicine, or psychiatry; subsequently complete one year of approved training in addiction psychiatry; and successfully complete a certification exam. To find someone who specializes in "addiction medicine," go to www.osteopathic.org and use the "Find a DO" search tool, which allows you to search according to geographic area and "primary specialty" (un-check the "search all specialties" option). The results also indicate whether the person holds the addiction certification.

- The National Association of Social Workers offers a special credential for members who apply to become Certified Clinical Alcohol, Tobacco, and Other Drugs Social Workers. To receive this, following acquisition of a Master of Social Work degree, they must document a minimum of 180 hours of education in this subject area and receive at least 3,000 hours of supervised practice experience in the assessment and treatment of substance use disorders.

DO CREDENTIALS MATTER?

When I asked Alexandria, the woman profiled in chapter 3, for any specific examples of how the last of many programs—the one that finally helped her daughter—stood out, she said, "Their group and individual therapy programs were run by credentialed people, and everyone was degreed. Most had master's degrees—but with years and years of experience. No one was fresh out of school. Yes, they were all recovering as well since that seems to be the recurring theme in all centers, but they also had the training. I believe that made a big difference."

While a higher level of formal education doesn't necessarily mean greater expertise, the consensus from the expert panel that developed the 2010 Treatment Research Institute report titled "Key Elements of Treatment Effectiveness for Adult Populations" was that for counselors, more education is better, with a master's degree being the preferred minimum level of training. Practical Recovery's Tom Horvath stated, "Addiction is no less complicated than any other psychological issue. So why wouldn't addiction treatment have the same minimum level of qualification as psychological treatment, where it's a master's degree? An addiction counselor without a graduate education is not prepared to respond to the co-occurring problems that often accompany addiction. In an extended surgical team licensed practical and vocational nurses have a place, but we don't expect them to perform the surgery." Addiction psychiatrist Dr. Mark Willenbring agreed that at least a two-year post-baccalaureate degree should be the standard, but said it's preferable that it come from a qualified institution of higher learning, not one that's affiliated with a treatment program. (Of course, there are exceptions—I came across some experienced, talented addiction clinicians who hold no more than a bachelor's degree.)

It's also important for counselors to have adequate clinical supervision, whereby a more senior person oversees and consults with a less seasoned counselor about his or her clients. I found that programs had a range of practices in this regard. At one high-end program, counselors received thirty minutes of weekly one-on-one supervision while at another place there was weekly group and monthly individual supervision. Caron was in the process of working with a nationally known expert on implementing a formal protocol for supervision that included taping client sessions and getting feedback.

An ongoing five-year nationwide research project expected to be completed in 2012 by John Gallagher, PhD, in which the number of ethics violations in the addiction treatment profession are being compared to those in other human-service professions (including licensed psychologists, social workers, professional counselors, and marriage and family therapists) suggests that the problems are worse in the field of addiction treatment. Dr. Gallagher's advice for consumers is "Check with state licensing boards to see if the counselor or agency has had an ethics violation; this is where I get most of my data."

To give some historical perspective to this field that I've sometimes referred to as the "Wild West"—with its inconsistencies and lack of rigor in many professional and facility standards—William White writes in his book *Slaying the Dragon: The History of Addiction Treatment and Recovery in America*, "The addiction treatment industry as a specialized field grew out of the contempt in which other helping systems regarded alcoholics and addicts. For generations, physicians, nurses, social workers, psychologists, welfare workers, and other service professionals barely masked their contempt for the alcoholic and addict. Beneath the veneer of professional discourse about addicts during the past century lies a pervasive undertone: Most professionals simply do not like alcoholics and addicts." White reminded me, "Other helping professionals failed disastrously in their efforts to help the addicted and their families and, as a result, did everything to exclude and extrude persons with such problems from their systems of care. Let's be very clear: If psychiatrists, psychologists, and social workers could have effectively treated addiction, there would have been no specialized field of addiction treatment. Whatever aspersions can be cast on the profession of addiction counseling with 'recovery status' its foundation, it should be acknowledged that it offered the first setting in which the addicted and their families could be treated in an atmosphere of moral equality and mutual respect."

THE COSTS AND BENEFITS OF BEING AN ADDICTION COUNSELOR

A seasoned master's-level counselor at an outpatient program said, "We're used and abused. There aren't a lot of kudos." Another young counselor, not yet licensed, stated, "You can't expect you're going to make money." All in all, it was clear from the staff people I talked to, and everything I read, that being an addiction counselor is no picnic.

It's a profession filled with well-intentioned people, often motivated by their own desire to "give back" after overcoming an addiction or watching a family member struggle through the process. Even a disgruntled ex-staffer of a residential rehab said of his colleagues, "Many of the staff were loving and caring—there were a number of extremely dedicated, hard-working, knowledgeable people who did a lot of good for a lot of clients." But it's also a field plagued by hard work, low pay and, often, little respect. It's not uncommon for staffing levels to be trimmed as a cost-cutting measure, while patient caseloads increase—as does the complexity of the problems clients face, from addictions to multiple drugs to complicated mental health issues to tough socioeconomic problems.

When I asked about the most difficult aspect of their jobs, a number of counselors complained about the burden of paperwork. One said that it took up about 20 percent of his time. At a staff meeting, someone said, "When I first came into the field, the expectation was 60 percent client contact, 40 percent paperwork. Now, it's the reverse, or worse." Mark Willenbring concurred. "A great deal of time (and money) is spent by multiple people to meet bureaucratic requirements of insurance companies and Medicare, while providing no benefit to patients whatsoever." He added that the individual professionals at all levels "seem to be devoted, careful clinicians and support staff who truly believe in what they do and want to provide the best care they can. The problem isn't the people in the system—the problem is the system."

In a recent *Counselor* magazine interview, Dr. McLellan went so far as to recommend that addiction treatment be formally declared "a distressed industry," explaining, "We don't have near the number of trained professional counselors, social workers, and psychologists working in the addiction field that we need right now. Second, a significant proportion of those people who are working are at or near the retirement age. Third, we don't see new people standing in line to enter this field." On another occasion, McLellan said, "Counselor and director turnover in addiction treatment programs is higher than in fast-food restaurants or among the help that clean hotels." When I asked Homer L. what happened after leaving his outpatient program, the first thing he told me was that the counselor he liked so much had left for another job; so did the next counselor.

A 2010 study in the *Journal of Addiction Treatment* that examined annual turnover rates over a two-year period within twenty-seven public and private addiction treatment organizations across the United States found it was about 33 percent for counselors and 23 percent for clinical supervisors. Research finds that people stay in treatment longer if they have the same counselor and have more therapeutic contact with longer-tenured counselors. High turnover may reflect low remuneration for the difficulty of the work. A 2009 government report on our addiction treatment workforce cites a survey of counselors that found that 30 percent had no medical coverage, and, ironically, more than half were not covered for services for substance or mental health problems.

When it came to compensation, salaries at programs I visited ranged from $28,000 for a starting counselor at an outpatient facility to about $100,000 a year for doctoral-level therapists at some high-end places. But most counselors indicated that typical salaries were in the high thirties to low forties. (At one outpatient program, site administrators only made about $40,000.) According to the U.S. Bureau of Labor Statistics, in 2011 the average annual wage estimate for substance abuse and behavioral disorder counselors was $41,030 ($19.73 per hour) and the median was $38,560, meaning half of counselors made more than that and half made less. When you consider the complexity of the responsibilities of an addiction counselor and their clients' needs, it's low compensation.

So why do counselors keep doing their jobs? And how do they feel about them? I wondered just that after meeting a young client who was physically scarred from abuse and who was giving her counselor a hard time during a group session. Yet the counselor told me, "I get gratification from someone having a good day, when they get through the weekend."

Another said, "The best part of my job is getting to see successes, to see people face the dragon and then have a good life. It keeps me coming back." A counselor assistant at an adolescent residential program summed it up this way: "This is the only job where you can have your heart broken and filled with joy at the same time! Yet we still love our jobs."

CHAPTER FIVE

REHAB ISN'T FOR EVERYONE

IN FACT, IT'S NOT FOR MOST PEOPLE

In a 2011 write-up at cbsnews.com about Whitney Houston's last treatment for her struggle with addiction—this time, reportedly in an outpatient program instead of a fancy residential rehab—the medical director of Hazelden's Center City programs was reported as indicating that relapse is common and that the only real failure is failing to get treatment in the first place. It seems to be a well-kept secret, however, that most people overcome alcohol and drug problems without ever setting foot in an addiction treatment program. So why was Charlie Sheen attacked for his decision, after trying numerous times to deal with his drug troubles the rehab way, to have "in-home" rehab? In fact, when it was announced that Sheen would not be getting help in a group setting, Dr. Drew Pinsky was quoted as saying, "Treatment of addiction is a group process when done properly—not an individual thing at all." For most people with substance problems, both the medical director *and* Dr. Pinsky are wrong.

SAM D.'S STORY: QUITTING WITHOUT REHAB, THE TWELVE STEPS, OR GROUP TREATMENT

As a kid, Sam D. excelled at just about everything he did—from scoring touchdowns to his blue-ribbon-winning science fair projects. Even though later in high school he started smoking pot and experimenting with illicit drugs, he graduated among the top members of his senior class. But during his first semester at an elite college, he got so involved with drugs that he flunked out. Shortly afterward, high school football injuries led to the need for knee surgery. While awaiting surgery, it didn't take much arm-twisting for Sam to convince his orthopedist that he needed more than acetaminophen with codeine to dull the pain, and he went home with a prescription for Percocet, a combination of the opioid oxycodone and acetaminophen. Sam said, "It started out as a legitimate need for pain alleviation, and no doctor behaved irresponsibly. As time went on, though, I started manipulating the system to get more than I needed." It all led to a three-year painkiller addiction that, in the end, was costing Sam $100 a day. (He was also a heavy marijuana user, but through all of this, he was still functioning quite well in his job and had even assumed a responsible position at work.)

Finally, Sam became so worn down with the struggle to obtain Percocet from drug dealers (most of the time, he did not manipulate physicians to get it) and the battle to pay for it, that he decided to get help. Because he wasn't interested in going to a treatment program, he went for once-weekly individual sessions with a woman licensed as both a professional counselor (with a master's degree) and an addiction counselor. From the outset, he made it clear that he didn't want to attend twelve-step meetings and that he wanted to do things his way, on his terms. Because he'd had some limited success in previous attempts at weaning himself off Percocet, he told her he thought that path might work if he had a little help. The counselor was amenable and also helped Sam with his depression related to the death of a friend, as well as self-care. For instance, he told me, "The first thing she suggested was that I start eating breakfast, because I'd go all day without eating. We also worked on sleep because I wasn't going to bed until 2:00 or 3:00 a.m."

Sam made good progress, but when he couldn't get Percocet he'd experience horrible withdrawal symptoms, leading him to self-medicate even more when he finally could get pills again. That's when the counselor recommended going to a physician she knew at a local medical clinic to see if he'd help Sam with a prescribed reduction of Percocet. The doctor's conditions? Sam said, "He told me he'd help only if I went to a group-based addiction program and that I'd have to have weekly drug tests. He also required that I write down the name of my drug dealer, which he would seal in an envelope and, if I ever tested positive, the doctor would give the name to the police. Right off, this made me feel like he wasn't on my side and like he was treating me as a criminal. His only concern was supposed to be my health. The fact that the legal side would even concern him bugged me." When Sam refused to comply, the physician said, "You'll never do it without group treatment." But Sam told me, "I had already made up my mind that I was going to quit. I had made the decision. I knew that I had the determination and the willpower."

I spoke with his counselor, who said, "I was frustrated that the physician wasn't willing to work with Sam at all, except on his terms. He wasn't willing to budge, which is when I started searching for methadone/buprenorphine programs. At that time, the closest was ninety miles away, and it wasn't an option to drive that far." So Sam continued to suffer, getting pills when he could and slowly but surely continuing to wean himself off—under the supervision of his counselor—until he became drug free. The counselor recalled, "He even started documenting how many pills he took each day, as that was something that helped him with weight loss years earlier. He was determined and didn't vary from his plan. It took him much less time than I anticipated. That must be part of his personality—when he makes up his mind to do something, he does it." Toward the end of writing my book, Sam had been totally off Percocet for three years, then went on to quit a two-pack-a-day cigarette habit and cut back on marijuana use by what he figured to be about 80 percent. (See chapter 9 for information about how certain people can be considered sober and still intentionally use *some* drugs or alcohol.)

MOST PEOPLE DON'T NEED REHAB

Because this book is about rehab, the majority of interviewees went to a residential or outpatient program of some type, and it's impossible for me to determine whether they belonged there. Many of them no doubt did, and benefited from their experiences. But again, most people who overcome substance problems do it without going to any type of rehab. Looking at a major 2006 study published in *Addiction* from one of the largest and most ambitious surveys ever done on alcohol problems and treatment, called the National Epidemiologic Survey on Alcohol and Related Conditions* (NESARC), seven out of ten people who were in recovery for the previous year attained their status without seeking any help at all or by going to AA meetings, while only about three out of ten had recovered with the help of formal treatment or formal treatment plus AA.

Yet even government agencies, such as SAMHSA, seem to assume that everyone who struggles with a substance problem automatically *needs* treatment at a specialty facility. They make statements such as "Most adults with alcohol problems do not recognize their need for treatment," citing the National Survey on Drug Use and Health finding that only a small fraction of untreated people with alcohol use disorders felt they needed treatment or counseling in the past year. The NSDUH defines the "need for treatment" as meeting the medical criteria for an alcohol use disorder or receiving specialty treatment for alcohol use or illicit drug use in the past twelve months. I asked Nova Southeastern University's Dr. Mark Sobell, who has conducted research on people who resolved substance problems without treatment, what he thinks about the notion that all people with substance use disorders *need* formal treatment, and he responded, "I think they're making big assumptions. The main point they are trying to make, I think, is that few people become involved in treatment. The point they never make is that part of the reason this occurs is that specialty services are not appropriate for persons with problems that are not severe. And often those services are not appropriate for people whose problems *are* severe."

Several months before he went to get help for his addiction, Sam D. said, "I had made the mental commitment to quit, I just didn't know how to do it yet. The will was there, but the way wasn't. I kept going back and

---

* For the National Epidemiologic Survey on Alcohol and Related Conditions (NESARC), more than 43,000 people from all walks of life were asked, in face-to-face interviews, a battery of questions about their present and past alcohol consumption, tobacco and illicit drug use, alcohol and drug problems, use of treatment services, and psychiatric disorders. Because NESARC participants were a large representative group of people selected at random, the findings from the study can be generalized.

forth, trying to quit and then using again. Finally, the struggle became too much to bear and I just said, 'Fuck it, I'll quit.' I called my family and asked if they could help me find a counselor." Earlier, his mother had suggested considering a residential facility and Sam wanted no part of it. So she called around to mental health providers in their community and was fortunate to find one who not only had expertise with addictions but who had a cancellation and could see Sam immediately. Chances are good, however, that if Sam had gone for an assessment at a traditional treatment program—particularly with the long-standing nature and severity of his addiction—he would have been told that he needed at least a thirty-day residential stay. Tom Horvath of Practical Recovery, which provides outpatient, intensive outpatient combined with optional sober living, and residential programs, said, "People quit when it becomes important enough. We have *never* told a prospective client that treatment is essential to change. Our approach is more, 'You may find treatment valuable to help solidify the decisions you have made and to follow through effectively on these decisions—what kinds of experiences do you think would be most valuable for you?' In my opinion, professionals oversell treatment, as if it were essential. It's not."

In support of what Dr. Horvath says and in contrast to what you might suspect would be a "party-until-you-have-to-quit" mentality, alcohol researchers have noted that people commonly start making changes between the time they first decide to enter treatment (or go for an initial evaluation) and actually start treatment. Mark Willenbring said, "Change typically starts thirty to ninety days before seeking treatment, according to several recent studies. Rehab is a *result* of change, not an instigator." As further support, SAMHSA's Treatment Episode Data Set (TEDS), which tracks the yearly number of admissions to rehabs, revealed that in 2010 about 29 percent of the time people reported no use of their primary substance in the month before entering rehab. Some of these people were referred to rehab by the court system and were probably under some form of court supervision, while others may have transferred from another program or been less than truthful upon admission. However, it's likely that a number of them privately decided to quit using before entering treatment.

It is true that many people who would likely benefit from treatment don't participate, as shown in an analysis based on information from the NESARC and published in *Drug and Alcohol Dependence* in 2007. Of the 30 percent of people (yes, 30 percent!) who reported that they had an alcohol use disorder at anytime in their lives, only about 15 percent said they ever sought treatment, went to AA, or got help from a professional for their alcohol problem. Of the help seekers, only about 45 percent took part in a rehab, while about 37 percent got help from a private physician, psychiatrist, psychologist, or social worker. The most common type of help was participation in a twelve-step program—about three-quarters of them went to Alcoholics Anonymous. Compared to those who didn't seek help, people who did tended to have more symptoms of an alcohol use disorder—in general, they were older, divorced or separated, and male—plus they had lower income and educational levels and more psychiatric problems and drug use disorders than the go-it-aloners. The top three reasons people gave for not seeking treatment, even though they'd considered doing so, were that they thought they should be able to do it alone, that the problem would get better by itself, or that they had already quit drinking on their own. (Other reasons included thinking the drinking problem wasn't serious enough, being too embarrassed to discuss it with anyone, feeling unable to afford the bills, not wanting to go to treatment, and hating answering personal questions.) Contrary to the notion that being "in denial" keeps people from getting help, research suggests that this is not a primary reason people with drinking problems don't seek treatment. Studies indicate that the majority of people with alcohol problems are aware of the problems for as long as a decade before seeking treatment, indicating that opportunities exist for reaching at least some people earlier.

THE DIY (DO-IT-YOURSELF) WAY

More than ten years ago, when I first visited Hazelden's main campus in Center City, Minnesota—at their invitation, shortly after *Sober for Good* was published—one of their administrators seemed incredulous when I told her that twenty-five of my 222 book participants overcame their drinking problems solo—without AA, rehab, or addiction counseling. She said something to the effect of "They must all be miserable," reflecting the notion that someone who recovers on his own is what's called a "dry drunk." Yet I found no evidence that these people had any less joyful lives than those who had gotten sober with some sort of help. Nevertheless, an overriding theme that came across in my visits to rehabs was that people cannot overcome addictions independently and they need treatment to *get* sober plus the support of twelve-step groups to *stay* sober. At one of the residential programs, many of the activities—from rope-climbing exercises to group therapy interactions—seemed designed to illustrate that, as one counselor put it, "On our own we can't do it." And at a lecture for professionals about twelve-step recovery at another residential rehab, we were told that "over-reliance on self blocks the addict/alcoholic from the spiritual solution" and explains why change is not possible on your own. We heard, once again, about how miserable people will be if they recover on their own, how they will be unfulfilled, and how they will use again.

The idea that people can overcome addictions on their own challenges the fundamental concept of the twelve steps, which is that an addict is "powerless" and has "lost control." Despite the fact that studies suggest that 20 to 80 percent of those who overcome addictions do so without help (depending on which studies you consult, how long people have been in recovery, and what type of addiction we're talking about), the notion that people can "do it on their own" is at odds with the stereotypical thinking that drug addicts and alcoholics cannot make informed decisions and develop their own strategies for resolving them, as Swiss sociologist Harald Klingemann, PhD, and Drs. Mark and Linda Sobell pointed out in a 2010 article that reviews the scientific studies on "solo" recovery in the scholarly journal *Addiction*. The article indicates that having a shorter "career" of problematic substance use, less severe addiction, and more "recovery capital" make "DIY" recovery more likely, as does having fewer mental health problems. (In general, people who are able to overcome addictions have more recovery capital, which includes having good health, financial assets, safe and sober housing, education, vocational skills and credentials, problem-solving abilities, self-esteem, a sense of meaning and purpose in life, interpersonal skills, supportive relationships, and healthy leisure activities.) It makes sense that you're more likely to get sober with all of these things going for you.

Dr. Klingemann and the Sobells speculated that one reason why so many people go the solo route is that the available options are not all that palatable. They noted, "When treatments are perceived as overly intensive, demeaning, and requiring unnecessarily severe changes in lifestyle, they lack appeal and are unlikely to be utilized." And, as noted, the incessant message that "you can't do it on your own" may actually discourage some people from trying to get sober.

The Sobells run the research-based Guided Self-Change Program at Nova Southeastern University in Fort Lauderdale, Florida, that encourages people to take responsibility for their own change and offers tools for doing so. These experts talked about needing to get the word out that "you *can* do it on your own," sometimes with a little how-to guidance, for this to become an accepted and credible route to overcoming substance problems. This softer approach might help more people earlier in their substance problem "careers." Part of the message of self-change could be that, if you don't succeed on your own, then treatment is there as the backup plan.

None of this is to say that treatment can't be helpful; in general, research suggests that drug- and alcohol-addicted people who participate in professional treatment and/or self-help groups are more likely to recover than are those who do not—particularly when comparing people with drug and alcohol problems of the same severity.

LUCY K.'S "NOT YET" STORY

When she heard I was recruiting subjects for my book, Lucy wrote, "I have a drinking problem that would have become alcoholism, but I 'nipped it in the bud.' None of my friends went to treatment. We call ourselves the 'not yets.' We don't have any major health problems or history of mental health issues. We simply opened a bottle of wine every day, attended bunco [a dice game] and dinners in the neighborhood, and then somehow found ourselves spiritually bankrupt." She explained that an alcohol problem had "snuck up" on her, adding, "I had this internal 'gut' that there was a problem. This internal 'gut' was a whisper, so it was easy to ignore. I did, in fact, ignore it for ten years. I didn't seem to fit what was described in the 'alcoholism' books."

When I asked Lucy to describe her work five years ago with a psychologist who had an addiction specialty, she explained, "I wasn't a 'crazy drunk'—I was a professional woman who on occasion drank too much and used wine to relieve anxiety. He called it, 'Relief drinking.' What he did was monitor my drinking by checking in with me at each visit and asking important questions, such as about blackouts. As time went by, he gradually added rules, which were introduced so gently that I didn't get it at the time. The rules were, no drinking alone, limit your wine to no more than two glasses on *all* occasions, and no drinking on two consecutive days. He was testing whether I could moderate, and I was unable to follow his gentle recommendations." It was then that the psychologist said, "You are demonstrating over time that you abuse alcohol and at times I am worried about addiction." Lucy said she was "stunned" and that next she did a "quit and try it pattern." She explained, "I had to prove to myself that I couldn't control it. It was a powerful process because I struggled with him setting the limits, following the rules, and with myself. Eventually, the struggle became too much." When he asked her, "Don't you think it would be easier to not drink at all? Your life would be more manageable," she agreed. "It was not hitting me over the head with a baseball bat, a style I found in AA meetings I had attended." Altogether, she stayed with this therapist for four years and noted that she was fortunate that her health insurance paid for unlimited therapy sessions.

Yet when she "had the spaciousness of evenings with no wine," Lucy said, "I found that there was a 'hole in my soul.'" She began to fill this hole by joining a women's group taught by a personal coach who emphasized meditation and spirituality. She also left her church and began attending a

Quaker meetinghouse that had small "spiritual-nurture" groups that "filled the emptiness." But Lucy also learned that "emptiness is a *good* thing—emptiness becomes openness, and creative things flow in. I developed a prayer practice, my form of meditation, have friends who are on the same path, and attend conferences on spiritual topics. For me, spirituality was what I needed to fill the hole."

NOT ALL THE SAME

Not only is Lucy's story another example of the many paths leading to resolution of substance problems, it illustrates how people whose problems are not severe can benefit from professional help. In fact, substance problems fall along a wide continuum, ranging from relatively minor to very serious. Many people abuse substances in a way that's risky or hazardous but that doesn't meet the definition of a substance use disorder. For instance, when it comes to alcohol, "at-risk" or "heavy" drinking for a woman is considered having more than three drinks on any day or more than seven drinks per week; for a man, it's considered no more than four drinks per day or fourteen drinks per week.

Mark Willenbring explained that, in any given year, about 25 percent of adults are considered to be "at-risk" drinkers who meet these guidelines. They don't fit the criteria for an alcohol use disorder, but they're at risk for developing one. Another 4 percent of adults have symptoms consistent with an alcohol use disorder in any one year, but their problems are not incapacitating. They have a mild to moderate disorder and don't have severe alcohol-related relationship, health, work, or legal problems. Dr. Willenbring said, "The majority of these people are functional. They have jobs, health insurance, reasonably stable family lives, and go to church on Sunday. But that doesn't mean they aren't hurting." Note, too, that a NESARC study published in the *Archives of General Psychiatry* in 2007 suggested that about seven out of ten people who have an alcohol use disorder at some point in their lives have just one bout, lasting an average of less than four years, while the others who have multiple bouts have an average of about five episodes. All of this challenges the notion that "all alcoholics are the same" and that addiction is invariably a terrible, progressive disease that only gets worse unless one goes to a treatment program.

In short, most people with drinking problems are not like the characters depicted by Ray Milland in *The Lost Weekend* or Nicolas Cage in *Leaving Las Vegas*—only 1 percent of adults have a chronic or recurrent and severe alcohol use disorder in any one year. Despite the fact that people with such serious addictions tend to be a unique and small subset of the large body of people with substance problems in the general population, they're the ones who tend to get most of the attention, wind up in treatment, and about whom many of the stereotypes and assumptions about addiction and recovery are formed. Because treatment workers encounter harder-core cases over and over, it logically but falsely tends to shape their views and often those of the general public about all people with substance problems—and about how to overcome them.

What about illicit drugs? Was Charlie Sheen right when he suggested on the Dan Patrick sports-talk radio show that some crack users can "manage it socially"? Dr. Willenbring said while this may be true, especially for cannabis—and that although there are no doubt "functional" cocaine, methamphetamine, or opioid users—probably with illicit drugs, fewer fall into that category relative to the number who are impaired addicts. While the government doesn't issue cutoffs for risky levels of illicit drug use, many of us know people who used and abused drugs casually and didn't get hooked or who had a problem at one point and then seemed to outgrow it. However, it is surprising that so few studies have been done on the course of drug addiction and recovery in the way that alcohol addiction has been investigated.

GETTING HELP WHEN IT'S NOT "THAT BAD"

In my travels to treatment programs and in talking with experts in the field, I repeatedly heard that one of the biggest challenges facing the treatment industry is whether it will continue to focus on the relatively small number of people with advanced addictions or help the broader spectrum of individuals with substance problems. To be sure, a big problem with the drug and alcohol treatment system today is that it's not designed to help the "not yets," people like Lucy, whose substance problems are not "that bad." Many of them aren't comfortable with group treatment and programs that emphasize lifelong abstinence and attendance at self-help meetings. Although Lucy found that abstinence was best for her, not everyone who has an alcohol use disorder needs to resolve it by giving it up. A fair amount of research reveals that some people are able to resume drinking, in a nonproblematic way. (For more on this, see chapter 8.) And although people usually develop drinking problems in their early to mid-twenties, most of them "mature out" of their troubles without help.

When I first interviewed Dr. Willenbring, he had one foot out the door of the NIAAA, as he was returning to his Minnesota home where he is on a mission to modernize addiction treatment. One of his projects is working with the state and several large health-care organizations to see that the much greater number of people who have not hit their proverbial "rock bottom" get the help they need. It's this group that he's training—physicians, nurses, and other health professionals in everyday medical clinics to "screen, evaluate, and treat"—but not in the conventional way. His vision is consistent with that of other experts who see treatment of less severe alcohol and drug problems moving into the realm of regular medical clinics and hospitals. It's all part of a growing national movement to have substance use disorder treatment transition from its isolated domain to become more integrated within the larger health-care system.

Willenbring is training physicians and other health-care professionals in the appropriate way to help at-risk drinkers through "brief intervention" (BI), an approach that's been tested and shown in many studies to have positive effects. It entails brief, one-on-one sessions (usually one to four of them) between a client and a trained health-care professional. Often the goal is to help a person reduce risky alcohol consumption or discontinue harmful levels of use rather than to insist on abstinence, although quitting may be encouraged. BI gives people tools for changing their beliefs about substance use and helps them cope with situations that can increase the risk of harmful use. However, the long-term effectiveness of BI approaches is not clear, and there's been very little research on BI for use with drugs other than alcohol. BI isn't meant for people with more severe alcohol problems because it hasn't been shown to be effective for them. If you're uncertain about where you or someone you care about falls on the spectrum of alcohol problems and wonder whether BI might be an appropriate approach, the pamphlet "Rethinking Drinking," developed by the National Institute on Alcoholism and Alcohol Abuse, is a valuable resource. You can find it at www.rethinkingdrinking.niaaa.nih.gov.

When it comes to helping adults with mild to moderate alcohol use disorders—people whom we sometimes call "functional alcoholics"—Dr. Willenbring says, "Currently they're not getting treated at all, and they have nowhere to turn because their issues aren't severe enough for a rehab program. But they can benefit from help to quit or cut down their drinking. Similar to people with mild to moderate depression, this group can respond to medications and medical management from a primary-care doctor or psychiatrist. They may also benefit from therapy with a mental-health professional to learn skills for coping better with their drinking problem."

Finally, growing support exists for Internet- and phone-based interventions, which can be particularly attractive to those disinclined to seek help in a more traditional way. A number of Internet screening programs help people figure out if they have a drinking problem. One of them, AlcoholScreening.org, also provides links to help participants find services in their community. And the Drinker's Check-up, developed by psychologist Reid Hester, PhD, at www.drinkerscheckup.com, provides an in-depth assessment, personalized feedback, and a set of exercises to help users decide what to do from there. (In a 2005 study published in the *Journal of Substance Abuse Treatment* involving heavy drinkers, a single forty-five-minute session using the Drinker's Check-up helped participants reduce their alcohol use, and, after a year, they were still drinking about 50 percent less.)

THE ONE-ON-ONE WAY

I was struck by the number of people I heard from who resolved their drug and alcohol problems the one-on-one way—that is, with individual counseling. Some, like Sam and Lucy, used it as their sole route to recovery, while others found it to be more helpful than a previous stint at rehab.

Forty-year-old Ruth M. first went to an outpatient program and then to AA when she was in college. Of her overall experience, she said, "I hated it and in eighteen months was back to drinking." For ten more years, she continued to drink heavily and at her worst was consuming "half to three-quarters of a bottle of vodka a day and passing out most nights." Through most of this time, however, Ruth was "functional and by most standards successful in [her] life and career." Over the years, she went back to AA a few times, but just for a week or two. When she was thirty-one, she went to a psychologist who specializes in individualized approaches for substance problems. Of her experience with him, she said, "It took eight years to get to a life of happy abstinence. It was gradual, small goals sometimes achieved. I was drinking the whole time, sometimes not drinking for a few days, and maybe tempering it from two bottles of wine to one." At times, she saw the psychologist weekly; other times there were big gaps in their visits. But when she saw him, she drank less. Then about a year and a half before I interviewed her, Ruth had a night of excessive drinking that made her decide she never wanted to feel that way again, and she just quit. Her health improved dramatically (she lost eighty pounds), as did her relationships. In general, she said, "I am just kind of high on life."

Playing devil's advocate, I asked Ruth how she'd respond to someone who might say, "Well, if you'd gone to rehab, you might have gotten to where you are sooner." Her response? "This was the path I had to take, and I had to take it with someone who was going to allow me to do it my way. My therapist always left me with options and questions, and that felt safe to me. At some point, the sweater just unraveled and the relationship between my issues and my drinking was very clear. I'm very convinced I'm where I am because of the long, often winding and genuine path of self-discovery and acceptance led by a very wise and patient facilitator."

In the opinion of Thomas McLellan, "Most substance abuse counseling happens behind closed doors in private office settings, with a counselor or therapist—such as a psychologist, social worker, or other mental-health professional—who works with people one-on-one. And no one knows what they are doing. There are not studies on this. One thing that's likely is that the counseling or therapy is far different from what one gets in a typical addiction treatment program." Dr. James McKay, director of the Center on the Continuum of Care in the Addictions at Philadelphia's Treatment Research Institute, said, "If you talk to any clinical therapists, they'll say that about a third of their clients have substance problems, now or in the past. Usually, they go to see the therapist for other problems and substance abuse comes up."

To find a mental health professional who provides one-on-one counseling for substance problems, you can check the yellow pages of your phone book under such headings as "alcoholism," "drug abuse and addiction," "counselors," and "psychologists." However, in calling around, ask questions about any therapist's education, clinical training, experience, and philosophy. (I'm always leery when individuals claim expertise in treating a multitude of different disorders. I was amazed at how many people in my small city offer addiction counseling and, quite frankly, wondered about some of their experience.)

DOING AWAY WITH RESIDENTIAL REHAB?

"The best way to ensure a successful treatment outcome is to remove the person from the people, places, and things associated with their addiction," declares the Web site of a residential program boasting it was featured on A&E's *Intervention* and the *CBS Evening News with Katie Couric*. They go on to say, "This reduces distractions and gives the individual an opportunity to fully engage in treatment and to learn the coping skills necessary to stay clean and sober when they return to their home environment." Once again, however, studies have consistently failed to show that more intensive treatment settings, such as round-the-clock residential treatment, offer better outcomes than less intensive ones. Or, as Tom Horvath says, "For most individuals, outpatient treatment is as good as or better than residential. Residential involves so much withdrawal from the world that it can be counterproductive." (Again, Dr. Horvath runs both outpatient and residential programs.)

At an intensive outpatient program, I sat in on an interesting client discussion about the pros and cons of outpatient and residential treatment. A number of the participants had been to both types of programs. One person said that he thought "it was easy to stay clean in residential rehab" and that outpatient is better because "you are going on with life; it gives you practice to use your better judgment." After his experiences at several residential facilities, Homer L. said of this outpatient program, "You got to deal with your daily life along with your treatment. It was great." However, another client spoke very highly of her experience at what sounded like a high-end residential rehab, while yet another said she doesn't know if she could "stay clean" if she hadn't been through residential treatment first. She said, "I worked on me first, not just getting clean." In short, the clients I met expressed pros and cons of residential treatment, depending upon where they'd gone, but it may also have been a matter of where they happened to be when they were ready for treatment.

Dr. Willenbring goes so far as to suggest that we should do away with residential rehab altogether. He explains, "The idea of changing the life course for people with severe, recurrent forms of addiction through a time-limited intensive transformative rehab is a fatally flawed relic of ancient times. What other chronic disorder do we treat that way? There is no basis for a burst of intensive education and counseling. The idea of a sudden change leading to permanent remission is a fiction—it very rarely occurs." As a psychiatrist, he talked about how for decades the Menninger Clinic and other famous places often had patients reside for a year or more in inpatient treatment for various psychiatric disorders. "There is no reason to believe any of them had a lasting therapeutic effect," he said. "Everyone has to return home eventually, and my experience is that, with no continuity of providers or treatment, there is little or no carryover from what's supposedly learned in treatment to being back in the community." He feels the same applies to addiction rehab and maintains, "The evidence points to a much more individualized, outpatient, longer-term approach with a variable number of sessions. The length, not the intensity, of treatment predicts how well someone will do."

William Miller of the University of New Mexico concurred that "it's easy to feel like you've got it licked while you're in a secure residential facility, but ultimately you have to deal with it all back home. In outpatient programs, people can start to readjust their lives while living in their community and it's usually far less expensive than residential, while providing more time for the client and care providers to figure things out before hitting a funding ceiling."

When I asked staff members at a drug court outpatient treatment program—one that treats some of the toughest addiction cases to be found—what they thought about the need for residential treatment, one of the counselors said, "I wouldn't advocate doing away with residential rehab—we need that safe harbor for some people. There are advantages to having addiction, medical, and mental health care available all in one place. Sometimes, people just do better when they go away for thirty or sixty days and get right with themselves." The director added, "Sometimes, people need to go away when they just can't stop. . . . But I also wonder if some clients like this wouldn't do just as well in intensive outpatient treatment five days a week."

Nevertheless, according to Dennis Kivlahan, PhD, who chaired the working group that reviewed the research and came up with comprehensive clinical practice guidelines for treating substance use disorders for the federal departments of Veterans Affairs and Defense, there is little controlled research (meaning research designed to show cause and effect) supporting any added value of residential treatment, where you stay at a facility overnight and receive treatment for a set time period. The guidelines, however, state, "There is now a fair amount of research that indicates patients with greater substance use severity and co-occurring problems such as psychiatric disorders and housing problems will do better in more intensive forms of treatment. Conversely, those with lower severity levels will do as well *or* better in less intensive forms of treatment." Kivlahan stated, "Intensive treatment for the select group of people with severe problems can occur in different settings including traditional residential treatment or intensive outpatient treatment given housing in an environment supportive of recovery." (For more on who would be more likely to do better in residential treatment, see pages 197–99.)

A DIFFERENT REHAB MODEL

As a relapsed meth addict who'd been in treatment numerous times, Anna J. had the kind of problem that most would say warranted residential rehab. At her worst, she was a daily user, getting her fixes by snorting, smoking, or injecting meth. But when I met her, she was doing very well in the kind of situation that a number of experts advocate over the traditional residential rehab model—it was what Dr. Kivlahan referred to as "outpatient treatment . . . given housing in an environment supportive of recovery." When our paths crossed, Anna was living in a sober house that required her to attend a separate outpatient program. I sat in on her initial intake at the program (her second time through it) and then talked with her about eight months later when she was still living in the sober house with two of her children. At that point, she'd completed treatment at the outpatient program, which she'd attended for five months, three days a week for three hours a day. (She'd requested and been granted an extension of her treatment time.)

Of the total experience, Anna told me, "This was probably the best treatment I had—it was the longest. I think a lot of it was having a safe sober living facility, which allowed me to focus on treatment and not having to work. It was also about still living on the outside, being part of the community and not confined to an inpatient facility. It's part of building your self-esteem back up again when it feels like you're almost hopeless." She also said, "The home I live in gets you out there. We have to organize a community event—I did a bake sale for the humane society. We're expected to exercise four times a week. The parenting classes and living skills are to reteach our brains." She added, "Residential rehab is like you're almost institutionalized and then they boot you out. Here, you have time to look for a house. You're not kicked out of treatment to go back to only what you knew before." I spoke with Anna about a year later when she had bought a home, completed a year of college, and was approaching two years of sobriety.

"If both are well-run, the combination of going to intensive outpatient treatment plus living a well-run sober home can be a better model than residential rehab," according to James McKay, PhD, an expert on long-term treatment for people with substance use disorders. He added, "When a sober home works well, it's a longer stay than in a residential program. You get six months rather than twenty-eight days for a fraction of the cost." But being well run is a "big if," McKay pointed out, because sober homes generally are unregulated, which means there's a huge amount of variability in their quality. "And some are run like boot camps," he said. (For more on sober housing, see chapter 9.)

DOES *ANYONE* NEED RESIDENTIAL REHAB?

As mentioned before, I did come across people who appear to have "made it" after one thirty-day stay at a residential rehab. For a drinking problem that caused her to lose her job and led her to detox twice within a year, Lee Ann B. had a one-time experience at a high-end traditional residential program I visited, was still sober several years later, and had returned to college to complete the requirements for eligibility to become a licensed drug and alcohol counselor. She told me, "I knew that I needed to be admitted to inpatient treatment because that's the only way I could stay focused on *me*. Otherwise, with having three kids, a husband, and household duties, I would have gotten lost in all of that. I feel so blessed to have gone to this program and received quality care. I don't think the counselors did anything spectacular or that the treatment planning was anything 'grand.' The biggest factor was that I felt safe there, had great women in treatment with me, and a supportive family and network waiting for me."

Quite frankly, with the extent of their problems, it's hard for me to imagine some of the clients I met "making it" in their first round of care in an intensive outpatient program that allowed them to go home at night. Dr. Horvath, who for years has run an exclusive outpatient program with optional sober housing and then also opened a residential rehab while I was writing this book said, "For some individuals, 'retreat' is essential or at least helpful for establishing an initial period of abstinence and clear thinking. One of the clinical decisions to be made is how much retreat is useful. For some, living in a structured sober home and attending intensive outpatient treatment is sufficient. For others, residential treatment involving twenty-four-seven staff availability and more limited interaction with the world may be useful. Thirty days is much more time than many need for retreat, while months may be needed in other cases—depending on the environment someone is going to return to."

Horvath also pointed out that, despite the lack of scientific evidence that residential treatment is better than outpatient, residential remains popular with both clients and their families. He explained, "Addiction can be exhausting physically and emotionally, so for the resident, the retreat experience can be rejuvenating. For families, residential care can provide the relief of knowing 'someone else is taking charge for a while, so we can rest.'"

The question is whether it's worth refinancing your mortgage, giving up retirement funds, or spending the money, period, if you have no health insurance or your insurance won't pay for it. Also at issue is whether the third-party payer system should support this expense if there's not evidence supporting its efficacy.

Dr. Horvath responded, "Whether governments or insurance companies should pay for a treatment experience that may have a large component of 'retreat and rejuvenation' is an important question. But what happens if we don't pay for it? In selected cases, it might be more expensive over time not to pay for residential treatment. However, I would not recommend paying for a residential experience that is not primarily focused on working on underlying problems. It's the depressed, anxious, bipolar, and other clients with significant mental and emotional problems who may need the residential setting. Unfortunately, most U.S. residential facilities appear to have little capacity to address these issues." (For more on this topic, see chapter 8.)

RESIDENTIAL REHAB CHECKLIST

As director of the University of Pennsylvania's Center on the Continuum of Care in the Addictions and an expert on who should be placed where in the addiction treatment system, James McKay, PhD, seemed to be the logical expert to go to with the question "Does anyone really need to be in residential rehab as we know it—and if so, who?" He responded, "I believe that a case can be made for residential care, but for a pretty limited segment of people." In his opinion, this segment would include individuals who meet the criteria for a severe substance use disorder along with any of the following:

- Those with current and significant major mental illness that is not reasonably well controlled, such as severe depression, bipolar disorder, schizophrenia, or what mental health professionals term an "axis II disorder" (borderline, antisocial, or obsessive-compulsive personality disorders are examples) along with behavior that poses a significant risk to the health or safety of self or others
- Those who are suicidal, regardless of the nature of the underlying psychiatric disorder
- Those with significant medical problems that will be made much worse by further excessive alcohol/drug use and who have shown recent inability to stop drinking*
- Those unable to achieve abstinence in an outpatient program, especially if they have a recent history of significant dangers to self or others while intoxicated (such as committing acts of violence, drunk driving, etc.)*

* Assuming there is no availability of a safe, well-run sober or halfway house option.

CAN A BAD MIX CREATE AN ADDICT?

I became confused in my visits to a few, mainly outpatient programs, when I discovered that some people whose problems didn't seem that bad were mixed in with those with pretty severe problems. Is there any harm in going to rehab if you're struggling with a problem on the less severe end of the spectrum—or could it be argued that it will help you anyway?

When I posted a query on this topic on a professional e-mail list service, a psychologist who specializes in addiction treatment responded, "I have not met many individuals in treatment who did not benefit from it, regardless of their diagnosis. I feel their quality of life is elevated from the treatment they are willing to accept." However, a real concern in this regard, expressed by some clients I interviewed, was their exposure to hardcore addicts who introduced them to new drugs.

One of the more striking stories was that of Emily E., who said, "I think I'm an example of the system creating a drug addict." Before her first rehab experience, she was an award-winning professional woman who had never used drugs or abused alcohol during high school and college. But in 2000, afflicted by debilitating migraines she was told wouldn't respond to customary medications, she went to a pain clinic. Her physician prescribed two drugs in the opioid family—oxycodone and fentanyl—plus Demerol, a narcotic that's similar to morphine. When her pharmacist and her doctor eventually told her she would "have to be detoxed" because she was on too many drugs, Emily found that because of her high medication doses and other medical complications, the only place that would accept her was a residential state program for people with chronic addictions. Although her physician wanted her there for detox alone and did not see her as a "drug addict" or being more than physiologically addicted to painkillers, she received the same addiction treatment as the other clients, who had all previously been in treatment "at least eight times." Emily said she was the only client there voluntarily.

Her description of the place was that of a "twelve-step program, locked facility" where the group was told, "If you're here, this is your last chance—you have really messed up your life . . . except for Emily." She wound up staying there for sixty-four days and being detoxed on methadone, which helped alleviate the headaches. ("During that time," Emily said, "I learned from the other patients about all these drugs I didn't know about.") When she left the program, she was not sent home on methadone because "they wouldn't allow it" and her headaches had not been adequately addressed. But she faithfully attended AA meetings for four months, as she'd been instructed to do. However, one night when Emily was in terrible pain again from a headache, someone she'd befriended in rehab offered her heroin, which she reluctantly took for the pain and found relief. From there, a downward spiral began toward nearly five years of hard-core drug addiction, interspersed with periodic rehab stays. As the book was coming to a close, Emily told me that her involvement in an opoid treatment program, where she was placed on methadone on a long-term basis and was taking part in a non-twelve-step treatment program, had helped her "stay totally clean for thirty-two months, without testing once for [illicit] drugs in my urine." (For more about the complexities of opioid addiction and opioid treatment programs, see chapter 8.)

Of course, rehab can expose anyone who's in treatment—even those in the right level of care for their drug and alcohol problems—to multiple drugs of abuse. When she went to her first treatment program, Chantal J. had a serious drinking problem, was snorting cocaine, and smoking pot. While there, she said, "I learned more about drugs and where to get them than I did anything else." (Coming into contact with harder-core users can be a particular concern with adolescents. For more on this, see chapter 7.) I also heard reports of drugs being sneaked into certain rehabs (which is why programs conduct searches upon arrival). Because drugs can always find their way under the radar screen, it's important to ask any residential rehab about their security measures.

Dr. McKay has other issues with "lumping people with varying degrees of substance problems together, figuring that it's okay because 'they're all just getting a higher level of care.'" He said, "On the one hand, if you give them more treatment than they need and it's not what they need or want, more can be worse. For instance, if someone has no intention of adopting an abstinence-oriented lifestyle and you insist on a traditional abstinence oriented go-to-AA, change-your-whole-life kind of treatment plan, an awful lot of people will never opt for it. For people who do need the abstinence model, it undermines things to be mixed in with others who don't want that approach and are just paying lip service to it." He added, however, that when individuals who don't have a severe addiction decide they want all the help they can get and opt to go to AA, he doesn't think it will hurt them. Like many experts, he believes that what's needed are different tracks of treatment, according to the degree of severity of the substance problem, and some places have this. The reality, though, is that funds are often tight, as can be the case in rural settings with small programs that don't have the resources for multiple tracks. In one such setting a director suggested that they have to treat everyone similarly because, otherwise, clients complain about lack of fairness.

WHEN THE CHOICE TO GO TO REHAB IS NOT YOURS

Addicted or not, the choice to go to rehab was not their own for many of the people I interviewed. While it's impossible to know exactly how many enter treatment against their will, while writing this book I often heard it said that few "rehabers" want to be there. It's no fun to give up a love affair with your drug of choice, and even those who are worn down with the battle typically don't relish the idea of weeks or months of treatment. What commonly gets someone to rehab is arm-twisting of some sort—legal coercion or mandates such as court-ordered rehab, civil commitment, diversion to treatment as an alternative to criminal sanctions, or a mandate from a professional organization, employee assistance program (EAP), or social assistance program to avoid loss of child custody. The following individuals had "the assistance" of some outside force or incentive to attend rehab:

- Beth O. stayed in an unethical treatment situation (see page 28) because she feared that if she didn't complete the program, her child would be taken from her by social services.
- Because he thought it would help his legal case, Zack S. chose to go to an outpatient program following a drunk-driving arrest, and told me, "You just learn to play along with the system and get your certificate."
- At the tender age of fifteen, Elizabeth B. was sent to a juvenile drug court with an outpatient program that allowed her to live at home. But when she showed up with a black eye, she was placed in a residential rehab in a different state. That didn't go well, and, after mul-

tiple stays in a mental health facility and then time spent as a runaway meth "tweaker" (user), she wound up in a foster home with people who sent her to a teen outpatient program based on the Seven Challenges curriculum (see pages 287–88) that turned her around.

One reason people sometimes wind up in treatment when they don't belong there is that they're placed through the criminal justice system. For instance, Scott Stern, MSW, a New York–licensed social worker and addiction counselor who worked for more than twenty years in residential and outpatient addiction and psychiatric programs and now has a private practice where he offers both individual and group treatment, said that it's not uncommon for people arrested for drunk driving to be mandated to attend rehab, even though many such offenders would not be considered alcoholics. (The results of a survey published in a 2011 issue of *Addiction* suggested that the majority of nighttime weekend drivers on U.S. roads with high blood alcohol concentrations don't fall into that category.) Stern finds that "people with less severe problems, who experience an isolated incident, often benefit more from other interventions, such as individual counseling. They don't necessarily belong in rehabs or even AA meetings."

As a case in point, Stern recently worked with a young man with no history of abusing alcohol who went out one night with friends, drank too much, and had his first blackout. Then he got into a physical altercation with someone who afterward pressed legal charges. After this single episode of alcohol abuse, he was legally required to enter an outpatient rehab and encouraged to attend AA meetings. He was troubled that he couldn't relate to the addicted clients he encountered at the program, nor could he relate to the self-identified alcoholics he met at AA meetings. Stern said, "This young man clearly was not alcoholic." The man later pursued individual therapy with Stern, began to address his issues of stress and anger management, and had not had a drink for over eight months. Rather than use the same approach for everyone, Stern said, we need to educate the criminal justice system about different interventions to provide effective outcomes for each individual. The same could be argued for drug problems. (Again, some places do provide different kinds of counseling for problem drinkers.)

In 2010, 37 percent of admissions came through the door of treatment through the criminal justice system, according to the TEDS. Nearly half of adolescent treatment admissions were referred through criminal justice channels. It's safe to assume that the vast majority of these cases involved some direct or indirect coercion. While a small percentage of these people are in prison, the majority are not—they're under some kind of supervision. For instance, treatment may be required as a condition of probation or as part of drug court involvement. Drug courts provide comprehensive long-term treatment and rehabilitation to nonviolent offenders with addictions and serve as an alternative to incarceration. Mandated treatment has implications for the people who *do* want to be there, as registered nurse Bob Muscala, director of Muscala Chemical Health Clinic in Edina, Minnesota, points out. He finds that "when a significant portion of patients is there through the criminal justice system, the treatment tends to be less effective. It can ruin it for the others." He does not allow more than 20 percent of his client base to be legally mandated participants.

Given the widespread use of social pressure, such as drug or alcohol interventions by families, mandates from employee assistance programs, and legal sanctions, to get people into treatment, you'd think there would be solid research informing policy makers and treatment providers about whether such coercion is effective and ethical. However, a 2005 review article on that topic, published in *Addiction* by Canadian psychologist T. Cameron Wild, PhD, suggests there's a paucity of good studies on efficacy of coerced treatment and states that while U.S. reviews of research on legally mandated treatment conclude that coercion "works," non-U.S. reviews have pointed to inconclusive findings and suggest "a more cautious and critical stance." Dr. Wild's review concludes that "proliferation of social control tactics to facilitate addiction treatment is a worldwide social experiment" being implemented without compelling evidence that it's effective. Just as questions are raised about the efficacy of coerced treatment, the next chapter raises many more about the rehab industry's long-standing failure to individualize approaches to meet diverse needs.

CHAPTER SIX

ONE SIZE DOESN'T FIT ALL

HOW COOKIE-CUTTER APPROACHES AT REHAB
GET IN THE WAY

" I f you go to a hospital with a heart problem and they don't have what you need, they'll make it available or refer you to a place that has what you need," said Dr. Richard Saitz, director of the Clinical Addiction Research and Education Unit at Boston University School of Medicine. "But at drug and alcohol treatment programs, you get what they offer." And more often than not, what they offer is group counseling, the twelve steps, and all-around one-size-fits-all approaches to treatment that, from the stories I heard and studies I read, clearly don't meet the needs of a large number of people—or could meet them better if applied with more give-and-take and greater consideration for the individual.

VINCE T.'S STORY: HOW ONE SIZE DOESN'T FIT ALL

Vince T. is one of the first people I interviewed when I began writing this book. At that time, he was in rehab and had about a month of sobriety under his belt. He told me, "I'm seven-twelfths done with an intensive outpatient program (IOP). I was a drinker for twenty-four years and a hard drinker by my own estimation for the last five to ten years or more." As mentioned in chapter 4, Vince decided on his own that he needed help and was dumbfounded when his physician asked him why he wanted a referral to a treatment program. Vince said, "I get up the nerve to ask for treatment—and he's questioning it? Shouldn't the asking alone get your ticket to treatment punched?" Looking back on it, he now realizes that his physician might well have had difficulty determining how serious his problem was because he'd been lying about the fact that he was down-ing thirteen drinks a day.

Vince had no choice about what treatment facility he'd attend because his health insurance covered only one program. He said, "I just assumed that the program would be the right fit. If you go for a colonoscopy, you take whatever doctor works with your insurance carrier. And it's pitched to a price—there's a minimum that the insurance companies will cover, and they don't go over that number."

The month-long, three-nights-a-week IOP consisted of three-hour group sessions with about ten other people. The groups were run by two counselors. When I asked him about their backgrounds, Vince responded, "I have no idea what their credentials are. Both are in recovery, and I as-sume they have a BS degree." (In fact, in Vince's state at that time, you didn't even have to have an associate's degree to be a licensed addiction counselor.) When I asked him to describe the program, he told me, "One of the messages was this: 'You're at the base of a mountain and you can climb it, but you're very likely to fail and most people do fail. If you fail, you'll use again and die from it. You're in a hole you dug at the base of the mountain because you're an addict/alcoholic and a lowly worm with no arms and legs. So start climbing, you lowly worm. See you next week in group.'" He went on, "This is my interpretation of the message I received. Perhaps this message is necessary and helpful [for a person] to realize the gravity of addiction. But I didn't find the 'nearly impossible task/lowly worm' theme in group to be helpful, and it was surely less than empower-ing." About halfway through, it struck Vince that he was one of the few in the program who was driving to and from treatment. He realized that most "had lost their licenses, were broke, or had smashed up their cars" and therefore couldn't drive. So he was thankful to still be driving but re-sented the assumption that everyone was the same.

When I asked Vince whether the program was individualized and, if so, how, he replied, "Outpatient groups were not individualized, unless you had a question you wanted the group to provide an answer for. For instance, there was a woman that was considering working at a bar as a vocation. We all gave some advice on that question. And there were also folks who relapsed during treatment, and some of them shared about that." (In other words, the only "individualization" that Vince could discern came from the clients themselves.) He added that everyone in the group did the same assignments every week and the only tailoring that went on occurred in one-on-one sessions with a counselor. But this only transpired several times during the month-long program, and the counselor was not one of the ones who knew him from the group. (Unlike many programs that require everyone to attend twelve-step meetings, Vince wasn't required to attend any outside recovery group meetings, although he was encouraged to go to AA.)

As the program was drawing to a close, Vince's individual counselor (who had a bachelor's degree) asked him to come up with a written relapse prevention plan for himself, which he did. But when he shared it with her, she instead pulled out her own plan for him to use. I asked if it was generic or personalized and he replied, "Generic or nearly generic." Vince subsequently chose to follow up the IOP by attending a month-long relapse prevention program that the facility also offered.

A few weeks after our initial conversation, I spoke with Vince again, when he'd completed the relapse program and was almost three months sober. He said, "In my case, treatment was clearly necessary, and some ongoing plan afterward will be needed." Looking back on his outpatient rehab experience, he was feeling more positive about it and concluded, "Overall, it was helpful. The counselors were good at their craft, and I believe that they had my best interests in mind. I learned a lot about addiction and myself. On balance, it was helpful." At that point, he'd attended about half a dozen AA meetings and was considering getting a sponsor. But he was also going to SMART (Self-Management and Recovery Training) meetings. "I like both SMART and AA," he said. "Despite the differences, the primary purpose of sharing, helping, providing insight, and fortifying each others' sobriety is common to both approaches and is really helpful to me."

Vince is one of a number of rehab clients I was fortunate to be able to follow over the next several years as I continued writing the book. In time, he stopped going to SMART Recovery because he felt that AA offered him more structure, which he needed. With more than three years of sobriety at our last contact, he remained involved in AA and had just become the general service representative for his "home" group, an AA position under which he serves as the link between his group and the whole of AA and takes its vote to the larger organization.

COOKIE-CUTTER APPROACHES

Although the program Vince went to states on its Web site, "Services are individualized to meet your unique needs," his description of their overall approach is like that of many others I heard about—pretty much one-size-fits-all, with most of the interventions provided in group format, very little one-on-one counseling, and minimal individualization. As mentioned in his story, many other programs also include a greater emphasis on the twelve steps and going to twelve-step meetings outside of the program. Vince's description of the format and content of groups was much like what others shared with me: "There were times where the counselors just talked—those could be for an hour or longer. Other times, there were exercises, like 'draw a picture of your life when you were using and one of your life in recovery.' Everyone was required to write an exit letter and read it to the group on their last day. So I would say it was a combination of counselors 'teaching' and activities and lessons that the group participated in." It appeared to him that the program had a month's worth of material that was repeatedly recycled. He explained, "New people came at the beginning of every week, and people left at the end of every week. So everyone got a month of the same 'info,' but in an order determined by when they came in the program."

If anyone knows about one-size-fits-all practices, it's Shari P.'s mother, who said, "All rehab programs basically offer the same treatments." As mentioned previously, her daughter's residential experiences alone have added up to twenty stays. From high-end residential to low-cost outpatient programs, many of the stories about one-size-fits-all approaches were similar. Elizabeth F. found that at a prominent twelve-step residential rehab, "They only know how to work one way—it's a cookie-cutter approach. I felt like I was part of a herd." What helped her least was "the group counseling that everyone got—the traditional drug and alcohol counseling. It did nothing for me." When working on her assignments at night, she'd compare notes with her roommates and "everyone seemed to be working on the same thing; we all seemed to be on the same path." An example of an activity required of all clients was a "use history" or timeline of their drug and alcohol experiences—a common practice at traditional programs. She recalled, "It was terrible in that it was mandatory to do it in front of everyone. Women who'd been raped and abused and then drank 'around' it—and they were sharing this in front of people, some who were nodding off." In a few cases, women who were listening to the stories became so upset that they'd run out of the room because it triggered something for them. "It would be one thing if we were doing it in the privacy of a therapist's office," Elizabeth said, "but these were presentations done without a counselor in the room."

A number of people talked about how little individual counseling they received. Eddie F. attended an outpatient program whose Web site maintained that treatment is "individualized" and that they "focus on the strengths of each client." However, he said, "We were all grouped together as addicts who could all recover by the same program. I had two scheduled one-on-one meetings—in one, we talked about expectations for the group and the other was just to make sure I had all of my homework turned in and all of their i's and t's were taken care of. I really can't imagine how any of them could have known what my strengths or weaknesses were."

Sarah J. made the point that nontraditional programs can be one size fits all, too. After a relapse, she went to detox from heroin at a non-twelve-step residential rehab, which she chose because they claimed they used a "scientific" model. She said, "I was led to believe they had a two-week detox program"—for a cost of $17,000. But after the first two days, she was expected to take part in the regular program, which was not why she went there. She said, "We sat all day, doing group therapy—even while I was detoxing. We filled out SMART Recovery work sheets. I saw a counselor twice a week for forty-five minutes. I got nothing out of it."

Thomas McLellan of the Treatment Research Institute affirmed, "Most addiction treatment programs are structured to provide a single type of treatment or approach. If patients don't want it, they're told to come back when they're ready. A more consumer-oriented approach to treatment would be to offer different options. This would get more people into treatment and keep them longer."

WHY AND HOW ONE SIZE FITS ALL

Why and how did this come to be? Dennis McCarty, an expert on the organization and quality of addiction services at Oregon Health & Science University, speculates that the reason why "treatment centers all claim to individualize treatment, yet individualization occurs within a narrow range" is that "the field emerged as a grassroots initiative by women and men who used their personal experience with addiction and recovery as the way for others to recover. It was underfinanced from the start and has relied on a workforce dominated by counselors without much professional training. The thinking has been 'we have always done it this way,' and tradition is a barrier to change." Dr. McCarty maintains that until we have a better-trained workforce and improved financing of treatment, individualization will remain minimal.

Dr. McLellan, who's studied the ins and outs of addiction treatment for the better part of thirty years, said, "It's a fact that once you've seen any substance abuse program, you have seen the great majority of them." He believes this came about because the field was spawned in a vacuum— that is, in a world where there wasn't a body of research showing the best type of care for people with addictions. So the field "grew its own 'program'" with a model McLellan described as "peer-oriented, rule-oriented, and program-oriented. . . . Many who created the kind of care we have now felt deeply that alcohol- and drug-addicted individuals have significant personality problems and, therefore, need repetitive, simplistic rules, confrontation, and feedback from their failures to 'learn their lesson.' Under that model it's really necessary to 'follow the program' and to accentuate the similarities rather than the individualities associated with addiction."

Shelby W. confirmed, from her experience at an exclusive twelve-step rehab, that "a lot of the counselors were ex-addicts, and their attitude is, 'You're an addict—you have to do it exactly the way we say or you'll never get clean.' You're treated like a child; it's condemning." McLellan feels that it's difficult for many working in the field to view individuals "who either never wanted this protocol or didn't do well with it as people other than 'those who failed and are back'—usually because they 'didn't do what was suggested'—and to conclude 'it works only if you work it.'" He added, "They only recognize those who do well and benefit from their approach and then conclude, 'It works.'"

Dr. McLellan noted, too, that our nation's insurance reimbursement system, with its failure to pay for early intervention, compounds the one-size-fits-all problem by limiting coverage to "addiction treatment" for those who are clearly addicted, which is like saying, "We won't provide early intervention or office-based care for diabetic patients until they've lost a digit or their eyesight." (If the Affordable Care Act remains in place, the situation should improve.) For those who do have serious addictions, Dr. McLellan believes that rehabs' interpretation of "having a chronic illness" is "thirty days isn't long enough—the patient needs another ninety days." However, since such people are continually at risk for relapse, he said, "a program's goal instead should be to come up with individualized *ongoing* care, with interventions that can teach, motivate, and help clients connect with others while providing choices and options designed to attract and appeal to patients." He noted that similar options are quite common for diabetes and other illnesses and are often included in insurance benefits.

It also comes back to the notion that treatment specialists have "the answer" and clients don't know what's in their best interest. However, William Miller said, "Even acknowledged experts with a lifetime of experience aren't much better than chance at picking the 'right' treatment for clients. In cancer treatment, docs generally don't pick the treatment that a patient will receive. They give patients a fair description of the available treatments—probability of benefits and side effects—then the patient does the deciding. What we have in the addiction field is longstanding overestimation of our own wisdom and underestimation of the client's."

ONE NATION UNDER GROUP TREATMENT

Thomas McLellan is well known for saying this about group treatment: "If you go to just about any addiction program in this country, the major treatment activity is 'group.' If that doesn't work, then they'll try . . . 'group.' And when all else fails they'll suggest . . . 'group!'" He has long argued that scientific studies support the value of having more individual counseling than is customary in addiction treatment programs. But group therapy has been and remains the modus operandi, whether it suits clients or not. Addiction psychiatrist Mark Willenbring facetiously said to me, "In rehab, we do a comprehensive, individualized assessment and then send everyone on to group."

At the low end for group time at twelve-step residential programs, staff at an exclusive celebrity rehab said that their residential program consisted of about 60 percent group and 40 percent individual counseling. (I was told that clients in primary care attended twenty-one groups per week.) At the other extreme, a young woman went to a place (one I didn't visit) for extended care where they did "groups and paperwork from 6:30 a.m. until 9:00 p.m." She said to herself, "I can't believe I'm going to do this for sixty-five days. There must be something more for us to do." Initially, when his outpatient counselor first brought it up, Vince T. said, "I was dead set against group. I had no idea that the standard treatment was group therapy. I thought it was a scam and a way for them to bill for counseling twelve to fifteen people at a time with only two counselors." In the end, though, Vince thought the group was good for him and found, "Once I was in it, I was okay and shared pretty well for a newly sober guy. I remember a nurse in there who drank exactly like I did, a workaholic who drank at the end of the day to wind down. There must be a reason other than money why they use group therapy. Maybe we can only learn from other addicts."

Similarly, Rose T. found that group treatment was beneficial to her, despite her initial reservations. Previously, when faced with a social situation, she always had to have a drink in her hand, feeling that she had nothing of importance to say when she was sober and "needed the 'liquid courage.'" Therefore, she found it "most difficult," even "terrifying" at first to get used to talking about herself in a group setting and seriously considered quitting the program and working with an individual therapist. "With the support of counselors and other patients," she found, "I was able to work through my fear. IOP forced me to face this situation without a drink. I was able to learn coping mechanisms that led me away from drinking and built up the self-confidence that I'd often searched for in the bottle."

The problem, once again, is that group treatment isn't what's best for everyone. Sarah J. said of her experience at traditional programs, "I don't like groups—they make me uncomfortable. I have never shared in my life at a twelve-step meeting. It seemed that my stories were way worse than others', and it made me not want to share." When she went to a non-twelve-step program, "one of the most fantastic things" was that she didn't have to go to any groups.

Some rehabs that normally rely on group treatment do have counselors who find ways to meet the needs of people who don't do well in groups. At an outpatient program I visited, a counselor was working with a young man who'd been kicked out of two other programs because he wouldn't talk in groups. (He told her that, just when he was starting to feel comfortable, "it was too late" because the decision had already been made to remove him from the program.) As financially beleaguered and short-staffed as the program clearly was, the counselor worked out having all one-on-one counseling sessions until the client felt comfortable in group situations.

However, in observing programs with so much "seat time," I couldn't help but wonder who possibly conceived an outpatient model that required recovering alcoholics and drug addicts to sit through three hours of group treatment, three times a week. Dr. McCarty proposed that this model emerged as an alternative to residential rehab, stating, "It tries to mimic the intensity and relative duration of care provided in residential and inpatient settings in an ambulatory setting." Dr. McLellan added, "They do group treatment because it's much cheaper than individual sessions and to prepare clients for aftercare, which in many cases, is sending people to twelve-step meetings." As Vince and the experts suggested, there's no question that group treatment can be more cost-effective than individual counseling—for both the program and the client. After all, if providers can bill $70 per hour for fifteen clients in a group, the program obviously makes more than if they bill $180 for an individual session with a counselor—both approximate rates at an IOP that I visited.

I also wondered whether there's scientific evidence that group treatment is an effective way to help people with substance use disorders. Like so many other things in this field, despite widespread use, group therapy for addictions has not been well researched and we know relatively little about its effectiveness. It's been far less studied than individual approaches—in large part, because groups are more unwieldy to put under the research microscope. In the most comprehensive review of the limited research on group therapy for addictions, published in 2004 in the *Harvard Review of Psychiatry*, researchers concluded that there were few differences between group and individual therapy, suggesting that they might be equally effective when the content and length of treatment are equivalent. This conclusion challenges the argument of traditional treatment devotees that group therapy is critical to the recovery process. Still, I interviewed a counselor whose one-on-one program was in jeopardy because her state's licensure rules specify that treatment must consist of individual visits *and* groups. She said, "If I made an appointment to see a therapist because I was depressed, would I be told I have to do a program with everyone else?" After a long battle with officials, she got a waiver from having to offer groups.

There *is* evidence that cognitive-behavioral coping skills for preventing a return to substance use and improving quality of life can be effectively taught in groups, perhaps even more effectively than individually. However, Yale University's Dr. Kathleen Carroll points out, "This research involved using manuals, clinical supervision, and didn't bear much resemblance to what happens in a lot of clinical practice." She went on, "Programs get the same reimbursement whether they deliver this type of therapy with a highly skilled, more expensive clinician or if they stick as many patients in a room as possible with someone of dubious training, who can do pretty much anything he or she wants, with little or no accountability. Think about current programs, stretched as thin as possible, and guess what usually happens? There are doubtless some places that deliver terrific group therapy and have terrific group leaders; however, my guess is that what most consumers receive is a service with no evidence of efficacy."

As a case in point, Holly Y. went to an outpatient program, where she felt like more experienced people should have been doing the group counseling. She said, "Interns sometimes ran it. There were, like, little fifth-grader exercises—not coping skills." One of the exercises was that clients had to take turns leaving the room while the rest of the people in the room stayed behind and were told to come up with their perceptions of the individual who left. When the absent person came back, he or she had to listen to the descriptions, which Holly said might be "arrogant" or "smart ass." She added, "Sometimes it could be from a person who had just met you. I wound up feeling worse when I came out of there." To protect yourself, when considering a treatment program, Dr. Carroll advises asking about the qualifications of group leaders; the focus, goals, and orientation of groups; whether their approaches are scientifically supported; and for a summary of typical outcomes for the program's groups.

William White also made this important point: "The question is not, 'Which is superior—group or individual counseling?' The issue is, 'Are there particular types of people whose recovery outcome would improve with an individual versus group therapy format?'" He sees the need to move away from group-oriented programming to "an ever-widening menu of services" that allows for more individual counseling sessions in addiction treatment.

TREATMENT ACCORDING TO DRUG OF CHOICE?

The going philosophy at most treatment programs seems to be that drugs differ, but recovery from addiction is the same, regardless of the drug involved. Until I started interviewing people who'd been to rehab, however, it hadn't occurred to me how different and isolated some people can feel in rehab because of their particular drug addictions. Carrie G., who went to treatment numerous times for a heroin addiction, said, "Alcoholics feel terrific when they get sober. But I was on Suboxone [a brand name for a form of buprenorphine, which helps people withdraw from opioids] and felt terrible."

Several other former rehab clients told me that they think rehabs should treat people according to their drug of choice. Wyatt D. said, "Every substance is different and the approach to treat them should be different. If they don't know how to handle the monster they're dealing with, it's a waste. People on heroin and meth are completely different."

Is there any evidence that treatment should be according to a person's drug of choice? Most of the experts I consulted said that there isn't, aside from what we know about medications that can help people according to their particular addiction. (For more on this, see chapter 9.) However, Dr. Kivlahan emphasized, "There's evidence that people who remain engaged in care are more likely to have good outcomes. And those who feel different, alone, alienated, marginalized, or misunderstood in group-based treatment—whether it's because of the severity of their drug addiction, having a different drug of choice than other group members, or some other reason—are not as likely to stay in treatment. But good counselors and programs should be able to balance treatment principles common to everyone—such as learning how to recognize and manage relapse triggers—with helping people manage individual recovery challenges."

It occurred to me that "treatment by drug of choice" may be more of an early rehab issue. As mentioned in a previous chapter, I noticed that some people in residential rehab still seemed to be going through the detox process while participating in treatment. Former heroin addict Shelby W. said, "For me—and this is how it seems to be with most of the twelve-step programs—you have to go to classes all day long and you have to go to meetings every day. When still going through detox, to have mandatory schedules all day long was not what I wanted. It was too intense." She added that they gave her medication to help with withdrawal, but not enough to be effective. She said, "You're only in a hospital a few days for the really terrible part, but after that, you're out into the groups and you feel completely lost and hopeless."

At one program, a client privately commented to me that some people who were participating in treatment were "out of it" for a long time, and she didn't think it was fair that this counted as part of their treatment. When I ran this by a staff person, he acknowledged that there was some truth to the observation but explained that people exhibit varying degrees of ability to participate while going through withdrawal and that, depending on the drug(s) they're addicted to, complete detox takes longer in some cases than others. I was told that because someone "might not remember their treatment the first week," it might be recommended that treatment be extended by a week, but that people don't necessarily comply.

When considering the question of whether people need to be treated according to their drug of choice, a former administrator of a residential rehab said that "treatment is based on the alcohol model," but "all addiction is the same only after withdrawal." That said, Dr. Saitz believes that it makes sense to start some treatment while people are going through withdrawal. He said, "Although it doesn't make sense to do intensive cognitive work while someone is unable to concentrate or comprehend, the counselors may need to do some motivational interviewing with the goal of engaging the patient in ongoing care, so they stick with it once they're through detox."

THE UBIQUITY OF TWELVE-STEP PROGRAMMING

Only a small number of people I interviewed who'd been to rehab said they'd been exposed to any self-help groups or philosophies aside from the twelve steps. Some who were had first been to twelve-step-based programs; a few others were offered religious alternatives to AA. As I began writing *Inside Rehab* Dr. McLellan said to me, "I personally do not know of a single program—other than methadone programs for heroin addicts—that could reliably be characterized as anything other than twelve-step." At an outpatient program, when I mentioned to a counselor that I visited some non-twelve-step treatment programs, it was as if he couldn't conceive of it. He asked, "What would it be? Treatment came out of AA."

When considering the research on Alcoholics Anonymous, it's important, once again, to note the distinctions about AA as it exists in self-help groups, twelve-step treatment as it is carried out in residential and outpatient addiction programs, and twelve-step facilitation as it's been studied in research settings. Here are the differences:

• AA groups as popularly portrayed in meetings at churches, hospitals, senior centers, fire stations, AA clubhouses, and the like is a non-professional network of self-help groups, usually in community settings.

• Twelve-step treatment typically refers to programs in which clients receive a variety of interventions, but usually they're educated about AA and the twelve steps and may formally "work through" some of these steps. Clients often attend AA during treatment and are strongly encouraged to continue when the program ends. (Although members of various AA self-help groups often speak at treatment programs, AA itself is not affiliated with any professional entity or organization.)

• Twelve-step facilitation, or TSF, is a professional approach to treatment, usually done with the guidance of a manual and designed to facilitate, not pressure or compel client involvement in AA. (See chapter 4 for a description of TSF.)

In short, it's hard to find an addiction treatment program that doesn't include the twelve steps in some shape or form, although the numbers have dropped somewhat since I wrote *Sober for Good* in 2000, when more than 90 percent of rehabs in the United States were twelve-step based. The most recent statistics available on this subject come from the University of Georgia's National Treatment Center Study (NTCS), which conducts periodic surveys of nationally representative groups of addiction treatment programs. Researchers there compiled data on twelve-step pro-gramming in 2007–8 for private programs and found that nearly eight out of ten of them offered twelve-step-based treatment or included the twelve steps as part of their programming. Two-thirds of them required twelve-step meeting attendance, and almost as many held twelve-step meetings on-site. NTCS surveyed public programs in 2009–10 and determined that nearly seven out of ten were either based primarily on a twelve-step model or included a twelve-step component. Public programs were not asked about meeting attendance requirements or meetings on-site. But it's safe to say that, more often than not, even programs that are not heavily twelve-step oriented during treatment tend to refer clients to AA meetings in the community.

Thayer A. went to a number of residential programs where, she said, "All recommendations led to the twelve steps." But the steps were used to varying degrees. At one program, she found, "If you spoke against the twelve steps, it was like speaking against the Ten Commandments, and you didn't want to get better." However, at a youth program she attended, "if people resisted the twelve steps aggressively, it was, 'Let's talk it out, what's upsetting to you?'" And at yet another one, they didn't use the steps in treatment but, at night, took people in vans to twelve-step meetings if they wanted to go.

Traditional residential rehabs I visited made no bones about the fact that they were twelve-step based. I also got the sense that the majority of clients went to these places knowing and expecting this. (Of course, if you don't know there's any other way, why would you question it?) A long-time clinician at one place told me, "If someone comes in here, they know that we are heavily twelve-step based. Personally, I have never had a per-son who rejects the twelve steps. I've had people who reject portions of it—mostly 'god' or some concept of what 'god' is. But it's not like they are constantly getting beat over the head with the Big Book." A person who went to this rehab expressed dismay that, although something was men-tioned in a lecture about models of treatment other than the Minnesota model, when she asked what they were, she couldn't get an answer.

I suppose one might ask, why should a private program that's openly twelve-step based have any more obligation to tell people about alternative approaches to the twelve steps than the Catholic church has to teach its members the tenets of Islam? When I first interviewed Dr. Willenbring, he said of traditional residential programs, "People think of them as the churches of AA." However, it becomes an issue when someone pays for the same twelve-step-based treatment over and over again and is offered no alternative—not to mention the fact that hefty sums of public and health insurance funding are often involved. As illustrated throughout this book, individuals repeatedly go through twelve-step treatment that changes little time after time. This practice also violates one of the National Institute on Drug Abuse's fundamental principles of effective addiction treatment, which states, "No single treatment is appropriate for everyone." When Dr. Willenbring left the NIAAA in 2009 and returned to full-time clinical addiction psychiatry, he regularly e-mailed me about his frustration with this system. In one of our exchanges, he wrote, "I saw another patient today with the same story. She said, 'I've been through at least ten twelve-step programs. I hear the same thing every time. It's a waste of time. I don't like AA.'" (Of course, many people do benefit from twelve-step meetings, and it's the people who don't who might wind up with experts like Dr. Willenbring or at a non-twelve-step program.)

As mentioned in chapter 2, practices involving twelve-step meetings and emphasis on the twelve steps in treatment at the programs I went to varied. Some places held meetings there, while one took clients to outside meetings every day. A few exposed clients to just one or two outside meetings during treatment. The outpatient programs I went to appeared to place less emphasis on the twelve steps during treatment time, but some required clients to attend a specified number of outside twelve-step meetings on their own.

Sometimes, messages I got from administrators and counselors didn't quite match my observations. A number of them at traditional programs verbally expressed support for other routes to recovery, but I saw no sign of this in practice. At one residential rehab, I was told by an administrator, "We're not all about 'the twelve steps are the only way'" and that they'd work with people when they went home if an interest was expressed in a non-twelve-step support group. However, a doctoral-level staff person who used to work there said, "We never had any discussions of treatment models other than the disease model and the twelve steps. The place had a cultlike feeling. At one point, professional staff were forced to attend meetings where we had to talk about how we were working the twelve steps. We were given backpacks and had to carry AA's Big Book around at all times. I wasn't in recovery, and I wasn't going to walk around with the Big Book in a backpack."

The director of one of the few programs—an outpatient facility that didn't seem to work from the disease model—explained that they work from "the recovery model" and that treating addiction as a disease "makes the client powerless, reduces the client's ability for self-determination, and sends a 'we'll fix you' message." I was confused, however, when I noticed a number of disease-model and twelve-step influences during my visit. For example, I came across a handout on the "disease of addiction," and one of the counselors told me he gives a lecture on the same topic. Another counselor's office had a list of "character defects" on the wall, a reference to one of the twelve steps, while a group lecture I attended had NA readings. And clients were regularly referred to twelve-step meetings outside of the program. When I asked about this apparent conflict, I was told that twelve-step meetings are used to build a network of external peer support but that "staff should not be preaching disease" or "twelve-stepping within the program."

HOW DID THE TWELVE STEPS BECOME UBIQUITOUS?

How did it come to be that treatment programs adopted the disease model and the twelve steps lock, stock, and barrel—before they were tested to see if they were effective for most people? How did this become a near-universal approach to treatment, the one that almost everyone who goes to rehab "gets" whether or not they connect with it? Some professionals have even described AA as "institutionalized," not only in addiction care, but in places like prisons and jails. (I've given presentations at national professional conferences on addiction that hold AA meetings for attendees, which would be analogous to holding Weight Watchers meetings at conferences for obesity professionals.)

More than once while writing this book, I heard people talk about "what treatment has done to AA." Salina S., who went to several twelve-step rehabs, said, "There are parts of the twelve steps that are a beautiful concept, but I think that the creators of them would roll over in their graves if they knew what treatment programs were doing with it." A psychologist who currently works at a twelve-step residential rehab—maintaining that its overall approach benefits most of its clients—even said, "In truth, much of the cynicism about AA really should be directed at the treatment industry and other systems external to AA. One-size-fits-all is insane. Much of the treatment industry perpetuates this, but this should not be an indictment of AA itself."

The fact is that a good number of the principles and original teachings of AA are inconsistent with many of the ways treatment programs employ AA in practice. Psychologist Fred Rotgers, PsyD, past president of the Society of Addiction Psychology, said, "If you read the Big Book carefully, you will see that AA as originally conceived, but now sorely corrupted by the treatment industry, was purely a self-directed, self-elected program—no pressure to attend, no pressure to admit being an alcoholic. The only approach was an invitation, not a prescription. All the prescriptive stuff came from treatment providers who decided that if something was good, it should be required as a part of treatment. And, of course, they 'knew' it was good because they got sober while they were doing it. And if it worked for them, it would work for everyone. But AA makes no prescriptions about how it should be used, or even that it should be used."

Dr. Rotgers is correct. Bill Wilson and AA's Big Book, *Alcoholics Anonymous*, repeatedly "preached" tolerance of other viewpoints and declared that AA is not the only way to sobriety. And when people are "required" to meet certain step-related obligations in treatment, it conflicts with AA's other guidebook, *Twelve Steps and Twelve Traditions*, where it's stated, "Alcoholics Anonymous does not demand that you believe anything. All of its twelve steps are but suggestions."

AA certainly wasn't conceived for every degree of alcohol and drug problem. Yet one rehab clinical supervisor told me, "We recognize the twelve steps as a valuable set of tools that when utilized can be a positive experience for individuals despite their level of involvement with alcohol." As pointed out by a number of experts, AA was designed for people, men in particular, who had severe alcohol problems, described in the Big Book as "He is always more or less insanely drunk." Dr. McLellan said, "Bill W. had it bad and he came up with a treatment meant for people like him."

How AA and its commingling with the disease concept came to be sacrosanct in today's rehab system is a long story, well documented in William White's book *Slaying the Dragon: The History of Addiction Treatment and Recovery in America*. As he reports, much of it is intertwined with the emergence of the Minnesota model at Hazelden and several neighboring programs in the late 1940s and early 1950s and the subsequent proliferation of this approach over the next several decades. White explained that, at that time, twelve-step-focused residential treatment was perceived to be one of the only approaches that could address problems of severe alcoholism. And such programs achieved dominance "because there were few alternatives, the success stories that came out of them were often dramatic and remarkable (lots of analogies to Lazarus rising from the dead), and they provided immediate relief for the backlog of chronic alcoholics whose addiction was disruptive and costly to the community." Advocacy for a national system of alcoholism treatment was also afoot, and its champions had gotten sober through AA. Thousands of community representatives then traveled to observe Hazelden's program, went home to replicate what they'd seen, and, White said, "That process was replicated exponentially for more than two decades." This movement shaped public and medical conceptions of alcoholism and led to the application of these approaches to drug addiction as well as to other problem behaviors, such as gambling addiction.

As for "what treatment did to AA," White explained, "rather than use AA as an *adjunct* to treatment (via linking people in rehab to AA), programs began injecting ideas and practices into treatment in the name of AA that were alien to the fellowship—for instance, the idea that alcoholics needed to be coerced into treatment and into AA and confronted until their defense structure collapsed." Another concern was exploitation of AA's spiritual approach to recovery "by modifying, commodifying and commercializing it."

A psychologist I spoke to who works at a twelve-step rehab believes that coercion is a significant problem. She said, "If people are coerced into AA, it doesn't work. AA describes itself as a program of attraction. Although motivational interviewing has spread and our staff has been trained in it, confrontation is still pretty common. I see it all the time where I work. Often, people in positions of authority have gotten sober in AA and don't see beyond that." As a case in point, when I asked a doctoral-level CEO of a multisite government-funded treatment agency how she felt about the prospect of sobriety without the twelve steps, she said, "I think it's very difficult to achieve true sobriety without working the twelve steps. . . . It has been my personal experience through working the twelve steps that I came to believe that I could stay clean and sober, and it has worked for me for twenty-six years." The "AA is the only way" tradition then gets passed on in the education of new counselors, as experienced by a woman I interviewed who was in training to become a drug and alcohol counselor. She had twelve years of sobriety and, for one of her classes, wrote a paper about how not going to AA helped her recovery process and explained why she doesn't think AA is the only way. Her professor "chewed her out" for what she wrote.

WHAT DOES THE RESEARCH SAY ABOUT AA?

In my opinion, AA has every right to be whatever it chooses to be and does not owe us "proof" of anything, any more than an organized religion does. However, the treatment industry's adoption of AA as its primary approach for recovery makes it imperative to put AA to the test. (Of course, most treatment programs use other methods to help people, too.)

Despite coming on the scene more than seventy years ago and dominating alcohol and drug rehab, it's only been quite recently that AA has been subjected to rigorous scientific study—in part because only recently have academics begun to see AA as worthy of study. It certainly isn't easy for researchers to try to determine how effective the program is when participation is anonymous, and some of AA's operational rules make it difficult to study and recruit research participants. But a substantial amount of respectable research on AA has been published in what Harvard University's John Kelly, PhD, has referred to as an "empirical awakening" for recovery support groups, AA in particular. William White has noted that, while many in the scientific community expected "AA and AA-oriented addiction treatment approaches to be blown out of the water, the growing body of more rigorous studies on AA has revealed that what started out as folk wisdom is now turning out to be pretty good science as well." (Most of the research on support groups has been on AA—little is known about NA or the twelve steps as applied to problems such as eating or sexual disorders. For more on this, see chapter 8.)

RESEARCH ON ATTENDING AA GROUPS

Numerous studies have examined the relationship between attending AA meetings and sobriety. Overall, according to the University of New Mexico's Scott Tonigan, PhD, a prolific AA researcher, such studies show "a positive but modest association between AA attendance and abstinence." In general, this research has shown that people who attend AA frequently are more likely to become abstinent and remain abstinent over the short and long term. And at least several studies indicate that clients in treatment programs have better outcomes when they also attend AA meetings. Some research also suggests that being involved in AA may substantially reduce the need for more costly professional care.

In one of the only long-term studies done on participation in AA, Stanford University's Rudolf Moos, PhD, and Bernice Moos studied a group of 628 people with alcohol use disorders who sought help for their drinking problem. They found that of the 269 individuals who participated in AA in the first year of the study, nearly half of them still participated in AA two to three years later, while about 40 percent did so between the nine- and sixteen-year follow-up. At all follow-up periods over the course of sixteen years, the longer people participated in AA, the higher the likelihood of their being abstinent or drinking in a non-problematic way. It's not just showing up at the door of AA meetings that appears to be important—there's evidence that involvement in the program makes a difference. "Involvement" includes things like having a sponsor, reaching out to others for help, and beginning to work through the steps. Of course, these findings are not necessarily unique to twelve-step groups—it's just that almost all of the research has involved AA alone. It's entirely possible that the findings would apply to non-twelve-step support groups as well. (See "AA Alternatives" discussion below.) Note, too, that these studies on AA did not involve randomly assigning participants to take part in AA versus different treatment situations. Such research shows a correlation, not cause and effect, and doesn't prove that AA participation caused the positive outcome. Perhaps people who go to AA and stick with it are more highly motivated in the first place, or that those who are doing well continue in AA.

It's also important to bear in mind that even though people who go to AA regularly and get involved tend to do better than those who do not, many people who start out in AA don't stay with it over the long term. Dr. Tonigan's recent review of the scientific literature led him to conclude, "Overall, studies suggest that between 55 and 80 percent of alcoholics encouraged to attend AA while in treatment will stop attending AA within nine months." And according to Thomas McLellan, "Studies to date generally show that only about 25 to 35 percent of those who attend one meeting of AA go on to active participation." Of course, attendees do commonly go to meetings for a few months, drop out, and then come back at some later time. And, in all fairness, early and high dropout rates are not unique to twelve-step group participation. Dr. Kelly noted, "It should be remembered that many people don't benefit from cognitive-behavioral therapy either, and nearly half drop out within ninety days of starting treatment."

RESEARCH ON TWELVE-STEP FACILITATION

When it comes to twelve-step-facilitated treatment, or TSF, there have been about eight randomized controlled trials in which TSF was compared to and generally found to be at least as effective as other professional approaches that didn't involve the twelve steps. For instance, in a large, widely cited study called Project MATCH, TSF was as effective as cognitive-behavioral therapy and a version of motivational interviewing at reducing the quantity and frequency of alcohol use when the treatment ended and one and three years afterward. Moreover, during three years of follow-up, the TSF group had about a 10 percent advantage over the other groups in the proportion of people who were continuously abstinent.

Unfortunately, TSF as tested in most studies doesn't represent what goes on in the real world of rehab. In Project MATCH, for example, all of the counseling was provided by highly trained and supervised counselors who used a manual to guide their work. Moreover, all of the counseling was provided one-on-one, not in groups, as is the case at most rehabs. Even though eight out of ten programs reported in the 2010 National Survey of Substance Abuse Treatment Services that they used twelve-step facilitation at least some of the time, and more than half said they used it "always or often," experts in the field point out that when counselors attempt to involve their clients in twelve-step self-help groups, they rarely use scientifically supported methods.

Certainly, a good time to introduce people to twelve-step meetings is while they're in treatment. That way, they can turn to counselors for questions about how to pick a sponsor, how to find personally suitable meetings, and how to handle difficult situations. When I asked Dr. Miller if he thinks that when shopping for rehabs, one should be on the lookout for programs that regularly take clients to meetings, he said, "I don't personally favor programs *taking* people to AA meetings because it should be their choice whether and what meetings to attend. Good advice is to encourage everyone to try twelve-step meetings, particularly while they're in treatment, but no one should be required to do so." In *Treating Addiction*, Dr. Miller and his coauthors advise a "three-strikes" approach to recovery support meetings. Accordingly, counselors are advised to try three times, in a non-adversarial way, to refer clients to groups like AA. If a client refuses after the first try, he or she might be asked to revisit the idea a bit later in treatment. Continuing to advocate beyond three tries may damage the client-counselor relationship, and it would be better to help clients engage with supports of their own choosing.

What about the value of the twelve steps for addictions to illicit drugs? As with drinking problems, there's some evidence that NA and Cocaine Anonymous attendance is associated with better drug-related outcomes. NIDA's "Principles of Drug Addiction Treatment" includes TSF as an evidence-based approach for stimulant and opiate addiction but states that the research on other abused drugs, albeit promising, is more preliminary.

AA ALTERNATIVES

I was amazed at the number of rehab staffers and administrators I met—some of whom had worked in the field for many years—who were completely unfamiliar with or knew little about the non-twelve-step abstinence-based support groups SMART Recovery, Women for Sobriety (WFS), Secular Organizations for Sobriety (SOS), and LifeRing Secular Recovery. While AA and NA both use a twelve-step "spiritual" program that encourages long-term membership in their fellowships and the acceptance of a higher power, these other support groups offer a secular approach, one that does not rely on a higher power:

- SMART stands for Self-Management and Recovery Training. Its four-point program uses tools based on cognitive-behavioral principles and motivational interviewing. (However, according to its Web site, the SMART Recovery program will evolve as scientific knowledge about addiction and recovery evolve.)
  — Web site: www.smartrecovery.org
- Specifically for women, WFS is a support group that employs thirteen statements or affirmations emphasizing increased self-worth, emotional and spiritual growth, not dwelling on the past, personal responsibility, and problem solving.
  — Web site: http://womenforsobriety.org
- SOS considers recovery an individual responsibility separate from

spirituality and uses a cognitive approach. Members are encouraged to develop their own program of recovery.

— Web site: http://www.cfiwest.org/sos/index.htm

- LifeRing uses the group process to empower the "sober self" within each participant to work out his or her own path to sobriety. Its philosophy is summarized in the three words "sobriety, secularity, and self-help."

— Web site: lifering.org

- Finally, Moderation Management (www.moderation.org) is a self-help group for people who abuse alcohol but are not addicted to it and who want to reduce or stop their drinking and make other positive lifestyle changes.

All of these organizations have face-to-face and online groups, and none of them charge fees (although they may "pass the hat" to help pay for expenses), require appointments, or place limits on numbers of visits. The organization Faces and Voices of Recovery offers a comprehensive "Guide to Mutual Aid Resources" (both online and in person) that it describes as a "one-stop resource for people in or seeking recovery from addiction, their families and friends, and for addiction treatment service providers and other allied service professionals" (http://www.facesandvoicesofrecovery .org/resources/support/index.html).

Although almost no research has been conducted on AA alternatives, in discussing them at a 2007 conference at the Betty Ford Institute, psychologists and AA researchers Keith Humphreys, PhD, and Lee Ann Kaskutas stated, "By analogy, one can reasonably argue that these organizations probably benefit participants because they share curative features (e.g., abstinent role models, social support) with organizations that have been shown effective in longitudinal research. For some organizations, like SMART Recovery, an even stronger argument through analogy can be made for effectiveness because the organization's change technology is adopted from well-established treatment approaches."

In one of the few studies that did involve alternative support groups,

Randolph Atkins Jr., PhD, and James Hawdon, PhD, conducted a national survey of more than eight hundred men and women in AA, NA, SMART Recovery, WFS, and SOS to identify differences in people attracted to various recovery support groups and published their findings in the *Journal of Substance Abuse Treatment* in 2007. The researchers found that involvement in any recovery group directly increased the amount of time participants stayed sober and that there were no significant differences between the different support groups. In general, neither the respondents' level of religiosity or belief in a higher power had anything to do with their remaining sober. However, religious respondents were more likely to be actively involved in twelve-step groups or Women for Sobriety, while nonreligious people were more likely to actively participate in SOS and SMART Recovery and significantly less likely to participate in twelve-step programs. Given that involvement in support groups is associated with increased abstinence, the authors concluded that matching a person's philosophical beliefs to those of their support group can indirectly increase the number of days they remain sober.

Yet research efforts continue to be devoted to the study of twelve-step efficacy—in large part, because it's so widely available, with meetings night and day, seven days a week in many areas—while the benefits of alternative support groups, with totals in the hundreds for most of them, remain unknown. Accordingly, most rehabs continue to put all of their proverbial eggs in the AA basket. Clients are seldom told about AA alternatives, the groups fail to proliferate, their existence remains in obscurity, and the many people for whom AA doesn't resonate but who might connect with a different kind of support group fall through the cracks. This scenario was illustrated by an administrator and counselor who had worked at a prominent rehab for many years who said to me, "I wouldn't recommend that someone go to SMART Recovery. I don't know anything about it." Unfortunately, clients can pay the price for this. The 2012 CASA Columbia report on addiction treatment stated, "The research evidence clearly demonstrates that a one-size-fits-all approach to addiction treatment typically is a recipe for failure." Indeed, Rose T. felt that her relapse following her first treatment experience might have been prevented had she been told about Women for Sobriety at that time. When she went to a second program, she said, "The counselor provided information on AA, gave me a copy of the Big Book, and material regarding alternative groups was available upon request." On her own, she explored alternatives to AA and found Women for Sobriety to be the most helpful. She said, "To sit in a room with others like me, makes me feel less alone. I've found such a beautiful community of sober sisters, and I've got such a strong support group standing behind me."

MY WAY OR THE HIGHWAY

Not informing clients that there are alternatives to AA and the disease model can actually harm people when they're led to believe that if they don't connect with the established approach and (therefore) don't do well in treatment, it's because of some personal failing. *Celebrity Rehab's* Dr. Drew Pinsky—who's been known to say that the twelve steps are "mandatory," "the cornerstone of sobriety," and that you can't stay sober without them—illustrated this blame-the-victim mentality in a CNN interview shortly after the death of Amy Winehouse when he said, "People look at these stories and go, 'Oh, addiction treatment doesn't work.' The crazy thing about addiction is, part of the disease is a disturbance of thinking where the addict themselves convinces themself [sic] they don't need to listen to or do what they're being told to do and if they simply do the recovery process on a daily basis, just simply do it, they will be fine, just the way a diabetic is fine if they take their insulin three times a day." Dr. Drew just doesn't seem to get it that, sometimes—dare I say, oftentimes—it *is* the treatment and "what they're being told to do" that fails the addict.

When faced with a my-way-or-the-highway attitude, people can feel hopeless. Carrie G. said of an exclusive celebrity rehab, "Aside from a spiritual counselor who was amazing, it was entirely twelve-step based, and we had to get through three steps. I hated doing it. I let them know that I hated AA meetings and told the tech that it wasn't working for me. I felt punished, and was told that if I wouldn't do it, I wouldn't succeed. People were crying because of that. It wasn't like this was my choice. I was made to feel like there wasn't a lot of hope."

After attending more than a dozen traditional programs—from top-of-the-line rehabs to "street places"—for his heroin addiction, Wyatt D. felt hopeless, too. He was sometimes "kicked out," usually because they didn't like his personal attitude to "the twelve-step stuff," which was "infecting the other people." Until he went to the non-twelve-step program at which I met him, he wasn't introduced to any other approaches for recovery and said that if he brought up alternatives to AA, he was told they wouldn't work. He found the message to be "The twelve steps are the only way . . . It's this dogma and if you don't accept it, they tell you you're going to die. But if it's the opposite of how you think, then what hope could you have?" Of the non-twelve-step program, he said, "This is the first time I've been offered an alternative. The difference here is like night and day—at other places, it seemed like they were on a power trip. Here, they're not married to one philosophy." What was helping him most was "the individualized therapy that doesn't insult my intelligence so I can be more engaged in it."

A psychologist who used to work at a high-end twelve-step rehab said that when the twelve steps are imposed on clients without presenting them as a choice, "It conflicts with the principles of motivational interviewing"—an approach that many of these places now tout in their evidence-based repertoire. He described the case of a man who'd abandoned his religion. "For thirty days, all we did was argue about accepting a higher power. If not for that, I think he might have stayed in treatment longer." The psychologist wondered, "Couldn't we have found a different way to reach him? The clear message at the rehab, however, was that the only curative treatment for addiction is the twelve steps . . . 'you will believe or else,' as opposed to a client searching, questioning, and discussing."

Some people who went to traditional rehabs were afforded leeway in their choice of support groups. For instance, despite the apparent one-size-fits-all focus of most of his program, while he was there Vince T.'s counselor told him about SMART Recovery and didn't pressure him about AA. At one point, she suggested that maybe he should try an AA meeting.

Vince felt, "It was almost like she just said it in passing, which is good. I was much more likely to take a mild suggestion than a mandatory requirement. . . . They really did not push AA at all. If they did, I probably would not have gone." Similarly, after attending a residential rehab that, in her words, used a "treat-every-addict-the-same" philosophy, Aurora S. went to an outpatient program where she found that "they didn't push any particular group just as long as you were involved in attending meetings like Women for Sobriety online."

HOW NON-TWELVE-STEP PROGRAMS HANDLE THE TWELVE STEPS: A ONE-WAY STREET?

What about non-twelve-step programs? Are they resistant or receptive to sending people to twelve-step groups and programs? In answering that question, Tom Horvath said, "Most people who come [to Practical Recovery] have exhaustively searched to find us. Consequently they know all they need to know before they get here—essentially, that we use a highly individualized, non-disease-model approach that fits the client rather than making the client fit into a preexisting plan. From our residential facility, we take clients to a SMART Recovery meeting once or twice a week, but it's optional. (Dr. Horvath is also the president of SMART Recovery.) If someone seems to be having trouble, however, we sometimes suggest twelve-step groups in addition—even if they arrived opposed to them— or switching entirely to that approach, which might entail leaving our services, but not necessarily." (It's not uncommon for programs to refer clients to other programs, especially if they need a different level of care than their original program can provide.)

Nearly a dozen interviews with active and former clients confirmed that Practical Recovery does not work from the disease model or use the twelve steps and that this is a major reason people seek them out—often after having been unhappy with traditional approaches. And one of their clients confirmed that the staff is supportive of AA attendance if a client chooses that. He said, "They thought it was fantastic that I started going to AA. I have a sponsor, I've gone to hundreds of AA meetings, and I've done all twelve steps." He added that he was also attending SMART Recovery meetings and told me, "I have a hybrid approach. At Practical Recovery, they're open to anything that works for you."

Likewise, Bob Muscala, owner of Muscala Chemical Health Clinic, has referred clients to twelve-step groups and programs many times when he feels that it's in their best interest—even though he openly challenges the Minnesota model on his Web site. When I visited his clinic, he introduced me to a young man who he was encouraging to go back to a twelve-step treatment program because of the severity of his alcohol addiction and because he felt the young man needed the support of the twelve-step community. Muscala also described a situation involving one of his clients who had an adult child at a twelve-step residential treatment program. Muscala encouraged the parent to take part in the family program at his child's rehab. However, when the tables were turned and it was the child's turn to take part in his parent's treatment at Muscala's clinic, Muscala told me that the child's treatment program discouraged him from taking part and from even talking to Muscala.

Therein lies the rub—there's virtually no reciprocity. Both Muscala and Practical Recovery refer clients to twelve-step programs and groups when they feel it will be good for the client, but this practice doesn't seem to happen in the other direction. Muscala said that over the course of more than thirty years, although he's referred hundreds of clients to twelve-step rehabs, AA, and NA meetings, twelve-step rehabs don't refer clients to him. Dr. Horvath's comment about referrals from twelve-step programs was similar: "We infrequently get referrals from twelve-step programs—at this point maybe a handful. I'm sure we had years where we had none."

AA: YOU CAN'T MAKE ME, CAN YOU?

After a drunk-driving conviction (with charges for criminal damage to property), Jessie C. was court ordered to complete a ninety-day residential program. Pending successful completion of the program, she would not have to fulfill a jail sentence. As is often the case, she wound up at a private rehab, but her treatment was paid for with public funds. She happens to follow an unusual, unconventional religion—which she'd indicated on her intake form—and she did her best to follow the program's twelve-step approach in the context of her religion.

What happened toward the end of her rehab stay so disturbed her social worker that he referred her to me so she could tell her story for the book. Jessie felt she was doing well in the program and was three days away from graduating, when, without warning, she said that police arrived and took her to jail. She told me, "I didn't know why I was being kicked out. I asked my counselor, 'What's going on?' and she said, 'You'll find out soon enough.'" Jessie explained that the paperwork for her removal from the program indicated that she wasn't following the program rules and that she'd "failed to accept a higher power that coincides with their twelve-step program." She felt this "totally violated my religious beliefs." Because she was forced to leave treatment early, her probation officer took her to court for violating the terms of her court order to complete a ninety-day treatment program, but her social worker intervened and was successful in placing her in treatment elsewhere. He told me, "Human rights people in the department that licenses addiction programs in Jessie's state agreed with me that the actions of this rehab were absolutely inappropriate. The fact that the rehab literally put its reason for discharge in writing illustrated clearly why the program was culpable and unable to later retract what they did. The client's basic human rights were violated."

I wondered if it's legal—particularly in a case like Jessie's, where she was in a private rehab, but her treatment was being paid for by government funds—to require adherence to the twelve steps and then to kick people out if they don't subscribe to the twelve-step philosophy. I already knew that higher courts in a number of jurisdictions had ruled that people in the criminal justice system cannot be required to attend twelve-step groups without being given the alternative to attend secular support groups. In a 2009 review article on this topic in *Counselor* magazine titled "Choice of Support Groups: It's the Law!" Martin Nicolaus, MA, JD, who's affiliated with LifeRing, noted that multiple federal courts of appeal ruled that the AA/NA program is religious in nature. He concluded, "The courts have consistently found that the number of 'religious components' in the

AA/NA approach is not merely token or trivial, but is substantial; and that is enough to offend the Constitution." (As suggested earlier, AA devotees will often say, "AA is not religious, it's spiritual," and that although the twelve steps frequently make mention of "God," this "higher power" can pretty much be whatever you want it to be.) The rulings indicated that requiring twelve-step participation specifically violates the Establishment Clause of the First Amendment to the Constitution, which says: "Congress shall make no law respecting an establishment of religion. . . ." Nicolaus also cites similar court rulings against other programs that either required participants to participate in a non-twelve-step, faith-based program or used state funding for a faith-based program.

As Nicolaus points out, the court decisions do not prohibit referral to twelve-step groups—in fact, AA and NA are cited for their "fine work." But what the rulings mean, said Nicolaus, is that "if you are a state actor, and if you require clients to attend treatment or support groups (or else!), then you must offer not only twelve-step but also a secular alternative. Or you and your agency may be sued for monetary damages and attorney fees." (While there are many states where the religious nature of AA/NA has been settled, the issue remains undecided in others.)

So what's a "state actor"? Nicolaus explained that it's a legal term with still-evolving parameters but that criminal justice officials at all levels would be included under the term and that counselors in government agencies other than the criminal justice system, but where governmental coercion of some kind is involved, appear to be subject to the same interpretation.

And what about private programs that require people to subscribe to twelve-step principles or go to twelve-step meetings? In the article, Nicolaus said, "Employees of private programs operated with substantial government funding and with government oversight . . . are also liable to fall within the 'state actor' definition." On the other hand, professionals in private practice without government funding would not be affected, nor would private facilities without public funding. In a case like Jessie's, Nicolaus told me, "The key is whether the government imposes sanctions for noncompliance with a religious program. Whether the program itself is privately or publicly funded is secondary. If the state required her to be there, the program didn't provide a secular option, and the state punished her for non-participation in it, her first-amendment rights would be violated. However, her social worker was able to get her referred to another program."

Nicolaus chided the addiction counseling profession for largely remaining silent about the rulings on twelve-step coercion, but as he notes, secular alternatives are hard to come by in most communities. Furthermore, many people in the criminal justice system don't even know about these rulings, nor do they have the financial means to fight for them.

Even if pressuring someone to go to AA were legal, it's unwise. Of the few respected studies on coerced AA attendance, none showed a differential benefit with the treatments to which it was compared. And mandated attendance is actually inconsistent with one of AA's self-styled traditions, which states, "Our public relations should be guided by the principle of attraction rather than promotion." (Accordingly, some twelve-step groups and members refuse to "sign" for people who are required to get documentation proving their attendance at meetings when they're legally required to attend or to keep their professional licenses.)

BRANDON G.'S EXPERIENCE AT A FAITH-BASED PROGRAM

When Brandon G. was sentenced to attend a year-long drug and alcohol program following a felony DWI charge, his social worker told me that he lined up a primary care residential rehab stay, followed by extended care and time at a halfway house. But he said these were rejected by both the judge and the prosecuting attorney because the treatment wasn't all at one place. Both Brandon and the social worker said that the judge then ordered Brandon to thirteen months at a recovery program that is tied to a Christian organization. Brandon said, "I had no choice. It was that program or fifty-six months in prison. I struggled from the get-go."

It started with an order to cut his long hair. Having grown up in a

Christian church, he told the staff, "Nothing in the Bible says you have to have short hair." But when the choice became a haircut or going to prison, Brandon let them get out the scissors. The first week he was there, Brandon said, he was required to sing in a choir that traveled around to different churches—sometimes many in one week. He said, "While at the churches, they made different people tell their story—tell what a low-life you were and how, by the grace of God, you're better. Then we'd have to beg for money."

Of the program itself, he said, "It's religion-based. They believe God can cure you of your addiction. They were trying to convert you. You have to speak in tongues. They expect it of you—you're probably not going to graduate if you don't." The most disturbing thing Brandon found was unwanted baptisms. He said, "I saw people dragged up a ramp and then pushed into a pool."

He also talked about a visitor who would come and "put his hand on your forehead and expect you to fall down. . . . All of us would have to line up in rows and he'd hit us all in the head [not in a painful way]. If you didn't fall down, they'd say, 'You're not getting it.'" Brandon learned to con his way through the program. "I wasn't the only one. We knew it was bullshit."

Brandon said he was also required to do physical labor. "They'd work you, man, they'd work you. Part of the time, I got sent to remodel a building and then I had to help dig out an inner courtyard. You don't have a choice, and you don't get paid. And if you don't do it, they'll set you back. If you were openly resistant, they'd have the cops come haul you away."

When I asked if he completed the program, Brandon's response was, "I left on my graduation day without graduating. They didn't approve of where I was going to live, so they weren't going to graduate me." Their rationale? He said that the people he was going to move in with weren't "acceptable" because they weren't married and, therefore, were "living in sin." At that point, he called his probation officer and went to see him right away. The officer said, "I'm not a big fan of that program, and I'm not going to violate you."

That was the end of the residential program for Brandon, but when I last spoke with him, he was still on probation and had been ordered to attend twelve-step meetings.

I interviewed one other person who attended this program several years before Brandon, who said he'd had a positive experience there. Although he didn't like having to memorize Bible verses, he didn't feel that "the Bible or giving your life to the Lord was crammed down your throat." He also said that he didn't witness any forced baptisms. Nevertheless, Brandon's social worker told me that his account is consistent with everything that Brandon told him at the time of his treatment at the program and that other clients who went to this program reported similar experiences. While writing the book, this program approved my request to come visit. Later, a voice mail message indicated that the offer had been withdrawn.

When I asked program representatives for a response concerning Brandon's description of his experiences, I was informed that no clients can be court ordered to their facilities unless they specifically request their program as an option in court and that as part of the admissions process, applicants are made aware of the faith-based nature and requirements for the program. I was also told that faith is not required for entry or graduation and that in the admissions process, applicants are asked to sign off on policies such as dress code and personal appearance, choir participation, chores, and volunteer opportunities. They said, "Participation (beyond attendance) at in-house chapel services, worship experiences, or baptisms is completely voluntary."

KEEPING MEN AND WOMEN APART

Some rehabs have blanket guidelines about male-female relationships designed to separate men and women or, in rehab lingo, to prevent "fraternizing." "We couldn't even look at the boys," said one young woman of her rehab experience. Another woman shared her program's written rules, which stated, "Fraternizing: You are in a gender-specific program. Clients may not approach any non-staff male while in treatment [here]. This includes on field trips, at the YMCA, grocery store, and AA meetings." According to the Web site of one facility I came across, the rationale for the no-fraternizing policies is that "all emotional energy needs to be concentrated on recovery."

While it might make sense to discourage clients from getting involved in romantic relationships or sexual activity when they're at a short-term residential program, the strictness of some of the rules struck me as unrealistic and unreasonable, particularly when important life skills in recovery involve developing healthy social and relationship skills.

To find out if there's any research-based rationale for keeping men and women apart, I turned to psychologist Barbara McCrady, PhD, director of the Center on Alcoholism, Substance Abuse, and Addictions at the University of New Mexico, who studies the role of couples therapy in addiction treatment. When it comes to forming romantic relationships in rehab, she said, "There aren't scientific studies to guide the answer. I think it depends on the function of the relationship and the timing. Many people use short-term sexual relationships as a way to cope with negative feelings or to avoid other problems in their lives, so from that perspective, it makes sense to use time in intensive treatment (which usually is pretty short) to help clients focus on their major presenting problems. But there is some evidence that developing a new love relationship can be a major factor in long-term, successful changes in drinking." (Dr. McCrady added that the frequent advice to newly sober people to avoid new, romantic relationships until they've been sober for a year "seems completely unrealistic.")

Another common residential rehab practice regarding male-female relationships is to split up couples when both partners struggle with addiction. I learned about this when I spoke with a couple who, after an exhaustive search, found a place that would treat them together. Shelby W. told me, "We called everywhere. There were so many times we wanted to go places to get clean, but time would go by and the moments would pass because they wouldn't take us as a couple. And we were willing to pay whatever it cost." When Shelby and her partner finally did find a place that accepted both of them, she said, "Getting sober together was what worked," even though they eventually went their separate ways.

Dr. McCrady said, "There are not scientific data backing the notion that couples should be separated in treatment, so flexible decision-making rather than a blanket rule makes the most sense. Clinical lore would suggest that having intimate partners in the same groups might create problems—for example, they'd bring their relationship conflicts into the group, might ally with each other, or might not bond with others in the program as much as the staff would see as desirable. However, I've had married couples in residential treatment together, and, although there are some complexities to consider, my *own* 'clinical lore' is that it's do-able. What makes the most sense is to do some work together and some separately." It's obviously a complex issue, particularly in programs that rely on group treatment. David Sack, MD, CEO of Elements Behavioral Health, the organization that owns Promises, said, "We have reviewed this question extensively and will not admit couples to the same campus, although we've had them attend simultaneously but split apart at our two different facilities. The reason is that each member may disclose confidential information in his or her respective therapy groups that they may not be ready to share with their spouse or partner, and we feel that it is unrealistic and unfair to expect that their peers will be able to keep this information confidential."

JUST FOR WOMEN

A practice that *is* gaining research support is providing separate programming for women with substance use problems. There's evidence that women may fare better and be more likely to stay in same-sex groups than when treated with men, while men appear to do equally well in mixed or all-male groups. According to the 2010 N-SSATS, 32 percent of addiction treatment facilities provided programs or groups specially designed for adult women, while 25 percent did so for adult men. Among rehabs I visited, smaller and outpatient programs tended to treat men and women

together, while larger residential rehabs like Hazelden and Caron had separate units for men and women.

One reason why women may have better outcomes in groups just for
women is, in part, because of the high rates of physical and sexual trauma,
followed by post-traumatic stress disorder (PTSD), in women seeking
treatment. For that reason, groups created just for women allow them to
feel more comfortable discussing details of their personal lives that im-
pinge upon recovery. However, it's not really clear whether special treatment for women is superior; there have been only a few well-designed
studies comparing it to mixed-gender treatment. One such study by Harvard Medical School's Shelly F. Greenfield, MD, MPH, and her colleagues,
published in *Drug and Alcohol Dependence* in 2007, revealed that women
who took part in a group treatment program specially designed for women
not only used significantly less alcohol and drugs during the months following treatment than did women who took part in a mixed-gender counseling group, but were significantly more satisfied with their treatment.
Also, it should come as no surprise that women who are able to keep their
children, or retain custody of them while in treatment, are more likely to
stay in rehab.

> **Women are less likely to enter treatment than men are, with about
> twice as many men in the system at any one time. Although much
> higher rates of substance use disorders have been reported in men than
> women, women who have substance use problems tend to experience
> faster progression from the time when they first start using alcohol or
> certain drugs to the onset of addiction and their first time in treatment.
> Therefore, when they enter rehab, women typically have more severe
> problems than men, despite having used less of a substance and for a
> shorter time period.**

It was interesting to observe the dynamics of a mixed male-female outpatient group for an entire week, where two counselors indicated that,

ideally, they'd like to see this balanced with some single-gender groups. One did point out, though, that "women will go places that men won't. Women open up the men and talk about relationships more."

Although twelve-step groups help many women, some feel that meetings and materials are male dominated and that women—particularly those who were abused or have low self-esteem—struggle with the themes of powerlessness, making amends, and humility. Norman Briggs, EdM, Director of Addiction Services for the ARC Center for Women and Children in Madison, Wisconsin, said that they ask women to give twelve-step meetings a try because some do find support there, but added, "We often find that women who try AA or NA hate it. We try to discourage feelings of powerlessness, and having women absorb that as a tenet of recovery conflicts with our strength-based approach. Our clients come in so down and discouraged that they don't need to hear that they're powerless over anything. They need to hear that they can change things."

It's true that AA was first written by men, primarily for men, and that the program reflected this bias. Since then, AA literature has been revised, but some women still feel there's too little focus on cultural and social issues pertinent to women. The very limited research on the benefits of AA for men versus women has resulted in inconsistent findings.

DOES DIVERSITY MATTER?

In a move away from one-size-fits-all programs, some rehabs pay special attention to diverse groups of individuals who find their way to addiction treatment—from bisexual, gay, lesbian, and transgender (BGLT) individuals to aging baby boomers. (Nationwide, the 2010 N-SSATS found that 7 percent of addiction treatment facilities provided programs or groups specially designed for seniors or older adults and 6 percent did so for BGLT clients.)

While there are rehabs especially for BGLT clients, no program I went to specifically catered to this group, although some places did offer to take clients to meetings for gay people. I was surprised to find, with their strict rules about fraternization in straight couples, that residential rehabs tended to room gay and straight people together. A psychologist at one place said that the ideal is to give gay people private rooms. The National Association of Lesbian, Gay, Bisexual, and Transgender Addiction Professionals at www.nalgap.org is a resource for sexual minorities.

Way ahead of the game with the aging of the nation's baby boomers and a concomitant rise in drug abuse among people age fifty and older, the Fountain Centers program in rural Minnesota has for some time had a state grant to provide one-on-one services for older adults with alcohol and drug problems that also addresses their health and social service needs. They also offered a culturally and language-sensitive residential program for Hispanics on their adult men's unit.

How important is it to find a program that caters to racial, ethnic, sexuality, or age differences? While more research is needed in this area, the general consensus seems to be that well-trained counselors and programs that truly meet the needs of individuals preclude the need for special programming for people based on these variations. In their book, *Treating Addiction: A Guide for Professionals*, Dr. William Miller and his coauthors emphasize that, outside of recognizing language differences and the need for clear communication, there's little evidence that treating people in racially or ethnically uniform groups improves treatment outcomes. They stress, however, that it's important for treatment providers to be respectful of cultural traditions and differences when approaching issues like anger and assertiveness.

They go on to note that individuals with the *same* skin tone or socioeconomic background are otherwise quite *diverse* and stress the importance of "regarding each person as unique and the expert on his or her own life," which once again contrasts with how many rehabs approach their clients. For instance, when I asked a clinical supervisor at a prominent residential rehab whether they had any special approaches for gay people, people of different racial or ethnic groups, or the elderly, he replied, "Every addict thinks their situation is different. We don't want to focus on differences. We want to focus on similarities."

Regarding baby boomers, a 2010 government report revealed that the number in this group entering treatment more than doubled from 1992 to

2008. And estimates suggest that the count of those in this age group with substance use disorders will climb from about 2.8 million to 5.7 million per year in the first two decades of this millennium. Rehabs are heeding the call, as reported in a 2008 *New York Times* article on treatment for the aging that stated, "Across the country, substance abuse centers are reaching out to older addicts whose numbers are growing and who have historically been ignored. There are now residential and outpatient clinics dedicated to those over fifty, special counselors just for them at clinics that serve all ages, and screenings at centers for older Americans and physicians' offices to identify older people unaware of their risk." Nevertheless, according to NIDA's "Principles of Addiction Treatment," research to date indicates that current addiction treatment programs can be as effective for older adults as they are for younger adults. It makes sense, however, that older people may respond better to treatment that takes place in groups with people of the same age.

————

In the end, the question for the rehab consumer may not be, "Do you individualize treatment?"—because most rehabs will tell you that they do—but "How will you individualize treatment for me and my needs, and how will you involve me in the process?" Tom Horvath shares his philosophy this way: "There are as many roads to recovery as there are individuals. Therefore, there are just as many 'treatments.' The primary role of the provider is to collaborate with the client to discover the client's road. Hence, treatment should be completely flexible with respect to nearly every aspect, including orientation, length, frequency of visits, counseling approaches, group versus individual sessions, choice of therapist or counselor, return visits, support groups, medications, and holistic services. And if we try something that doesn't work or seem to be the right fit for the client, then we should try a different approach."

CHAPTER SEVEN

WHEN IT COMES TO REHAB,
TEENS ARE NOT JUST LITTLE ADULTS

MORE QUESTIONS THAN ANSWERS?

Want a "luxurious setting" so your teen can "relax and rejuvenate" while recovering from a drug or alcohol problem? The Web site for one adolescent rehab suggests that they offer just that. Or maybe you think your kid needs more of a tough-love approach, perhaps at a place with a camplike or wilderness atmosphere. How do parents know what's best for a teenager with a drug or alcohol problem and what their role in the process should be? Should they just drop their kids off at the door, or even ship them across the country, and then let the rehab do all the work? Parents may breathe a sigh of relief to be told, as a Web directory suggests, that just by removing the teen from the family, both will have an opportunity to heal. On the other hand, as with adults, maybe a local outpatient program for teens would be just as effective as an overnight rehab—or perhaps even better, at least in part because families could be nearby and easily get involved in the treatment process.

Then there's the issue of the twelve steps for teens. One Web site acknowledges controversy over such programs for adolescents, with their philosophy of powerlessness and admission of being a lifelong alcoholic or addict who will never again be able to take a drink, then goes on to argue in favor of twelve-step programs by noting that "no one has come up with anything better" and that the approach is among the cheapest. Is that how you should choose a treatment program for your child—by default and because it's "cheap"?

After visiting teen drug and alcohol treatment programs at six different sites, three of them residential and three of them outpatient, I wondered how common it is for rehabs to offer special programming for young people. I also had questions about whether kids belong in rehab at all, and, if so, what approaches have been shown to be most effective and how parents are usually involved in the process (if they are). When I began to dig into this topic I soon realized, as experts had warned me at the outset of my project, that drug and alcohol treatment for young people easily warrants a book in itself. As such, in this chapter, I only scratch the surface of some of the important issues, share stories of young people and parents who addressed the issues in different ways, and provide pointers for families looking for help. The chapter opens with the stories of two young people who had completely different experiences with high-end residential twelve-step-based treatment.

LUKE G.'S STORY: THE QUINTESSENTIAL
RESIDENTIAL REHAB EXPERIENCE

Many would say that Luke G. had the "quintessential" rehab experience, certainly the type that most traditional rehabs advocate for their clients. He first spent a month in primary residential care at a highly regarded twelve-step-based youth treatment program, followed by three months in the same rehab's extended-care facility. From there, he lived for four months in a halfway house he described as "almost opulent" that had "wonderful" counselors, allowed him to work part time, required AA meetings four times a week, and included "healthy and enjoyable" wilderness therapy. I interviewed both Luke and his mother, who said that her health insurance company had no in-network coverage for a youth rehab. She said, "I was going to be damned if he was going to be in a program with fifty- to sixty-year-old alcoholics dealing with alimony and losing jobs while my son was dealing with separation issues. When I found a youth program, I didn't care that it wasn't in-network and handed over my check for $1,000 a day." I would have guessed the three rehabs, amounting to eight months of treatment, would have cost much more than the $40,000 or so the family spent—$5,000 was included for travel expenses. (This took into account a large deduction on their taxes the following year because the rehab expenses were considered medically necessary.)

What landed Luke in rehab was a combination of Klonopin (a benzodiazepine), prescribed by psychiatrists for anxiety and panic attacks, plus two to three bottles of wine nightly, and a lot of pot smoking. Luke said, "I was one big depressant head." His mother told me, "Aside from the times we'd let our kids have a little wine at family dinners, I'm pretty sure that every time Luke had a drink it turned into fifteen." When I asked her how she knew this, she responded, "Because he told me."

As a twenty-two-year-old college student and one of the oldest people at the youth rehab, Luke felt it was the right fit to be at a place with so many younger kids because he was emotionally immature. Plus it gave him the opportunity to be in a leadership role. (The program accepts teens and young adults through their mid-twenties.) Although the place largely used group treatment for substance problems, Luke felt that its strength was "the continuity between addiction treatment and mental health." He explained, "They do a great job with dual diagnosis. In the beginning, I saw a psychologist once a day and a psychiatrist every two weeks or so. The psychologist talked me through my four months there and gave me constant support. She knew I'd understand cognitive-behavioral therapy. I'm an academic at heart, and she gave me things to read." (With time, he saw her once a week.) Luke also really connected with his extended-care addiction counselor, about whom he said, "He did more than anyone else to get my life back on track and help me live a life not on drugs. He did cognitive-behavioral therapy. I did a 100-question relapse prevention packet with him that was really helpful."

Of the twelve steps, Luke said, "At first, it seemed like another one of those crackpot things that you see someone selling on TV at 3:00 a.m., like power blenders. And as a staunch agnostic when I arrived, there was that terrible three-letter word 'God.'" However, he said that reading the Big Book and doing related assignments "kept him going" in the beginning and appealed to his studious nature. For the first two months, the treatment center was his "higher power."

When I spoke with Luke almost ten months later, after he'd completed his time at the sober home and graduated from college, he told me that he was attending about two AA meetings a week and had a sponsor. He said, "I know that the AA program was written by a bunch of white guys in Akron, Ohio. But the language appeals to me—the old-fashioned, old-boys-club language. And I am the target audience. It didn't feel like normal self-help stuff." I contacted Luke again by e-mail about sixteen months after that, when his feelings about AA were still evolving, and found that he felt that, "it serves a purpose that I imagine a tight-knit church congregation, fraternity/sorority, or neighborhood would. In a time of increasing digitization and depersonalization, the beauty of AA/NA recovery is that it lets you talk to other people . . . honestly, personally, and face-to-face." While he loved his time at both the rehab and the sober home, he feels that he would have had "a good shot" at getting sober without them. He added, "By that same token, could I be sober right now without AA? I doubt it, and, if I was, even I probably wouldn't want to hang out with me."

HALEY B.'S STORY ABOUT HER DAUGHTER'S EXPERIENCE AT A HIGH-END REHAB

The first person I talked to about adolescent treatment for this book happened to be someone I know personally. One day when we got talking about our kids, she confided that her two daughters had struggled with drug and alcohol problems. In searching for a treatment program for their younger daughter, Logan, Haley B. and her husband kept in mind their dissatisfaction with the rehab the older daughter had attended as a teen. She told me, "We didn't want our younger daughter, who was addicted to cocaine, in with adults who were alcoholics in their fifties." So, when nineteen-year-old Logan came to them and said, "I was going to ask you guys if I could go to treatment," they followed a psychologist's suggestion to place her in one of the top teen residential rehabs in the country, one that's twelve-step based. They didn't find out until the end of her four-week stay, when they met with their daughter's counselor, that Logan hadn't accepted the twelve steps, which they were told meant she wouldn't be ready for any continued treatment at that time. (Haley added, "I think any program for teens should have continuing contact with parents during treatment." But they weren't told how their daughter was doing until a week before she was to be done with her stay, and, as Haley recalls, Logan had given her permission for the staff to talk to them.) They were advised, "You have to let her fall, let her fall hard, and hope that she doesn't die." Haley said, "We were astounded. We felt so helpless and like it was so hopeless—this place was supposed to be the pinnacle of rehab. Did they do what they needed to do for Logan? Logan has always been complex and complicated. They detoxified her, but I don't know that they 'got' her. It's like educators who teach to the mainstream, who may not help kids who learn in a different way. But we weren't going to give up on our daughter."

So after the rehab helped them draw up a contract about what their mutual expectations would be, they decided to bring Logan home. This entailed a requirement for Logan to attend twelve-step meetings in their community. "There was never any suggestion that there was another way than the twelve steps, so we didn't know to question that," Haley recalled. "We didn't fully appreciate that she didn't buy into it." When they discovered Logan was lying to them about going to meetings, she told them, "It's just the same people talking about all the drugs they used to do and all that they used to drink." Haley added, "She didn't like the fact that you have to say 'I'm powerless' over it. She told us, 'It's my responsibility. I can fix it, and I'm the one who has to do it.'"

Logan did attend their weekly family meetings, which was a stipulation of the contract if she wanted to live at home and have access to a car. Logan had a few lapses in which she used drugs shortly after she completed treatment. But she never went back to rehab, eight years have passed now, and she's married to the guy whom Haley believes first gave her the ultimatum to get help. "We think she's doing okay, but we worry if she has a glass of champagne," Haley said. "However, she's back in school, on the dean's list every semester, involved in her church, and seems to be happy. I look at each day as a blessing."

SPECIAL PROGRAMS, JUST FOR YOUNG PEOPLE

No question about it, Luke and Logan's families were wise to seek out re-habs specially designed for teens. Experts agree that adolescents should be treated apart from adults, as they were at the six sites I visited.

Daily schedules at residential programs were similar in many respects to those at adult facilities, with early morning wake-up times, numerous group counseling sessions, time for doing recovery-related assignments, readings from recovery literature (commonly from AA or NA materials), periodic individual sessions with addiction counselors and mental health professionals, and recreational activities. Differences I observed from adult programs included fewer lectures and the provision of on-site schooling, with licensed educators, for young people still in secondary school, as well as counseling and conversation at a young person's level. I got the impression that some facilities were more creative with recreation than others. For instance, at one place, when kids complained about boredom, they weren't happy about being told to play board games and do cross-word puzzles. Another place had a state-of-the art gym; yet another had recreation specialists who facilitated activities such as drumming and arts and crafts. However, boredom was a theme at more than one rehab. Efforts were made to take young people off-campus for fun-in-sobriety activities such as miniature golf and laser tag, things I was told they might not have previously experienced sober. Some places had strict limitations on television watching and music—at one place, I observed a discussion about their ban on popular music and certain movies because these might trigger a desire to use drugs, a challenge I'd think you'd want kids to learn how to handle in negotiating the real world. Reading materials were limited, too—at least one facility allowed only AA or "spiritual" material.

Two of the residential facilities, Caron and Hazelden, had separate programs for males and females. Some rehabs, such as Caron, offer special programs for men and women in their early twenties. I got to observe some sessions at Caron's Young Adult Male Program. (Since they've been offering separate programs and housing with specially trained staff for young adult men and women, Caron has found that fewer than 10 percent leave against medical advice—a dramatic decline.) Other facilities accept young adults in their youth treatment programs along with teens. Hazelden, for instance, accepts young people from fourteen through twenty-five into its youth program, and counselors individualize treatment plans and assignments according to age. (More mature young adults might be recommended for their adult programs.)

Much like adult programs, the bulk of what goes on in adolescent rehab is group counseling. Staff at two residential places told me that their young clients receive a minimum of one hour of individual counseling a week. Overall, from what I observed in sitting in on group sessions, counselors seemed compassionate and used what would be considered cognitive-behavioral and motivational interviewing-type skills, as kids were encouraged to express their feelings and talked about their desires to use drugs and alcohol. Counselors sensitively worked with their young clients on conflict resolution, improving communication, coping skills, and their anxiety about not wanting to move from primary to extended care (a common theme). While they seemed open to the kids' concerns, I did wonder—as I had at adult rehabs—about the frequency with which personal issues were addressed in front of a group of peers. With psychologists and psychiatrists on staff, the high-end residential rehabs paid particular attention to dealing with psychological problems that accompany substance problems in the majority of their clients, and many of their clients had at least weekly visits with a psychologist. Outpatient programs tended to refer young clients elsewhere for psychological counseling.

As with adults, many people think of adolescent rehab as synonymous with residential treatment. But experiences like Luke's and Logan's are not typical—it's also the case with teens that drug and alcohol treatment largely occurs in outpatient settings. According to the 2010 National Survey of Substance Abuse Treatment Services (N-SSATS), 87 percent of clients under age eighteen who went to rehab were in outpatient treatment, 11 percent were in residential (nonhospital) rehab, and 2 percent were in hospital inpatient facilities. The few outpatient sessions I observed seemed to be unstructured, and I couldn't tell if that was just because I was there or if such was always the case. At one of them, the counselor spent a great deal of time doing a hard sell for attending a lot of twelve-step meetings and having kids get a sponsor. At another outpatient program, kids just seemed to casually and comfortably "shoot the breeze" with the counselor, while at a program for young men—most of whom came from heavy crime areas and were mandated to attend—the counselor gave more of a "lesson" on the harmful effects of marijuana. Using motivational inter-viewing strategies, she tried to get the boys to weigh the costs versus the benefits of drug use, but it was clear that most weren't ready to change. The counselor said, "My main goal is to teach them they have choices."

WILL T.'S STORY: A TEEN IN AN ADULT OUTPATIENT PROGRAM

I met Will T., an eighteen-year-old high school senior, when he was taking part in a twelve-step-based adult outpatient rehab. His response to my question about being the sole teen in the group was that, on the one hand, it was "weird" to be so much younger than the others. On the other hand, he said, "It was kind of like a family. You could talk about what you wanted and got feedback. Most of the others had been through it before." For Will, it was his first time in treatment. He started smoking pot when he was ten and from there, he and his cousins "did other stuff—pills, alcohol, and got in a lot of trouble all the time." One night, when they were running from the police, he assaulted an officer and resisted arrest, which landed him in a juvenile detention facility. While waiting for a court date, the judge ordered him to attend this particular outpatient program.

During one of the group sessions I got to observe, Will was confronted by his counselor about not doing his assignments. After not getting much of a response, the counselor then asked him, "What would help you?" and asked what he thought he needed to work on, which seemed like a logical approach for a resistant adolescent. *That* then became his new homework assignment. Will's experience at an NA meeting also engendered a lengthy group conversation about how the speaker at the NA meeting (not specifi-cally for young people) seemed to have singled out Will in an accusatory way and made him feel uncomfortable.

About three months later, I spoke with Will after he'd completed six months in this program, and he said he was still abstinent. When I asked him what helped him most, he said, "My counselor being a hard ass, having her push me" and "talking to people who would understand." In an interesting twist, he also said that the fact that it was "a twelve-step program that emphasized powerlessness over addiction" helped him—but not because he believed that. He explained, "I thought it was bull crap. But it became a challenge to me. I can control it. It's not that I feel I can use; it's that I'm not powerless over my addiction. It was this challenge that helped me." After he completed treatment, he didn't attend twelve-step meetings but was going to weekly aftercare sessions at the outpatient program. As a result of treatment he found, "A lot of good things started happening for me. My grades went up, I was participating in sports, and I have some new friends—people that were kind of friends before but who seem more accepting now."

WHY TEENS NEED THEIR OWN PROGRAMS

Although Will seemed to benefit from his experience in an adult program, according to psychologist Sarah Feldstein-Ewing, PhD, an expert in adolescent substance use and treatment at the Mind Research Network of the University of New Mexico, "Just because we've found something to be effective in adults, we can't say 'that's how it will work for kids.' We know enough to be certain that adolescents and adults are different in lots of critical ways (how they use, who they use with, how their brains are). But, because there hasn't been much research in adolescents, we are only beginning to know the nature of these differences and how they might affect treatment." Obviously, teens are different from adults developmentally, and, therefore, things need to be made relevant to their everyday lives in order to motivate them to stay in rehab.

Psychologist Ken Winters, PhD, a leading expert on adolescent substance problems and treatment based at the University of Minnesota, added, "Mixing young people with adults is bad clinical practice. Adults can make kids uncomfortable and less likely to open up. It may also make teens feel less than safe." He said that exposing teens with less severe substance problems to adults (or even older teens) with more severe ones could make the younger teens' problems worse, particularly if counselors are not skilled in dealing with this situation. (See "Group Treatment for Teens: For Better or Worse?" on pages 269–70.)

From the 2010 National Survey of Substance Abuse Treatment Services findings, which showed that nearly half of the 13,000-plus respondents accepted adolescents, only about 60 percent of them (or almost 30 percent of all facilities) offered a specially designed program or group for teens. Of the 5,500-plus programs that accepted both adults and teens, 45 percent did not indicate that they offered special programming for adolescents, so it's likely they were treated similarly to adults or perhaps together with them.

Unfortunately, separate programming for teens offers no guarantees. Mindy G.'s daughter was sent to a residential adolescent rehab for a month, during which, Mindy said, "At first, they put you through a 'blackout' period where you can't have any contact. And my barely fourteen-year-old daughter, who was a marijuana smoker, was housed with violent adolescents who had a history of doing hard-core drugs. Most kids in the program were there because they had committed crimes. Some were gang members. I think in this type of setting, kids will learn more about drugs and violence than they likely would have learned if they were kept at home and in outpatient treatment."

DO ALL TEENS WITH SUBSTANCE PROBLEMS *NEED* REHAB?

As mentioned in chapter 1, the number of teens who go to rehab each year is surprisingly small—just 138,000 according to the 2010 National Survey on Drug Use and Health. But far more young people have drug and alcohol problems. That same year, 1.8 million twelve- to seventeen-year-olds (about 7.3 percent of them altogether) were reported to have a substance use disorder. The situation is even worse in young adults—about 20 percent of eighteen- to twenty-five-year-olds had a substance use disorder in 2010.

Once again, frequently the assumption is made that all of these young people need treatment. For instance, the NSDUH report, which equates having a substance use disorder to "needing" treatment, indicates that when you subtract the teens who received treatment from those who, by their definition, "needed" treatment in 2010, you're left with "1.7 million who needed treatment for a substance use problem but did not receive it at a specialty facility." Such figures can readily be employed by rehabs in their marketing efforts. But do all of these teens really *need* to be helped at a drug and alcohol treatment program? As is the case with adults, substance use disorders in young people fall along a continuum of severity—and regardless of how bad the problem is, not everyone needs help from a residential or outpatient rehab.

In a joint interview, Drs. Kathleen Meyers and John Cacciola, psychologists at Treatment Research Institute in Philadelphia who study adolescent drug and alcohol treatment, expressed their opinion that young people who have substance use disorders need some form of intervention, but not necessarily at a drug and alcohol program. Unless a young person has a very severe drug or alcohol problem, before going the rehab route, they said, they'd first seek out a mental health professional with expertise in substance use disorders for a comprehensive assessment, including a thorough psychological evaluation. Dr. Meyers said, "Based upon the results, a variety of treatment options could be explored. Depending upon the constellation of issues the young person is struggling with, individual psychotherapy and/or family therapy with a mental health professional knowledgeable about substance use disorders may be more appropriate than going to a drug and alcohol rehab."

Dr. Cacciola added, "Some studies show that as many as 95 percent of teens with a substance use disorder have some other mental health disorder. Substance abuse is often the overt thing that gets them into treatment, but it's an underlying problem, such as depression or sexual trauma, that's really the issue. Substance abuse can be a symptom and is often not the primary problem." (He did caution that if the drug and alcohol problems are not dealt with, they may become more and more entrenched in a teen's lifestyle so that by the time adulthood is reached, substance abuse might trump the other problem[s].) Dr. Cacciola maintains that rehabs tend to see things the other way around—that is, they see the substance use disorder as the primary problem. He added, "If you take your child to the addiction place as your first course of action, they're not likely to say, 'Oh this isn't an addiction'—unless there's really nothing there in terms of alcohol and drug use or there's a severe mental health disorder, such as psychosis." That's why he recommends a good mental health evaluation and an attempt at therapy with a therapist skilled in addiction and family issues as a possible first course of action.

In reality, research suggests that many teens diagnosed with an alcohol use disorder will outgrow it. Duncan Clark, MD, PhD, at the University of Pittsburgh Medical Center, conducted an extensive review of scientific studies on teen alcohol problems that was published in *Addiction* in 2004. From his findings, he estimates that of teens in the general population with an alcohol use disorder, about half will continue to have a problem in young adulthood and half will not. And of teens with an alcohol use disorder, fewer than 20 percent will become and remain abstinent through young adulthood, while about 30 percent will go on to drink in a non-problematic way, a phenomenon often referred to as "maturing out" of a substance problem. (This review did not address drug use disorders.)

NICOLE A.'S "MATURING OUT" STORY

As children of a single mom, Nicole A. and her brother were unsupervised at night, and at the age of thirteen, Nicole became a daily pot smoker and a regular weekend drinker. At this young age, she also had her first treatment experience when she was sent to a residential teen program for five weeks. (She said that her mom had no say in the matter; the county made the decision.) From there, her course was a three-month stay at a halfway house, AA and NA meetings, more alcohol and pot use, a "locked-ward" adolescent addiction facility, several group homes, and an outpatient drug and alcohol program. It was sad to hear about how much time she spent in rehab when she was so young. She said, "Part of me is cynical that I was taken out of my home and told all these terrible things about me—that I can never do this, never do that—because they're not true." She remains in touch with others who were in various rehabs with her, and they had the same experience. She added, "When I was a teenager I didn't have the insight to realize that maybe I really wasn't an alcoholic who could never ever drink again. Even if I had, I would have most certainly been told that I must be in denial and that denial is a classic symptom of alcoholism. But that's not my experience. I've never had any adult problems." Today, Nicole is a social worker, the mother of two children, and about to start work in a doctoral program. She said, "I might drink once a week, occasionally twice a week. When I do, I have a couple of beers while I sit on the patio. I don't smoke pot or do other drugs."

WHY GETTING A GOOD ASSESSMENT COUNTS

Dimitri R., who spent months of his adolescence and young adult life in and out of rehabs, said, "I saw a lot of kids who drank and smoked weed too many times and their parents overreacted and sent them to rehab where they were told they had a disease. These kids would be truly, truly confused. They were trying to comprehend that they're drug addicts, and it was really sad. You're getting all this stuff from the techs about 'this is your disease talking,' and if you're not sure if you have one, it can be confusing. I knew I was an addict and needed help, but I think it's a lot more harmful than helpful when it's someone who doesn't have that much experience with drugs. People in that category are screwed over for life in some ways, and their parents are getting all this education. It must feel like they're in a nightmare."

Maia Szalavitz, author of *Help at Any Cost*, and a journalist who specializes in addiction, wrote an excellent *Time* magazine "Healthland" blog about adolescent addiction, treatment in which she stated, "Appropriate assessment of teen behavior is crucial because the line between normal and unhealthy behavior can be hard for parents to discern. Since many treatment programs focus on getting teens to accept that they have a drug problem, it's important to determine first whether or not that is truly the case." She quotes Ken Winters as saying, "A lot of things can look like drug abuse when they're not—including just being a normal, healthy teenager. A good assessment can help minimize over-pathologizing."

When it comes to assessment practices, however, it appears that adolescent rehabs aren't any more state-of-the-art than adult programs. In 2010 Dr. Winters and colleagues published a survey of assessment practices used by 120 "highly regarded" teen treatment programs in the *Journal of Child & Adolescent Substance Abuse* in which they found that more than two-thirds of facilities used questionnaires developed in-house— very few used gold standard tools designed for adolescents—and numerous programs were using assessment instruments that were not uniquely designed for teens. They concluded that "many of the most highly regarded treatment programs in the country were not adequately assessing adolescent clients." Dr. Winters noted that this survey was conducted in 2005 and that, since then, he'd seen signs that significantly more programs were using standardized, objective assessment tools rather than simply relying on untested and potentially unreliable measures. His advice to families seeking a good assessment for young people is to follow the same general guidelines as for adults but added that it's important to find out whether the tools used in the assessment are validated and developed specifically for use with youth. And ideally, the person doing the assessment should have experience with young people.

HOW PROGRAMS USE THE TWELVE STEPS FOR YOUNG PEOPLE

As with adult rehabs, most programs that treat young people involve the twelve steps in some way. The 2010 N-SSATS revealed that of the 6,368 facilities that accept adolescents, 46 percent indicated that they used twelve-step facilitation "always" or "often" while 31 percent indicated that they used the approach "sometimes." And in a national survey of 154 adolescent treatment programs published in 2009 in the *Journal of Substance*

Abuse Treatment, it was determined that 85 percent of programs linked kids to community-based twelve-step meetings after discharge from treatment.

In my visits to teen rehabs, teens did not seem pressured to accept the tenets of AA or to attend AA meetings, except for one outpatient program where a counselor devoted more than half of a lengthy group treatment session to trying to persuade attendees to go to meetings. At one residential place that uses the twelve steps, I was struck by how little talk I heard on the topic. At another twelve-step-based rehab, young people were allowed to challenge the disease model, although it remained clear that this philosophy was predominant.

Unlike some adult rehabs, none of the adolescent programs had a goal of getting young clients through a certain number of steps; the objective seemed to be more to introduce them to the first few steps and to link them to twelve-step programs after they left treatment. An administrator at one of the residential rehabs said that twelve-step facilitation is used by all of their clinicians and that they individualize the approach. But it was clear that the twelve steps were integral to their treatment when he added, "Obviously, understanding the principles of Step 1 (admitting you're powerless over alcohol or your addiction) are high priority. All patients start with Step 1 and progress as they're able through the next steps until the time of their discharge. The twelve steps are introduced as a framework for living that, if understood, can be used as tools to live by and deal with life's situations in ways that lead to more positive outcomes than the 'tools' the person has been using or just isn't equipped with yet. The clinicians are trained to interpret the steps in a way that fits the person's developmental level and takes them from the abstract and puts them in concrete, practical terms." Young people also attended some outside twelve-step meetings in the community—two or three times during a typical primary stay and several times a week when in extended care. In addition, volunteer speakers from the twelve-step community came on campus to share their stories, and a "Big Book meeting" was held on-site by returning alumni. (Another residential rehab had similar practices, but an administrator there told me, "The 'Big Book' is a turnoff—it's like

War and Peace. The Big Book Unplugged: A Young Person's Guide to Alcoholics Anonymous grabs them more.")

Despite his own positive experience with the twelve steps, Luke G. thinks that, in general, "Most kids aren't ready or willing to grasp recovery and, as a result, counselors end up talking to a wall for twenty-eight days and then letting them out with a renewed zeal to get fucked up." However, if a young person was having difficulty accepting a higher power and there was genuine effort and desire to work the twelve steps, it was his impression that "although the staff might try to persuade him otherwise, they still would say that he was doing a good job and progressing in the program. So long as he relied upon others within the program/treatment center, set up an extensive support system, and managed to become integrated into a sober community, then there probably wouldn't be any problem." He added, however, that although the rehab "uses a good deal besides the twelve-step model, it's the foundation, and other things are integrated. I don't think the program believes you can get sober without the twelve steps."

It was my impression that young people are not told about alternative approaches to the twelve steps, and I suspect this is common nationwide, as with adults. Twelve-step meeting attendance is sometimes required, and it may even be mandated by the criminal justice system. When I asked at one place whether young people are presented with any other self-help choices, such as SMART Recovery (which has a handbook for adolescents) or Women for Sobriety, I was told, "We cannot force the twelve steps down their throats" and that they might promote other support groups in the community, but not alternative recovery groups. The administrator also said, "It all comes back to the twelve steps in the end."

YOUNG PEOPLE SPEAK OUT ABOUT
THE TWELVE STEPS AND THE DISEASE MODEL

Experiences of young people with the twelve steps and the disease approach are just as varied as those of adults. Here are two different perspectives from people who attended twelve-step-based programs:

KELLI O.'S PERSPECTIVE

Both Kelli O. and her father had nothing but good things to say about her experiences as a twenty-two-year-old at a highly regarded high-end twelve-step-based residential program for youth. Kelli began drinking heavily when she was seventeen, after her mother died. She regularly went in and out of detox at a respected psychiatric and substance abuse hospital and told me, "I probably did this six times in a year, thinking it would be different each time." Her last detox episode occurred right after she celebrated her twenty-second birthday, and she started thinking, 'This is not how I want to live my life.'" Her psychiatrist then told her about the youth rehab, where she stayed for a month. Her experience overall was "absolutely wonderful." Of their twelve-step approach, she said, "I heard a lot of God stuff and wondered if I'd have to go to church. But it wasn't a problem. It did make me feel better." She said that some other young people there had trouble with the twelve steps, feeling that they were religious. When they were told, "It doesn't have to be God, it could be an ocean wave, a power greater than yourself," Kelli said. "It seemed to help." (The program also addressed Kelli's other issues, placing her in a grief group and having her see a therapist twice a week and a psychiatrist weekly.) Anticipating going to community AA meetings after she got out of treatment made Kelli feel scared and think of "old people from skid row who had been drinking for years and years." But at her first meeting, she felt at ease as soon as she arrived. She explained, "There were a lot of people my age, and I could relate to what they were talking about." In our last communication, she was two years sober and still regularly attending twelve-step meetings.

DIMITRI R.'S PERSPECTIVE

Even though he'd had a lot of therapy to help him believe otherwise, Dimitri R. was struggling to get out from under the admonition he'd received during his traditional treatment experiences that he would fail if he didn't accept the twelve steps. He told me, "It's like a curse to put on teens. Something like the twelve steps is a big, big commitment. Before you leave treatment, they tell you that you have to go to meetings every day, do ninety in ninety. You have to call your sponsor every day. For teens, it's hard enough to do homework." He had an especially tough time with the relapse message. "With the twelve steps, you can never use again. And if you use, they tell you it's going to ignite everything again. I see it as a set-up for disaster. Young people are going to have slip-ups."

When Dimitri connected with a clinical psychologist at a non-twelve-step practice at the tail end of his third twelve-step rehab experience, the psychologist said, "At this point, he was feeling hopeless and demoralized. When he asked about whether he'd have to do the twelve steps if he came to our place and I said we use a different approach, he was ecstatic." (As suggested before, Dimitri was eventually diagnosed with mental health problems that had probably fueled his drug use for years.) His therapist added, "I think pushing only the twelve-step philosophy sets many young people up for going underground later when they're struggling with normal young adult ambivalence. Kids often assume any error will result in getting shipped off, so they hide their errors and don't get help learning how to live. They think they're failing or an addict in denial when they may just need help making big decisions in this time of life. If they lapse or something else flares up, I think many resist the help they need moving forward."

In the end, Dimitri said that his rehab experience made him "a people pleaser" and left him confused because he had learned that "there's what people show to the staff and there's what's really going on. Among patients, you start to figure out that if you tell them you're really starting to like AA and believe in God again, then they'll let you leave. I think a lot of my brain power was spent on 'what can I do to get out of here?'" Now, Dimitri has to ask himself, "Who am I doing this for, who should I get sober for—myself or my parents? I think about the fact that my parents have spent so much money on all of it, and it makes me feel so much pressure."

RECOVERY FOR LIFE AND POWERLESSNESS

In addition to having trouble with the idea of a higher power, I was told that teens tend to have a particularly hard time with the "step one" concept of powerlessness and the notion that they're in recovery for life, which means they can never use again. Psychologist Steve Sussman, PhD, of the University of Southern California, Los Angeles, noted in a review of the scientific literature on twelve-step approaches for teens that admitting to being powerless doesn't fit with the normal adolescent search for autonomy. Dr. Wilkens added, "The fact that programs so often focus on instilling the belief that young people should sign on to and embrace the twelve-step, lifelong commitment philosophy for the rest of their lives is a ridiculous expectation. Teens can't see into next month, much less their whole lives. Many of them outwardly embrace the philosophy when in treatment because they realize that doing so is the key to getting out of rehab. But internally, they are full of doubt, questions, and ambivalence, which all gets played out the second they get discharged."

When I asked if the notion of "recovery for life" for teens isn't a tall order, an administrator at a high-end twelve-step residential youth facility candidly replied, "If a kid says, 'I'll do this now, but I'll drink when I'm twenty-one, you take it.' If a teen leaves rehab, is around friends who use, slips, then gets back on the wagon, that's success. But it takes an artful clinician to explain that to parents."

As Dr. Clark noted in his review of research on teen alcohol problems, "In most treatment programs, the goal of abstinence from alcohol is promoted." However, "while indisputably a successful treatment outcome . . . long-term abstinence is atypical." He added that other outcomes for adolescent alcohol use disorders need to be considered and that for many teens, a reduction in alcohol use to what's typical for most young people, as well as elimination of alcohol-related problems, may be achievable goals that will have acceptable outcomes as time goes on—for instance, as adults, some teens who had alcohol use disorders will be able to drink moderately.

The clinical director of one of the outpatient programs I visited said, "I honestly believe that most of the kids we see are not addicts. They have drug problems. We tell them, 'Just for today, just for this week.' If you replace it with something positive—an adult mentor and activities like sports, dancing, fishing, etc.—and teach them life skills, decision-making, and drug refusal skills, hopefully they choose to stay drug/alcohol free. If you tell teens, 'You have to go to meetings and stay sober for the rest of your life,' they walk out the door."

WHAT DOES THE RESEARCH SAY ABOUT THE TWELVE STEPS FOR TEENS?

I find it alarming, given how common twelve-step approaches are for young people, that when you read reviews of the scientific literature on what works for drug and alcohol problems for adolescents, the twelve steps are mentioned little, if they're mentioned at all. No randomized controlled trials have ever been conducted comparing twelve-step interventions with other approaches. In fact, as I was coming down the home stretch with this book, John Kelly, PhD, associate director of the Center for Addiction Medicine at Massachusetts General Hospital and a Harvard Medical School faculty member, was just starting the first experimental study ever on twelve-step facilitation in young people.

In an effort to scope out the studies that have been conducted on AA and NA programming for teens, Steve Sussman searched the scientific literature through mid-2009 and published his findings in 2010 in the journal *Evaluation & the Health Professions*. He was able to find only nineteen studies of high enough quality for the review. In his summary, Dr. Sussman concluded that, on average, 30 to 40 percent of teens were abstinent in studies involving evaluation of professional twelve-step-oriented treatment programs at various time points at the end of the studies. However, he noted that this may be "overly optimistic" because most of the studies included only youth who completed treatment and, therefore, excluded dropouts who likely were not doing as well.

When it comes to having teens attend AA and NA meetings in the community, a number of research studies suggest that those who get involved after treatment and stay involved are much more likely to remain abstinent than those who don't. Sussman's findings suggested that AA/NA attendance predicts abstinence by two- to threefold or that young people who were abstinent attended twice as many meetings per week. Most teens don't affiliate with twelve-step meetings, however, and many who do, drop out over time. For instance, in a study by Dr. Kelly and colleagues, only one third of teens who'd been to a twelve-step-based inpatient program were attending weekly AA or NA meetings six to twelve months after treatment. Similar findings have been reported in a number of studies involving teens in outpatient programs. Dr. Kelly notes again, however, that the dropout rate from professional treatment is generally about 50 percent or more during the first ninety days, so it's difficult to get anyone to stay involved in anything related to recovery, even over short periods. Kelly has conducted numerous studies on involvement of young people in AA and NA and has found that those with the most serious drug and alcohol problems tend to be more likely to attend meetings and receive the greatest benefit from them, while those with less serious problems tend not to attend or stop going.

It's quite clear that teens are more likely to attend twelve-step meetings set up explicitly for young people and to rate such meetings as important. But special groups like this can be few and far between, particularly in rural areas. (In the United States and Canada, less than 3 percent of AA members are under the age of twenty-one.) To keep young people engaged in twelve-step meetings, Kelly said that it's important to facilitate a good match between a teen's primary substance—marijuana, other drugs, or alcohol—and the group to which he or she is referred, such as Marijuana Anonymous, NA, or AA. Failure to do so can lead to a poor initial match, which can be difficult to overcome. He's also found that teens benefit from having an adult take them to their first meetings to facilitate introductions with existing young members and help them become actively involved in twelve-step groups.

CONCERNS ABOUT TEENS AND TWELVE-STEP MEETINGS

Some experts have concerns about the amount of emphasis some programs place on the twelve steps. Dr. Winters said, "Putting a lot of time and energy into the twelve steps may not be time well spent. Often, they're not doing enough with the approaches that help young people change behavior. It's always been my spiel that programs need to help kids do more with skill-building—decision-making, dealing with triggers, and negotiating life better. You can learn some of these skills with the twelve steps—they provide a new roadmap for life. However when we look at accepted treatment for other adolescent problems, such as anxiety and ADHD, they're organized around skill-building strategies. The addiction field should be that way."

Another issue raised in a 2011 article on the topic of teens and twelve-step recovery in *Counselor* magazine by addiction counselor Thomas Greaney, MEd, is that while adults may hear "war stories" told by peers at meetings as cautionary tales about the negative consequences of drug or alcohol use, teens may think to themselves, "I've never done that. That sounds neat." Minimizing their own behavior may be another teen response. For instance, the thought may be, "Oh, I have a long way to go before getting *that* bad."

Having attended many AA meetings, and knowing that twelve-step meetings are largely made up of adults, one of the first concerns that crossed my mind about having teens attend twelve-step meetings was the issue of safety. But raising this issue with some experts and treatment professionals, I found it was as if it had never occurred to them. However, several people who'd been to adolescent rehab shared my concern. Nicole A. said, "Due to the anonymity in the groups, it's impossible to know the histories of the attendees and what their motives are in attending. On the other hand, anyone could attend the groups and say anything he or she wanted to." She noted that because many twelve-step meetings are closed (literally) to nonalcoholics and addicts, it's "difficult for the parents of teen attendees to be aware of group happenings." Nicole also raised concerns about teens having adult sponsors, saying, "This is meant to be a close, confiding relationship—and because it's between an adult and a teenager, there's an added vulnerability of the teen due to the age difference." Luke G. added, "Just because people are sober doesn't mean they're good people. I would not allow a kid to go to an AA or NA meeting unaided. There's wide potential for malfeasance, mainly with women who, post-treatment, may be sexually or emotionally taken advantage of by predatory AA/NA members."

One small study addressed safety concerns of teens attending twelve-step meetings and was published in 2011 in the *Journal of Substance Abuse Treatment* by John Kelly and colleagues. Out of 127 teens who attended twelve-step meetings, 20 percent reported at least one incident of feeling intimidated, threatened, or sexually harassed at a meeting, more commonly at NA than AA meetings. (Young women were no more likely than young men to report this.) However, the authors make the point that consideration should be given to whether being alone or in another social or physical environment constitutes higher or comparable risk for such teens. As the mother of a teen once said to me, "My child is much safer at twelve-step meetings than she ever was when she was out buying and doing drugs on the street."

Still, many parents are unaware of how twelve-step meetings work and who attends them—and they may not know that sponsors aren't trained professionals. Nicole A. advised, "Risks could be reduced by having the adult sponsor also develop a relationship with the teen's parents and agreeing to a background check." Luke's recommendation was for parents to accompany teens to "open" meetings that allow nonmembers to attend but also to help teens find a trusted adult in recovery who can accompany them to the wider variety of closed meetings. When I asked for other recommendations from staff at rehabs, suggestions included steering kids to young people's twelve-step meetings, seeking twelve-step members with long-term sobriety as sponsors, not accepting sponsors who approach the teen (in other words, it should be up to the teen to make the approach), and having parents invite sponsors into their homes to meet them. One staff member said, "If your kid won't bring a sponsor home or the sponsor won't meet you, that's a huge red flag."

GROUP TREATMENT FOR TEENS: FOR BETTER OR WORSE?

"I learned a lot of ways to get high," Dimitri R. said of his experiences at a high-end adolescent rehab. He warns, "You're throwing your kid into a batch of kids who started using drugs young. I learned a lot of stuff I didn't know before. And I wound up using drugs later on with kids I met at rehab." While we touched on this topic in chapter 5 (Can a Bad Mix Create an Addict?), possible concerns about drug ideas "rubbing off" from one person to another should be greater with regard to impressionable young people than with adults. Experts refer to this phenomenon as "deviancy training," as addiction journalist Maia Szalavitz reported in her 2010 *Time* magazine article titled "Does Teen Drug Rehab Cure Addiction or Create It?" She wrote, "Many programs throw casual dabblers together with hard-core addicts and foster continuous group interaction. It tends to strengthen dysfunctional behavior by concentrating it, researchers say." She quoted Nora Volkow, MD, director of the National Institute on Drug Abuse (NIDA), as saying, "Just putting kids in group therapy actually promotes greater drug use."

Despite concerns voiced about group treatment for teens with drug and alcohol problems, the jury seems to be out about whether it's helpful or harmful. Ken Winters said, "Group therapy is commonly practiced in adolescent drug and alcohol programs, but there's still only minimal evidence one way or the other. The negative 'contagion effect' is a concern, and some youth may be more susceptible to this than others. It takes a good counselor to avoid it. Parents may want to ask about what training counselors have had to deal with the issue." Rather than mix young people with substance problems of varying degrees of severity together, rehabs may be wise to separate high- versus low-intensity users.

Gayle Dakof, PhD, is part of a research team at the University of Miami Center for Treatment Research on Adolescent Drug Abuse, where they've conducted studies comparing a family approach to group treatment for teens with substance problems. While they found that teens who took part in the family approach did better than those in the group intervention, both groups showed some improvement. And group treatment did not lead to a worsening of symptoms at discharge. Dr. Dakof concluded, "These studies at least do not support the claim that groups make kids worse."

A LEVEL OF DISCOMFORT

As with adults, confrontational approaches in addiction counseling for teens are considered passé and ineffective. Dr. Winters pointed to research showing that positive reinforcement, such as rewarding them, is more effective than punishment in helping young people change their behavior. At Fountain Centers in Albert Lea, Minnesota, I observed the psychologist/clinical director working with the staff on using positive reinforcement versus punitive measures for resistant behavior. There, young people were rewarded with leadership roles and titles including "junior rep" and "senior rep" that seemed to have a big impact. Dr. Winters noted, however, that confrontational interventions are still in effect at some teen addiction programs. For instance, not long ago, he observed a rehab session during which the counselor was quite confrontational, eliciting tears from a female client—the apparent goal of the counselor, who believed the approach was therapeutic.

While I witnessed few overtly confrontational episodes, there were a number of experiences that left me feeling uncomfortable and would have made me think twice had one of my own children experienced them in a counseling situation. (And I do have some experience both as a counselor, and as in the role of "counselee.") The following episodes at teen rehabs were unlike anything from any of my own mental health interactions:

- One program held a family session with a female teen and several family members who shared their feelings about her drug use and behavior in front of male peers. (A fair amount of personal information was divulged.)
- At several programs, individual teens' positive drug test results (meaning they had used drugs) were shared before the entire group, and the kids who tested positive were challenged about their results.
- Several young people read letters detailing the consequences of their drug use, sent by their family members and not seen by the teens before, out loud in front of their treatment groups.
- A young man who had some behavior issues was asked to stand up in front of his treatment group to say things he needed to be accountable for.

Knowing how sensitive teens are to peer opinions and relationships, my main discomfort was that these events took place in front of a group. If nothing else, parents and teens should be prepared for the fact that such practices go on. When I ran this list by several experts, one of them said, "I am not a fan of these approaches, nor do I see their clinical value." Another said, "In general, the scenarios do not appear to reflect the commitment to patient-centered care (including respect) that I would consider fundamental to an effective therapeutic relationship." Another said, "Strategies designed to make teens feel bad, embarrassed, or ashamed are not beneficial, may be detrimental, and don't help them to change. And challenging teens in front of a group is not likely to be a helpful strategy either." A tip for parents would be to ask if you could have regular communication with your child while in treatment so you can check in about specific activities that went on that week and how your child felt about them afterward. (It's up to the child to decide how much to share.) If the program declines, one expert said, "I would never send my child to a program that did not let me talk to him or her." He added, "Your child should be feeling better, not worse about himself or herself as a result of treatment. Teens should feel supported and understood by their counselors, not intimidated or frightened by them. Don't turn your child over to a program designed to 'scare them straight' or 'buy' a program that claims to 'break them down' in order to rebuild them."

The advice for regular parent-child communication assumes at least a somewhat healthy and trusted relationship, which is not always the case. Jim Steinhagen, MA, executive director of Hazelden's youth programs, said, "Because we view addiction as a family disease and treatment works most effectively when all family members are involved, we engage parents (or guardians) and siblings in the recovery process whenever possible. But there's no one-size-fits-all approach, and such involvement will always be based on individualized assessments and treatment plans. Unfortunately for some kids, dysfunctional family situations sometimes dictate that involving parents or guardians may not be appropriate at that immediate time." If that's the case, some other trusted adult could be the outside contact person for the child—for instance, a grandparent or social worker. And sometimes, child-parent interactions warrant supervision by rehab staff.

A WARNING ABOUT TOUGH-LOVE PROGRAMS

If you're considering a residential wilderness, military-style, emotional-growth, "boot camp," or troubled-teen treatment program, particularly for a young person who's been "a handful," think twice, because not everyone has had the positive experience Luke mentioned in his opening story. Such programs provide a range of services, including drug and alcohol treatment, military-style discipline, and psychological counseling for troubled youth who have a variety of substance, behavioral, and emotional problems. As a case in point, consider the aftercare plan established by Anne E.'s ex-husband for their fourteen-year-old son following a month-long stay for a marijuana use disorder at a traditional residential teen rehab. The plan included two months in a wilderness program, followed by three months in a "therapeutic boarding facility"—over Anne's objections and counter to the rehab's recommendation that her son be placed in a lower level of care. At the wilderness program, the boy was subjected to what many would consider psychological and physical harm. For instance, Anne reported that the staff used food and water restrictions to "motivate" children. And when they were "snow camping," there was no access to warm shelter or running water. Children were also sent on a "solo" experience—totally alone—where they were forced to camp for several days in isolation from the rest of the group. Communication with family was severely restricted—counselors reserved the right not to forward any family communications they deemed "inappropriate." And at the boarding facility, minors and adults were housed together. Anne added, "The judge involved in our case felt that my advocacy against these programs and my repeated requests for evidence-based treatments showed that I was in denial about my son's issues. At the end of all of this, my son is receiving absolutely no counseling even though he suffers from depression and anxiety."

I was shocked to learn that situations like the one Anne described were still going on in 2011, even though in 2006 Maia Szalavitz published her investigative book—*Help at Any Cost: How the Troubled-Teen*

Industry Cons Parents and Hurts Kids—exposing the practices of such programs. And in 2007 the Government Accounting Office (GAO) released a report concluding that there had been thousands of allegations of abuse at certain residential programs across the country for troubled youth such as boot camps and wilderness programs. Szalavitz states in *Help at Any Cost*, "There is no 'FDA' that approves behavioral programs that are safe and effective and rejects those that do harm or don't work. There is no requirement that psychotherapies—even for children—be proven safe and effective before they are marketed." In fact, a 2011 Medscape review article (www.medscape.com) on "conduct disorder"— a mental health problem marked by defiant and antisocial behaviors, such as lying, stealing, running away, and physical violence that may determine whether a child is sent to a boot camp—concluded that although such solutions may initially result in a good outcome, in the long term, the result is worse, "with higher rates of arrests and serious crimes found in boot camp graduates."

In its "Treatment e-book: Time to Get Help" for parents with kids having drug and alcohol problems, the Partnership at Drugfree.org (at drugfree.org) admonished, "Although you may have heard success stories or read about how great boot camps are, we strongly suggest you look very carefully into any boot camp or wilderness program before sending your teen for substance abuse treatment." They advise that if you're seriously considering one of these programs you should check with the Better Business Bureau for any complaints against it. They offer a host of questions to ask, including "Has a child ever died in their care and if so, why?"

The full GAO report can be found at http://www.gao.gov/new.items /d08146t.pdf.

The "Treatment e-book" can be found at http://timetogethelp.drugfree .org/.

The Building Bridges Initiative offers information and helpful tip sheets on residential programs for young people and their families at http://www.buildingbridges4youth.org/.

The Alliance for the Safe, Therapeutic, and Appropriate Use of Residential Treatment, or ASTART, is an organization that seeks to increase

awareness of problems in this industry, promote protections for children and families, and provide information about residential programs
and community-based alternatives so that parents and youth can make
the best choices at http://astart.fmhi.usf.edu/.

For questions parents and guardians should ask when considering
residential treatment programs for troubled teens go to www.ftc.gov/bcp
/edu/pubs/consumer/products/pro27.pdf.

HOW TEEN REHABS STACK UP NEXT TO "WHAT WORKS"

When I spoke with Dimitri R. about his many trips to rehab and how parents sometimes force kids to go there out of fear and concern, he responded, "Through all the kinds of rehab I went through, I'd say the
number-one thing I'd want if I were a parent would be to reconnect with
my kid. Kids need to talk with their parents about where they are. Parents
need to find out what their kids are about. Instead of programs trying to
get me to work the steps and throw these drastic lifestyle changes at me, I
wish I could have had more family therapy and talked with my parents
about why I was using, why I was upset. I kind of felt like a leper being in
rehab. I needed to get closer to my family." Dimitri hit the nail on the head
for what "works best" when kids have drug and alcohol problems.

Hot off the press, as I was writing this book, came two new reviews of
the scientific literature on adolescent substance use disorder treatment
suggesting that the most effective way to help teens is with family therapy,
based on the premise that the family carries the most profound and long-
lasting influence on adolescent development. Family therapy, which requires special training, typically includes the teen and at least one parent
or guardian.

One of the reports was the most comprehensive review of studies on
adolescent substance use disorder treatment ever, conducted by Vander-
bilt University's Emily Tanner-Smith, PhD, Sandra Wilson, PhD, and Mark
Lipsey, PhD, and expected to be published in the *Journal of Substance
Abuse Treatment* in late 2012. They completed what's known as a meta-

analysis—a statistical "study of studies," but only well-designed ones—to determine which approaches result in the best outcomes for teens with substance problems. Their review was limited to research conducted in outpatient settings because so few studies meeting their standards have been conducted in residential programs. The researchers concluded that the most effective approaches are family therapy, cognitive-behavioral therapy (CBT), and motivational interviewing alone or in combination with CBT. Bear in mind that, overall, there haven't been many studies on adolescent drug and alcohol treatment and that almost all of the studies reviewed were short-term studies, with outcomes measured just following the end of treatment. So it's not known how teens fared over time. (There was little or no information in either of the two new reports about twelve-step-based treatment because so little research on this met the standards for inclusion.)

How do programs stack up when it comes to using the most effective interventions? In a 2011 review article on adolescent drug and alcohol treatment published in *Current Psychiatry Reports*, Dr. Winters and colleagues listed key elements of effective teen rehab—including comprehensive assessment and treatment, family involvement, developmental appropriateness, and qualified staff—and stated that although national data are not available on community programs that treat teens, "We suspect that most programs fall short of offering all or nearly all of these services in their program." Over the course of the past ten years, several studies have suggested that adolescent rehabs do, indeed, fall short. The most recent national study of adolescent programming was the one mentioned earlier, in which 154 rehabs with separate programs for teens were surveyed about their services and practices. Researcher Hannah Knudsen, PhD, found that "educational programming was highly prevalent," and that fewer than six out of ten included families or caregivers in some of the nongroup sessions. Only about a third held counseling sessions with the family or caregiver alone, without the teen present. On the four-point scale used to measure family involvement in the treatment process, on average, programs scored about 2.2. More positively, nearly two-thirds of the programs said they treated both substance use and mental health disorders—a good thing given the number of teens who have both problems. While many programs said they used a cognitive-behavioral approach, most studies of CBT (as well as motivational interviewing) in adolescents have used one-on-one approaches, so it's not known how effective it is to use CBT in a group format, as is commonly done in teen treatment programs.

Susan Godley, PhD, at Chestnut Health Systems in Bloomington, Illinois, codeveloper of a respected research-based approach for teens called the Adolescent Community Reinforcement Approach, or A-CRA (see pages 293–94) thinks that the failure to use approaches shown to be most effective stems from "a strong belief by program staff that what they're already doing is effective because programs have histories, and staff have seen some individuals improve with the approaches they've used." She added, "In general, the work is difficult and there's a human tendency to resist change—it takes strong and consistent leadership in a program to change the therapeutic approach."

When it comes to the training of drug and alcohol counselors, Dr. Godley maintains that there's not enough emphasis on teaching research-based approaches and that it's more complicated to implement treatments like A-CRA and science-based family approaches the way they're supposed to be used—that is, with ongoing professional supervision and coaching by skilled supervisors. In reality, she said, when insurance companies and public funding pay for treatment, "they may say they value evidence-based treatment, but most do not investigate whether a provider is implementing such treatment appropriately—so the financial incentives for implementing research-based approaches are lacking." (Most of the places where A-CRA has been implemented have received federal grants for training and proper implementation.)

Dr. Godley thinks parents need to educate themselves and advocate for research-based treatment approaches. She said, "If a child had a physical medical problem like diabetes, wouldn't parents want the physician to treat their child based on the latest scientific approach? Parents should demand the same rigor in treatment for alcohol and drug problems." Although parent advocacy groups are somewhat in their infancy, probably because of the stigma associated with going public about one's child having this type of problem, Dr. Godley said that parents are beginning to speak out about the need for more and better treatment.

HOMING IN ON FAMILY THERAPY

Knowing that family therapy consistently ranks at the top of the list of effective interventions for teens with substance use disorders, I was surprised to learn that none of the programs I visited used the type of family therapy shown to be most effective in research studies—that is, individual (not group) family therapy sessions, held at least weekly. The family component during primary care at two residential rehabs consisted of parents coming on campus for four-day family programs that consisted of psychoeducational lectures, group sessions and exercises, and one individual family session. (At one place, local families had the option of ongoing family therapy available through the facility's mental health clinic.) Throughout the client's treatment stay, there was also regular phone contact between counselors and parents. Yet another residential program held five-hour group family education sessions on Saturdays and, for each young client, twice during a thirty-day stay a group session took place that included the client's family members, fellow clients, and addiction counselors. (A counselor at this program told me that no true family therapy took place.)

A psychologist formerly on the staff at a high-end rehab and who worked with all age groups there, said, "My take is that what happens at the psychoeducational family program at the rehab where I worked had healing or therapeutic value but that the amount of time for the entire family to participate together was brief, an hour or two. And I would question the credentials of the people doing the 'family therapy' during the family program—most of them, when I was there, did not have family therapy training. Those of us trained in family therapy are aware that effective family treatment typically occurs in a number of sessions over a period of weeks, months, or years. Typically, people who provide this have masters or doctoral degrees, as well as extensive training in a 'school' of family therapy. For the life of me, I do not understand why genuine family therapy provided by adequately trained therapists is not provided. I think the reasons have to do with money, territoriality, ignorance, and apathy."

Indeed, when I read about the family approaches with sound scientific backing, it became clear that they are *entire approaches* to treating substance problems, not short sessions that a counselor does here and there. To truly implement them would involve a paradigm shift in the way traditional rehabs go about treatment. For instance, while most rehabs do the bulk of their counseling in groups, I repeatedly came across this description of the various family approaches: "not designed to be conducted in a group setting, and has not been tested for use in a group setting."

I asked Gayle Dakof, PhD, who runs the highly regarded Multidimensional Family Therapy (MDFT) program (see pages 294–96) at the University of Miami's Center for Treatment Research on Adolescent Drug Abuse, if it surprised her that the adolescent programs I visited weren't doing state-of-the-art family therapy. She said, "No, I'm not surprised. This is especially true in the private sector—many privately funded adolescent programs are not implementing evidence-based treatments and evaluations. But these programs think they're doing a great job. Families mortgage their homes and borrow money from relatives to send their children to outpatient, day treatment, and residential programs, and often, they're not receiving the best treatment available. This upsets me very much." She added that most of the MDFT programs are in the public sector, where agencies get funding from their state or county governments. Dakof believes that "none of this will change until the insurers demand evidence-based practices. And I am not sure how this will happen, but perhaps one avenue is through activism from families."

Dr. Winters agreed that "getting parents and kids in the same arena, where a professional person is mediating," leads to better outcomes, but he also raised the question "How would a residential program do family therapy when a kid is away from home? It would be hard for a place like that to pull it off. Usually, family therapy is done in outpatient programs, when families live close by. If residential programs mandated family therapy, it would restrict families who would realistically be able to attend these programs. It's just not what they do in residential." (I have to say, however, that at high-end residential rehabs, it was clear that a number of the young people came from wealthy families—I was told just that by one administrator. My guess is that some parents would be able and willing to come from a distance for family therapy sessions. (See pages 294 and 295 for a description of how both MDFT and A-CRA *have* been implemented in residential rehabs.)

A MOTHER'S INVOLVEMENT IN
HER SON'S REHAB EXPERIENCE

Grace G., Luke G.'s mother, couldn't have been more involved in her son's rehab experience—at least as allowed by the format of a traditional twelve-step-based residential program. Knowing that he struggled with separation anxiety, Grace initially wrote to Luke every day, took it upon herself to visit him twice during his four-month stay, and (with her husband, who visited Luke separately once) also attended the rehab's psychoeducational program for families. Overall, Grace saw her role as "to let him know I was there for him, in whatever way he and the staff needed me to be, because they were the experts in this. I was not abandoning him." She added, "There was considerable communication—a weekly phone call from his wonderful counselor, who met with me each time I visited. He was instrumental in getting me to let go of Luke." She also spoke with Luke regularly.

When I asked Grace about family therapy during Luke's four months at the primary and extended-care programs, she said, "We had no family therapy other than one session during the parent program. If we'd been local, there might have been opportunities for us to schedule extra family therapy sessions, at additional cost, but since we were not local, there wasn't. When my husband and I visited on our own, therapy sessions were not suggested. We kept it strictly fun."

Grace then offered the following description of the parent program that she and her husband attended at about the midpoint of Luke's first twenty-eight days in rehab:

They offered an exceptional program that was held over a four-day period, and it was included in the cost of Luke's twenty-eight-day program (with the exception of our lodging and evening meals). It was really great to get to see Luke, but, of course, that really wasn't the intent. It was to educate us as parents about the disease of addiction and how we could deal with it as parents, as a family, and how we could cope as individuals and as a couple to keep our marriage healthy. It was absolutely a Godsend in terms of educating me about the realities of addiction and its impact on the person: body, mind, and spirit. I was quite shocked, literally shocked. In fact, I could barely make it through the first afternoon. The news, the data, and the stats were SO dismal, that when the program ended in the afternoon, I ran from the room to the car and wept. I just sobbed. My husband had to comfort me. I could barely cope with the awful reality of the ravages of this awful, horrible disease. The program educators pulled NO punches. The first day, they gave it to us completely straight, no sugar coating, the pure science, all the facts—right in order, from top to bottom. . . . Day one just about destroyed me.

The next three days were much better and I left buoyed by a sense of great hope. One of the pivotal facts was that emotional development stops when the young person becomes a user. So, if your kid became addicted at thirteen but is now twenty-two, emotionally/maturationally, he is still only thirteen. Well, that explains a lot of behavior and poor choices and decision-making by so-called adults, doesn't it? Additionally, the parent program emphasized the helpfulness of support groups like Al-Anon. As a result, I found an Al-Anon group near me and attended the entire remaining seven months Luke was in rehab [and extended care programs]. I got myself a sponsor and worked the twelve-step program just as Luke was doing. It only did me good. Finally, during the parent program we met with Luke's treatment team (individually)—the psychiatrist, psychologist, and counselor. All were helpful.

The only real family therapy I can recall took place during family week—it was a ninety-minute session with us, Luke, and his counselor. I remember that it was a really cathartic session, with an opportunity for Luke to share with us some really honest feedback about how he felt about needing to be in rehab and a chance for us to share feedback with him about his needing to be there. It was a difficult session, but it ended with a lot of hugs and all of us crying and reaffirming our love for one another and recommitting ourselves to our family unit and the importance of our family.

SITTING IN ON FAMILY PROGRAMS

I had the opportunity to observe the family component at two residential programs, one for adolescents, the other for adults. Grace G.'s experience is consistent with my observations at the adolescent program, where parents were told, "Addiction is a progressively pathological relationship with a mood-altering substance that negatively impacts most areas of one's life. Yet, despite an awareness of this negative impact, one is unable on his or her own to refrain from using." It was mentioned that addiction has a "predictable course and outcome," and reiterated, "Everyone progresses."

A typical course of events at such programs includes an educational lecture series, counselor-led group discussions of the material, and group activities—some just for family members and others also involving the client. Large group lecture themes included the disease of addiction, co-occurring psychological problems, continuing care possibilities (following primary treatment), how addiction impacts teen development, setting boundaries, the need for family members to take care of themselves, and introduction to Al-Anon.

When parents introduced themselves and talked about what they hoped to get out of the program, the pain in the room was palpable as they shared fears about the phone ringing in the middle of the night, a near-death overdose experience, and even relief at having their children out of the house and in rehab for a while. In smaller "process" groups, I could see the need parents had to connect and commiserate. (Haley B. said, "The parents' program when Logan was in rehab was very helpful, not just in terms of understanding what goes on in the psyche and the brain of someone who's an addict. It was support for the feeling of 'Gosh, what did we do wrong?'") Parents also shared their parenting war stories—taking away cell phones, cars, the Internet—and how none of those strategies stopped their children's aberrant behavior with drugs and alcohol. In "Dr. Phil" style, one counselor asked, "How's it working for you to focus on the addict? You need to take the lantern off them and put it on you." (He did not advocate tough love but instead let parents know that they needed to find their level of comfort with the process. At one point, he said to me privately, "These kids have a disease; if your child had cancer, you wouldn't expect rules and regulations to work.")

After parents shared how their repeated efforts to manage their kids' behavior didn't work, the message became one of acceptance of "powerlessness" and "there isn't much we can do to change the addict, but we can change ourselves and live happier lives." Al-Anon's first step was described as admitting your powerlessness over your child's disease and behavior and that your attempts to control it made your life unmanageable. Parents were urged to stop trying to keep their kids sober because that ball was now in the child's court, and to focus instead on limits and expectations within the household as well as on their own "recovery." In the end, I was left with a feeling that any sense of self-blame was lifted from parents' shoulders but that there was little more they could do for their kids, even though it was made clear that the chances of relapse were high.

JUST THE FACTS, PLEASE

As mentioned in chapters 5 and 6, it's just not true that addiction has a predictable course, nor that it gets progressively worse in all people. And it's particularly not true in adolescents. William Miller, who's been following the science on substance use disorders for decades, said, "'Everyone progresses' is one of those old chestnuts that's amply refuted by research. The hope is to scare people into abstaining for life. If the strategy fails, however (as it does most of the time), imagine how it leaves you feeling."

In reviewing Grace G.'s recap of her time at the adolescent family program, Dr. Susan Godley said, "I feel really sad for this mother, who had to experience the negative emotions she described. In meta-analyses, which examine outcomes of many studies, psychoeducational approaches are usually near the bottom in terms of effectiveness. And I haven't seen any data that support the efficacy of emphasizing such a dismal prognosis for young people. Besides, by the time they get to residential treatment, parents already are painfully aware of many consequences related to their children's use of drugs and alcohol. So I'm not sure why there's a need to put parents through this type of experience."

She added that, in contrast to the Al-Anon message that there's nothing a parent can do to change the addict, "There *are* ways that parents can react to their youths' behavior that might be more helpful than others." For example, with the CRAFT approach described in chapter 4, parents would be taught how to reward a teen for desirable behaviors like not using and to minimize friction in the household by ignoring rather than nagging or blaming, as well as to take care of themselves. Godley added that the approach described by Grace "seems more typical of many programs that have just slightly tweaked the traditional twelve-step approach that they have always used with adults and relabeled it as an adolescent program—instead of implementing an evidence-based approach for adolescents that's been shown to be effective." Another concern is that although Al-Anon seemed to be of value to Grace, it's again an example of a rehab offering a one-size-fits-all approach that won't resonate with all parents.

It turns out that not only has CRAFT been shown to be helpful to parents in engaging their resistant teens in treatment, but it has now been pilot tested for teens who are already in recovery programs. The results were not available at this writing; however, based on what appear to be promising findings, CRAFT strategies have replaced the psychoeducational parent program at a residential adolescent drug and alcohol rehab at Chestnut Health Systems, which is the organization for which Dr. Godley works.

What about the notion that active addiction sets an adolescent "back in time" psychologically? Another father who attended the same program I did, said, "I remember vividly this information being conveyed at the family program and elsewhere. My daughter often reflects on this very point, that she is developmentally delayed for each year as a user with an addiction." But is *this* true? Addiction psychiatrist Mark Willenbring said, "I've found that it holds some validity, in that there are developmental landmarks that are not accomplished while someone is addicted—or ill with something else, for that matter. So it's safe to say that a young person with severe addiction has to catch up in some ways when it comes to psychological, emotional, and social development, when he or she stops using. As for scientific evidence, there's only preliminary research examining the effect of especially heavy drinking on brain development. My concern is when these things are presented as scientific facts." Dr. Sarah Feldstein-Ewing, who studies the relationship between what happens in the brain and how adolescents respond to addiction treatment, agrees that there's something happening in the brain, but contends that it is likely to be more of a chicken-and-egg question, meaning the brain differences may very well be there before a teen starts using. She added, "There are no data supporting the common claim in the world of adolescent addiction treatment that a person with a substance use disorder is emotionally stuck at a certain age."

WHAT'S IN A NAME? THE ADDICT LABEL

Thayer A., who went to a residential youth rehab at the age of twenty-one, and later to several adult programs, talked about the "culture of treatment" in which people introduce themselves according to their labels. At one place where she was also treated for an eating disorder, she said, "My list got longer there. I remember saying, 'Hi, I'm Thayer, and I'm an anorexic, bulimic, alcoholic, drug addict.' It was really hard, and some days I didn't go to group because of it." When I asked if she was told to use these monikers or if clients just assumed the habit from others in treatment, she replied, "I think it's a little script people pick up."

I wondered about the impact this might have on adolescents as I observed a ninety-minute group session at a youth residential program in which a boy introduced himself as "an addict" every single time he spoke—about ten times. Afterward, when I asked his counselor why this was done, she replied, "It's to remind them of why they're here." A psychologist at a non-twelve-step program thinks it hurt can young people "to frame their identity around whether you're an addict or not. After a lot of time in traditional rehab and twelve-step groups, they may not get exposure to other ways young people get a sense of identity—for instance, being a student." (Although twelve-step meetings typically open with attendees' going around the room introducing themselves by their first names, followed by "and I'm an alcoholic" or "an addict," labeling yourself this way is not required.)

Paul Hokemeyer, JD, PhD, a New York City marriage and family therapist and addiction specialist affiliated with Caron Treatment Centers, said, "While I agree that it's a bad idea to dehumanize people by attaching labels to them, in my experience, putting a label on conditions—not the person—enables them to contain the seemingly overwhelming nature of the disease. In my work, I try to always put the person first or separate the person from her illness by using language such as "Do you think you suffer from alcoholism?" or "Has alcohol caused problems in your life?" I do, however, slip (quite frequently) and refer to people as alcoholics. While there's certainly stigma attached to the label of alcoholic, I have found that people experience a great sense of relief by having a professional name the state of despair and chaos that has plagued their lives. When conveyed in the context of a trusting and respectful relationship, these labels do much more good than harm."

While the intent is partly the opposite, several studies suggest that the "disease" label may actually further stigmatize people with mental health issues such as drug and alcohol problems. In a 2010 study published in the *American Journal of Psychiatry* that attempted to determine whether public health stigma reduction efforts have paid off, researchers compared the levels of stigma associated with alcohol addiction, schizophrenia, and major depression in 1996 with those in 2006 and found that overall, "No significant decrease was reported in any indicator of stigma, and levels remained high." Of the 630 people surveyed for their views on alcoholism, the percentage who believed it was a brain disorder increased from 38 percent to 47 percent, but that shift was not linked with a decrease in stigma. To the contrary, the percentage of people who thought alcoholism was linked with "bad character" actually increased significantly, from 49 percent to 65 percent, over that time period.

Some adolescent programs steer away from using labels. Mike Panico, MS, LPC, director of the Seven Challenges program at Providence Service Corporation in Tucson, Arizona, said, "We don't use the word 'addiction' at all. Defining someone in terms of their problem is a great injustice." He went on to tell me about an incident with an intern who was working with a woman whose son had a fairly serious substance problem. The woman was ambivalent about the severity of her son's problem, and the intern said, "Your son is an addict, and he has to come to terms with this first." The woman became defensive and Mike stepped in "to act as referee," at which point the boy asked to go to the bathroom, and then went out the window, never again to be seen by the program. Mike said, "When you try to get people to admit to having a problem, they're defensive. We're talking adolescents—they've been called terrible names their whole lives—losers, druggies. We want them to look at their strengths. You don't have to admit to having a problem to be successful here. It frees them up. They need to believe in themselves to be successful. And I think the labeling interferes with that."

ELIZABETH B.'S STORY: THE SEVEN CHALLENGES WAY

By the age of seventeen, Elizabeth B. could have written a book about her drug and rehab experiences. She wanted me to tell her story in the hope that it will help other young people. With her mother on meth and knowing that her "grandma died on meth," Elizabeth vowed she'd never go that route. But by the time she was fifteen, she was using marijuana, pills, and cocaine. After winding up in a court-mandated outpatient program, she told herself she was going to stop but then started abusing painkillers, which her mom was using and selling. Next, she was sent to a residential rehab in another state, where she tried to get high by snorting medications that were prescribed to her. When she got into a fight with another girl, she was kicked out and sent to a behavioral hospital for youth with mental problems. She went there seven times altogether. Of those stays, she told me, "A lot of the times I was sent there because of me doing stuff caused by drugs but I didn't say why—stuff like attempting suicide and being promiscuous. They never drug-tested me."

In between stints in the mental hospital, Elizabeth would live in foster homes, then run away. As a runaway, she said, "I'd use every drug in the book. But meth was my drug of choice—I was using it, selling it. The things I could tell you, you wouldn't even think are human." Eventually, she got arrested for being on the run and was put into a detox facility and then a hospital. From there, she said, "I made the decision that I would never do it again. I realized how close I came and how lucky I am to be here."

Her most recent foster parents sent Elizabeth to an outpatient program for teens with drug and alcohol problems called the Seven Challenges. When I spoke to her, at seventeen she had just completed the program. (While it takes most kids three months, she was in the program for six months.) Initially, she went three afternoons a week for three hours each time, participating in group counseling, with about seven to nine kids per group. On Friday evenings, they did something fun, like eat at McDonalds, go to the movies, or go rock climbing. Elizabeth said that every **teen was assigned** a counselor who "checks in with you now and then **and who you talk to** when you need them." After graduating from the program, she said, "You meet with your counselor once a week—to tell her any concerns, how you're doing and feeling, regardless of whether you're sober. There are still feelings about using, and we talk about them. And I still have journals to do, which I go over with my counselor."

She explained how the Seven Challenges approach compared to others: "At other programs, we did the twelve steps. At one rehab, I went to all their groups and learned the Serenity Prayer. But I didn't pay attention. I tried talking to them once and they drug-tested me. No one wants to talk to someone who gets them in trouble. The message was, 'Don't do drugs, it's bad for you.' It doesn't work when adults tell you it's bad. We all know it's bad. At the Seven Challenges, they don't tell you, 'You need to stop using.' They help you figure that out for yourself. And if a teen does use, it's not the end of the world. At one point, I smoked a joint and they didn't freak out like at previous facilities, where they'll drop you or you'll go to detention for a week."

Elizabeth concluded, "It's easier to stay sober than it ever was before. Now, I think through, 'Oh, it won't hurt this time.' I realize that that's where use will start. The Seven Challenges really makes you realize what to look for right before you're falling. They help you think through why you're doing what you're doing. You have to want to change for yourself, and the Seven Challenges helps you do that."

CONSUMER QUESTIONS FOR CHECKING OUT YOUTH PROGRAMS

The list is long—you may want to pick and choose according to your top concerns—but here are some specific questions to consider when checking out drug and alcohol treatment programs for an adolescent or young adult. (Some of these questions are not relevant for an outpatient program.)

- How will you assess my child's substance problem? What tools will you use, and who will be doing the assessment? What will you do with the information—for instance, if you do psychological testing, how are those test results used?
- How is your program designed to meet the unique needs of adolescents and/or young adults? What are some of the therapies you use that are evidence based, and how are they tailored to meet the needs of young people?
- What are the qualifications of the counselors who will spend the most time with my child? Do they have special training in adolescent development? How are these counselors supervised, and by whom? (They should receive regular supervision by more experienced staff. For more on staff issues, see chapter 4.)
- How does your program address co-occurring psychological problems in young people?

- What type of professionals provide medical and psychiatric care? What is their availability? How often do they see the clients? Is there emergency coverage?
- Can the staff/program manage all of my child's medications, if necessary? What is your philosophy about the use of psychiatric medications? Is the staff knowledgeable about and willing to consider the use of medication that may help treat addiction?
- How would you describe your program philosophy and your overall approach to treatment—for instance, is it twelve-step-based, cognitive-behavioral, motivational, or family-based? About what percentage of time do you spend in each area?
- Are counselors free to do their own thing or do they follow a curriculum? Has the curriculum been tested in any studies?
- What is your client-to-staff ratio? (The lower the better.)
- What's the schedule like—how much of the time is structured lectures versus group counseling versus individual counseling? How much free time do kids have and what do kids do during that time?
- How is the family involved in the treatment process and what is the family component of your program? For instance, does it consist of family therapy or education? Is counseling group or individual? What special training does your staff have in family counseling?
- What opportunities do you provide for recreation, exercise, and learning to have fun as a sober person?
- What are your program's rules and regulations and what are the consequences for violating them? How does the program discipline young people? (How do you and your child feel about these aspects of treatment and how will these rules help your son or daughter negotiate the real world?)
- How are young people involved in decisions about their treatment? What kinds of choices do they have? To what extent are they supported in making their own choices and decisions?
- For residential treatment, do young people who are still in secondary school attend classes in the local community, or does the rehab

offer on-site classes with credits that can be transferred to the student's home school?

- Do you offer separate, single-sex treatment? How do you address the unique needs of males versus females? (Single-sex group sessions allow for discussion of issues that might be difficult to address in co-ed groups.)
- Do you separate youth within your program in other ways, for instance, according to age, severity of drug and alcohol problems, or according to co-occurring mental health issues? If so, how does that impact programming?
- What precautions do you take to keep kids with more severe drug and alcohol problems from having a negative influence on those with less severe problems?
- How do you handle relapse prevention and prepare clients for what to do if they use again?
- What happens if a client uses drugs or alcohol during treatment?
- How does your program or staff address the unique needs of minority groups, including youths who are not heterosexual?
- How much will my child be expected to share in front of the group, for example, with impact/cost letters? What is your philosophy about confrontation?
- Do clients have assignments, and, if so, what are they and who goes over them with the young person?
- How much time do young people spend with counselor assistants/ technicians, what is their training, and what is their role?
- How will you communicate with us and how often?
- Can I contact my child freely by phone or e-mail when I want to and can my child contact me the same way when he or she wants to?
- Can my child switch counselors if there's a legitimate need, concern, or conflict? What do clients do if they feel they are being treated unfairly or if they find something to be unhelpful? Whom do they approach with their concerns?

- How will your program follow up with my child following completion of treatment and how is continuing care addressed? Do plans include aftercare or alumni groups/activities, checkups at regular intervals, and/or referral to community resources such as mental health, employment, education, social, and/or medical services?
- If you connect young people with twelve-step meetings, how does that process occur and how do you ensure their safety?
- How will my child's progress in treatment be measured and how will that feedback be communicated? (For instance, does the program report on behavior change? Is drug testing routine?)
- What factors determine length of treatment and how will it be communicated to our child and us (when appropriate) that treatment goals have been met and that he or she has successfully completed treatment? (Depending on a teen's unique needs, the recommended length and intensity of treatment will vary widely.)
- What evidence do you have that your program is effective? Why will this program be a good fit for my teenager?

You can ask if the program has conducted any studies measuring its success, but given that few places have, another way to assess program effectiveness is to ask about dropout rates; keeping teens in treatment is related to better outcomes. Good questions to ask are about how many young people drop out of treatment, how long participants typically stay, how many actually complete the program, and if there's a waiting list. According to Drug Strategies, "Even without formal evaluations, programs should be able to provide accurate information on client retention and completion." Dr. Kelly notes that nationally about half of people don't complete treatment, so if a program's completion rate is less than that, it may be an indicator of lower quality. However, you have to take into account the kinds of clients the program treats. For instance, if a high proportion of referrals come from the criminal-justice system, completion rates may be higher simply because clients are forced to remain in treatment.

RESOURCES

- The Partnership at DrugFree.org is a resource to help parents and caregivers of teens and young adults with issues related to substance use disorder prevention, treatment, and recovery: www.drugfree .org.
- SAMHSA's Substance Abuse Treatment Facility Locator can be used to narrow down a search for programs serving teens. (After clicking on a state and entering an address or zip code, choose "select services" to find adolescent facilities.) Note that these programs are just listings, not recommendations or endorsements by SAMHSA: http://findtreatment.samhsa.gov/TreatmentLocator/faces/quickSearch .jspx
- The California Evidence-Based Clearinghouse for Child Welfare (CEBC)—http://www.cebc4cw.org/topic/substance-abuse-treatment -adolescent/—lists and rates various approaches for treatment according to supporting scientific evidence and provides detailed information about each one, including training and supervision that professionals should have to implement each approach.

ADOLESCENT PROGRAMS WITH RESEARCH BACKING

The Adolescent Community Reinforcement Approach (A-CRA) was adapted from the well-researched, longstanding Community Reinforcement Approach for adults. (See chapter 4.) As with the adult version, A-CRA co-developer and researcher Dr. Susan Godley said, "The goal of treatment is to help teens learn how to have a worthwhile life that's fun without having to use alcohol or drugs." She explained that A-CRA therapists work with young people individually, understanding that they keep using because they like something about it—for instance, how it helps them escape, that they are hanging out with their friends while using, or that it helps them "chill out." A-CRA therapists help them identify these reinforcers for substance use and then learn how to engage in more positive activities that have similar results. Therapists also help young people develop friendships and activities more conducive to having an alcohol- and drug-free life.

Recognizing the important role of parents, at least four A-CRA sessions involve them—two with parents alone and two including parents and the teen—with an emphasis on skills such as more effective communication and problem solving. A-CRA therapists also help adolescents identify areas of their lives they may want to improve that have nothing to do with their alcohol or drug use. One young woman who participated in A-CRA said, "I learned a lot of skills that can help me in life in general. It's not just about not using drugs; it's about changing your life for the better."

A-CRA usually involves a one-on-one approach, but parts of the treatment can be used in a group format. Sessions are scheduled once a week for fifty to ninety minutes, and the program usually lasts for three months. Although some therapists have a bachelor's degree, the majority have a master's in a mental health–related profession, and a training and certification process is required to call yourself an A-CRA therapist or provider. Like the adult model, the adolescent model has been found effective in randomized clinical trials. Long-term follow-up of young people who participated in A-CRA in these studies showed that they were equally or more likely to decrease their use of alcohol or drugs than young people who participated in other, more expensive treatments. A-CRA has also been shown to be among the best approaches designed for reducing symptoms of co-occurring mental health disorders, such as anxiety and depression, in adolescents with substance use disorders. (Dr. Godley estimates that the client cost for completing the fourteen outpatient sessions involved in A-CRA treatment is about $2,000.)

Although usually an outpatient approach, A-CRA has been implemented in residential rehabs, where teens can then practice new skills at different times of the day with staff and fellow residents. In residential settings, A-CRA has helped staff reward kids for positive behavior rather than punish them for undesirable actions.

When funding is available, a separate continuing care component is built into the program that allows clinicians to work with teens and their families in home and community settings to accomplish such goals as going back to school, getting a GED, learning skills to seek employment, and linking with mental health services. Dr. Godley added, "This may also include twelve-step or other mutual help meetings in the community—if there are adolescent-appropriate groups available and a teen has an interest in attending them. However, we know from research that not all adolescents want to go to these groups, so no one recommendation fits all." Other possibilities might be encouraging participation in enjoyable activities that put teens in contact with nonusing peers, such as sports teams, paying or volunteer jobs, or bodybuilding.

To learn more about A-CRA, go to www.chestnut.org/li/acra-acc. To find out if there's a location near you that's using A-CRA, contact Susan H. Godley, PhD, at Chestnut Health Systems; sgodley@chestnut.org; (309) 451-7802.

Multidimensional Family Therapy (MDFT), in a nutshell, is a comprehensive program for adolescents who abuse drugs and alcohol and for teens who also have mental or behavioral disorders. Working with the individual youth and his or her family, MDFT helps the young person develop and improve coping and problem-solving skills; work on regulating emotions and social competence; and develop alternatives to substance use and delinquency. For parents, the focus is on improving parental teamwork and parenting practices, decreasing family conflict, developing better family communication, and self-care. (There's also a component of the program to help parents who have problems with drugs or alcohol or have mental health issues.) The mix of sessions is about 40 percent youth, 20 percent parent, and 40 percent family, with phone calls between sessions. Extra family sessions with school, juvenile justice, and child welfare personnel may also occur. Typically, MDFT takes place in a series of weekly or twice-weekly sixty- to ninety-minute sessions over the course of three to six months. Therapists must have at least a master's degree in counseling, mental health, family therapy, social work, or a related discipline. Numerous well-designed studies, including randomized controlled trials, support the use of MDFT. According to Gayle Dakof, one of the main researchers for this approach, an intensive training program leads to certification in MDFT, and programs that have gone through it are the only ones that can honestly claim that they have an MDFT program.

Although MDFT is not meant to be used in a group setting, Dr. Dakof explained, "We have been collaborating with folks in the state of Connecticut to develop and pilot two MDFT residential programs, and I am happy to report that these programs, although new, have done very well. So we hope to do some research in this setting and perhaps do more dissemination." Knowing that the teens in this study were in the residential program for four months and that residential rehabs are often far from home, I wondered about the logistics of having parents involved to the extent that MDFT requires. Dr. Dakof replied, "The MDFT residential programs in Connecticut are close enough to home that parents can come to the facility for weekly family sessions, and after the first thirty days, the teens begin getting day and weekend home passes. Therapists often go to the homes and conduct family sessions on the weekends." She added, "What we'd like to see is a revolution in private substance abuse treatment. I think the idea of shipping youth to programs far from home is ridiculous, and there is no science to show that these programs are effective. The whole idea of sending teens far away from home is a very anti-MDFT concept."

When I asked Dr. Dakof about the continuing care component of MDFT after the program ends, she replied, "Remarkably the MDFT follow-up studies indicate that the treatment effects last for up to two to four years, which is as far out as our studies have gone, but we all know there is a need for continuing care. In the MDFT model, supports might include enrollment in a good school or vocational program, involvement in healthy social activities, employment, and twelve-step meetings for youth. We incorporate some of the twelve-step philosophy in our treatment, and, when it seems appropriate, we encourage teens and parents to go to meetings, especially teen-focused meetings, since young people generally do not like being with the old folks. We don't force it and don't recommend it for everyone. If they go a couple of times and don't like it, then we drop it." To locate MDFT programs that use certified therapists, contact Gayle Dakof at gdakof@med.miami.edu; (305) 243-3656. In Connecticut:

Robyn Anderson at randerson@abhct.com; (860) 638-5302. In Riverside County, California: Craig Lambdin at craiglambdin@mfirecovery.com; (951) 683-6956.

The Seven Challenges is unlike twelve-step programs that immediately require abstinence because, according to program materials, it "starts where youth 'are at' (usually resistant and reluctant to change), not where adults wish they might be or where young people often pretend to be." Robert Schwebel, PhD, a psychologist who studied under the famous child psychologist Jean Piaget, set out to develop a more developmentally appropriate approach for teens than the traditional model, which, he said, tries "to teach them to be drug- and alcohol-free before they've decided they want to be. But they really don't think their lives will be better without drugs and alcohol." Although most teens are far from ready to quit using, many are under intense pressure to abstain—from probation officers, courts, school, or other authorities. Dr. Schwebel explained, "In the Seven Challenges, these circumstances are brought to the attention of youth, and we try to help them identify an 'impulse to quit' that will at least temporarily help them succeed. While we support abstinence, we know it's usually a Band-Aid solution in response to pressures, and there is much work to be done before teens will arrive at their own fully informed decision about drugs."

The "challenges" include having teens talk honestly about themselves, alcohol, and other drugs; look at what they like about using and why they're using; examine the impact of drugs and alcohol on their lives; consider their responsibility and the responsibility of others for their problems; think about where they're headed, where they want to go, and what they want to accomplish; make thoughtful decisions about their lives and how use of substances plays a role in that; and follow through on those decisions. Dr. Schwebel pointed out that traditional approaches to teen drug and alcohol treatment usually play up the negative aspects of use, and young people subsequently "are surprised by their desires to use and unprepared to cope with them." Then, when kids use again, there's a tendency to say, "More treatment is necessary" rather than "maybe we didn't do a very good job in the first place." However, because the Seven Challenges acknowledges the "benefits" of drug and alcohol use and addresses them with teens, they're better prepared to handle urges to use. The program also gives kids tools for solving problems that make them want to abuse substances. Sometimes, family participation is integrated into sessions. In addition to participating in counseling sessions, youth write in a set of nine Seven Challenges journals, and counselors and youth engage in a written process called "supportive journaling." (Because "kids are not going to find Seven Challenges meetings in the community," the director of one program that's had good results with the Seven Challenges said, they try to connect kids with twelve-step meetings and sponsors when they leave their program.)

The program has been used in approximately thirty-five states by more than three hundred agencies and organizations and implemented in settings ranging from outpatient programs to residential rehabs, drug courts, and schools. Independent studies funded by SAMHSA's Center for Substance Abuse Treatment and published in peer-reviewed journals showed that the Seven Challenges program significantly decreased adolescent substance use and improved their overall mental health status.

Mike Panico said, "Something magical happens when you stop telling kids what to do. The old, traditional model was to break kids down, show them ninety in ninety. And kids would say what they want us to hear to get out. With Seven Challenges, we honor them to make their own decisions. We don't drug-test kids, and most come in and tell us when they use. They know we're on their side—not there to be informants. Most kids seem to like groups and keep coming, and many keep extending times past the minimum we'd require." (The vast majority of participants are supported by public funds.)

Panico added that the toughest part of his job is addressing the concerns of other professionals who feel that teens must be drug free immediately upon entering treatment. He said, "I often have to deal with probation officers, teachers, and counselors who don't understand that everyone should not have to go to a 'rehab'; change is a process, and good counseling (based in integrity and relationships) takes time."

Organizations that provide the Seven Challenges must be licensed, which requires staff training and annual site visits from the Seven Challenges' clinical support team to ensure the program is being implemented in the way it was designed. To locate a program, contact the director of program services, Sharon Conner, who can be reached at (520) 405-4559 or at sconner@sevenchallenges.com.

For more information, go to www.sevenchallenges.com.

CHAPTER EIGHT

WHEN IT'S NOT "JUST"
A DRUG AND ALCOHOL PROBLEM

FROM DEPRESSION TO SEX ADDICTION

Addiction and mental health problems commonly go hand in hand. When someone has both going on at the same time—for instance, a serious drinking problem along with depression—it's said to be a co-occurring disorder or "dual diagnosis." People struggling with two demons are not likely to do well if they go to rehabs that neglect the "psych" component, and the same goes for such people in mental health settings not prepared to treat substance use disorders. As things stand, both rehab scenarios are the case more often than not, and the client often becomes the casualty of separate systems of care. While lip service abounds about the need to treat two problems when they occur together, big concerns exist about the adequacy of commonly available treatment in terms of what that treatment should be, who's providing the care, and what intervention should be provided and when. On the bright side, over the past decade, a significant nationwide effort has gotten under way to improve help for people with co-occurring substance use and psychiatric disorders.

ROSE T.'S STORY OF BACK AND FORTH
BETWEEN TWO SYSTEMS

When Rose T. and I first communicated, she affirmed, "I have alcoholism and bipolar disorder and am working hard at controlling both. I am not drinking, and I am taking my medication. I have wonderful doctors, plus supportive friends and family. I am not ashamed and will not be ashamed. But damn, sometimes this shit leaves me feeling pretty beaten down." Within that year, Rose T. had been to an outpatient program that, in her words, "focused on mental health issues and just touched on addiction," then had a stay on an inpatient psychiatric ward, followed by attendance at an intensive outpatient addiction program. All of this was to deal with what she refers to as her "two diseases" or "dual diagnoses." As I was finishing up the book in 2012, she was well into her third year of sobriety.

Rose's alcoholic father refused to admit he had a problem and Rose swore that she wouldn't follow in his footsteps. She kept her vow until she was nineteen, when she had her first drink. She described her initial experience this way: "I drank until I vomited and then passed out because my mind had never felt such relief. I remember thinking that my dad was really on to something. I was holding on to a lot of pain, and I realize now that the mood swings I'd been dealing with were part of bipolar disorder that had yet to be diagnosed." (Bipolar disorder, which used to be called manic depression, is in the category of mental health problems called mood disorders and is characterized by extreme mood fluctuations—from euphoria to severe depression—interspersed with times when mood is normal. When one's mood is elevated, it's considered a "manic" phase.)

From then on, Rose drank for the sole purpose of getting drunk and by the time she turned twenty-one, drinking had become a daily habit. At twenty-three, she said, "I became a sideshow. I'd built up such a tolerance that I could out-drink men twice my size." Looking back, she realizes that alcohol helped her deal with her as-yet undiagnosed bipolar disorder by calming her racing thoughts and making sleep come more easily. The psychiatrist she'd been seeing for anxiety and depression was aware that she had an alcohol problem, but Rose hadn't been forthright with him about how much she was drinking. Therefore, he unwittingly prescribed antidepressants at levels adjusted according to the huge amount of alcohol she was regularly consuming.

After one particularly rough evening, Rose asked her psychiatrist for a referral to an outpatient program that was "dual diagnosis." She found the staff to be "warm, welcoming, and comforting," but she said she couldn't relate to most of the patients "because the focus was primarily on mental health issues." She added, "They did not directly address the addiction in group therapy—they directed me to AA." Within six months of completing the program, she was drinking again.

At this point, Rose's situation was a complicated mix of undiagnosed bipolar disorder and a lack of recognition about the severity of her alcohol problem. And after her time at the outpatient program, both proceeded unchecked. She said, "Not having the right diagnosis left me self-medicating in the way I knew how. I would be awake for days at a time and would drink until I passed out just to get some sleep. Had the mania been properly diagnosed and treated, I may not have kept drinking to bring myself down." Although she believes she initially drank to dull her emotional pain and to calm her frequent mood swings, she said, "By the end of my twenty-fourth year, I was drinking because I didn't know how not to. Without a drink, I was shaky, spacey, and absolutely physically and emotionally miserable." On her last night with alcohol, she had two drinks on the way home from work, two bottles of wine once she got there, and then spent more than $100 buying herself drinks at a bar. She said, "When last call came, I was still standing, talking, walking, and hell-bent on driving myself home. I woke up the next morning having blacked out for the very first time and with no memory of anything after leaving the bar. I was so frightened that I went to the emergency room."

When she arrived at the ER of the same medical facility where she'd attended the first outpatient program, she was in such terrible physical condition that she "never saw the waiting room." She remembered, "I was in the middle of a manic episode, with my heart rate and blood pressure off the charts. Having lost forty pounds, I was malnourished, dehydrated, and vomited up anything I tried to consume. I couldn't stop shaking for anything, and my once-sharp mind was in a fog. I'll never forget the looks on the faces of the nurses—in triage, they gave me an IV and a number of drugs, then pushed me right through to a bed to be seen immediately." Rose was placed in a psychiatric ward, where, she said, "they did a pretty intense series of interviews, reviewed my records, and spoke with my psychiatrist. That's when they changed my diagnosis to bipolar disorder, started me on lithium for that, and began decreasing my antidepressants." A week of hospitalization was needed to deal with alcohol withdrawal and her newly diagnosed bipolar disorder.

Upon discharge, it was decided that Rose needed to be in an intensive outpatient program (IOP) that focused solely on addiction because they "couldn't deal with the effects of the bipolar disorder until I was sober." So Rose was referred to an IOP at a different facility, one she described as "a place where all of the patients were being treated for addiction." She found she could relate better to the people in this program and preferred its open discussion format to the prescribed curriculum of the other program. Of her overall positive experience, she said, "Group therapy was great for me during recovery, because it played a huge role in teaching me that I was sick, and not just making bad choices. It helped me to understand that I wasn't alone."

Although the IOP did not specialize in treating dual-diagnosis clients, they offered a weekly one-hour group for people with co-occurring mental health problems that Rose described as "not really helpful at all." She added, "The groups were run as an open discussion, which was helpful when everyone was on the same page, but when you have a group of addicts who are each dealing with a different mental health diagnosis, the discussion just kind of turns into a mess. It was led by one of the counselors at the program, and I think it was meant more to be supportive and let us know that we were not alone than to actually help with a diagnosis or treatment." All in all, most of her mental health care occurred outside of the addiction treatment program, where she saw her psychiatrist and another therapist two to three times a week. When I asked about how all this was financed, Rose explained that she had health insurance, but her co-pay for each program admission was about $900, plus her weekly visits to mental health professionals had co-pays. She also had a large deductible for addiction and mental health care, and she was out of work for periods of time while she was getting better. All together, she said, "I'll probably be paying this off for years to come."

When the IOP ended, Rose got involved with a local Women for Sobriety (WFS) group and its online community and also saw a counselor, who helped her recognize that her manic symptoms (sleeplessness and the racing thoughts) could be triggers for drinking. As she approached her third year of sobriety, Rose no longer felt the need to be involved in WFS, explaining, "I think that's the beauty of the program—it's not *meant* to be used for life, like AA. But it's always there." With her counselor no longer in the picture, she still saw her psychiatrist regularly and was happy to declare, "My treatment is going really well and I'm feeling *great*."

HOW TWO SYSTEMS FALL SHORT

Rose's story exemplifies the all too common back-and-forth between two systems that aren't well prepared to handle the many people who have both substance use disorders and mental health problems—at a cost to these individuals timewise, emotionally, and financially. In short, we have two systems that tend to treat addiction and mental health problems separately, and people in both fields often lack adequate training to treat the other problem. Of the first program Rose attended, the one that was "dual diagnosis," she said, "I don't know if they were trained to deal with addiction, but all they ever did was give patients AA fliers. It was only AA and NA. And I was not set up with proper aftercare for addiction." And because the IOP she went to next, for addiction, made no claims about treating mental illness, it seems somewhat surprising that that's where Rose got referred by a psychiatric unit that had just diagnosed her bipolar disorder. Granted, she needed to get sober, but Rose was disappointed in their lack of attention to the mental illness side of things. She explained, "The professionals at the IOP were trained *only* in addictions. I think that having a trained psychiatrist—even if just to talk to, even if he or she didn't prescribe medication, would have made a huge difference. They asked us about our appointments outside of the program but didn't provide any coordination of the care. It felt unfair that I had to be the liaison between the IOP and my psychiatrist. I understood that it had to be done, and so I did it."

How did it come to be that two problems so commonly experienced together are so often treated in two different systems of care that are frequently in different locations? Historically, the limited care that existed for people with addictions was housed within the mental health system. For instance, well into the 1900s, if someone with a serious alcohol problem received any care at all, it was likely to be at a place like a psychiatric asylum or sanatorium. Later in the twentieth century, alcohol treatment parted ways from mental health care with the establishment of separate programs, proliferation of addiction self-help groups, and creation of two government organizations for the study of alcohol and drug problems—the National Institute on Alcohol Abuse and Alcoholism (NIAAA) and the National Institute on Drug Abuse (NIDA)—that are separate still from the National Institute of Mental Health. The services grew further apart when separate public systems of care for each problem became largely funded by different federal government block grants.

Since addiction treatment and mental health services are often in different locations, people in need of services often have to pick one or the other and then wind up going back and forth between the two systems and even coordinating their own care, as Rose did. Because this can be especially difficult for people impaired by substance use or suffering from mental health problems, the result often is lack of follow-through or falling through the cracks for either or both problems.

To make matters worse, "it tells people nothing when programs say they are 'co-occurring' or 'dual diagnosis'—we really don't know what programs mean when they call themselves this," said Dartmouth Medical School's Mark McGovern, PhD, a psychologist and leading expert on co-occurring disorders who is spearheading a national effort to improve care for people with both addictions and mental disorders. He said, "Neither the substance abuse treatment system nor our mental health system are prepared to address both issues. It's a mess for the consumer. I get four to five personal calls or e-mails each week from people asking about programs that address co-occurring disorders, and they usually have tales of woe." (A problem I discovered is that when you go to Web sites or check state listings of rehabs, there are inconsistencies between the way programs describe their services for co-occurring disorders and the way they list themselves at SAMHSA's Treatment Facility Locator.)

Unfortunately for individuals with co-occurring mental illness and substance use disorders, according to the 2010 National Survey on Drug Use and Health, less than 8 percent of them received treatment for both conditions, with more than half receiving no treatment at all. Even fewer people get *integrated* substance and mental health help—that is, assistance for both conditions in one setting, during the course of the same treatment episode, and by the same team of clinicians—even though this kind of scenario is associated with lower costs, reduced substance use and increased abstinence odds, improved psychiatric symptoms, and better quality of life. (Contrary to this well-documented information, according to the 2012 CASA Columbia report on addiction treatment, in some states, treatment facilities and programs cannot be dually licensed to provide both mental health and addiction treatment services.)

THE DISCONNECT BETWEEN WHAT'S SAID AND WHAT'S DONE

"There's a disconnect between what programs say they provide and what clients report happening when they receive treatment," stated Dr. McGovern. Two people who affirmed this were Joni A. and Jackie H.

• Joni A.'s young adult daughter had seven addiction treatment experiences over the course of five years, and at the end of her description of almost every one of them, Joni said, "My daughter immediately went back to excessively using alcohol to deal with her emotional pain." In addition to her long-standing alcohol and drug problems, her daughter had been diagnosed with borderline personality disorder and also suffered from anxiety and panic attacks. Of several programs that were chosen because they were identified as dual-diagnosis centers, Joni said, "Unfortunately, there were not enough staff services available to handle everyone's needs so some, like my daughter, went without receiving the services. They did transport or allowed us to transport her to her psychiatrist." When her daughter did receive mental health services, it was helpful. Overall, however, Joni said, "This was very inadequate. The focus of these programs was addiction rather than mental illness, so they were not designed to help with co-occurring issues. My daughter's mental illness drove her addiction, so that needed to be addressed first rather than minimally or not at all."

• Jackie H. went for thirty days to a well-known high-end residential rehab that touts its ability to help people with both addiction and mental health issues as a service that sets it apart from other treatment centers, and that's why she chose it. After going through their extensive assessment process, it was determined that her primary problem was post-traumatic stress disorder (PTSD) caused by "complex trauma" from both childhood and recent experiences. She'd been coping with her pain by drinking heavily and taking high doses of benzodiazepines prescribed by her psychiatrist for anxiety. At the rehab, she said her only treatment for the trauma was "I was given medication for my depression, saw a psychologist once a week, and participated in two hours of group therapy [total] about trauma." In describing the approach used by her primary addiction counselor, Jackie said, "Her focus was solely on the twelve-step model of change, and her goal was to get me to realize how much I drank and used drugs, as well as how impossible it was for me to stay sober without attending AA meetings and working the steps." (As suggested in chapter 2, Jackie did not find this approach to be helpful.) Jackie didn't question her need to become completely sober at that time—"to learn to manage and tolerate the really disturbing symptoms of my mental illness"—and the rehab helped her accomplish that. However, she said, "It would have been helpful to talk more about how I felt in general and *why* I drank." In describing one of her in-depth assignments in which she divulged "painful and shameful memories and secrets," Jackie said that this counselor's only response was to tell her to remember all of the things she screwed up and how much time and money she wasted on alcohol and drugs. Jackie reflected, "At the time, I was shocked and am now repulsed that every event, thought, and emotion in my life was chalked up to my being 'an alcoholic.' The main reason for my substance abuse, I think, was that I was in so much pain that I preferred a drug-induced, zombie-like state to reality."

After treatment, the rehab recommended that Jackie go for a month to another rehab that specialized in treating co-occurring disorders and then go back to live with her parents. She said, "Living with family might be a good recommendation for someone from a stable background. However, for me, who has PTSD rooted in ongoing abuse throughout my childhood at the hands of my parents, this was a horrible recommendation."

When it comes to the disconnect between what's said and what's done, Dr. McGovern explained that most of what we know about the treatment of co-occurring disorders comes from information that addiction treatment programs *provide about themselves in surveys* such as the National Survey of Substance Abuse Treatment Services (N-SSATS). (No comparable information is gathered from mental health facilities, so we know even less about their treatment of both problems.) In the 2010 N-SSATS, which included the vast majority of programs in the United States, 61 percent of facilities said their *primary* focus was substance abuse treatment, while only 31 percent indicated it was a mix of substance abuse and mental health services, and 6 percent said it was mental health. Just 37 percent of programs said they provided programs or groups specially designed for clients with co-occurring mental health problems. And slightly more than half of all facilities reported that they provided a "comprehensive mental health assessment or diagnosis."

To assess how competent rehabs are at treating both addictions and mental illness, Dr. McGovern developed a scientifically based tool called the Dual Diagnosis Capability in Addiction Treatment (DDCAT) index with a rating system for outside observers to employ as they gather information from program administrators, clinicians, patients, medical records, and clinical observations. In 2012, the DDCAT had been used in more than thirty-two states and internationally to determine program variations and improve services for individuals with co-occurring disorders. (Some states are further along in the process than others. To find out about your state's progress and its rules having to do with co-occurring facilities, contact your state substance abuse agency, which can be

located at http://findtreatment.samhsa.gov/TreatmentLocator/faces/quick
Search.jspx.)

Both addiction and mental health facilities tend to see themselves as
more capable of treating people with co-occurring problems than they actually are, according to several studies involving Dr. McGovern. For instance, he and a colleague reported at the Addiction Health Services
Research Conference in 2007 that when addiction programs were asked
how they saw themselves, out of sixteen facilities, 75 percent of their leaders said they were "dual diagnosis capable" while 25 percent reported they
provided "alcohol only services." However, when the researchers actually
visited the programs, using the DDCAT to assess their services, they found
just the opposite of what was reported—that is, about 25 percent of them
were "dual diagnosis capable" and 75 percent provided "alcohol only services." More recently, in a study submitted for publication and presented at
the annual meeting of the American Psychiatric Association, Dr. McGovern
and fellow researchers assessed the ability of 256 addiction and mental
health programs nationwide to help people with co-occurring disorders
and found that fewer than one out of five addiction programs met criteria
for being at least dual diagnosis capable. The mental health facilities were
even more inadequate, with just 9 percent meeting the same benchmarks.
The researchers concluded that their findings "are not congruent with previous self-reports from providers about the co-occurring capability of their
services" and suggest that the odds of having both disorders addressed adequately in such programs are just one to two out of ten.

THE BARE FACTS: WHEN MENTAL ILLNESS AND
SUBSTANCE USE DISORDERS GO HAND IN HAND

Not surprisingly, it's usually tougher to help clients with a pair of problems rather than a drug or alcohol problem alone. And compared to
individuals with substance problems in the general population, more
people in addiction treatment programs tend to have mental health
problems, often more than one. Rehabs attract clients who may have a

wide range of co-occurring mental health problems; however, most do not suffer from severe mental illnesses. People with severe mental illness and addiction are more likely to wind up in the mental health system.

So just how common is it for addiction and mental illness to go hand in hand? Although it's sometimes said that nearly everyone who struggles with addiction has another "psych" problem, that's an exaggeration. While Dr. McGovern maintains that "upon arrival in treatment, just about all clients have depression or anxiety symptoms," the rate of these problems goes down as the effects of alcohol and drugs wear off. In actuality and generally speaking, about half of people in addiction treatment programs also have another *independent* mental disorder—that is, one not induced by drugs or alcohol. Anxiety and mood disorders, such as depression, are particularly common in people with substance use disorders, with mood disorders seen more frequently in women than men. Rates of physical or sexual abuse are also high in women who seek treatment, ranging upward of 55 percent, with many showing symptoms of trauma and PTSD. And among people with a serious mental illness, such as bipolar disorder, schizophrenia, or severe depression, substance use disorders are the most frequent co-occurring problem. (About 60 percent of people with bipolar disorder also have a substance use disorder.)

WHEN REHABS DROP THE BALL—
OR NEVER PICK IT UP IN THE FIRST PLACE

More than one person shared a story about mental health needs being overlooked or completely ignored either when they were in rehab or by the mental health system. One young man's brain chemistry was "all over the map" long before he started using drugs, according to the clinical psychologist and addiction expert he found after going to a string of high-end rehabs. The psychologist told me, "He simply became the master at treating his symptoms with illicit drugs. I think he did need to be in residential treatment of some sort because he was really out of control and could have hurt himself in a variety of impulsive ways. But he got into the traditional addiction rehab system, which told him that all of his problems were the result of his drug use, and that if he just did the twelve steps, all would be right with the world. That simply wasn't true. There was structure and he was safe, but his psych problems were not adequately addressed, and his family's communication problems were not targeted enough. So when he went back out to the world, with lack of structure, his psychological issues just led him back to drug use, and his family didn't have any different skills to deal with it except to send him back to rehab." The psychologist said that because of what the young man was told at rehab, "He now has a hard time seeing himself as anything other than a relapsing, screwed-up addict who simply doesn't want sobriety bad enough. What's been helpful is reframing things so that he and his family can see that his mental health problems drive his desire to use. If we treat the psych issues, he doesn't chase the drugs." The psychologist concluded, "This client has felt unnecessarily bad about himself for a long time. It all makes me sad and pretty mad at the system that's out there."

Will R. comes from a family "rife with depression, addiction, and suicide," in his own words, and is one of three brothers, all of whom suffer from depression—"sometimes quite debilitating." When I first interviewed him, he'd just completed a twelve-step treatment program, even though he felt he had no problem with alcohol. He'd long been a daily drinker, but rarely had more than a few glasses of wine. The year before going to rehab, however, he went through a period of depression and anxiety that he said "were killing me, and the wine provided the only way I could sleep." Then, when his mother died, he suffered "a major depressive crash," and the drinking continued. (Addicted to alcohol and prescription drugs, she was mentally ill throughout her life, and, from childhood, Will had been subjected to her destructive behavior, plus he often took on the role of being her caretaker.) After losing a summer teaching job as a result of his crippling depression, his wife said, "Don't come back home unless you go to rehab first." Once severely addicted to alcohol, she'd gotten sober with the help of a residential addiction rehab, so that's where he went for three weeks, followed by several months of outpatient care.

Although he "tried really hard to see what there was to learn—out of respect to the other people there and the counselors who were well-intentioned," Will found "very few of the staff had a college education, and they wouldn't allow you to ask a question. They were putting us in this one-size-fits-all, do this and don't ask why framework." When he told them he wasn't sure if he had an alcohol problem, "they tried to shame me by saying I'd let the group down. They were bullying and abusive." The program director's response when Will shared that he was filled with depression, panic, and anxiety and suggested that maybe his problem wasn't alcohol, was "You're a hypochondriac"—and walked away. Despite still feeling "miserable and upset" as treatment drew to a close, Will said, "there was absolutely no individual counseling—I never saw a psychologist, psychiatrist, or social worker. Only group counseling was provided."

After leaving rehab, he continued to feel "totally hopeless, about to explode, and miserable—I couldn't shower or brush my teeth. Plus, I had an angry wife and a pile of bills." When his father offered to foot the bill, Will decided to take part in a comprehensive, cognitive-behavioral substance use disorder and mental health program. The focus was on assessing and managing his long-standing mental health problems, while the alcohol issue was considered secondary. Will explained, "We dealt with the things that had been bothering me my whole life. They trusted my need to understand and interact with professional psychologists who would work with me as I tried to build a new, individual, and healthy model of approaching the world." He allowed me to talk with the psychologist-director of the program, who said, "Will didn't belong in a residential addiction rehab. His drinking problems were of recent onset, not severe, and clearly tied to emotional problems. The point of attack he needed was these issues."

Whether or not a rehab adequately addresses a specific person's mental health needs may depend on the complexity of the problems. For instance, I interviewed a woman who'd started drinking heavily in response to a personal tragedy, who said of her rehab experience, "They helped me deal with my grief as well as my anxiety, depression, and attention deficit disorder, which they diagnosed. If they had just treated my alcoholism and not the reasons for it, I would not be in recovery and doing as well as I am today." However, another person with several serious mental health problems who went to that same rehab expressed dissatisfaction with the many hours of group counseling, once-a-week meetings with a psychologist, and the type of counseling he received there.

TEASING OUT OTHER PROBLEMS FROM ADDICTIONS

Chronic use of alcohol and/or drugs can lead to temporary changes that make it look like a person has a co-occurring mental illness when, in fact, he or she doesn't. Consider, for instance, that alcohol acts as a depressant, and that heavy and chronic use of certain drugs, including phencyclidine (PCP), methamphetamine, and alcohol can cause temporary psychosis that may take months to subside. Hence, the importance of getting a good assessment of both substance and mental health problems cannot be overemphasized. Part of the process often entails carefully monitoring a client's symptoms during a period of abstinence, but also taking into account whether the mental health problems were present before the drug or alcohol problem, whether a family history of such problems exists, whether symptoms continue during the period of abstinence, or if the symptoms are in excess of what would be expected given the type and amount of substance used—all of which point to a mental disorder independent of the substance problem.

The problem is that it can take quite a while to distinguish the chicken from the egg—that is, to know if symptoms suggestive of a mental illness are present independently or are caused by alcohol or drug abuse. According to the *American Psychiatric Publishing Textbook of Substance Abuse Treatment*, for most substances of abuse—aside from those that cause psychosis when used heavily—"a general rule of thumb is to wait two to four weeks after acute withdrawal before diagnosing a mental illness." Petros Levounis, MD, director of the Addiction Institute of New York and chief of the Division of Addiction Psychiatry at St. Luke's–Roosevelt Hospital Center, said, "Unless the symptoms are severe enough that psychiatric treatment—typically with psychotropic medications—is needed right away, I think a better rule of thumb is to wait three months before making a formal psychiatric diagnosis." His reasoning is that it can take this long for what's known as "protracted (or post-acute) withdrawal syndrome" to subside. While acute withdrawal refers to immediate symptoms that occur when someone stops using drugs or alcohol, protracted withdrawal refers to continuing unpleasant symptoms such as mood instability, depression, anxiety, hostility, and irritability that may continue for weeks or months after someone stops using—all symptoms that can mimic mental disorders. When my reaction to Dr. Levounis's waiting period was that most people aren't in treatment for three months, he said, "If treatment professionals are confident in a client's history, you don't have to wait that long to make a diagnosis. For instance, with a history of suicidality, there's a good chance someone has a co-occurring disorder." And some mental health problems, such as PTSD, are never caused by the use of drugs and alcohol.

After stressing that "we can no longer tolerate treatment that simply ends in thirty days," Dr. Richard Saitz, director of the Clinical Addiction Research and Education Unit at Boston University School of Medicine, said that a careful clinical interview might reveal whether other mental health problems preceded addiction and that sometimes family members are consulted for information. However, he pointed out that just because it's unclear whether a co-occurring problem is caused by addiction or is independent doesn't mean that the mental health symptoms don't warrant treatment—for instance, with medication or cognitive-behavioral therapy—"and one can sort out the actual diagnosis later." Dr. Saitz also cited evidence that, at least in some circumstances, medications for co-occurring disorders in people with addiction can improve substance use and mental health symptoms regardless of whether the mental health disorders are independent or temporarily caused by drug or alcohol use.

TIMING, TESTING, AND TREATMENT IMPLICATIONS

Vince T. had mental health problems in his "history," yet during his outpatient treatment, his psychiatric needs seemed to go unrecognized for too long in the mistaken notion that his symptoms would subside after he was sober. Throughout his second month or so of sobriety, however, Vince was having serious suicidal thoughts, such as "I was ready to drive south of town with my shotgun and shoot myself." At his first appointment with his primary counselor—his assessment—he told her that he'd made a suicide attempt as a sixth grader, "and she did not blink," so he thinks that may have held him back from disclosing his suicidal thoughts during their subsequent visits. But he did tell her he was miserable and recalled, "She said something about chemicals in my brain adjusting to no alcohol." It wasn't until his second to last of about ten individual appointments with her, or at least two months from their first meeting, that the counselor told Vince she thought he suffered from depression. "But her diagnosis was linked to the fact that I was always angry; I was just perpetually pissed off," he said. At that point, the counselor referred Vince for mental health help, and, finally, he was formally diagnosed with depression and placed on a number of different antidepressants. The psychiatric professionals pointed to the suicide attempt in his youth, noting that he'd probably suffered from depression for decades until they treated it. After several weeks on the medications, he thought, "Holy crap, is this what normal civilians feel like all the time?"

"Looking back," he added, "I'm frustrated that it took so long to diagnose or even mention depression."

Richard Zwolinski, author of *Therapy Revolution: Find Help, Get Better, and Move On*, said, "My clinical experience has led me to believe that many addiction treatment clinicians are simply not equipped to diagnose mental illness. And in fact, that's really not their job." Moreover, as a licensed mental health and credentialed substance abuse counselor in New York with more than twenty-five years of experience in addiction and mental health settings, he's found that psychiatrists at most outpatient addiction treatment programs are primarily there to prescribe, not to diagnose, and often rely on previous diagnoses from other doctors. Zwolinski added, "Other licensed mental health professionals in outpatient settings who have the appropriate training to evaluate and diagnose mental illness, such as social workers and mental health counselors, are in short supply—they're frequently in administrative positions and don't always do clinical work with patients." The result is that, in many cases, when clients have co-occurring disorders, no mental health diagnosis is made, and, therefore, those problems don't get treated.

When I asked a psychologist at a high-end residential rehab about their practice (and that of other facilities like theirs) of administering a battery of psychological/psychiatric tests at the beginning of residential treatment, when many people are still in the throes of withdrawal or post-acute withdrawal, he admitted that giving the tests too soon lessens their validity. However, in a time-limited program such as a thirty-day rehab, waiting for the person to "clear" may make it too late for the test results to be useful in formulating a treatment plan. Moreover, he said that their state regulations commonly prevent the test results from being used this way because they require that the client's treatment plan be developed within less than a week of admission, and the tests may not even be administered by then. On a more global scale, he believes, "Most of the psych testing* is a waste of time and money—both ours and the patient's. It doesn't really help with a psychiatric diagnosis or give a better clinical picture of patients after the psychologists have already spent an hour or so with them in our evaluation in an interview." He feels that, to a certain extent, this testing goes on as a form of competition between rehabs—if one does it, so does another.

He then raised a question I'd had as I visited programs and interviewed staffers. "The real issue is: Does any of this information (testing, diagnosis, etc.) influence the treatment of any individual?" He went on, "Sometimes it does, but usually it doesn't. Depression, anxiety, or PTSD might get referenced on the treatment plan, but it's rarely a major focus of treatment. If it's referenced, it might result in [the individual] being referred to the psychiatrist and given psychotropic medications. Or a patient might get some extra time with the psychologist or get biofeedback for anxiety." He sees the services of their psychiatrists and psychologists as "ancillary—to help

---

* This refers to standardized psychiatric/psychological tests, such as the MMPI (Minnesota Multiphasic Personality Inventory), not to recognized assessment tools that address substance use disorders and related problems, such as the Addiction Severity Index (ASI) or Global Appraisal of Individual Needs (GAIN).

keep the patient together to be able to participate in the primary addiction treatment, and to serve a role of being a sort of 'advisor' to the counselors, which is not necessarily a bad thing in a facility where the primary focus is on recovery issues." Affirming this last statement, a woman who went to the rehab where this therapist works said, "The psychologists helped me to utilize strategies and techniques when my ADD became severe during meetings and long periods of sitting."

ON MY TRAVELS

This psychologist's remarks are consistent with my observations of how several of the traditional residential adult rehabs I visited handled treatment of clients with co-occurring disorders and of the mental health professionals' role at their facilities during primary care. They also offered specialty groups, such as body image groups, trauma groups, and DBT-type groups, for people with certain mental health issues. And after their initial month or so stay, clients who went to these rehabs were often referred to extended-care facilities that focused more closely on co-occurring mental health problems.

Although one of these rehabs did not tout itself as a program for co-occurring disorders, I was told that as many as 80 to 90 percent of its clients had such problems. Another rehab represented itself quite differently. For instance, it was stated in program materials that it fully integrated assessment and care for co-occurring mental health problems and that one-on-one sessions with a mental health professional were provided as often as once a day. Yet several people who went to this rehab described disappointment in what they felt were limited services for their co-occurring mental health problems, and no one told me they saw a psychologist more than once a week. On the other hand, some clients indicated that these needs were better met here than at other programs they'd attended.

Promises Treatment Centers offered clients more individual therapy with mental health professionals than any of the other residential rehabs I visited and routinely referred clients to specialists for co-occurring mental health disorders that they felt warranted specialty treatment, such as eating disorders and sexual compulsivity. (This was individually tailored and may or may not have incurred an additional charge.) In order to ensure that clients could continue in therapy with their referring therapists or psychiatrists, Promises provided transportation to scheduled appointments for those whose therapists were local and recently added video conferencing for clients who come from outside the Los Angeles area.

As for outpatient programs, Practical Recovery offered one-on-one therapy with mental health professionals as its predominant form of treatment—so its model was completely different from that of any of the other programs. Its overall approach is to focus at least as much on co-occurring psychological problems as on substance use disorders. (At its newly opened residential programs, individual therapy time varies from an hour a week to several hours a day at its high-end facility.) The stated view of Hope by the Sea is that they recognize substance problems as a symptom of underlying psychological issues and "equally treat the psychological disorders." African American Family Services in Minneapolis and the STOP program in Philadelphia were licensed in their states as both addiction treatment and mental health facilities, easing participation in both types of services for clients. However, one can't assume that access to an on-site mental health facility means that you'll get integrated dual disorders treatment. At another outpatient program that had a partnership with an adjoining mental health facility, their general philosophy was that if a client had an addiction and other mental health problems, "treating the drug and alcohol problem is primary because the danger to your life has to stop," and people often were referred for mental health care *after* addiction treatment. Of their adolescent program, I was told that once kids had thirty days of sobriety, they might get referred for psychological services.

Some rehab staffers told me they were "certified co-occurring disorders professionals," a credential bestowed by the International Certification and Reciprocity Consortium (IC&RC), which, as mentioned in chapter 4, is one of the main credentialing bodies for addiction counselors. While it may sound impressive, you can get this credential with just a bachelor's degree in a related field, to include a specific number of hours of coursework or educational training that focuses on both substance use and mental disorders. The equivalent of three years of related work experience and two hundred hours of clinical supervision (qualifications of supervisor unspecified) are also required, and then an exam must be passed and yearly continuing education is mandatory. Yale University's Dr. Kathleen Carroll, an expert who studies the addiction treatment field, said, "My take on credentialing is that while it's clearly better than none, it by no means assures that the clinician is actually competent to deliver care. Credentialing offers less assurance than board certification or licensing that a clinician has expertise in scientifically validated interventions." (IC&RC also offers a certified co-occurring disorders professional diplomate certification for people with advanced degrees.)

WHEN THE MENTAL HEALTH SYSTEM IS OFF THE MARK

As mentioned earlier, it's not just the addiction treatment system that falls short in helping people with co-occurring problems. Dr. McGovern said, "The mental health system, with its highly educated and trained providers (psychiatrists, psychologists, and master's-level clinicians), is probably less prepared than is the addiction treatment system to deal with the opposite side of the co-occurring disorder street." Rose T. affirmed, "The first time I tried to stop drinking, my psychiatrist was helpful, but when I relapsed, he was real quick to hand me over to the addiction program."

Thirty years after the fact, Lumen F. wonders if her serious drinking problem would have become as bad as it did had a prominent psychologist affiliated with a university addressed it in a different way. She knew she was struggling with both alcohol and depression when she sought his help and was relieved when he told her that treating her depression would take care of her drinking problem. After the psychologist had her keep records of how much she drank, Lumen was even more relieved when he reassured her that she was not an alcoholic and did not suggest that she stop drinking. Looking back, she said, "He was dead wrong. I continued to see him for three years, as my drinking problem got worse, and continued to do so for a number of years after I stopped seeing him." When she finally went for individual counseling with a drug and alcohol counselor, he asked to see her past drinking records and was shocked that she'd not been told she was an alcoholic, given how much she'd been drinking. She often wonders, "What would have happened if the psychologist had addressed both problems at the same time and early on? By the time I saw the addiction counselor, the drinking problem was so firmly entrenched that abstinence was my only option."

Dr. McGovern indicated that situations like Lumen's are not uncommon. He said, "Many mental health professionals continue to operate under the self-medication myth—that is, if a person drinks because she's depressed or uses oxycontin to deal with nightmares and flashbacks, the thinking is that all you need to do is get to the bottom of the problem (whether by medication or psychotherapy) and the need to use substances to cope, will dissipate. However, there is absolutely no evidence that this approach works for people who are addicted to alcohol or drugs." He added that this is not to say that therapy, psychiatric medications, and/or evidence-based approaches for specific co-occurring mental health problems would not be beneficial. It's just that addressing mental health issues without addressing addiction (or the other way around) usually is not effective.

WHEN VIEWING ADDICTION AS THE PRIMARY PROBLEM GETS IN THE WAY

Just as mental health professionals can miss the mark by focusing on a psychological problem to the neglect of a substance use disorder, a rehab philosophy that can get in the way of optimal care is "We treat the addiction as the primary problem"—meaning that's the one that assumes priority and needs to be addressed before dealing with other problems. (Exceptions are is usually made for people with severe psychological problems such as schizophrenia or someone who's made multiple suicide attempts—cases like this would likely be referred to special programs.)

While addiction often is the primary issue and, in many cases, getting a person free of alcohol and drugs is needed to make progress, focusing on the substance problem as the one that must be dealt with ahead of all others (which often goes hand in hand with the belief that certain tenets of the twelve-step philosophy must be accepted) means that addiction treatment programs too often ignore or delay help for co-occurring disorders.

This practice can have unfortunate consequences, as illustrated by Caroline R.'s story, which was told to me by her mother, Sylvia. Caroline passed away about five years ago, in her midthirties, because of medical complications related to a severe alcohol use disorder. Although Caroline had had some periods of anorexia nervosa and depression in her early twenties and was hospitalized for a short time, it wasn't until her late twenties that she started abusing alcohol. With a strong family predisposition, Sylvia said, "Caroline's addiction progressed rapidly by her early thirties, took hold, and owned her for the rest of her life." Not one for "denial," Caroline shared with her mother early on that she thought she had a serious problem and embarked on what would become a seven-year process of engaging in addiction treatment programs, relapsing, and then repeating the cycle. Sylvia recalled, "She always had high hopes that she'd recover fully."

Her excessive drinking periodically caused serious esophageal bleeding requiring hospitalization, and after one such episode she was immediately transferred directly to, in Sylvia's words, a "gold standard" residential rehab. When Caroline died several years after attending this rehab, Sylvia obtained Caroline's records to try to understand the findings of her assessment and what treatment had been provided to her there. The records indicated that their comprehensive assessment of Caroline's addiction and mental health status had uncovered severe clinical depression and anxiety, as well as low self-esteem and family relationship issues. However, at this "gold standard" facility, as at the four other programs Caroline had attended, Sylvia described her experiences as "brief thirty-day stays in one-size-fits-all programs where the primary treatment was the Big Book, treatment groups, AA groups, and working the twelve steps from morning until night." Sylvia felt, "There was no individualized plan of care, no help or medication for her depression or anxiety, no therapy to improve her thinking patterns or coping skills, no family or relationship therapy, no information about how to deal with cravings or about medication to prevent them, and no professional follow-up except recommending AA meetings."

Caroline's battle with addiction ended following a bad bout of depression, which led to relapse. Two months later, after a month in the hospital, she died of liver and kidney failure. Sylvia said, "I truly believe if she had received the right treatment—especially medication to address the intense cravings, depression, and anxiety; cognitive therapy to address her depression and anxiety; problem-solving skills; and long-term medical management of the chronic brain disease of addiction with a plan to help her navigate life—she might still be alive."

After Caroline's death, Sylvia went back to the "gold standard" rehab to meet with an administrator and share her frustration that, despite what their comprehensive assessment had revealed, there was no record of Caroline's having had psychological counseling for her problems, even though a psychologist who wrote a report about Caroline had recommended one-on-one therapy sessions twice a week. Sylvia told the administrator, "All of the information was there about her problems—over and over the same things came up. And there was input from your multidisciplinary team of experts. Out of that should have flowed Caroline's treatment plan. But all you did were the twelve steps. Yes, Caroline needed to be in a safe place, but this isn't what she needed." Sylvia said the response she was given was "I'm sorry." Then the administrator added, "We have to treat the addiction first. That's what's primary."

Institute of Medicine recommendations for implementing quality care for individuals with co-occurring disorders clearly state that all types of disorders should be treated as "primary" and that "no program, patient, type of disorder, or approach to treatment is considered more important than others." Dr. McGovern added, "The primary-secondary issue is moot and an artifact of the bifurcation of the treatment delivery system. It's not based on any evidence.

SOBRIETY DOESN'T *HAVE* TO COME FIRST

Salina S. talked about how freeing it was that, at the most recent program she attended, she didn't have to get completely sober before dealing with her mental health problems. She found, "Once you get mentally healthy, it makes it easier to be sober. But at other programs they think it's the other way around—that sobriety brings the mental health." Indeed, people are often told they have to "get clean" before dealing with their psychological problems as part of the "treat addiction as primary" philosophy. While it's certainly difficult (or even impossible) to work with someone whose addiction is way out of control, several experts affirmed that a "come back when you're sober" policy should not be applied across the board.

When I asked Dr. Levounis whether a person has to be abstinent to effectively begin to deal with a co-occurring disorder, he said, "Ideally, you'd like them to be sober, but this is real life. We can certainly address co-occurring disorders before people are sober and often work on both at the same time." While some rehabs don't tolerate mixing of nonabstinent clients with those who are, Dr. Levounis said that there's no evidence that they have to be separated and that, at his facility, they're typically treated together. He added, "If someone becomes toxic to the group—maybe talking about how great it was to have a glass of wine on Saturday night and glamorizing it—then we need to address that problem."

Practical Recovery's approach, according to Tom Horvath, is "If a person is unwilling or unable to abstain, we might make the focus entirely on underlying psychological issues or focus in a more balanced fashion on both addiction and underlying issues at the same time, depending on the client. Clients like this may need a sense of hope as much as anything, that there are effective ways to address underlying issues without having to use substances." (His facilities also allow nonabstinent clients to be in the same groups as those who are abstinent.)

In fact, a 2011 study published in the *American Journal of Psychiatry* by Denise Hien, PhD, and colleagues from Columbia University College of Physicians and Surgeons in New York found that treating PTSD symptoms first in women who suffered from both a substance problem and

PTSD led to a reduction in substance problems. Often, however, individuals who suffer from both disorders are not treated for PTSD until they receive addiction treatment and stop using drugs and alcohol—based on the assumption that addressing trauma could worsen a person's substance problem. Yet the study found little evidence that treating substance problems first improved PTSD symptoms.

The bottom line, according to the National Alliance on Mental Illness, is that while abstinence may be a goal of an integrated dual diagnosis program, it "should not be a precondition for entering treatment. . . . An illness model of the problem should be used rather than a moralistic one. Providers need to convey understanding of how hard it is to end an addiction problem and give credit for any accomplishments."

ALL-IN-ONE CARE

Many programs now recognize the downside of separating addiction and mental health care and are trying to integrate the two in various ways, largely as a result of national and state efforts to change things. Some programs address both problems at the same time but in separate, noncoordinated venues. Others have separate but well-coordinated, closely linked addiction and mental health systems. Research suggests that the most effective way to treat people with co-occurring disorders is through *integrated* treatment—which, again, is when both mental health and substance use disorder services are offered at the same time and seen as "primary," with one or more clinicians or a team that has expertise with both disorders, and in one setting.

Most people I interviewed who benefited from some semblance of integrated treatment came to it the hard way, after first stumbling through multiple programs that focused on addiction and neglected to adequately address their mental health needs. I followed Eddie F. through much of this process. When I checked in with him toward the end of writing this book, he said, "I've been through treatment five times now and it wasn't until this last time that the concept of having to treat both mental illness and alcoholism equally at the same time came to my attention." When he began drinking again and was "about as desperate as I could get; it got to the point where I was considering suicide," he had his sister take him to a facility that provided multiple levels of addiction treatment. The program's Web site said it had a dual disorder program with a goal of addressing and stabilizing both issues at the same time and where clients would receive medical care, addiction services, and psychotherapy—an apt description of the help Eddie described. He said, "What an amazing place. I was in detox for four days, where I met with doctors, social workers, psychologists, and evaluators." He subsequently decided to attend their twenty-eight-day residential program, even though it would cost him $26,000 out of his own pocket, which was not easy for him.

He explained that, right off the bat, "They treated my depression and my addiction at the same time—this was the first time it was addressed as part of my recovery plan." During the first two weeks, he met with a psychiatrist and psychologist three times each. Prior to leaving, he met with them once more. "After extensive evaluation," he said, "I was placed in a small group of guys with lifelong depression and alcohol or pot abuse and received much more education and more small-group therapy than in previous treatments. We met two and a half hours each day and spent equal time on chemical dependencies and mental health." He found great benefit in being with other clients like him and immediately noticed the sense of community among the patients and staff.

Even though Eddie couldn't afford any continuing treatment at the end of his stay, the program allowed him to audit their entire outpatient program, free of charge. After that, he took advantage of their free aftercare group, which is available to clients for five years, and continued to see a psychologist and psychiatrist regularly, which he paid for himself. Traditional thinking in twelve-step lingo would be that Eddie had to "hit bottom" in order to get well. Early on in dealing with his problems, however, he wanted to go to an addiction program that provides one-on-one treatment, and his insurance wouldn't pay for it. And before that, he tried to get into the inpatient program that finally addressed his depression, but they didn't have a bed for him. Who knows what would have happened if his needs had been met earlier?

FINDING A GOOD PROGRAM THAT DOUBLES UP

If you know or suspect that you or a loved one needs treatment for a substance use disorder *and* a mental health problem, how do you find a program that treats both and does that well? Dr. McGovern believes that many programs have taken great strides to improve their services and stated, "I often feel inspired by the work people are doing. Some places are doing great stuff." The list below suggests components that an ideal program would include, certainly a tall order and not easy to come by. You can decide which features are most important to you.*

- Specializes in treating clients with co-occurring disorders (some facilities are certified or licensed to provide both addiction and mental health services)
- Multidisciplinary team involvement with professionals working in one setting who regularly discuss client progress and coordinate all aspects of treatment
- On-site psychiatrist(s) or other prescriber(s) of psychotropic medications who are involved with the treatment team
- At least half the clinical staff have master's- or doctoral-level training as well as mental health licensure (or substantial experience) and are provided with routine clinical supervision
- Integrated screening and assessment practices that address both substance and mental health disorders using standardized tools (such as the GAIN or ASI—see chapter 2)
- Treatments (in addition to medication) that focus directly on mental health problems such as depression, anxiety, and PTSD. Ask about qualifications of those delivering these treatments.
- Treatment that routinely addresses both disorders equivalently—in addition to recognized addiction treatment approaches and medications when appropriate, clients should receive specialized mental health interventions such as symptom management groups, individ-

---

* Sources: The Dual Diagnosis Capability in Addiction Treatment (DDCAT) index and *Treating Addiction* by William R. Miller, et al. (Guilford Press, 2011).

ual therapies focused on specific mental disorders, and education about mental health disorders and how they interact with substance use disorders.

- Collaboration of clinicians with the client (and often the family) to develop a treatment plan for both problems that's tailored to the individual
- "Stagewise" treatment, recognizing that clients are at different points in their readiness to deal with their problems and that focusing on one problem over another is helpful at different stages of recovery
- An approach in which clients are not discharged if they stop taking their medications or continue to use substances
- Comprehensive approach, taking into account social networks, employment, housing, and recreational activities
- Family education and support programs specifically for co-occurring disorders
- Continuity of care after treatment, recognizing both problems as primary, with plans for on-site or off-site follow-up and formal plans for indefinite management of mental health needs (ideally in the same facility)
- Treatment that facilitates the use of addiction peer support groups geared for people with co-occurring disorders, such as Dual Recovery Anonymous, Double Trouble in Recovery, and alumni groups.

You can also ask program staff if they've had a DDCAT assessment and what the results were, but they may or may not know. (When I asked an administrator about this at Eddie's inpatient program, she didn't know.) A group of organizations recently joined hands to establish a Web site called Focus on Integrated Recovery to provide resources for co-occurring disorders that include a listing of many of the programs that have had an independent DDCAT assessment. (Many programs in the United States had yet to be assessed.) Here's the link for the directory:

http://www.integratedrecoverynow.org/resources/#Integrated Treatment Directory

GETTING OUT YOUR SECRETS

Salina S. described a practice that some rehabs believe to be therapeutic for emotional problems as "this thing where you had to share secrets, this deep shit. If you don't participate, it goes on your report." She said that at an outpatient program she went to, addiction counselors pressed clients to share secrets, "yelling at people who weren't sharing the right thing." At one point, when she shared something about her brother, they said, "No, Salina, we mean deep secrets." She told me, "I didn't want a bunch of strangers knowing these things about me. It was bad enough that we had to share, but nothing seemed to be secret enough. The theory is that secrets harm you when you keep them in. You have to get them out. They said secrets can kill."

Administrators at two prominent traditional residential rehabs I visited also described this practice. One said, "Twelve-step treatment is based on honesty, so we do a lot of work around secrets." Another told me that step work included "telling secrets to peers" and said that "part of recovery is getting out secrets." She added, "We're as sick as our secrets."

Petros Levounis said this type of practice might benefit one person yet make another individual worse—for instance, someone with a particular type of PTSD. He said, "Some counselors may not be adequately trained on how to handle such matters." Dr. Jeffrey Foote, codirector of the Center for Motivation and Change in New York, took a more critical stance, describing his experience with having people divulge "secrets" when he was a clinical director at a large facility years ago. He was not pleased when he discovered that, in group sessions, clients were being asked to share their three worst family secrets—and then confronted if the secrets weren't "good or dark enough." He said, "It stems from the idea that 'addiction is a disease of dishonesty, which must be counteracted by revelation of your secrets so as not to let your addict brain keep you isolated and dishonest.' Also, the act of putting forth really shaming, embarrassing experiences and feelings is seen as sort of a 'cleansing' that can feel intuitively correct to counselors and patients alike. Although treatment programs seem to love a lot of catharsis, they often don't really help people do anything constructive with it." As a clinical psychologist who specializes in treating people with addictions and co-occurring psychiatric problems, Dr. Foote explained, "The complicated part of this is that people who abuse substances have often experienced terrible, shameful, traumatic things in their lives, and they've often done things when they were abusing substances for which they felt guilty and ashamed. But this gets wrapped in as part of their 'addiction' instead of what it is—trauma. While processing shame and trauma is an incredibly important business (to be dealt with in professional individual therapy), it is incredibly complex and is *not* a business that should be happening by the forced divulging of secrets in substance use disorder groups." He added that this approach could be retraumatizing, shows no evidence of effectiveness, and can be counterproductive to progress—particularly when confrontational.

LETTERS FROM YOUR FAMILY

Perhaps the most uncomfortable practice I observed in my rehab visits was the reading of "cost" or "impact" letters that went on at several traditional residential programs, whereby clients shared with their treatment groups letters received from family members—and then fellow clients reacted to them. Instructions given to relatives at one rehab were that they were to write their loved ones in rehab about how their use of alcohol or drugs "negatively affected you." The letters were not to be "shaming and blaming."

I wondered if there was any scientific evidence that such practices are therapeutic or, on the other hand, could even be harmful. In one instance, when I asked these questions of two administrators, I was met with silence. When I asked about several women who shared impact letters in peer groups, without a counselor present, I was told, "They're supposed to be shared in group therapy. If they chose to share in peer group, it was on their own and their choice." Another time, when I gave a staff member the example of a woman I'd met who was worried about the possibility of traumatizing her thirteen-year-old son by having him write such a letter, the staff person mockingly said (in front of other professionals) something to the effect of, "Imagine, she's worried that this might traumatize her kid," implying that it didn't seem to bother the woman that her addiction had already hurt the child. I responded that the mother had told me that she had terrible remorse about her drinking and what it had done to her family. I was subsequently told by the same staff person that the impact letter practice "hasn't traumatized anyone."

It turns out that this person was mistaken. While some of the letters I heard shared before groups seemed relatively benign, others clearly made some people distraught. (In some cases, clients hadn't seen the letters before they were shared before their groups.) Jackie H. said that her "most damaging rehab assignment was and has been to ask my family for impact letters." She explained, "To a woman who has PTSD from the childhood abuse she endured at the hands of her parents, this is NOT a good 'assignment.' I still think of how horrible and mean those letters were—I was blamed for mental illnesses of relatives, my brother's addiction, and other family problems."

Because "there's no evidence either way" about the practice of receiving and sharing family impact letters, according to Barbara McCrady, director of the University of New Mexico's Center on Alcoholism, Substance Abuse, and Addictions, I asked her for her opinion about it. She responded, "There may be times when it's cleansing. Other times, it's terrible. The problem is the cookie-cutter nature of things—this is what we do and this is the best. Treatment needs to be more nuanced."

ON TREATING "SEX ADDICTION" AND OTHER "PROCESS ADDICTIONS"

Residential drug and alcohol rehabs sometimes incorporate strategies for addressing "behavioral" addictions, or what they often refer to as "process addictions," including compulsive gambling, shopping, and Internet use, as well as what's often termed "sex addiction." With the exception of Promises, however, none of the primary-care residential programs I visited offered specific treatment for such problems. Hazelden assessed clients for such issues, viewing them as co-occurring disorders, and made recommendations accordingly. This might include individual counseling with a staff mental health professional or advice to seek twelve-step support. Caron's approach was similar and might include individual counseling, twelve-step support meetings, and "specialty" groups. At both Caron and Hazelden, if a client's process addiction was determined to be the primary problem, and a substance use disorder was not, he or she would likely be referred to a facility that specializes in treating that disorder.

For clients whose addictions are complicated by compulsive sexual behaviors, Promises offered individualized approaches that might include trauma treatment groups and EMDR for those who experienced childhood physical and sexual abuse, individual psychotherapy, and new coping strategies. (EMDR stands for "eye movement desensitization and reprocessing," a scientifically supported therapy for treating PTSD.) As at many places that treat sexual compulsivity, twelve-step principles and support at meetings such as Sex Addicts Anonymous were incorporated and encouraged. More serious cases were referred to the nearby Sexual Recovery Institute, which Promises' parent organization purchased after my visit.

Dr. Levounis pointed to the controversy over putting these "behavioral" addictions in the same category as addictions to alcohol and drugs. He said, "Gambling has the most evidence to be considered this way; sexual and Internet compulsivity have less evidence; next may be compulsive shopping. (At this writing, the only "behavioral" addiction that's been proposed for inclusion in the forthcoming DSM-5 is "gambling disorder." And "internet use disorder" was proposed for placement in a section of the DSM about conditions that require further research, as was "hypersexual disorder" or what's commonly called sex addiction.)

Dr. Levounis said there's no question that people can suffer from compulsive engagement in these behaviors and that loss of control—the hallmark of addiction—can be quite similar in the case of these activities and substance use. But because we really don't know much about them and where to draw the line to determine when they become pathological—undoubtedly, sixteen hours a day of Internet use is a problem, but what about four or eight?—he said, "Then, we're flying by the seat of our pants when it comes to treatment." Because we really don't know what works, "we're forced to extrapolate from treatments of substance use disorders with proven success records—for instance, twelve-step facilitation, motivational interviewing, and cognitive-behavioral therapy can be applied."

Some rehabs have gone so far as to adopt an approach for the treatment of behavioral addictions that looks like it's out of the pages of traditional drug and alcohol rehab, just tweaked here and there. For instance, a famous program for sex addiction and other sex-related problems—one after which other programs model their approaches—at a large behavioral health and addiction treatment facility, said at its Web site at press time that its treatment is based on a twelve-step program and includes Big Book and step study, relapse prevention counseling, a "spirituality" group, a family program, EMDR, cognitive behavioral therapy, psychoeducational lectures, art and drama therapies, and experiential trauma work. Its approaches are primarily offered through group therapy, and the Web site mentions having patients do sexual timelines and "secrets lists."

Several experts told me there is no research support for this overall approach. One of them, Rory Reid, PhD, LCSW, of UCLA's Department of Psychiatry and Biobehavioral Sciences and an expert on hypersexual behavior and pathological gambling, said, "Sadly, many of these residential and inpatient programs for 'sex addiction' charge exorbitant amounts of money for their 'treatments,' and, to my knowledge, not one of them has invested in or published outcome research to show efficacy of their interventions." Psychologist David Ley, PhD, author of *The Myth of Sex Addiction*, added, "They'll argue that they've done their own studies, but these haven't been peer-reviewed and have only been described in pop psychology journals and books." Both Dr. Reid and Dr. Ley also raised concerns about certification programs for sex addiction therapists that train people in these approaches.

Dr. Reid has found that cookie-cutter approaches similar to those endemic in the drug and alcohol rehab industry are the rule rather than the exception in sex addiction rehabs when, in fact, the nature of hypersexual disorder, like substance use disorders, is highly variable. He also pointed out that there have only been about a dozen outcome studies on hypersexual behavior, and most of them weren't rigorously designed. Therefore, rehab claims of using research-based approaches are misleading because such interventions just don't exist.

As principle investigator of what's known as a DSM field trial to test out the proposed criteria for diagnosing people with hypersexual disorder in treatment programs, Dr. Reid has worked with patients from around the country, conducting back-to-back assessments with as many as twelve patients in a day. In some situations, he found that intake workers failed to diagnose major psychiatric conditions. Although he acknowledged that some facilities are doing good work, he commented, "It's astounding that someone can pay $30,000 a month and not receive routine psychological testing and a diagnostic interview from a doctoral-level clinician." In certain cases, clinical interns at the beginning of their careers made up a significant proportion of the staff at sex addiction programs and were not capable of diagnosing the complex issues in their clients.

WHEN EATING DISORDERS AND ADDICTION GO HAND IN HAND

Because the residential rehabs I visited required that substance use disorders be the primary problem in order to attend their facilities, anyone with a serious, active eating disorder was referred to a facility offering specialized care. However, it's not uncommon for people who have an eating disorder in their past to show up at an addiction rehab. One study showed that as many as 40 percent of women who received drug and alcohol treatment also had an eating disorder at some point in their lives, and eating disorders sometimes resurface as substance problems begin to be resolved. (Men with eating disorders often have substance problems, too.) As mentioned earlier, some of the programs I visited offered special groups for clients with body image and eating issues. Weekly individual counseling with a staff mental health professional was sometimes offered as well. Rehabs often encourage twelve-step support at such groups as Overeaters Anonymous or Eating Disorders Anonymous meetings. If they feel it's warranted, Promises arranges private therapy with an eating-disorders specialist.

Some rehabs that treat drug and alcohol problems have separate eating-disorders programs. However, in a recent scientific review on women and addiction, Harvard Medical School's Shelly F. Greenfield, MD, MPH, and colleagues concluded that there are no integrated, evidence-based approaches for substance use and eating disorders when they occur together. That stated, components of a science-based program for eating disorders should include medical care and monitoring, nutrition counseling and rehabilitation, cognitive behavioral therapy, interpersonal therapy (having to do with relationships), psychiatric medications (usually antidepressants), and family therapy (which is not the same as a "family week" in rehab).

Although rehabs commonly use and recommend twelve-step approaches for eating disorders, several experts at university-based eating disorders treatment programs told me they knew of no supporting evidence for this practice. Carlos Grilo, PhD, director of Yale University's Eating Disorders and Obesity Research Program, said, "I'm not aware of any research or data on the twelve-step approach for treating eating disorders. We do not use it here." It's interesting to note that the mother of a young woman who had been to both eating-disorder and addiction rehabs found that "none of the stand-alone eating-disorder facilities used twelve-step methods in their treatment. However, the drug and alcohol facilities did introduce twelve-step eating disorders treatment for their dual-disorder patients like my daughter. It was no more effective in helping the younger folks with their eating disorders than it was for their substance problems."

Going by my rule that the burden of proof is on the claimant, I turned to a prominent addiction rehab (not one that I visited) with a separate eating-disorders program, asking if it could provide me with any supporting peer-reviewed studies for their use of the twelve steps for eating disorders. Nothing they sent me qualified. In practice, however, their approach seemed flexible. I was told that although all eating-disorders clients get some exposure to the twelve steps, if it doesn't work out, they "move on." One young woman I interviewed who went there for help with an eating disorder (who also had an alcohol problem) said they did not emphasize the twelve steps for her eating disorder.

This is not to say that twelve-step groups, in addition to science-based approaches, might not be beneficial to certain eating-disorder clients. The 2012 SAMHSA advisory listed below on substance use and eating disorders states, "Although research on mutual-help groups for clients with eating disorders is virtually nonexistent, these groups may be useful for clients in long-term recovery from eating disorders." SMART Recovery, which uses cognitive-behavioral approaches, also welcomes people with eating disorders, although it doesn't have groups specifically for people with these issues. Following are two good resources on treatment of eating disorders:

http://store.samhsa.gov/product/Advisory-Clients-With-Substance -Use-and-Eating-Disorders/SMA10-4617

http://www.nimh.nih.gov/health/publications/eating-disorders /complete-index.shtml.

CHAPTER NINE

HELPING PEOPLE STAY THE COURSE

ON USING IN REHAB, REPEAT VISITS, "SUCCESS," AND IMPROVING THE ODDS

The client who holds the record for "most times in rehab" of the more than one hundred people I interviewed for this book is a man who was in treatment at least thirty times. When I met him, he'd had a six-year period of sobriety after three stays at the same high-end rehab within the space of one year. The truth is that 40 to 60 percent of people treated once for a substance use disorder go back to using substances again. Unfortunately, however, phenomenal "cures" are still the expectation when one goes to rehab—not only by many in the general public but sometimes by health-care professionals and even those working in the addiction field. Such unrealistic expectations inhibit some from seeking help in the first place and keep others from going back for assistance if they start using drugs or alcohol again.

Given the nature of the problem—that it's chronic for many individuals—and that most addiction programs say they recognize it as such, a lot of what goes on in the world of rehab doesn't make sense. For instance, are short-term programs reasonable when they expect nothing less than abstinence as the end result? What about the policy of kicking people out when they engage in the behavior that characterizes their illness? And where's the logic when someone goes through rehab multiple times (and then slips back to his old ways) in using the same treatment formula over and over again until *the client* gets it right?

This chapter looks at rehab policies that may actually interfere with recovery and explores more productive ways of helping people stay the course.

FRED B.'S STORY OF STAYING THE COURSE AND HELPING HIS SON DO THE SAME

Fred B.'s story caught my attention because, even though his rehab experiences took place some time ago, he had a varied and interesting history of addiction, treatment, and going in and out of recovery before he finally "stayed the course"—one he's maintained for about ten years. He's also had recent experience with the addiction treatment system both as a drug and alcohol counselor and as a parent who wrote me, when we first communicated, "I have a twenty-three-year-old son who's been struggling with this disease for over five years. He's been in short-term primary care programs several times as well as extended-care programs. He's also lived in a variety of halfway houses—a few good, most bad. I've done exhaustive searches to find the places that I felt would most likely be able to help my son and feel fortunate that, having gone through this myself and working as a substance abuse counselor for some time now, I believe I know the right questions to ask and what to look for in trying to find appropriate treatment for him. However, I wish I could claim more success than I've had. Despite the ups and downs with treatment, he's made so much progress and I'm optimistic for his future."

Fred began using drugs regularly when he was fourteen, starting out by trying LSD and soon smoking marijuana daily and drinking on weekends. During high school, he continued to do "a lot of acid and got heavily into barbiturates as well as amphetamines." When he was eighteen, his parents kicked him out of the house and he went to live in a sort of "urban commune" where "people would come from the suburbs every night bringing all kinds of drugs and alcohol, and it was a year-long party." His first experience with heroin felt so good, it scared him, so he promised himself he'd never use it again. He then moved away with his girlfriend and eventually went to college, but continued smoking weed daily and drinking on weekends. He also started selling coke and using it daily. Nevertheless, he graduated summa cum laude with a 3.95 average when he was twenty-seven. Toward the end of his senior year he just decided one day (literally) that he didn't like smoking marijuana or doing coke anymore and hasn't touched either drug since. He then went to graduate school, drank on weekends—"nothing out of the ordinary"—and as he got older, his drinking decreased to a couple of beers or glass of wine with dinner or on weekends.

At thirty-eight, everything changed again when he had his wisdom teeth pulled and his oral surgeon gave him a prescription for Percodan, an opioid. He said, "I had found my drug of choice. I got the prescription refilled as many times as I could, then began forging prescriptions and did that daily until I was arrested and convicted about two and a half years later. That's when I went to my first treatment program, simply to detox and deal with withdrawal. I thought I'd go for ten days or so, get through the physical part of it, and just stop, the same way I stopped the coke and weed, but it didn't turn out that way. I did the whole AA/NA thing and went to an outpatient program, but it wasn't long before I started forging prescriptions again." A businessman at the time, he regularly traveled to countries that sold opioid pain medications over the counter. This enabled him to fill up his suitcase and bring home enough to get by until his next trip. Despite his addiction, he excelled at work and was offered the opportunity to run a large project overseas—in a country where he could continue to obtain these medications over the counter.

In 1999, when he moved back to the United States, on his first night home he decided to go looking for some heroin, which he found. He recalled, "I liked it, no, loved it for quite a while—several years—and was still travelling, and now to countries where heroin was readily available. I'd buy enough there and bring it back. Fortunately, I was never caught." But at some point, "it stopped being fun," and Fred started a several years-long process of going to rehab for two to four weeks, staying sober for anywhere from a few days to a few months, using again, then returning for more treatment. (Some of his outpatient experiences were longer.)

Throughout all of this, Fred said, "I appeared to still be a good dad, spending lots of time with my kids, and was affectionate both to my wife and to them. But she saw me losing my soul. For a long time her attitude was 'It's your issue, you need to fix it.' She was always very supportive when I went to treatment, but I think eventually she realized it wasn't working. Toward the end, she was about ready to leave with my youngest son. (My older child was away at college.) The thought of my wife leaving motivated me in a way that being arrested, convicted with a felony, or getting fired and losing my job and career didn't." Fred added that his downfall came very quickly when he went from snorting heroin to injecting it. In a matter of months his life "spun totally out of control" and he was fired from his job after he nodded off in an important meeting.

Altogether, Fred went to the same outpatient program three times. He also went to residential rehab seven times, sometimes to the same place more than once. His description of his treatment experiences was much like that of others in this book who went to traditional programs. Of several, he said, "It was a standard program—learned about the steps, getting a sponsor, disease concept, defense mechanisms. Same stuff they all talk about." (Fred never did any extended care or lived in sober housing because he didn't want to be away from his family for that long.)

After returning to drugs following all of these experiences, Fred traveled to a now-closed clinic on Saint Kitts Island in the Caribbean to take part in a study by a University of Miami Medical Center researcher on the use of ibogaine, a plant-derived hallucinogen that's not approved for use in treatment in the United States and that the FDA classifies as a Schedule I controlled substance. (Safety concerns have been raised about ibogaine, and NIDA rejected clinical trials for it years ago.) Each time, Fred found that ibogaine eliminated his drug cravings for months, apparently because of a metabolite that stays in the body for some time. But when it wore off, he said, "I was unprepared and went back to using heroin." Then, five months after that last treatment, in late 2002, the FDA approved the use of the medication buprenorphine, which is available as Subutex or Suboxone, for opioid addiction. (Suboxone is a combination of buprenorphine and the medication, naloxone, which is added to decrease its potential for misuse.) Fred exclaimed, "Suboxone saved my life!" He's been on Suboxone and off illicit drugs ever since.

Shortly after this, Fred decided to go back to school to become a certified drug and alcohol counselor in his state, and he'd been working in the field for about three years when we first communicated in 2010. At that time, he was actively involved in AA and NA, but he felt he had to keep the Suboxone "a secret because so many people don't believe you're really 'in recovery' if you're taking it." When we spoke again two years later, he'd stopped attending meetings because he no longer felt the need. (But he said he wouldn't hesitate to go back if things got rocky.)

When his son started having problems with drugs in his late teens, and heroin became his drug of choice, Fred and his wife decided to send him to a prominent high-end residential rehab that has a program for young people. After completing their month-long primary program, it was recommended that he go into their adult three-month extended-care facility. However, after about two and a half months of doing well, Fred said, "They kicked him out because he used heroin when someone else went home on leave and brought it back. I recall being irate that they'd kick someone out for relapsing and arguing with the counselor for hours about it. But I was told that was their policy and nothing could be done." So their son left, didn't stay off drugs for more than a few weeks, and almost right away, Fred and his wife sent him to another long-term program, where he again did well but was made to leave after several months because of what Fred said the place called an inappropriate relationship with a female. (According to Fred, although they were just friends and not romantically involved, they'd been warned about not spending time alone together. When they wandered off someplace alone, Fred said, "That was it.")

Next, their son had his first of many experiences in a sober-living facility, where he did quite well for about five or six months but relapsed on crystal meth and wound up at another rehab. Fred said, "From there, it was more sober houses, back to using, more treatment, more using then detoxing, and more sober houses." Eventually, he went to a nine-month program that Fred described as "one that doesn't spend a lot of time in group counseling and education about addiction. Our son has been there, done that, many times. He needs to learn how to live life without drugs, and that's what this program strives for—to help clients develop problem-solving skills and clean up the wreckage of the past. It's expensive, and we're paying for it. But it bothers me that there are very few people fortunate enough to pay for something like this."

When I was wrapping up the book, Fred's son had completed the nine-month program and moved into an apartment with a friend from the treatment center when he had a relapse that lasted a couple of weeks. He then moved into a sober house and had been off drugs for about six months when he used heroin one time. To quell his cravings, he told his dad that, for most of that six-month period, he'd been taking Suboxone that he'd obtained without a prescription. He felt he couldn't go to a physician for a prescription because the sober house prohibited taking medication for addiction, and his counselor didn't approve of Suboxone. He also felt he couldn't tell people at the AA/NA meetings he was attending because of the stigma attached to medication-assisted treatment.

Of his personal experiences with treatment and as both a father and an addiction professional, Fred said, "It frustrates me to no end that, when the science is clear that medication-assisted treatment saves lives, this information is close to completely ignored by much of the treatment and recovery communities. Yet I do see people who make it without medication, so I know it can be done. One thing that I have more and more clarity about is that there's no "right" way for someone to get and stay off drugs and that it's truly harmful to talk as if there is."

THE ON-AGAIN, OFF-AGAIN NATURE
OF ADDICTION AND RECOVERY

All in all, Fred said, "I think from late 1999 until I got clean it was just a cycle of treatment, relapse, treatment, relapse." The truth is that continuous, ongoing abstinence from alcohol and drugs is relatively unusual for most individuals following one-time treatment. Numerous studies have shown that, on average, people reach sustained abstinence only after three to four episodes of different kinds of treatment over a number of years. Even though the majority of addicted people who go to rehab experience on-and-off using, they often have long periods of stability and improvement, as was the case with Fred B.'s son.

This may seem rather a bleak picture, but it's now argued that addiction is best viewed the way other medical illnesses—such as type 2 diabetes, hypertension, and asthma—are viewed. Tom McLellan and other experts have found very similar patterns in the experiences of people with these problems and those of individuals with substance use disorders in that their symptoms come back just as frequently and they tend to have similar issues with adhering to treatment recommendations.

The good news is that, even though many people with serious drug and alcohol disorders require multiple episodes of treatment before they reach at least a year of sobriety, a 2012 review of scientific studies for SAMHSA by William White revealed that, on average, about half of adults who received professional treatment did achieve recovery. (In the many fewer adolescent studies, the recovery rate was 35 percent.)

One way to look at it is that the impact of multiple rehab experiences can be cumulative. Milwaukee psychologist and addiction expert Dr. Ned Rubin said, "Learning to change addictive behavior is difficult, like learning to ride a bike. And most of us fall off a few times when we're learning. But to get it right, you have to get back on again and keep working at it until it becomes second nature. It's important to keep getting back on the bike and to find someone or someplace where you're comfortable to work and that seems to fit with your style or personality. There's no one right way to do this."

Although the benefits of repeat visits to rehab can add up, and sometimes people just aren't ready for the help that's extended to them, I have to wonder if perhaps the picture might be rosier if expectations were different, policies about "using again" were changed, and there was more of a willingness to try something new for people who've been around the rehab block more than once, twice, or thrice.

ON USING IN REHAB

Most of the programs I visited consider themselves to be abstinence-based—certainly all of the twelve-step rehabs did—but administrators at several of the outpatient programs told me they really had to accept less than abstinence. One said, "To be licensed, we have to be drug-free, abstinence from everything. But we don't kick people out if they lapse." Another stated, "We preach abstinence but there are times when all we can hope for is harm reduction." (Harm reduction generally means "meeting clients where they're at," which translates as lowering drug and alcohol use and the harm they cause rather than stopping completely.)

Some view resumption of *any* use of drugs or alcohol as a relapse. Others who work in the field view a brief episode of use as a lapse or slip, while a relapse is considered a return to more extended and excessive use of alcohol or drugs. When I asked staff at twelve-step-based residential rehabs, "What happens if a patient has a slip or relapse while in the program?" the typical response I got was that they'd handle it on a case-by-case basis. There seemed to be an understanding that "use" might be part of the process for some people but also that only so much could be tolerated for the "safety" of other clients in the group. It might also depend on the stage of treatment—for instance if someone is new, tolerance for use may be higher than for someone further along in rehab. At one place, I was told that if people were further along in treatment and used, they'd probably be discharged and placed at another facility because their motivation would be questioned. Another rehab said that a person's treatment stay might be extended.

At programs for young people, I sensed a fair amount of tolerance. One administrator said, "That's what addicts do. An addict who's new [to treatment] is not going to refuse a substance. We try to use it therapeutically, not punitively." Another staff member said that he did not feel a slip was a relapse and added, "If you have two months of sobriety, then one slip, it's cause for celebration that you had two months. The point is not to blow the slip out of proportion."

Because the occasion didn't arise, I did not witness firsthand what would actually have happened in an incident of use at any of the adult rehabs, although in two different groups where someone was suspected of using, what transpired ranged from a confrontational, rather shaming situation at a traditional program to more of an attempt to not draw attention to the person at a non-twelve-step program, where I was told the person was addressed more privately.

KICKING PEOPLE OUT OF REHAB

Sadie A., profiled in chapter 4 for her "rehab shopping" savvy, found that in most cases when she asked programs about their relapse policies, "If a client was suspected of using and tested positive, they would be kicked out. This means they would have to restart a new program or wait a period of time prior to reentering that one. This made no sense to me as a person trying to get and stay sober. I believe that helping someone after a relapse is the key to a stronger program rather than disappointment that leads to continued use." (In some instances she was told that a client would be moved to a more intense program after the first relapse—"and then you'd be done if another one happened.")

Here's how and why two individuals were terminated from rehab:

- When Eddie F. had finished an outpatient program and was in its aftercare group, he had a "one-night slip" with alcohol. Feeling very guilty, he shared the incident with fellow clients, only to be pulled out by the counselor and told he needed to sign "a zero tolerance agreement or be kicked out." The next week, Eddie felt it was more important to attend his son's birthday party than the aftercare meeting that took place at the same time. Even though he hadn't consumed any more alcohol, Eddie said, "This resulted in my being kicked out of aftercare, which at the time was the one place I felt I could connect with people and share my feelings."
- Alexandria was surprised at how easily her daughter was removed from a famous residential rehab when she used drugs that her boyfriend sneaked in to her. Alexandria said, "It's a substance abuse

treatment program, for goodness' sake. Don't they anticipate that addicts are going to do whatever they can to get drugs?" Her husband added, "Unfortunately, many twelve-step programs still do not have a psychotherapy component. If they did, they would appreciate better the effect of 'kicking someone out' for displaying the symptoms that they came to get help for. It would be like a psychiatric hospital kicking someone out for being 'crazy.'"

As an addiction counselor working in a strict traditional program, Fred B. said, "A few of us think that it's the nature of the disease and that discharging them isn't helping them. But most of the people I work with feel that someone who uses has to be immediately discharged, no questions. They argue that not doing this sends a message to the rest of the community that they can do whatever they want and know they won't get discharged, so why bother to try to do the right thing? Funny thing is that a lot of the clients feel that way. A lot of them say, 'I'm doing the right thing, why should someone who relapses be allowed to stay?' There's also the whole argument about the safety of the community—and that's something I'm concerned about." (As a case in point, one of Fred's young clients overdosed and died after he used drugs that someone brought into the rehab.)

Some experts argue that many of the ways in which rehabs handle use during treatment run counter to the rehabs' own view that addiction is a disease. Even the words "relapse" and "lapse," some say, have moralistic overtones, perhaps less obvious than words like "clean" to refer to drug-free individuals and "dirty" to refer to those still using. They argue that "relapse" is a term that isn't defined (is it one drink or five? Using drugs once or for three days in a row?), implies complete success or total failure (rather than acknowledging shades of gray, such as the value of using less or using once and then deciding to quit), and may impart feelings of shame having to do with complex behavior that's more likely to change incrementally.

In a 2005 article in *Counselor* magazine titled "It's Time to Stop Kicking People Out of Treatment," William White and colleagues note that expelling clients for manifesting the main symptom of the disorder for which they were admitted to rehab—that is, using alcohol or drugs—is "illogical and unprecedented in the health care system." They state, "We know of no other major health problem for which one is admitted for treatment and then thrown out for becoming symptomatic in the service setting. For other chronic health care problems, symptom manifestation serves as a confirmation of diagnosis or feedback that alternative methods of treatment and alternative approaches to patient education and motivation are needed."

They also criticize the practice of discharging clients for rule infractions that have little to do with recovery from addiction. For instance, regarding rules about fraternizing, the authors said that while sexual activity may need to be addressed clinically as part of the treatment process, "One is hard-pressed to find other arenas of health care in which sexual prohibitions are a condition of continued service access."

TEACHING PEOPLE HOW TO HANDLE SETBACKS

Most programs spend a lot of time teaching you how to prevent relapse—for instance, by having a plan in place before you leave rehab for identifying and avoiding the "people, places, and things" that might trigger urges to use alcohol or drugs and for what to do if and when the urges come back. Typical plans include going to twelve-step meetings, going to ninety meetings in ninety days, calling a friend, or seeking out your AA sponsor. But given the frequency with which people go back to using drugs and alcohol, there seemed to be a lot of fear—and not much practical help—around what to do if you actually *did* use again. I spoke with one woman shortly after she left a rehab I visited who seemed absolutely terrified of what would happen if she were to drink again. And the warnings were quite dire at one family program I attended, where the instructor said, "If your [family members] relapse, they may die—they may not get another chance at recovery."

Sadie affirmed that at the conventional residential and outpatient rehabs she attended, "You learn how to *prevent* relapse—but they're afraid to say what happens if you *do* relapse. Even the workbooks are all before it would happen; they're not, 'Where's your plan if you do relapse?' The counselors are trained to not let clients fail." She added, "You hear people say, 'I don't think I have another relapse in me.' But you know what? We all probably do. Look at the statistics—it's more likely to happen than not." Because of all this, she advised that a good question to ask programs is "How are you going to prepare me if I do have a relapse?" Having *first* been to a non-twelve-step program that taught her what to do if she did drink again, she said, "There was acceptance of relapse and working through it. At the nontraditional program, you weren't one step out the door if you used, as in a conventional program. Being prepared was more than just 'call your sponsor.' For example, if I drank, I knew to call my counselor as soon as possible and would get to the clinic to meet with him if he could be available. Even if I was still impaired, I knew I could ask for help without judgment. (In contrast, my AA sponsor wanted me to call her after I sobered up, which might be too late, in my case.)" Because this was not a program with a beginning and an end, Sadie's relationship with the counselor was ongoing and she could continue to see him as needed. On the other hand, when the conventional six-week outpatient program ended, she was frustrated when she was told that there was no way to continue seeing the counselor with whom she had had a relationship.

In an effort to focus more on what's being embraced rather than on what's being avoided, White offers the novel suggestion that instead of "relapse prevention programs" rehab clients would benefit more from "recovery support programs" that help them seek broader dimensions of personal and social well-being such as wellness, quality of life, meaning and purpose, and citizenship. He also advocates abandoning the oft-espoused notion that "relapse is part of recovery" because "using again" is an expression of the disorder, not of the recovery process.

GOING TO REHAB AGAIN AND AGAIN

At twelve-step meetings, you often hear the saying, "Insanity is doing the same thing over and over again but expecting different results." Several experts told me this applies to rehab, too, referring to the lack of logic in putting people through the same kind of treatment repeatedly—where they're offered the same interventions without much consideration about whether they're the right fit. Wyatt D., who went to thirty-day traditional rehabs at least a dozen times yet never connected with the twelve-step philosophy, said that he was labeled "a chronic relapser because I wasn't accepting the program."

A physician who used to work at one of the high-end rehabs I visited said, "Nowhere else in medicine is it okay to blame the patient when treatment doesn't work, to say things like, 'You didn't really work step one.' And the program was rife with it when I left." Dr. Mark Willenbring maintains, "Rehab is one of the few treatments where the less effective it is, the more you need it. You gotta admit, it's a great business model!"

Sometimes, people who aren't ready the first time around do benefit from another period of treatment at the same type of facility. Margaret F. said that when she first went to a famous residential rehab, "I wasn't fully convinced that I couldn't drink ever again. I thought I could get a better handle on it and drink like a normal person." After she relapsed and went back there, she said, "My second time through, it was definitely more tailored to meet my needs, which were relapse, dishonesty, and the PTSD I was dealing with. And I got into specialty groups more quickly—for instance, a grief group and a dual diagnosis group." And at Caron, some repeat clients go to Caron's separate relapse unit that offers somewhat different programming than that of regular primary care.

Dr. Rubin often finds that it's difficult to tell whether clients are not ready to change or "if they're just demoralized because they've tried and have now given up." He said, "I frequently encounter people who had prior treatment experiences where they were criticized and chastised for lapses and relapses." Psychologist Paul Rinaldi, PhD, clinical director of the Addiction Institute of New York, said, "Rather than reinforce someone's shame when they return to rehab by saying things like, 'You didn't listen before,' we should celebrate when they come back." With people in this situation, his staff is trained to think more about "what didn't we consider last time—what did we miss? What stressors are the same and what's different? Maybe the person needs more family work, or we may give them more individual treatment."

You'd think that after many times of doing the same thing, more rehabs would adjust their treatment plans for clients who've been through it before. Fred B. said, "I do feel that treatment for people who are chronic relapsers should be handled differently. And there was no different treatment for me than for clients in any given program for the first time. I eventually figured out, pretty much on my own, that self-esteem was a big issue for me. If I were designing a program, lots of therapy would be involved—to address issues like trauma, anger, being insecure, and lack of coping skills."

Dr. Rinaldi affirmed that sometimes people who've been through rehab repeatedly haven't had a good psychological evaluation and may need more help with co-occurring disorders. In their programs, they also try to recognize what went right, not just what went wrong, for such individuals. He explained, "Even if it's just been for a day, we need to ask what it was like when they weren't using and what the circumstances were." And although they let clients know that people who have outside support tend to do better, they don't "preach the twelve steps are the only way," and encourage clients to try different options.

CAN AN ALL-OR-NOTHING VIEW OF RELAPSE SET PEOPLE UP FOR FAILURE?

A contentious issue in the field of rehab is whether intentional use of *any* drugs or alcohol counts as a relapse. Some people told me that a "one drink/one drunk" message led them to a downward spiral. Dimitri R., for instance, figured that since he'd been taught this philosophy—requiring him to "start all over again"—by multiple rehabs, he may as well go wild if he used. He told me, "Why not just keep doing what I was doing until I got caught? I hated so much starting at 'day one' again and hearing that I must not be ready to be sober, that lying was just easier." He added, "No one ever asked me much about how I was feeling before deciding to use.

They just told me to tell my sponsor or call someone." When he started going to a group at a cognitive-behavioral program, Dimitri said, "If there was any drug use, the group talked about it and analyzed it. That's where I had a breakthrough because I had a safe place to go when I used drugs, rather than feel guilty and let it propel and get out of control."

Research supports the notion that believing in the idea that either you abstain or you use out of control can become a self-fulfilling prophecy. More than fifteen years ago, in a study published in the journal *Addiction*, Dr. Miller and colleagues found in a group of people entering treatment for alcohol problems that those who more strongly endorsed the all-or-nothing disease model of alcoholism were more likely to relapse at six months than were those who didn't endorse the model.

Sadie said that at the non-twelve-step program she attended, it was helpful for her to get away from the idea that if she drank, she had to "start counting all over again," as if she had lost the sober time that she already had. She added, "We don't have sobriety dates; we talk about when we started improving our chemical health." At the traditional programs she attended, "they acted like it was cheating if you did this."

Another point of contention is the requirement that "abstinence from *everything* is necessary." That is, when I asked counselors about the greatest form of resistance they faced from clients, a number said it was failure to recognize the need to give up all substances—for instance, someone who's addicted to prescription painkillers might think it's okay to still drink alcohol or smoke marijuana. In an interview for *Counselor* magazine, Robert DuPont MD, the first director of NIDA, said, "To me, any use of addicting drugs is incompatible with recovery. That means that for heroin addicts to be in recovery, their sobriety date is when they last used any illicit or unprescribed drug, including alcohol and marijuana."

However, Sarah J. told a story of falling back into serious drug use after two and a half years free from her crystal meth addiction because she'd been told at a famous residential rehab that use of any substance was a relapse. Although she'd never had a drinking problem, she said, "They scared me so much about alcohol that I was afraid to go into grocery stores. My dad had to go with me." At one point, when she did drink, she figured "Oh well, I've done it now; I'm using, so I may as well use meth and keep using before they make me stop." This led to a lengthy return to heavy drug abuse, including eventual use of heroin. As mentioned in chapter 4, after finding her way to a non-twelve-step program, she at first still struggled with drugs, but the program continued to work with her. She thought, "You mean I'm not a bad person? I'm not gonna die?" Yet "they just moved on and the only negative consequences were the true negative consequences, like feeling sick after using." With time, the relapses became less frequent and less severe. In the end, she said, "Their reaction to my relapses made me get sober."

Mark Willenbring said, "There is no clear scientific justification for telling people addicted to one substance that they have to be abstinent from everything forever. Someone with opioid addiction may well be a social drinker with no proclivity towards alcohol addiction. This needs to be individualized." Fred B. still has the occasional drink without any problems, but he said he waited until he was very secure in his recovery before he picked up a glass of wine again. Sarah J. wound up being able to drink this way, too, although at the recommendation of the non-twelve-step program she first had a long period of abstinence (eighteen months) from alcohol. The last time we spoke, she told me, "When I go out, I occasionally have a few drinks or a glass of wine with dinner. If people wonder how I can say I'm sober when I drink, I tell them, 'because I don't use heroin or meth.'" However, as an addiction professional now, she does believe that "some people can't use any substances and that, for them, one drink will lead to using." A counselor who works with young adults also made the point that part of the problem with using substances that aren't your drug of choice is that it may put you back in the environment or circumstances that place you at risk again.

After carefully considering the history of this issue and reviewing the scientific literature in this area, William White concludes, "Some people possess a unique vulnerability to addiction to one substance or a particular class of substances that fits them like a lock and key—with other keys simply not fitting. Others bring vulnerabilities for addiction to multiple substances and other excessive behaviors." So how do you know which description fits you or a loved one? White said that long-term studies have not been done to answer that question. However, he believes there's evidence suggesting that the more of the following characteristics an individual has, the more likely he or she is to be prone to being addicted to more than one type of substance: A family history of alcohol and drug problems, a high tolerance to alcohol and drugs at an early age, a drug or alcohol problem that started during adolescence or earlier, an early experience of some sort of trauma (such as sexual abuse), a psychiatric problem, close ties to friends and family who abuse alcohol and/or use drugs, and euphoric memories of your first experience with alcohol or drugs. Given the reality that many people with a risky history won't follow the advice to give up all drugs and alcohol, he thinks the best approach is ongoing "recovery check-ups" that allow for nonpunitive monitoring of use of any substances and early intervention should problems occur. That's how Sarah J. handled her return to drinking. She explained, "I still see a psychologist and closely monitor my feelings to pay attention to why I'm drinking. I have to think about my motives and keep myself in check."

A psychologist who works at a traditional rehab said her advice about drinking for clients who are newly abstinent from drugs is, "In the beginning you don't know what you can and can't do. Do you want to play Russian roulette? You may want to experiment with that, but don't do it for a couple of years."

Research clearly shows that people who were once addicted to alcohol are sometimes able to drink again without problems. However, a 2007 study published in the journal *Alcoholism: Clinical and Experimental Research* suggests that abstinence is the most stable form of recovery for most people with drinking problems. In a study that followed nearly eighteen hundred individuals who were in recovery from what would be considered alcoholism over the course of three years, researchers found that "low-risk drinkers" (people who had been consuming alcohol in a nonproblematic way at the beginning of the three-year period) were about six times more likely to experience a return of some symptoms of an alcohol use disorder than were those who had been abstaining. Note that this study drew from a representative group of people in the general population. Individuals who seek treatment tend to have more severe alcohol problems, and people with more severe problems tend to be less likely to be able to drink moderately.

FINDING A PROGRAM WILLING TO MEET YOU WHERE YOU ARE

What if you (or a loved one) have a substance problem, you're not ready or able to give up drugs or alcohol entirely, but you still want to work on it? How do you find a place that doesn't require abstinence—one that will meet you where you are? It may take some searching, but here are places I visited that would fall into this category:

• **PRACTICAL RECOVERY** offers care primarily from doctoral-level therapists who use a range of scientifically supported approaches from which they "construct a completely individualized treatment plan which fits you, rather than making you fit a preexisting plan." They describe their overall philosophy as "self-empowering" and specialize in helping people with co-occurring disorders, using a unique "collaborative approach" that enables each client to work with a team of therapists who consult with one another about the best way to help him or her. Clients set their own goals, in collaboration with professional staff. In the outpatient program, some clients have an abstinence goal, while others choose to moderate their use of alcohol and/or drugs. Although all clients are expected to be abstinent while in Practical Recovery's residential facilities, some may be contemplating moderation as an acceptable goal at some point after discharge. I had the opportunity to observe a few of their therapy groups that mixed abstainers and moderate users in the same groups. Although some abstinence-based programs couldn't conceive of this model working, it seemed functional in this setting. Psychologist Daniel Galant, PhD, told me, "Often, moderators convince abstainers that they've made the right decision. And it's not unusual for moderators to eventually choose to stop drinking." Dr. Galant added that if an abstainer is early in the abstinence process and having strong cravings, he or she might be discouraged from attending a group like this.

• **MUSCALA CHEMICAL HEALTH CLINIC** is run by a registered nurse who specializes in drug and alcohol treatment and provides one-on-one motivational interviewing and cognitive-behavioral counseling as well as several weekly groups to about fifty individuals and families each week. Bob Muscala said, "The goals are different for every person and may change—complete abstinence and partial abstinence are seen as legitimate goals." In contrast to the Minnesota model, which "prepares people for a lifetime of involvement in AA," Muscala has coined the term the "American model" to describe his "low-structure, progressive/incremental change program that helps the client achieve a lifetime of freedom from the problem behavior." He said, "I prescribe the least amount of services per week for however long is needed for a particular client. It is 'in vivo' work, keeping clients as involved and functional in their lives (work, family, social groups, activities, etc.) as possible, at the same time slowly shifting them away from enjoyment of the undesirable behavior toward acceptance and enjoyment of life with either no use or less use of the addictive substance."

• **THE HEALING JOURNEY PROGRAM AT MINNESOTA INDIAN WOM-EN'S RESOURCE CENTER** is a grant-funded program designed to improve the overall quality of life for Native American women who have chronic drug and alcohol problems. Many of the participants have been in and out of traditional addiction treatment programs and experienced tough times, such as extreme poverty, physical abuse, and loss of custody of their children. Describing their approach to drug and alcohol problems as "harm reduction" rather than "treatment," the director told me, "It's the women's program, not ours. They're not 'out' if they use. We just say, 'Don't be high when you get here.'" Twice a week, the women come together for multiple activities that often occur while they do crafts. The day I attended, events started with a sage-smudging ceremony, followed by a meditation/reading and then a check-in period that allowed each woman to give a personal update. For an hour each week, there is usually some sort of presentation—for instance, from a nutritionist, nurse, therapist, or sexual assault advocate. Or they might have "a woman who was raised in traditional ways" as a speaker. Because Healing Journey is part of a bigger agency, the women also have access to individual mental health therapy once a week.

THE HARM REDUCTION FOR ALCOHOL Web site offers the following "harm reduction therapist" finder: http://hamsnetwork.org/therapist/.

DRUGS THAT HELP PEOPLE WITH DRINKING PROBLEMS GET SOBER AND STAY SOBER

During the decade that passed between my writing *Sober for Good* and *Inside Rehab*, I'd heard over and over about how infrequently medications shown to facilitate recovery from addiction were being prescribed. In the 2010 N-SSATS, only 23 percent of facilities reported using at least one of the FDA-approved drugs for treating alcohol problems. So I was pleasantly surprised to learn that most of the traditional residential rehabs I visited were making these medications available to their clients at the time of my visits. In 2011, Hazelden informed me that they were using Acamprosate (campral) and naltrexone in about 30 percent of their patients, and Caron offered people these same drugs plus topiramate and disulfiram. Promise's Web site indicated that they prefer not to send clients home "taking yet another drug" and an administrator said that although they do a lot of education about drugs for alcohol problems, many of their clients would rather not be on medications.

Several of the outpatient programs I visited were not routinely using medications to treat addictions. In fact, at one place, the director was unfamiliar with drugs that have long been approved by the FDA for treating alcohol problems. One program told me there were barriers: "These medications are not on Medicaid's approved list." Another suggested that cost was a factor. (Medicaid coverage of addiction medications varies considerably by state and by whether or not the state's Medicaid plan is offered under managed care or HMO arrangements. Medicare coverage varies also.) Even when you factor in the cost of the medications, however, several recent studies indicate that the use of medications to treat addictions can significantly lower overall health-care costs. Counter to what you might expect, a 2010 study in the *Journal of Addiction Medicine* suggested that state- and county-owned addiction treatment centers were more likely to use the five FDA-approved medications for treating addiction than were privately owned facilities. The researchers also found that, overall, the presence of staff physicians and nurses was quite low and said, "Without increases in the employment of physicians, nurses, and other medical personnel, there are likely to be ceiling effects on the percentage of organizations that can offer medication-assisted treatments."

A 2012 *New York Times* article on drugs for alcohol problems illustrates that some rehabs are still opposed to using these medications. In a remarkable twist of incongruity at a place invested in the twelve steps and the disease model, Harry Haroutunian, MD, physician director at the Betty Ford Center in Rancho Mirage, California, was quoted as saying, "When you medicalize the disease and pay a lot of attention to the biology, it's easy to get a patient to say, 'Well, my cravings are gone, there's nothing else I have to do.' We try to use the principles of the twelve-step program as a source of strength during times of craving, to deal with the inevitable stressors." (It was suggested in the article that AA is opposed to such medications, but this is untrue—AA leaves that decision to members and their physicians.) Although patients who arrive at Betty Ford already taking some kind of prescription drug for addiction won't be asked to stop, others are unlikely to be prescribed such medication.

DRUGS FOR DRINKING PROBLEMS

Currently three drugs are approved by the FDA for the treatment of alcohol use disorders:

- **Disulfiram** (trade name Antabuse)—can deter people from drinking by causing anticipation of the unpleasant symptoms, including nausea, vomiting, palpitations, and headache dizziness that occur when people drink alcohol while taking it. (Although currently there are no FDA-approved medications for cocaine addiction, disulfiram also appears to reduce the craving for cocaine by diminishing the high produced by this drug.)

- **Acamprosate** (trade name Campral)—is thought to reduce relapse risk by reducing subtle but unpleasant symptoms associated with early abstinence. It is most likely to work with people who have had severe physical withdrawal symptoms such as morning shakes.
- **Naltrexone** (available for oral use or in monthly injectable extended-release form under the name **Vivitrol**)—blocks receptors involved in the pleasant sensations associated with drinking (so it's easier to stop before intoxication) and can reduce alcohol craving.

Topiramate, another drug that two studies showed to be effective for people with alcohol use disorders, is believed to act by decreasing the urge to drink. It's approved by the FDA for the treatment of seizures and migraine headaches but can be prescribed "off label" for those with alcohol problems. Overall, Dr. Daniel Kivlahan said, "The approved drugs for alcohol use disorders have not been shown to have blockbuster effects in the way that antibiotics do for bacterial infections, nor are they as effective as the medications we have for opioid addiction (see the next section). But they do boost the odds of success on average, and some individuals consider them to be a critical tool in their recovery."

DRUGS THAT HELP PEOPLE WITH DRUG PROBLEMS RECOVER AND STAY RECOVERED

A wealth of studies show that the use of two FDA-approved drugs—methadone and buprenorphine—for treating people addicted to opioids, are highly effective not only for making the initial medical withdrawal or "detox" phase more comfortable, but when used as part of "maintenance treatment" after leaving rehab, they also help people *stay* recovered.

Unlike medications for alcohol problems, in the United States methadone must be dispensed or prescribed by state- and federally regulated clinics—opioid treatment programs (OTPs)—or, in the case of buprenorphine, by specially certified physicians. Fred B. tried getting off heroin by using methadone, which would work for periods of time, but because he'd have to go to a clinic daily to get methadone, it was too difficult to stick with it and keep up a career that involved so much traveling. "With Suboxone," he said, "a doctor can write a prescription for a month, and you don't have to go to a clinic every day." And his health insurance pays for it. While we typically think of OTPs as treating heroin addicts, they also help people addicted to prescription painkillers such as OxyContin and Vicodin, as well as morphine and codeine. Actually, far more people abuse prescription opioids and seek treatment for addiction to them than use heroin and go to rehab for heroin addiction.

In Internet searches, if you come across so-called ultrarapid detox that offers "painless detox" for heroin-addicted people and takes place under general anesthesia to sedate the client for several hours while an opiate blocker precipitates withdrawal, be aware that research challenges the value of its use and raises questions about its safety. The method was designed in the hope of mitigating the discomfort of withdrawal and expediting initiation of relapse prevention therapy. However, after a 2005 National Institute on Drug Abuse–funded study compared this detox method with two others, one of the researchers concluded, "Although providers advertise anesthesia-assisted detox as a fast and painless method to kick opiate addiction, the evidence does not support those statements. Patients should consider the many risks associated with this approach, including fluid accumulation in the lungs, metabolic complications of diabetes, and a worsening of underlying bipolar illness, as well as other potentially adverse events."

DRUGS FOR DRUG PROBLEMS

Typically, the changes in the brain caused by opioid addiction don't correct themselves until some time after drug use has stopped and can trigger cravings for the drugs months and even years later. Currently, the following medications are approved by the FDA for use in treating opioid use disorders:

- **Methadone**—can be used for medically supervised withdrawal ("detox") alone or for long-term maintenance treatment. In use for more than forty years, methadone has been shown to be effective for both heroin and prescription drug addiction. For maintenance, it must be taken daily.
- **Buprenorphine** (trade names Subutex and Suboxone)—can be used for medically supervised withdrawal alone or for long-term maintenance treatment. However, unlike methadone, buprenorphine can be prescribed in a doctor's office by specially certified physicians, where clients should receive or be referred for outside counseling. (Typically, Subutex is given during the early days of treatment, while Suboxone is used during the maintenance phase.) Some OTPs also prescribe buprenorphine.

Methadone and buprenorphine are substitute drugs that block cravings and drug seeking for illegal and unauthorized drugs—they're legal and do not produce a high or impair functioning when properly medically prescribed. When used correctly, they allow people to live normal lives. If a person treated with these medications takes an opioid such as heroin, the euphoric effects are usually dampened or suppressed. To achieve stable recovery, some people need to stay on these medications for long periods of time or even for life.

- **Naltrexone**—blocks the effects of opioids, but its effectiveness depends largely upon patient motivation and social support because users must abstain or detox from opioids for at least seven days before starting treatment and then take the medication regularly. (Again, Vivitrol is the injectable extended-release form of naltrexone, and one injection blocks the effects of opioids for about a month.)

Given all the talk about escalating pain-reliever misuse, it's rather alarming that so few programs are available to treat opioid addiction. For instance, even though clients receiving methadone or buprenorphine in

OTPs accounted for 28 percent of all individuals in treatment in the year 2010, OTPs were available in only 9 percent of all substance abuse treatment facilities, according to the N-SSATS. And as of early 2012, a spokesperson for the National Alliance of Advocates for Buprenorphine Treatment reported that, nationwide, with only about eight thousand physicians prescribing buprenorphine, there were not enough services available to meet the demand.

At least as alarming is the fact that a number of rehabs refuse to send people home on these medications. An administrator at one residential rehab told me, "No one leaves on Suboxone because that's a recipe for disaster." As of August 2011, all of the residential adult rehabs I visited were using buprenorphine for detoxification purposes, but none were sending people home on opioid maintenance medications.

In the summer of 2012, Promises' Web site stated, "Although Suboxone and Subutex are approved for maintenance treatment . . . we only use the drug for the detoxification period." The site said at that time, "We do not want to send you home taking yet another drug" and warned that you should "beware" of drug rehabs that tell you you'll be taking detox drugs when you return home, adding, "This is not a full detox and does not give you the best chance for success." (Promises did indicate that for people concerned about relapse, they can develop a plan using a medication such as Vivitrol for three to six months.)

This assertion is in direct contrast to research findings and what numerous experts told me. In 2009, the United Nations' World Health Organization (WHO) published guidelines for treating opioid use disorders based on an international consensus that concluded maintenance therapy with either methadone or buprenorphine produced far better outcomes than withdrawal and detoxification alone and that "opioid withdrawal (rather than maintenance treatment) results in poor outcomes in the long term." The report found maintenance treatment, combined with psychosocial assistance, to be the most effective of all treatments examined. Not only that, but a number of studies show that such treatment markedly lowers the death rate in people addicted to opiods—by as much as 50 percent.

Although most research on treatments for opioid use disorders has been conducted with heroin-addicted people in methadone clinics, the value of "maintenance" treatment in people addicted to prescription pain-killers was supported in an important 2011 study published in the *Archives of General Psychiatry*. Nearly half of participants reduced painkiller abuse during extended (at least twelve-week) Suboxone treatment, but the success rate dropped to less than 10 percent once Suboxone was discontinued. And participants who received intensive addiction counseling fared no better than those who didn't receive counseling. Referring to this study, Brown University addiction expert Dr. Peter Friedmann concluded in the online newsletter *Alcohol, Other Drugs, and Health: Current Evidence* that "a tapering detoxification strategy, regardless of duration, fails the majority of patients. As with the treatment of hypertension or diabetes, as long as the patient takes the medication, it works; when the medication is stopped, the disorder returns." In light of such mounting evidence, it will be interesting to see if rehabs that use the detox-only approach change their policies. At one rehab I visited, where I was somewhat adamantly told, "Our goal is to use as few medications as possible," I was informed less than a year later that while they still were not routinely using such medications, some of their clients were participating in a medication study. At press time Hazelden announced that, for the first time, it was starting to use buprenorphine for select patients.

Curtis M. considered going to a famous residential rehab for his forty-year opioid addiction and was told that they used buprenorphine for detox, then weaned clients off it by the end of thirty days. Instead, he went to an outpatient drug and alcohol program and separately saw a physician who prescribed maintenance Suboxone, which Curtis described as "a miracle drug." He added, "In the past, I always wanted to use—it always consumed me before. This is the one thing that Suboxone has taken away from me. Now, I can sit and read a book."

Mark Willenbring, who earlier in his career was director of a Veterans Administration rehab that included a methadone treatment program, said, "When addiction treatment providers 'don't believe' in maintenance treatment, it's like a doctor 'not believing' in chemotherapy for cancer. These medications allow many people a chance at recovery who otherwise would fail at quitting." Boston University School of Medicine's Richard Saitz added, "If this were viewed like other health problems, patients addicted to opioids who are not offered the opportunity to be on maintenance medications would sue their providers and win. These maintenance drugs prevent death, HIV infection, and all those other things rehabs care about—dozens of studies affirm this. At the very least, patients should be linked with places using methadone or buprenorphine after they leave their initial treatment."

If you go to a residential rehab that uses buprenorphine for *detox only* but you'd like to try it long term, ask if they'd be willing to keep you on it during your treatment stay and then refer you afterward to a physician in your area who's a certified buprenorphine provider. Another way to go about it, advises Dr. Kivlahan, is that before going to residential rehab, find a physician in your community who will get you started on buprenorphine—then if you still feel that residential treatment is needed, go to rehab with a plan in place for resuming treatment with that doctor after you're discharged from rehab. Dr. Kivlahan said, "That would provide continuity and should clarify up-front whether the residential program is needed and, if so, whether they are willing to work with you toward maintenance treatment with buprenorphine." (Note that when a rehab says it provides "buprenorphine services," it could mean either detox or maintenance services, so be sure to ask.)

Unfortunately, stigma and stereotypes abound about opioid replacement therapies. Several people described past experiences in which they or a family member went to methadone clinics that provided little or no counseling, seemed like places where "providers were in it for the money," and/or where they could buy drugs right outside the door. However, according to William White, who's written extensively for government agencies on the topic of opioid maintenance treatment, professionalism has evolved with the creation of advocacy groups, treatment associations, and accreditation standards. He said, "My experience suggests that the number of very high quality, recovery-focused OTPs is greater than it has ever been in both the public and private sectors."

A huge remaining problem is the stigma of being on medically assisted treatment (MAT) within the treatment community itself. Fred B.'s initial hesitation to tell me that he was on Suboxone was emblematic of that. When he was still attending AA and NA, he told me, "Being on Suboxone is not something I'd announce at a meeting. I tried to stay away from discussions about it because it's looked down upon." Also, Fred found that his use of MAT prevented his admission to a prestigious addiction-training program. He said, "They actually sent me a letter stating they wouldn't accept me as a student due to my use of Suboxone." (An advocacy group offered to defend him free of charge if he wanted to fight this, but he decided not to.) Fred's son's problems with housing show stigma of a different nature. The government brochure *Know Your Rights* states that it is illegal to exclude people who live or want to live in halfway houses, recovery homes, or other residences because they are on methadone or buprenorphine, "even though this type of discrimination occurs with some frequency."

RESOURCES

- A federal government Web site with resources on medication-assisted treatment for substance use disorders: http://www.dpt.samhsa.gov/
- To find a physician certified to prescribe buprenorphine, go to suboxone.com and put in your zip code.
- You can contact the SAMHSA Buprenorphine Information Center by telephone toll-free at 1-866-BUP-CSAT (1-866-287-2728), or by e-mail at info@buprenorphine.samhsa.gov
- The National Alliance of Advocates for Buprenorphine Treatment is a nonprofit resource: http://www.naabt.org/
- For the brochure *Are You in Recovery from Alcohol or Drug Problems? Know Your Rights*: http://pfr.samhsa.gov/docs/Know_Your_Rights_Brochure_0110.pdf
- The National Alliance for Medication-Assisted Recovery, or NAMA Recovery, is an advocacy organization of medication-assisted treatment patients and health-care professionals at www.methadone.org.

PROGRAM SPOTLIGHT:
SPECIALIZED TREATMENT SERVICES (STS),
WHERE CHOICES COUNT

I wasn't sure what to expect when I visited the opioid treatment program Specialized Treatment Services in Minneapolis, the largest facility of its kind in Minnesota, owned and directed by Carrie McGregor, a drug and alcohol counselor with many years of experience in this line of work. I first learned about STS's philosophy, which is quite different from that of a number of other OPT facilities that require abstinence from illicit drugs and alcohol. While abstinence is the goal at STS—and regular drug screens are done for this reason—they "do not kick clients out the way other clinics do for drug use." I was told, "If they use, clients are not punished; we use it as a teaching moment. We meet people where they are." (The caveat is that clients who have county funding *are* required to be abstinent from other drugs. If they can't remain abstinent, they may be referred to an outpatient or residential treatment program, most of which won't accept people on opioid replacement drugs and, therefore, wean clients off them.)

I got to see medical cubicles at which either methadone or buprenophine are dispensed to clients by nurses and required to be taken (orally) in a nurse's presence. (This is to avoid on-the-street sale of the medications as illicit drugs.) Clients who consistently have negative test results indicating they're not using illicit drugs can earn "take-home" privileges, meaning they're given short-term supplies of prescribed opioid replacement drugs to self-administer.

I also met with the clinic's medical director, a physician, who conducts an initial medical evaluation on each client and then periodically monitors his or her replacement medications and related health concerns. Clients also receive counseling: for the first ten weeks in the program, they're required to see a licensed addiction counselor once a week for an hour; after that, visits become less frequent. If they've never been in addiction treatment before, it's "strongly recommended" that clients attend an outpatient treatment program—either the "Six Dimensions" non-twelve-step program housed within STS or an outside program. STS also offers education and counseling groups on such topics as stress management, women's issues, positive self-image, living skills, recreation, family education, and career building.

Ultimately, the goal is to wean clients from the opioid replacement drugs, but that doesn't always happen. McGregor said, "I've known people who've been on methadone for twenty years, and they're successful, functioning members of society. If they went off methadone, they'd be out on the streets." In cases like this, she said, "it's like someone with hypertension needing to take medication to control blood pressure."

It became apparent almost immediately upon my arrival at STS that a glaring difference between their approach and that of many addiction treatment programs is that they allow clients far more choices, and the program seems open to whatever works. McGregor unofficially described their philosophy as "If you listen to the clients, they tell you what they need. You have to set aside *your* ideas." In the first place, clients may choose their own counselors and are allowed to switch counselors if it doesn't work out (a client confirmed this). They also have a say in whether they're prescribed methadone or buprenorphine as their opioid replacement medication. Aside from the required one-on-one sessions with a counselor, the group counseling and education programs that STS offer are suggested but not required. As far as the twelve steps are concerned, McGregor said, "We try to connect people with some kind of outside community group when they leave here. If ninety meetings in ninety days works for you, that's great. But we're open to other options." Demonstrating this openness, McGregor agreed to allow the operation of a separately run, non-twelve-step outpatient program under the STS roof.

THE MEANING OF "SUCCESS RATES"

An amazing 76 percent of our graduates choose to remain drug free and become productive members of society.

Drug rehab programs with this method are having a success rate of over 70 percent.

How do you know if claims like these, taken from programs boasting about their success rates on the Internet, are legitimate? How can you tell if a rehab has a good track record at helping clients stay the course? I can tell you that no place I visited made any claims close to these. In fact, when an administrator at a residential program I was visiting said to me, "A rehab that says 'we have a 75 percent success rate' is full of shit," I thought, *Now there's forthrightness for you!*

Treatment success has traditionally been tracked by keeping tabs on how many people continuously stay abstinent, in part because disease-model proponents often believe that anything less than that signifies failure. Also, abstinence is a lot easier to track than "slipping and getting back on the wagon" or "using less." (Interestingly, quantity and frequency of alcohol and drug use are not even mentioned in the DSM definitions used to diagnose people with substance use disorders, aside from the criterion that specifies "the substance is often taken in larger amounts or over a longer period than was intended.")

Some studies have grouped people in such categories as "abstinent recovery" and "nonabstinent recovery," the latter describing those who once were considered addicted but subsequently resumed drinking without having any problems. Taking into account the fact that people may have a few difficult days interspersed with use-free periods of time, other studies look at a percentage of days people are abstinent during a period of time following treatment.

After reviewing more than one hundred studies on how people fare in abstinence-oriented addiction treatment programs, both high- and low-end, and concluding that, overall, roughly 50 percent of their clients use again over the course of the year following treatment, Dr. McLellan concluded, "This isn't a bad track record, particularly when you consider some of the challenges in the field." However, he agrees with many experts who say that it's a mistake to look just at abstinence from alcohol and drugs as the only marker of success and added, "We need to ask, 'Are clients actively participating in treatment, *reducing* their use of chemicals, improving their health and social functioning, having fewer legal and social problems, becoming employed, or going back to school?'" And, indeed, studies that measure the outcome of various treatment interventions often examine how people are doing in multiple areas of life.

The bottom line, however, is that without general agreement on accepted benchmarks, such as we have in other areas of medicine—for instance, the number of successful heart procedures for a specific clinic—we lack a system that enables people considering addiction rehab to make informed decisions. Harvard addiction expert John Kelly, PhD, said, "Without high-quality systematic and standardized measurement and program evaluation, consumers will always be at the mercy of the word of program directors selling their particular programs. I think the only way around all this is to measure program effects and outcomes. But most programs don't do this. Those that do some kind of evaluation often claim outrageously high 'success' rates without telling you how they got their numbers or how 'success' is defined." For example, is it a one-month, one-year, or a five-year abstinence rate? Does it take into account everyone who entered treatment at a particular time—if the dropouts aren't included, "success rates" will be falsely inflated.

When I asked the rehabs I visited, "How do you monitor the quality and success of your program?" a number of them said they conducted client satisfaction surveys, which, according to Dr. Adam Brooks of the Treatment Research Institute (TRI), "are generally not a very good way to measure quality of care because clients typically give high ratings regardless of the quality of treatment they're receiving." Even though they're not very effective, for instance, people may like (or even prefer) common rehab activities such as seeing films and hearing lectures. As lead author of a study of outpatient programs described in chapter 4, Dr. Brooks and coauthors found that despite the fact that clients agreed that counselors rarely employed science-based strategies, the clients still gave them high satisfaction ratings.

When I asked Promises for outcome information, they told me that they survey clients ninety days after leaving the program by telephone and through written surveys. For each quarter in the year 2009 (the year I visited them), they could tell me what percentage of clients reported achieving ninety days of sobriety (defined as abstinence), as well as details about their involvement in twelve-step meetings. They also provided information about what percentage of admitted clients completed the survey. For instance, for each quarter, at least two-thirds to three-quarters of their clients completed the survey, and, of those, more than eight out of ten had ninety days of sobriety and were attending twelve-step meetings. (Several administrators raised the issue of paying for outcome evaluations. A director of an outpatient program told me, "There is no funding for outcome follow-ups.")

A REHAB THAT DOES REAL RESEARCH

To its credit, Hazelden is one of the few addiction treatment facilities that has a research department, Butler Center for Research, and publishes studies of its treatment outcomes in peer-reviewed journals. At its Web site, under the heading "Why Choose Hazelden?" it said, "Hazelden treatment works. . . . Our scientific evidence-based treatment methods get results. Over 80 percent of our adult patients either remain continuously abstinent or dramatically reduce their use in the year after treatment." The study from which those statistics were drawn, published in the journal *Addictive Behaviors* in 1998, followed 1,083 people admitted to their Center City Minnesota-model-based residential program, which found that one year after treatment ended, 53 percent reported abstinence and an additional 35 percent reported reductions in drug and alcohol use. (It's interesting to note that although the cornerstone of successful treatment at Hazelden is considered abstinence, the "using less" statistic is also used to promote their program.) However, at this one-year follow-up point, only about 70 percent of the initial group of people were still involved in the study.

Based on his knowledge about treatment outcomes, Mark Willenbring, MD, former director of NIAAA's Division of Treatment and Recovery, said that it's reasonable to believe that of the 30 percent of clients who could not be contacted for follow-up, "More people were probably not abstinent than were the ones who were contacted, and that would make the abstinence rate lower than reported." We don't really know how those who couldn't be reached were doing, and there aren't studies on people who can't be located after treatment. But a number of studies have found, and numerous experts I consulted agreed, that people who are more difficult to contact for follow-up tend to have worse treatment outcomes than do people who are followed up more easily. Willenbring added, "Unless you assume that the people they couldn't contact had identical outcomes to those they could reach, it's likely their actual outcomes aren't as favorable as they report." This is not to denigrate the Hazelden study, but to make the point that outcome results are often presented in a selective way, depending on the group being followed. Willenbring also pointed out that the higher socioeconomic status of clients who go to programs like Hazelden makes their prognosis better at the outset of treatment than that of clients in a program with less-advantaged people.

In their latest research update report on their 2011 outcomes for adults attending their Center City, Minnesota, facility, Hazelden not only notes continuous abstinence rates but also compares percentage of days clients were abstinent from alcohol before and after treatment. At the outset, on average, the more than four hundred clients surveyed by telephone by Hazelden's Butler Center for Research said they'd been abstinent from alcohol on 38 percent of days. A year after treatment, the report indicates they were abstinent on 95 percent of days, a significant increase. However, Audrey Klein, PhD, Hazelden's research director, informed me that about 40 to 45 percent of such clients are usually not available at the one-year follow-up, information that was not included in the research update. (Their research studies generally have better response rates.) Dr. Klein said that while Hazelden consistently provides such information when its studies are published in scientific journals, it was not included in the research update because it's intended for a lay audience. One could argue that because these latter figures were not included, the outcomes look much better than they probably were. However, as Dr. Klein notes, "The reality is that we have no way to know how the people we don't reach are doing. They may be doing worse than the ones we reach or they may be doing better."

It can also be helpful to know what percentage of clients complete a rehab's program. I found that the high-end residential rehabs I visited had completion rates of about 90 percent while some of the outpatient programs were in the 55 to 60 percent range. It's not possible to know, however, if the differences have to do with program quality or other factors, such as the very different backgrounds of the clients in the programs. And completion rates aren't that relevant to programs that don't have "set" schedules and with more of a policy that encourages people to come indefinitely or on an "as-needed" basis.

Finally, licensed treatment programs in some states report yearly "performance outcomes" having to do with various aspects of patient treatment. In Minnesota, for instance, you can look up each program to find out what percentage of clients improved in such areas as drug and alcohol use, employment status, self-help-group participation, family support, and relapse potential. And the state of New York offers a program-by-program "scorecard" that reveals such information as completion and abstinence rates and employment status of clients after treatment. The problem with reports like these is that they tell you how clients did while they were in treatment for a recent time period, but not later in time—for instance, a year after treatment ends. Again, to find out if your state has any such reports, the easiest way to access your state's drug and alcohol agency is to go to SAMHSA's Substance Abuse Treatment Facility Locator and click on the link for "State Substance Abuse Agencies": http://findtreatment.samhsa .gov/TreatmentLocator/faces/quickSearch.jsp.

BEYOND REHAB: THE "CONTINUING CARE" EXPERIENCE

Inside Rehab has primarily focused on the first stage of addiction treatment or what's commonly known as primary care or "phase one." Unfortunately, most clients don't even make it to the end of primary care in any one treatment episode, as mentioned in chapter 4. However, a whole other book could be written about "beyond rehab" or what many people call aftercare. The preferred term is actually "continuing care" and it includes *extended-care programs* (for people referred for more or specialty treatment after primary care, sometimes involving longer residential stays); *aftercare groups* (for "graduates" of rehabs following residential or outpatient treatment); and *sober-living facilities* (such as halfway houses and sober houses). While some people I met told me that their continuing care experiences consisted of "Go to AA and good luck"—and that does actually work for some—sending clients to twelve-step meetings is not considered continuing care treatment.

As stressed throughout this book, there's growing recognition that many people who struggle with substance use disorders need much more than a finite, short-term rehab experience. Bruce O., who's had two daughters in and out of various types of addiction programs, says that "aftercare is as important as initial intervention, detox, and treatment." As mentioned in chapter 4, the National Institute on Drug Abuse says, "Generally, for residential or outpatient treatment, participation for less than 90 days is of limited effectiveness, and treatment lasting significantly longer is recommended for maintaining positive outcomes." Experts who are developing ways to keep people in treatment longer say that we need to move away from providing an initial "burst" of rehab toward more of a *continuum* of care. And, indeed, an administrator at one of the rehabs I visited said, "One of the problems is that we as an industry have not educated the public that twenty-eight days doesn't do it. We need to see it as short-term and long-term needs."

Sadie A.'s experience at the high-end rehab mentioned earlier followed the typical course of a month of intense Minnesota-model-based primary care treatment at their residential facility, followed by six weeks in their outpatient program (in a different location), which was very much "more of the same." When the outpatient program ended, it was recommended that Sadie attend the same rehab's "continuing care" groups, but her health insurance wouldn't cover them. So Sadie went back to the non-twelve-step outpatient program where she started her treatment because it was "open-ended and you can keep going as long as you need to."

Several of the high-end rehabs I visited told me that although they refer 25 to 50 percent of their clients to extended-care treatment (which may mean several more months in a residential facility), only about 30 to 50 percent of them follow through. Some clients are resistant to the notion of needing more treatment, especially if it means being away from home longer. And as mentioned previously, funding for continuing care through insurance, public funds, and personal funds is often inadequate. As Fred B. suggested earlier, continuing care can come at a steep personal cost. At one point, Bruce O. had both daughters in sober-living facilities to the tune of $1,900 per month, combined, not including living expenses of another $200 per week.

Residential rehabs sometimes have specialists who help place clients in various continuing-care options following primary care. And they may have their own residential extended care programs and/or sober residences, to which clients may be referred following their initial thirty-day stay. A continuing care specialist at Hazelden's youth program told me that they have a list of extended-care rehabs (in addition to their own) to whom they make referrals and that they have "outreach people" across the country who do site visits to these rehabs.

Some rehabs offer telephone follow-up and support. Caron provided free monthly checkup calls for a year after residential rehab, while Hazelden had a free eighteen-month online continuing recovery service with various tools and activities, plus a personal recovery coach who could be contacted daily. Other places offered free aftercare groups, some of them professionally run, others peer facilitated.

There isn't much research about "what works" for continuing care— only about twenty controlled research studies have been conducted since the late 1980s to examine the various types of help available following the completion of residential or outpatient treatment. They suggest that interventions lasting at least twelve months or in which greater efforts were made to reach and engage clients—for instance by visiting the home, approaching clients by telephone calls, use of incentives such as money, or involving significant others—appeared to be the most effective. And two studies showed that "recovery management checkups" can help get people back in treatment when needed and significantly increased days of abstinence following treatment.

CONTINUING CARE FRUSTRATIONS

Some people expressed frustration with their continuing care experiences at a high-end rehab. Elizabeth F. said, "They didn't seem to have a lot of data about programs far away or follow-up once you got there. So ask rehabs questions about this and, when they refer you somewhere, also find out, 'When was the last time you were there?'" She mentioned that a family member checked out a sober home the rehab recommended, and after going there, said, "No way." Another woman said, "I really can't stand how these residential places all commonly recommend patients stick around for further treatment. I suspect they have a cross-referral system." She's gone on to receive training in the field and added, "The most frustrating thing in all of this is that when a patient doesn't agree to the recommended additional treatment, it gets labeled as 'resistance.' Then these resistant patients are also told that they will never stay sober and that they are manipulative liars."

Several professionals raised concerns about the "business" of sending clients to residential extended-care facilities that often last as long as ninety days. Marriage and family therapist and addiction specialist, Paul Hokemeyer, JD, PhD, appreciates this need for some patients, but isn't convinced everyone who winds up there needs this level of care. "In effect, what they often turn out to be are expensive baby-sitting programs that indulge their patients' narcissistic needs to feel coddled and pampered. Even patients with co-occurring disorders, who require a higher level of care, can usually be effectively stabilized in thirty days." He believes it's important for people to get back to their lives. He added that these ninety-day programs are expensive "both in terms of real dollars and human resources that need to be invested in repairing families, careers, and individual lives." Hokemeyer noted that rehabs have an incentive to keep people in treatment for as long as possible, explaining, "Not only does it improve their bottom line through additional fees, but it improves their 'track record' by keeping people sober longer." His advice to people considering the ninety-day option is "Make sure the treatment center has a robust family program and a reputation for solid psychotherapeutic work. If it doesn't, save your time and money."

A longtime clinician at a prominent residential rehab felt it was a conflict of interest that many of their clients get referred to the rehab's own extended-care programs. She said, "It would be different if we also referred them other places, but the directive comes from higher up, and the counselors have become convinced that it's necessary. So what happens is that although patients are supposed to come up with their own goals, if they say they want to go to outpatient treatment next, that doesn't fit with our business plan. So we browbeat people into extended care." She's found that during the last two weeks of primary care, a lot of time and energy winds up being spent on trying to convince clients they need to go to extended care rather than on "preparing people on what they need to do to go home."

REHAB THAT COMES TO YOUR DOOR

What if you had a drug and alcohol counselor willing to show up at your door—one who'd personally come to your home to help you get back on your feet after you've struggled with addiction? You might think it would be something only the elite could afford, but I learned that my own county has just such a "community-based treatment" program, and it's usually covered by private health insurance as well as by public funds. I spoke with Jason Hoffman, the Minnesota-licensed addiction counselor who runs the program, who explained that it was designed for people who "are constantly in the system—people who often do well when they're in treatment programs but can't do well when they go home." However, he added that it's not just for people who've been through treatment multiple times. Most of his clients are dual diagnosed with psychiatric problems, and some have anxiety when they're in group settings. Some can't access treatment programs. For others, AA isn't the right fit. When I wondered about the expense of a model like this, Hoffman responded, "We're finding it can be just as cost effective as sending people to treatment and then having them come home." Hoffman works for a large HMO, and his supervisor told me, "Payers began covering this service as 'individual' treatment several years ago, when they recognized its value."

Hoffman often feels "like a life coach" as he helps people in different dimensions of their lives, for instance in building relationships, solving problems at work and school, and teaching them better communication skills. He sees his clients anywhere from twice weekly to once a month and their relationship can go on for months or years—there's no set end date. With different goals for each client, he said, "It may be sobriety or not ending up in the hospital. We're looking at other measures than abstinence." Personally, he tries "to get them excited about something they have fears or concerns about" and is gratified when they "see things in a different light." He said, "I have quite a few clients who have gone back to school, are being successful, and heading in a direction that they never thought possible."

I came across people in my area I personally knew could benefit from this program who had no knowledge of it. If you are interested in such services, ask around in your area about "community-based treatment" at rehabs and public-health agencies.

LIVING IN A SOBER FACILITY

Sometimes, the "beyond rehab" experience includes moving into a sober-living facility—a place that may go by names like "halfway house," "recovery home," or "sober house." (In chapter 5, I discussed doing this while in outpatient treatment, but often people find that it's a helpful way to ensure their sobriety following rehab.) According to Beth Fisher, LCSW, president of the recently formed National Association of Recovery Residences (NARR), "These monikers lack common definition and clarity, not to mention clear professional identity in the field of recovery services, and the meaning often depends on the system or area of the country in which one operates." Such housing services may be directed by a staff, professional or otherwise, or managed by recovering peers. Preferring the term "recovery residence" for such facilities, NARR also includes under its umbrella facilities that provide residential treatment and extended care.

Fred B., whose son has lived in more than half a dozen recovery residences, points out, "In theory, sober living is a great thing—it provides safe, structured living for people in early recovery and requires both personal responsibility and accountability. But when you put a lot of people in early recovery together, there are going to be a lot of relapses. When people do relapse, they tend to take others down with them. I can't tell you how many times I've seen that, either with my son or with others in houses where he's lived."

So why did Fred continue to support his son's living in these facilities? He responded, "Despite all of the negatives, there's some level of accountability." As someone familiar with dozens of them in California and Florida—two states known for having a proliferation of such establishments—Fred said, "The intentions of the owners vary tremendously. Some are owned by people who truly care and want to help residents stay clean and sober." His son had two very positive experiences, which Fred described as "the ideal of what sober living should be. They had regular (weekly) drug testing, curfews that were enforced, groups run by a professional therapist a couple of times a week, and owners and on-site managers dedicated to ensure the houses were well run." But he found that "those houses are very rare. Many are run by greedy people who don't care about addicts and are just in it for the money. The dirty little secret is that there's a lot of money in it and it draws some pretty unsavory people in early recovery who have money to invest." Adding that certain sober-living places charge $4,000 to $5,000 a month, he said, "When people are paying that much money, the owners aren't going to hold residents accountable or they'd just move elsewhere, which can mean that they can just do what they want, with no consequences." Often, he added, "Sober houses are in pretty bad neighborhoods—what 'nice' neighborhood wants a house full of addicts? So they may be literally next door or down the street from crack houses and/or in drug-infested neighborhoods. And despite what the owners tell people, in practice, drug testing is very rare because it's too expensive."

Stories from other individuals who lived in sober housing ran the gamut as well—with conditions that ranged from rigid and demeaning to positive and life changing. Emily E. went to a halfway house that gave people demerits for things like not making their bed on time or misplacing their keys. She said, "They were very punitive—if you got three X's, you couldn't leave the house or watch TV. You'd have to go to your room, like a child." In contrast, Sadie S. wound up in a positive sober-living situation that she began during her outpatient treatment and continued afterward, which she found for herself after her high-end residential program pressured her to live in their own more expensive sober facility. After spending seven months there, Sadie said, "Sober living was the best thing I ever did. I removed myself from family stress, but I could still get my son off the bus and take him home after school." (Several people talked about how important they thought it was for sober-living facilities to be near a person's home, to ease the transition back to "real life.")

Sadie found that the sober houses in her city all basically had the same requirements, which I gathered were pretty typical: treatment ongoing or completed; attendance at three to four AA meetings a week (hers allowed attendance at alternative support groups); residents absent from the facility during the day—for instance, you had to be in treatment, at a job or looking for one; a mandatory house meeting at least weekly; random drug tests that clients had to pay for; and nightly curfews. After thirty days, residents could have one night outside the facility. Most homes allowed sober visitors in common areas with set guidelines, such as time limits and number of guests. Monthly costs, without food and including some personal supplies, ranged from $500 to $675 per month. Knowing that there can be residents from a wide range of socioeconomic backgrounds at such residences, I wondered how Sadie "rolled" with this as a woman with a professional background. She said, "The diversity is difficult, and you don't get to choose. However, most of the sober houses invite the prospective candidate for an interview. That can give a good sense of what's going on in that house. You could also ask if you can come to their house meeting prior to moving in to get a feel for what it's like."

According to William White, "The number of sober-living facilities is growing explosively. Most don't even show up on the radar of the majority of national and state policy makers or treatment experts." However, I heard from counselors in more rural areas who said that "beds" in such places are often few and far between. And depending on location, sober-living facilities range from what were described to me as little more than "flophouses" that provide "harm reduction" and safety to upscale, well-monitored homes. An example of a large national chain of inexpensive sober houses is Oxford House. Their Web site provides directories of the various houses around the country at www.oxfordhouse.org. Studies suggest that Oxford House has good outcomes; however, as an addiction counselor, Fred has found that in practice (at least in his area) their individual facilities are variable. He said, "I think sober living is a critical link in helping people in early recovery when it's done right. But I think people have to be so very careful because there are a lot of bad people out there just wanting to take advantage. The only way I know to protect yourself is to make sure that the sober-living facility is associated with a licensed or certified clinician or connected to a licensed treatment program. Every house I've seen that works that way has been a good one."

In addition to the tips above, those looking for a reputable sober-living facility should seek out one that . . .

- is one of a number of houses run by a business with a good track record in running such houses.
- is not under investigation or experiencing financial or staffing issues.
- comes recommended by someone (alumnus and/or a professional) who has knowledge of the house and its operations.
- has access to psychiatric and medical services in case of emergency.
- has staff with some training and that participates actively in setting and enforcing rules.
- is run in a reasonable fashion, not run like a prison.

- clearly describes expectations for behavior, up front and in writing, along with all rules and consequences for breaking rules.
- clearly explains financial matters—for instance, how much it costs to stay in the house whether this changes over time, how residents' income is treated (i.e., does the house take a percentage?), and whether refunds are given for early departure.
- provides residents with access to transportation, community services, and work opportunities in the surrounding community.
- belongs to professional organizations and, if so, whether that means they must adhere to certain standards.

For information about NARR, whose mission is "to create, evaluate, and improve standards and measures of quality for all levels of recovery residences," as well as to credential those who implement empirically based recovery principles and practice standards, visit their Web site at www.narronline.com. There, they offer standards for various levels of residential facilities that can begin to serve as guidelines for people seeking services.

CHAPTER TEN

GETTING WHAT YOU NEED

ADVICE FROM THE PROS AND A LOOK AT "DREAM" TREATMENT MODELS

I know we've come so far. But we've got so far to go.
—Hairspray

As I was finishing *Inside Rehab* and a friend called looking for alcohol treatment recommendations for his brother-in-crisis, it was painfully obvious that, at the end of four years, I didn't have much positive direction to offer. I found myself sending the message "Be cautious, and be skeptical." In short, almost everything I'd read, observed, and heard from experts kept arguing against the traditional rehab model—the one where people go away from daily reality for intense treatment for varying periods of time, be it thirty days or ninety days. And whether someone goes to a residential or outpatient facility, the model used is often too one size fits all and says addiction is a disease, but then doesn't treat it the way we treat other chronic illnesses. Common interventions include groups, lectures, rules, and "we-know-best" attitudes that aren't necessarily in the client's best interest and are often unsupported by science. The field is dominated by professionals who tend to be overworked, underpaid, and less than adequately trained for the complexity of the problems they face day to day. The system leads families of addicted loved ones to think they can't do much of anything aside from orchestrate sit-down "interventions" and learn about "the disease" in psychoeducational family weeks, when research studies show that other approaches are far more effective. But I knew there had to be good advice out there. So for this last chapter I decided to turn to the experienced and the expert—both people who have "been there" and movers and shakers in the field—for their wrap-up thoughts about getting what you need, given where we are.

PAUL S.'S STORY: ADVICE FROM SOMEONE WHO'S MADE THE ROUNDS

As a guy who has gone through nineteen residential rehabs since 1998—three of them more than once, so twenty-two times altogether (and that's not counting about twenty-five detoxes, four outpatient programs, and at least fifteen sober-living facilities), Paul S. offered to share his thoughts about getting what you need when looking for addiction treatment. Some of the rehabs were high-end, while others were run-of-the-mill facilities. Most were twelve-step based, but after realizing AA wasn't for him, he stayed at a few that were nontraditional. Paul estimates that more than $500,000 was spent on all of this, through a combination of insurance and private payment, some paid by him and some by his "ever-tolerant and loyal family," who never gave up on him.

While he was well aware of many shortcomings of the treatment system, Paul was amazingly unresentful about his experiences and said, "Though I wasn't in favor of each and every program, I did gain something from each one, sometimes very little and sometimes more, that has all 'built up' to leading me to the point I am now, where I am finally attacking my issues in each and every aspect of my life to complete a totally brand new future for myself in every way, shape, and form." When he and I connected, he'd just spent a month in an expensive residential treatment program that emphasized cognitive-behavioral approaches and was subsequently attending a nontraditional outpatient program and living in their sober house. He seemed the perfect person to provide advice about seeking help in the addiction treatment system that *is* rather than the one that we'd like it to be.

Paul went to his first rehab, a residential program, at the age of twenty-nine after his family confronted him about his drinking, which at that point was a daily and heavy habit. He said, "It didn't work because I had no desire to really stop. The staff didn't look into why I drank—I was told it was because I'm an alcoholic and that's what we do. Within a few days of getting out, I was drinking again." So Paul's first piece of advice was, "Only go to treatment if you truly want to change your behaviors. If you're going to appease someone else, it's a waste of time and money. If you determine that you definitely want to go, then look around at all of the options."

Paul feels that a big mistake families and individuals make is rushing into treatment, "thinking that the faster the person enters rehab, the better." He recommended, "Take time, at least a few days, if not more, and do research. You can never do enough research, both on rehabs and their methodologies, before deciding where to go. And don't fall for a pushy sales pitch. Call facilities, lots of them, and ask questions. Ask about how tailored their approaches are to each individual. If someone tells you that their approach and their approach only is what's best for everyone, I would politely thank them and move on." Realizing that geographic and financial limitations often restrict the ability to go exactly where one wants to go, Paul advised, "Research everything that's an option for you, make a list of those options, talk at length to each facility under consideration, and make a list of pros and cons of each one before you decide."

Paul's experience affirmed that the most prevalent and widely known approach available is the twelve-step approach. He said that's one reason why he wound up going to rehab so many times—despite a diligent, year-long effort to get involved, it wasn't an approach that worked for him. Nor did it work for him when he went to a non-twelve-step treatment program and then lived in a facility that required daily AA attendance and checking in with his sponsor. He stressed that you take into consideration transitional support or aftercare following the intensive treatment period to make sure that the two use approaches that are compatible.

If detox is necessary, Paul advised finding out whether the rehab will provide the services or if you need to take care of it beforehand. As also mentioned in chapter 6, Paul stressed, "The most important thing during detox is being safe medically, so it's important to research detoxes well."

Noting that many detox facilities have a full schedule for their clients, he added, "As wonderful an image as they believe they're creating for themselves, for me, the best approach was one where I was allowed to get medically cleared so that I could maximize subsequent treatment." In other words, he found that treatment activities, such as being involved in groups and lectures, during detox were not particularly helpful.

When it comes to paying for rehab, Paul found that cash-paying customers can usually negotiate the quoted rates down. In his experience, at most places, when paying privately, payment in full is expected up front—in many instances, after a set time (such as forty-eight to seventy-two hours) none of that is refundable. He recommended trying to negotiate out the "no-money-back" part of any agreement. "If you leave halfway through treatment, you should get half of your money back. But if they refuse to budge on that, be certain you're fully satisfied with the program during the time period they provide for a refund, and inform anyone else financing your treatment about this policy." Paul learned about this the hard way after agreeing to attend one particular rehab "at the last minute," where he'd been told they'd accept his insurance and then found out they didn't. When he discovered that the treatment approach was "the same old thing" and he wanted out, his family was stuck with the expense because the place had a strict no-telephone policy for clients—so he couldn't call his family to say, "Don't send the check." And by the time the family received his letter telling them not to pay, it was too late, and the money was nonrefundable.

Paul also found that clients are often told that "you may leave any time. However, you're often not informed that if you're being covered by insurance and leave before your discharge date, it's considered leaving against medical advice, or 'AMA.' If you leave AMA, the insurance company will almost always refuse to pay the bill, and you become liable for the charges."

Paul feels that "there's a lot of deception and greed in this industry. No matter what any of them claim, every private treatment center is in the business to make money. Their main goal could very well be to help people, and in a lot of cases it is, but unless a business is nonprofit and has deep-pocketed donors, and lots of them, they need to earn a profit to exist. It doesn't mean clinicians don't care about clients, because they do. But beware, as the almighty dollar usually wins out over any amount of compassion." He did say, however, that one of the rehabs he attended recommended that he "look for something more than they could offer" and that the rehab he was attending at the time of our interview was "ethical, caring, up-front and honest about all of the costs involved."

Paul also issued some warnings about the "rules of rehab": "Be sure to ask about what types of reading material you may bring, whether or not you can have your cell phone and laptop, and how much contact you may or may not have with the outside world. If you're a smoker, ask about smoking. If you like coffee, ask about caffeine. If you're anything like me and you care about these things, you'd better ask, because you could arrive and be stripped of all of them and also be removed from contact with society for the duration of your stay." Acknowledging some rehabs' belief that getting rid of "distractions" is good, Paul said. "To me, real life is full of distractions, so if you're in a protected environment and can't handle distractions, how are you ever going to be able to handle them after you finish the program you've entered? Also, many people who enter treatment have personal business to attend to, even though we're often told that it's acceptable to ignore all of that because of the sheer importance of getting into treatment. Some of us lose it all before getting effective help and changing, but why have outside things like jobs, homes, and relationships collapse if they don't have to?" He reminds rehab consumers to stand up for themselves and that it's acceptable to question things.

The bottom line, according to Paul, is "ultimately, after you've done all of your homework and laid out your options, *you'll* need to decide where you're going. A lot of people are going to chime in, saying they have 'been there' and thus they know what you ought to do. Remember, you're not exactly the same as they are, and what worked for them may not be what's best for you. In my opinion, the treatment center that listens to the client and tailors treatment to the client based on what they hear is the one that will probably be the most beneficial. This is about YOU. YOU are the most important person in this process. After all, it's your life."

DÉJÀ VU ALL OVER AGAIN

Paul S. is an expert from the "been there, done that" standpoint, whose suggestions nicely wrap up many of the practical questions, concerns, and considerations people should have in mind when looking for a drug and alcohol treatment program, be it residential or outpatient. His story also illustrates numerous problems and stories I heard that started me on the journey of writing *Inside Rehab*, and it strikes me as incredibly sad and unfair that he had to learn things the hard way—by unintentionally "doing his own research." Why would anyone wind up going to rehab more than twenty times for upward of $500,000? Why did he go to residential rehab so many times when research indicates that it's no more effective than outpatient treatment? Why did he have to go through so many programs before finding out that a big part of the problem was that the twelve steps weren't right for him? Why did he end up in continuing care that was incompatible with the treatment he'd received? In short, why did Paul have to discover on his own so many of the things *Inside Rehab* addresses?

With Paul's permission, I had the opportunity to pose these very questions, and more, by conference call to his team of therapists, all doctoral-level psychologists with addictions expertise, at the nontraditional outpatient program where, at the time of our interview, he was living in its sober home. He was also attending its outpatient program, which entailed going to ninety-minute group therapy sessions with one of these psychologists twice a week, plus two weekly one-hour individual therapy sessions. Recognizing the uniqueness of this program, and with his commitment to "get it right" with a "whole life and life balance strategy" this time, Paul relocated to be near this program and decided to approach his stay in thirty-day increments, reevaluating whether he needed more time as the process continued.

In response to my incredulity about Paul's treatment history and my question about how he might have been spared time and expense in rehab, I was informed that ongoing care with the same set of providers would have likely made a big difference for him. One of the psychologists elaborated, "Many personal problems take more than thirty days to un-fold, and it can take much longer than thirty days to build the rapport needed to work on serious issues. Although a longer residential stay is an option, that's really excessive for someone like Paul—his problems don't warrant that." Like others in this book, Paul hesitated to discuss deeper is-sues in the group settings of traditional rehabs. His program at the time of the interview afforded more opportunities for individual therapy with skilled mental health professionals who understood substance use disor-ders as well as the other issues he was facing, issues typically unaddressed or underaddressed in addiction treatment. The team explained, too, that repeating nearly identical rehab experiences multiple times "does not get to the heart of his or anyone's difficulties."

Finally, the director of this program explained that he finds that current private-insurance reimbursement rules often give individuals better resi-dential than outpatient coverage, providing people an incentive to go to residential programs, which are not organized to be part of local systems of care in the client's community. He reiterated the need to think past the thirty-day rehab model and added, "Rehabs tend to present themselves as 'solutions' rather than components of a longer process. The way most think about rehab suggests that it will be something outside clients— 'treatment'—that leads to recovery. Rather, people need a new harnessing of their *internal* resources, and this takes time and often ongoing care."

Before circling back to those with rehab experience, I next turn to ex-perts from four quite different settings, all of whom have devoted their careers to improving care for people with substance problems. They of-fered their thoughts about addiction treatment as it is, where it's headed, and how to get help when you need it.

A YALE RESEARCHER'S MISSION TO GET
SCIENCE-BASED TREATMENT TO REHAB

Dr. Kathleen Carroll of the Division of Substance Use at Yale University School of Medicine continues to work tirelessly to find new ways to get the approaches shown to increase the odds of success into the world of substance use disorder treatment. Her own research has helped to make many of these approaches available. Some of her latest efforts involve the use of computer-based interventions and training to ensure that scientifically backed practices are delivered to clients in a coherent and consistent way.

In seeking help, Dr. Carroll advised, "Like every revolution, change can spring up from all over, and one of the ways this can happen is that individuals can and should think of themselves as consumers. It's important to be a smart consumer—to remember that the most expensive treatment is by no means the most effective, to question prospective providers, to challenge insurance companies, and to demand quality and facts from the treatment system."

Dr. Carroll suggested selecting substance use treatment as you would a surgeon for a medical procedure, asking basic questions like "How do you know it works?" "What's your success rate and how do you know?" "How have you been trained in these procedures?" "What are my options?" Finally, admitting her own bias as a researcher at one of these places, she offered a good suggestion for increasing the likelihood of finding a treatment center that uses scientifically supported practices and employs clinicians knowledgeable and trained in their use, which is finding a program linked to academic medical centers that have strong treatment research programs. Her short, nonexhaustive list would include Columbia, Dartmouth, and Duke medical centers; the Harvard-affiliated programs; Johns Hopkins Medical Center; the University of California, Los Angeles; the University of California, San Francisco; the University of Pennsylvania; the University of New Mexico; the University of Washington; the Medical University of South Carolina; the Research Institute on Addictions in Buffalo, New York; Rutgers University; and Yale University Medical School. "These are essentially the 'teaching hospitals of substance use treatment.'" She said that programs affiliated with the National Institute on Drug Abuse's Clinical Trials Network (http://ww2.drugabuse.gov/ctn/index.php) and many U.S. Department of Veterans Affairs–affiliated programs are also good bets.

A VISIONARY'S QUEST TO TRANSFORM
THE ADDICTION TREATMENT SYSTEM

As former director of the Treatment and Recovery Research Division of the National Institute on Alcohol Abuse and Alcoholism (NIAAA), Dr. Mark Willenbring's focus was on alcohol use disorders, but he's had broad clinical and research experience with all addictions, including opioid addiction, as well as pain management. In addition to being dedicated to bringing science-based practices "from the lab to the trenches of treatment," Dr. Willenbring is also a compassionate clinician who's always personally worked with clients, especially those others had given up on. As I got to know him over the course of writing this book, I watched Dr. Willenbring grow increasingly antsy with rehab "as is"; and he was in the process of starting his own state-of-the-art treatment facility, ALLTYR.

However, as suggested throughout *Inside Rehab*, Dr. Willenbring envisions a very different "ideal" approach than our current model. Chapter 5 describes his work with professionals in the primary health-care system on ways to help those whose substance problems aren't severe. For those with severe disorders, he agrees with other professionals that most would benefit from care provided over years to decades, similar to that provided for diabetes or cancer. He finds that "this is a very ripe time for new ideas. Health-care clinicians are disillusioned with the time-limited rehab system, where there's only one option that doesn't change even after repeatedly showing lack of effectiveness. They want guidance on what to do next. Contrary to what many in the addiction treatment field believe, doctors and other primary care clinicians want very much to help but have pretty much been told to 'leave it to the addiction experts,' which for the most part means counselors alone, and for relatively short periods. However, patients spend much more time in primary care than they do in any treatment programs."

Dr. Willenbring's advice for people seeking addiction treatment?

- You are the customer. Ask questions and educate yourself the same way you would if you were going to have surgery or cancer treatment.

- Get a comprehensive evaluation from a professional trained to assess alcohol and other drug problems who's knowledgeable about treatment and who's not professionally or financially invested in a particular treatment program.
- Don't accept anything less than a master's degree-prepared therapist or counselor. (See chapter 4 for a discussion of credentialing of professionals.)
- If you don't like the therapist, counselor, or doctor—or you don't feel understood, accepted, and respected—get help someplace else.
- If the program doesn't routinely use medications such as naltrexone or topiramate for alcohol addiction and Suboxone or methadone for both detoxification and maintenance treatment of opioid addiction, look elsewhere.
- Rather than go through rehab over and over, which is senseless, find a professional with addictions expertise who will work with you on an ongoing or intermittent basis.
- Don't pay more for residential or "inpatient" treatment thinking the outcomes are better than in outpatient rehab because they're not. If you can't abstain without residing in a structured, sober-living facility, then by all means do so. But it doesn't need to be in an expensive rehab. (Paul said that he was aware of this, but that he "sometimes felt 'pushed' into rehab, as if it made everyone else happy to know that I was simply somewhere 'safe.'")
- Find a place that will aggressively help you with any co-occurring psychiatric and medical conditions. (Elizabeth F. learned from her experience trying to get help for her PTSD at a high-end addiction rehab, "There's no one there to advocate for you, so you have to be the squeaky wheel." She doesn't think she would have seen a psychologist after her initial visit if she hadn't pressed for special help.)
- Find help that's not time limited and engage in whatever therapy you choose (and use medication, if prescribed) for at least a year. Expect that you might relapse and have an emergency plan in place

in case you do. If it happens, stop it as soon as possible, pick your-self up and get right back on track, looking forward, not back. Noth-ing can take away every sober day you have—you don't have to "start over" after a slip or relapse. Paul S. figured this out for himself after a while and said, "I always got the feeling that since I'd started drinking again, it was back to kindergarten from twelfth grade; it was starting all over again. But every time I picked back up drinking and then stopped again, I tried to learn what I could from it. Some-times I felt as though I'd failed, but deep down knew I wasn't a fail-ure and wasn't inherently flawed, and that any work I'd done and progress I'd made before was not washed away and I was not 'back at the beginning.'"

A RESPECTED CLINICIAN'S PRINCIPLES FOR A STATE-OF-THE-ART REHAB

Early in his career, Jeffrey Foote, PhD, tried to transform rehab from the inside out when he spent nearly ten years as associate director of one of the largest addiction treatment facilities in the state of New York, where he tried to implement science-based treatment in a very traditional setting. Finally concluding that "the system as a whole was enormously difficult to make substantive, lasting changes in—even working from the inside out"—he left and, with fellow psychologist Carrie Wilkens, PhD, started the Center for Motivation and Change (CMC), a state-of-the-art outpa-tient practice that now has locations in Manhattan and White Plains, New York. That's the point at which I first met them—about twelve years ago, at a professional meeting, when they excitedly shared their ideas for a "dream" addiction treatment facility. Within five years, it was thriving.

Often, the clients who walk through their doors have not fared well at traditional treatment programs. Dr. Foote told me, "Almost every week, we hear unfortunate stories about more traditional, disease-model-based residential experiences. I experience the distinct pain these clients bring with them, not only from the struggles they're engaged in with compul-sive behaviors and substance use, but from the damage inflicted on them by the part of the treatment world that still lumps 'addicts' together in a messy, homogenous stew that says 'addiction is addiction, leave your uniqueness at the door.'" He also expressed frustration concerning the workforce in this field: "In few other fields do we place some of the most difficult and complicated patients in the health-care system with some of the least-trained folks among us."

In their effort to establish a practice that has all the pieces in place from scientific research on addiction treatment as it should be, Dr. Foote described what they accomplished as "a business with an untested business model in the heart of not the friendliest and not the least competitive city in the world, but one that's working astoundingly well." He shared the following principles, which are really guidelines for the treatment field—whether outpatient, as in Dr. Foote's programs, or inpatient—to better meet client needs:

PRINCIPLE #1   Hire highly qualified staff, pay them what their qualifications deserve, and keep them happy doing the very hard work they do. If treatment programs don't hire good folks—highly trained mental health clinicians who are eager to be trained in new treatment approaches—and pay to keep them, the system of care is constantly being gutted.

PRINCIPLE #2   Keep track of how you're doing and have it be a transparent, nonthreatening support system—not a judgmental, job-performance-related mechanism or a managed-care, pseudo-monitoring system built purely to *cut out* treatment. In CMC's case this includes a computer-tracking system developed by CMC and performed by clinicians in every session with their patients, so that not only are they tracking change in real time, but their clients are doing it as well. With this system, clients are asked to recount daily substance use and whatever else has been deemed clinically relevant to track in an ongoing way by the client and the clinician—for instance, strength of cravings, mood and anxiety, or self-harming behaviors. Dr. Foote notes that a growing body of evidence demonstrates that such tracking improves outcomes for patients and improves clinician performance.

PRINCIPLE #3   Make evidence-based treatments (EBTs) the foundation of your program, but give clients a choice in the matter. This includes cognitive-behavioral therapy and motivational approaches, as well as the non-stigmatized availability of medications, both addiction related and psychiatric.

PRINCIPLE #4   Train, supervise, and retrain staff in EBTs (a huge job). Dr. Foote added, "We know from research studies about 'therapist drift.' . . . It's 'I thought we trained that guy in CBT—what the hell is he saying to that patient?' and occurs when, over time, therapists drift away from the protocol in which they were trained. So, we need to train thoroughly (not in a one-day 'in-service'), watch what's happening over months and months (with supervision of a more senior staff member), and then require refresher training."

PRINCIPLE #5   Hire therapists who can demonstrate empathy and run an organization that backs up this value. This means treating therapists with compassion and having an organization that truly understands the difficulties of this job. Dr. Foote elaborated, "Having empathy is more than 'I've been there,' and it's not necessarily based on personal experience—it's an ability of the therapist to actually *listen* to clients and appreciate where they're coming from. Humility is important, too—we can be experts and humble at the same time."

PRINCIPLE #6   Work with families—and not just "our family worker will do some psychoeducation with you." He explained that therapists "are a bit reluctant to jump into the messy brew of family, especially if they don't have the tools." However, because families living with and interacting with clients twenty-four-seven have so much more impact on outcome than any professionals ever will, both positively or negatively, sound training in evidence-based family and couples approaches is essential.

PRINCIPLE #7   One size doesn't fit all. "If there is one thing our clients have repeatedly appreciated over the years, it's this," Dr. Foote emphasized. "We find it's important not to pigeonhole them, ask them to accept some common belief system about who they are, or follow some predetermined path of change. We don't know what will help them until we get to know them!"

PRINCIPLE #8   Address trauma. Many substance-using patients have histories of trauma and suffer accordingly. "Whether this has resulted in frank PTSD or just inordinately high levels of distress, living in their skin is a hard job," he said. "Assessing for this and training therapists in the use of therapies shown to help goes a long way toward not losing this big group of exquisitely suffering folks. It's not all about drugs."

PRINCIPLE #9   Embed treatment in life, understand substance use in the context of a person's life, and recognize the importance of helping clients develop a full life to compete with the pull of their substance use. At CMC, they often say to clients: "If using substances was like putting your hand on a hot stove, we wouldn't be having this conversation." Dr. Foote feels there's a need to stop placing so much emphasis on the pathology of addiction and understand better how clients' use of drugs and alcohol makes sense to them—then help clients see "if anything else could make more sense."

At CMC, they put into practice what Dr. Foote preaches, with staff consisting of doctoral-level clinicians, a research psychologist who manages tracking of their evaluation system, and lots of staff training and clinical supervision. They can afford this because the practice is largely client-paid, which means that they don't bill insurance companies. Since many people foot the bill for thirty-thousand-dollar residential rehab stays, I asked Dr. Foote what that amount would net them at CMC. He replied, "If you were coming for one individual session ($275) and two groups ($150 each), or if you were coming for two individual sessions a week and no groups, that would be about $2,300 per month. So you could do that for a little more than a year." He added that just under half of their clients receive a 40 percent discount, on average, which would enable someone to come for much longer. (But the typical length of treatment is about four to eight months.) And many patients do receive some out-of-network insurance reimbursement.

A FORCE BEHIND A MOVEMENT
TO HELP *SUSTAIN* RECOVERY

In a field of push and pull between experts whose research shows how rehab should be and clinicians working in the trenches of everyday addiction treatment, it became clear throughout the writing of *Inside Rehab* that William White has the rather unusual distinction of being held in high regard by both communities. Having worked in the field since 1969 and worn many hats—from "street worker" and counselor to well-traveled trainer and consultant—he's authored or coauthored more than four hundred articles, research reports, and book chapters, as well as sixteen books, including the award-winning *Slaying the Dragon: The History of Addiction Treatment and Recovery in America.* With his finger on the pulse of what's happening and about to happen in the field, his view for the future is one of optimism, having witnessed major improvements in the profession over the course of his career. He said, "Addiction treatment as it is designed today provides acute stabilization of alcohol and drug problems more safely and effectively than it has ever been achieved in history." However, he noted how slow things are to change: "If a mass conversion reaction occurred in the field's thinking today, it would still take ten to fifteen years to implement policy and practice changes in local programs across the country."

This hasn't held him back from devoting the most recent part of his career to helping bring about such a "mass conversion" in the field, working with others who recognize that it doesn't make sense for people to go through rehab only to have them return to communities that fail to support their recovery. As such, White is one of the forces behind the "recovery management" movement—an attempt to shift the emphasis of addiction treatment from one of *acute stabilization* of people in crisis to a model focused on *sustaining* recovery. He explained, "Rather than the current approach of 'admit, treat, discharge, and terminate the relationship,' the recovery management model forges a long-term partnership with clients, their families, and community support systems." Not only is he talking about adequate duration of treatment (for at least ninety days, when needed) but also actively linking people to recovery support services, such as self-help groups, alumni associations, religious organizations, ethnic and cultural resources, recovery support centers, sober-living facilities, recovery schools, and recovery job co-ops. The emphasis is on empowering clients to manage their own recoveries and moving away from authority-based relationships to ones based on mutual respect, collaboration, choices, and recognition of multiple styles of recovery.

Recovery management also includes years of after-treatment monitoring through such services as recovery checkups and ongoing peer support services or "recovery coaching," which is a role different from that of an addiction counselor or a twelve-step sponsor. White referred to a residential rehab that offered discharged clients six months of recovery coaching at a rate of $25 per session, while others use telephone or Internet coaching, as mentioned in chapter 9. Of course, this raises issues about the qualifications of people providing such services—that is, the sober coaches and mentors, recovery companions, and sober escorts who perform such services as taking clients to and from recovery meetings, having one-on-one in-home meetings, overseeing drug testing, providing sober companionship, and even live-in support. White notes, "Recovery coaching, like addiction counseling before it, is being promoted as a 'new' profession, one that seems to be a perceived zone of business growth by life coaches who previously provided intervention services for drug and alcohol problems and by addiction counselors frustrated with treatment organizations they perceived as caring more about paperwork than people work."

According to a November 2011 article at TheFix.com, sober coaches have reportedly served the likes of Lindsay Lohan, Robert Downey Jr., and Matthew Perry, and generally charge between $750 and $1,000 a day. But the article also noted that the business isn't regulated in any way. As such, White cautioned, "This new role of recovery coach is being rapidly commodified, professionalized, and commercialized, all resulting in a need for training and supervision so that people seeking recovery are not harmed in the name of help." Indeed, one couple I interviewed told me about a professional "sober companion" they hired who was supposed to stay in their home and get rid of all their drugs and related paraphernalia prior to a rehab stay. Despite having been told that he'd been in recovery for seven years, the couple went out for the evening only to come back and find "he got high on our drugs, when we were relying on him to help us get clean." To be sure, studies are needed to identify the appropriate qualifications for people working in this capacity to help bring about optimal long-term recovery outcomes for those in their care.

Given that the implementation of "recovery management" was just beginning to take hold as I was writing *Inside Rehab* and that comprehensive, professionally organized opportunities for sustaining recovery are available only in selected places, such as Philadelphia, where White has been working with colleagues to bring about change, I asked him for some practical suggestions for people who want to get on board with the recovery management concept now. He offered the following suggestions:

- Recognize that what it takes to successfully sustain recovery is different from what it takes to start recovery.
- Choose a source of treatment or recovery support that's committed to providing *sustained* contact and assistance—obviously, accessibility and affordability are important, too.
- Select a source of support that recognizes and respects multiple pathways and styles of recovery as well as the importance of personal choice in recovery initiation and maintenance.
- Combine professional treatment, self-help, and participation in other recovery support activities to increase the stability and quality of personal and family recovery.
- Locate a primary care physician or helping professional who's knowledgeable about addiction to help monitor and manage the recovery process.
- During periods of increased personal vulnerability, increase contact with professional, family, and peer supports.

As it turned out, in his many years in and out of rehab, Paul enjoyed one of his longest and most satisfying periods of sobriety for eighteen months in 2005 to 2006, when he established a scenario akin to what William White and Mark Willenbring describe. "I worked with a cognitive-behavioral outpatient therapist, kept busy, and had a purpose and more balance in my life. I also took naltrexone for twelve of those months and did SMART Recovery meetings as well. I think it also had to do with the fact that I wasn't bitter about having been forced into a rehab, since I just detoxed, got off the booze, and got back to real life. I was in an unhappy marriage, but still had things I enjoyed and pursued—like getting certified in building and repairing computers. I didn't make any money doing it, but I was enabling underprivileged kids who couldn't otherwise afford computers, to get them. I was helping people and felt good about my life as a whole. I didn't have all of the pieces in place, so it didn't last, but I was close to having a life I enjoyed. It came from within, and I believe that when we have a higher purpose in our lives, drinking and drugging becomes secondary and just detracts from achieving our goals."

———

Faces and Voices of Recovery is a national group that was inspired in part by the work of William White. It serves as a resource and advocacy group and works "to organize and mobilize the over twenty million Americans in recovery from addiction to alcohol and other drugs, our families, friends, and allies into recovery community organizations and networks."

http://www.facesandvoicesofrecovery.org/

ADVICE FROM PEOPLE WHO HAVE BEEN THERE

When I asked, "What advice do you have for others as they seek out or enter addiction treatment programs?" they shared the following words of wisdom:

- "Do your own due diligence based on recommendations from professionals and friends. But go to places first, interview the people, tour the facility, get a copy of what the program is, and find out if it's group or one-on-one." *Warren T.*

- "Find out everything about how you're going to be treated before you go somewhere, but don't just talk to the person on the phone who doesn't know the answers. Have a sit-down—with the person who is going to treat you—to find out what your treatment plan will be. Meet with the doctor who will treat you." *Brian A.*

- "Look at the program's board of directors and advisory board. Instead of 'follow the money,' follow the board. You can tell a lot based on this." *Wynn O.*

- "Research *very* carefully, asking very specific questions. Ask about what their philosophy is based on, how long they've been in business. Find out what your options are if you decide that this place isn't right for you. Fancy pictures and words are not enough—anything that sounds too good to be true just may be." *Nancy B.*

- "Get the rules—find out what you can and can't do and what they do on a daily basis." *Anna J.*

- "Find out how programs deal with each person as an individual—for instance, a sixty-five-year-old woman isn't going to do as well in a mixed-age group. They need to be with people like them." *Elizabeth F.*

- "Clearly understand the facility's approach to treatment—does it fit with your personal beliefs and values? Who are their typical clientele—are they of similar socioeconomic background, and is it likely you'll have things in common? Ask how meals and living situations work and how structured they are. Find out what type of post-treatment support they make available." *Peter C.*

- "Know who the clinicians are at the program before you get there." *Sarah J.*

- "Don't accept twelve-step just because it's the most prevalent approach if it really doesn't match your needs. But take from any program, including twelve-step, what works for you and don't feel like you have to accept all the program's mantras blindly." *Sandy B.*

- "Try everything, and don't knock it 'til you've tried it. Even though I was leery of AA, I tried it before writing it off. I think it's important to give everything a chance, because you never know where it might lead you." *Rose T.*
- "Seek out a comprehensive program that is long enough (three months to a year), has good twelve-step meetings, and [has] a clinical psychology component that includes individual psychotherapy." *Larry B.*
- "Don't just drop the kid off at treatment and breathe a sigh of relief. They're not always safe while they're there. Be involved." *Alexandria B.*
- "An ideal treatment program won't have a set amount of days, a predetermined treatment plan, or set of ideals to [help you] get better. Work with the counselor to understand what the process will be and what *your* responsibilities will be." *Jack S.*
- "Look for different types of programs and keep asking for help. Work as hard at getting well and help as you did at getting your drugs and getting high, and you will be a success." *Emily E.*
- "Don't give up—there is a treatment program for you." *Zack S.*

AT THE END OF THE TUNNEL

One of the most rewarding aspects of writing *Inside Rehab* has been my ability to follow treatment and recovery experiences over the course of years in a number of cases. It seems fitting to close with some "where-they-are-now" stories from some of these individuals. Although their experiences weren't all positive en route, I think that all of them would say that they benefited in some way—some of them in many ways—from going to rehab.

- After two short inpatient stays, two outpatient stints at the same program, and finally paying out of pocket for a residential program that treated his co-occurring alcohol use disorder and depression, Eddie F. had just landed a great new job as the book was coming to a close. He told me, "I'm proceeding with honesty and taking baby steps, not letting myself get too 'high.' I speak to groups at the rehab when I can, and that keeps me grounded. Meeting with the people in the trenches keeps me humble."

Eddie was just days away from getting his driving privileges back after a period without them and said, "This means another step toward self-respect and personal dignity. . . . I've also come to understand what the term 'higher power' means to me. Most of all it's being present in life—embracing what life has to offer, both the good and the bad."

• Anna J.'s treatment journey began in 2005, when, because of her meth addiction, she was court ordered to attend a residential rehab for two weeks. From there, it was outpatient, halfway house, outpatient, residential, and back to the outpatient program where I met her. This last time, she was also living in a structured sober home with her children— and she felt she was "ready." However, looking back, she feels that each treatment experience taught her something along the way. In mid-2012, Anna was working a full-time job, had completed her second year of college (toward her degree in drug and alcohol studies), and had purchased her own home. She said, "Life with school, kids, work, keeps me going all the time, but on occasion I'm able to get away with friends. Though I have my ups and downs, I'm able to cope and not use when life throws me a curve ball. I've maintained my sobriety since October of 2009 and do so by going to meetings, keeping in contact with my sponsor and fellow AA/ NA members, and my higher power. Most importantly, I'm honest with myself and others, regardless of what it is."

• Margaret F. doesn't think she'd be here today if she hadn't gone to the residential rehab she attended. She shared, "Actually, I probably needed both of my stays there and my two times through the outpatient program in my community afterward. Everything seemed to work together to get me one step closer to a sober and happy me." She still gets angry when she recalls her counselor's advice the second time around at the residential program to leave her husband, but overall, she says her treatment experience was positive. Margaret added, "We stuck together and through the rehab's family program and our sober network, mostly family and very close friends, we made it. Our two boys are amazing and we're closer than ever before." She doesn't attend AA, but surrounds herself with "a network of sober people," including her husband and brother, who both have many years of sobriety. And with an avid return to running, Margaret logged sixteen hundred miles in the last two years. She said, "I wake up every day refreshed and ready to face the day, but that's not to say that everything has been wonderful. My husband was out of work for two years and now is gone a lot on the road. For a while, I worked two jobs that totaled seventy hours a week. But we did what we needed to do. I couldn't have done that if I had still been using."

• Now in his midtwenties and more than three years sober, Luke G. is filled with gratitude for his experiences at both the youth program and the sober-living facility for young men he attended. He recently recalled an experience when he had seven months of sobriety under his belt, when "trekking" to the San Juan Islands with his sober housemates. "On one of the nights, I walked off to an outcropping of rocks on Orcas Island to meditate on how I got to where I was. As I sat there, and the sun began to set behind San Juan Island, I bathed in the hot orange light and looked at the water crash rhythmically into the rocks below me, over and over again. That's when I realized I had been given this—I had gotten here—by abusing alcohol and benzodiazepines. How blessed and lucky was I to be rewarded like this, for being an alcoholic? And so, almost three years later, I hold those trips we took dear to me and try to remember my friends who made it and my friends who are no longer with us." Luke said that on the one hand, he could spend the rest of his life trying to repay his debt to the professionals who helped him, but then concludes, "All I am responsible for is carrying the message and listening whenever someone has something to say." He's completed a year of grad school and stays sober by "going to AA meetings, working with alcoholics, addicts, and people in need in general, and by taking care of myself physically, spiritually, and emotionally."

• Since January of 2010, when Sadie A. made the decision to attempt sobriety, she said, "I attended four treatment programs on a continuous basis. This means I've been working on the recovery process the whole time—not simply relapsing and starting over by attending treatment again, but *enhancing my recovery with additional treatment.*" After doing well in a transitional job for people in recovery, she was granted an apprenticeship and is now being considered for a staff position. Sadie has moved from the sober-living facility back to her home to be with her young son and is trying to sort things out with her husband. She enjoys being sober and finds "every program I went to gave me something that I've been able to 'make a part of my own' for my program."

• Jackie H. stayed in touch for the three years following her stay at a well-known residential addiction facility followed by a month at a rehab that specializes in co-occurring disorders. She's pleased that she trusted her instincts and returned to the graduate program she'd begun at the outset of treatment, supported by one-on-one therapy with a psychologist who helped with her main problem, trauma. As for substances, she said, "I drink moderately with my friends on the weekends and have no desire to have more than two to three drinks on a given night. I enjoy the people I'm with much more than I enjoy any alcohol. This had always been the case, until I fell into an abusive relationship." Since rehab, Jackie did experience a brief period where she compulsively took prescription painkillers, which she said, "wasn't fun, not even for a minute." (She added, "Because of my propensity to become hooked on opiates, I now take Suboxone.") Overall, she finds, "There are so many difficult days, days when I want to crawl into bed and give up on my quest to be a human being who contributes to knowledge and science. But every time I meet one of these difficult days with a shower, a smile, and a commute to work, I feel like I've won another battle."

ACKNOWLEDGMENTS

My foremost appreciation goes to the hundreds of people—those who've sought help for their drug and alcohol problems, as well as rehab staffers—who entrusted to me their stories and confidential information. Although I wasn't able to include all of their stories, every one of them contributed to the wealth of information and research I collected for this book. In particular, the people profiled in each chapter devoted a great deal of time to answering my numerous questions. And the rehabs that so graciously allowed me to visit them showed courage and confidence in opening their doors to an author writing a book about their livelihood. I also appreciate the people, the programs, and the groups that helped me recruit interviewees for *Inside Rehab*.

I am indebted to the many researchers and clinicians who supported and reviewed my work. In particular, Tom McLellan, PhD, CEO and founder of the Treatment Research Institute (TRI) in Philadelphia, inspired me to write this book through his research on the state of treatment, along with his professional friendship, candor, and support. He and his wife, Deni Carise, PhD, currently the chief clinical officer of Phoenix House substance abuse services in New York, facilitated my visits to more "everyday" programs than those most people think of as rehab venues and welcomed me as a house guest during a hectic time when Tom McLellan was about to become President Obama's deputy drug czar. (He's since returned to TRI.)

So many other experts were available at just about any time of day (and often evening) to answer questions, offer direction, and review sections of *Inside Rehab*. First, I can't say enough about how much I learned from

Mark Willenbring, MD, former director of the Treatment and Recovery Research Division at the National Institute on Alcohol Abuse and Alcoholism (NIAAA), who was kind enough to review the corners and crevices of this book for accuracy. I was honored to have regular input from renowned researcher William Miller, PhD, Emeritus Distinguished Professor of Psychology and Psychiatry, University of New Mexico. With his infinite knowledge of the scientific literature in this field, the University of Washington's Daniel Kivlahan, PhD, sent me studies and answered my questions about almost anything. On this list, too, were Kathleen Carroll, PhD, director of psychosocial research at Yale School of Medicine's Division of Addictions and Dennis McCarty, PhD, professor and vice chair of the Department of Public Health & Preventive Medicine at Oregon Health & Science University, whose contributions were immense. John Kelly, PhD, associate director of the Center for Addiction Medicine at Massachusetts General Hospital and an associate professor at Harvard Medical School, was patient, thoughtful, and helpful with his expertise about both twelve-step programs and teen treatment. Another expert in substance use disorder in adolescents, Ken Winters, PhD, a professor at the University of Minnesota who is also affiliated with TRI, helped me from day one with this book and also reviewed the teen chapter. Last but not least in the "available night and day" category is the generous William White, MA, perhaps the most prolific writer and certainly one of the most knowledgeable on the topics of addiction, recovery, and treatment, and with whom I was most fortunate to strike up an ongoing professional relationship.

Thanks, too, to the following experts who reviewed sections of *Inside Rehab* according to their areas of expertise: Adam Brooks, PhD, a researcher at TRI; John Cacciola, PhD, an expert in the assessment of substance use disorders and co-occurring problems at TRI; Gayle Dakof, PhD, from the University of Miami Center for Treatment Research on Adolescent Drug Abuse; Deborah Dawson, PhD, a prominent researcher recently retired from the NIAAA; Barbara McCrady, PhD, director of the Center on Alcoholism, Substance Abuse, and Addictions at the University of New Mexico; Susan Godley, PhD, at Chestnut Health Systems in Bloomington, Illinois; Petros Levounis, MD, director of the Addiction Institute of New

York; Dartmouth Medical School's Mark McGovern, PhD; James McKay, PhD, director of the Center on the Continuum of Care in the Addictions at TRI; Robert Meyers, PhD, developer of Community Reinforcement and Family Training (CRAFT) and coauthor of *Get Your Loved One Sober*; Martin Nicolaus, MA, JD; Milwaukee psychologist Ned Rubin, PsyD; Richard Saitz, MD, MPH, director of the Clinical Addiction Research and Education Unit at Boston University School of Medicine; Mark Sobell, PhD, co-director of the Guided Self-Change Clinic at Florida's Nova Southeastern University; and LaVerne Hanes Stevens, PhD, owner of New Seasons Counseling, Coaching and Consulting in the Atlanta area.

Two other professionals who were tremendously helpful are Deborah Trunzo, chief of the Treatment Services Surveys Branch of the Substance Abuse and Mental Health Administration (SAMHSA), and Amanda Abraham, PhD, with the National Treatment Center Study at the University of Georgia. Both answered countless questions and even did some special data analyses for *Inside Rehab*. Several rehab staff people deserve special mention: Karen Pasternak at Caron, Christine Anderson at Hazelden, former Promises vice president Shari Corbitt, PhD, and David Sack, MD, CEO of Elements Behavioral Health, the organization that owns Promises, all endured my endless questions with patience and grace. For their help I'd also like to thank Jeffrey Foote, PhD, and Carrie Wilkens, PhD, of the Center for Motivation and Change in New York; A. Thomas Horvath, PhD, director of Practical Recovery in San Diego, California; psychologist Andrew Tatarsky, PhD, in New York; Tamara Grams of AA Alternatives in St. Paul, Minnesota; Henry Steinberger, PhD, of Madison, Wisconsin; the Seven Challenges; the Six Dimensions program in Minneapolis; and Women for Sobriety.

Next, I want to thank my family and friends for accepting the long work hours I devoted to this book. My daughter, Julia's, entire high school experience occurred while I was writing *Inside Rehab*, and I particularly appreciate her putting up with my countless days and nights at the computer. For letting me run ideas by him and taking care of math and statistics needs for the book, thanks goes to my son Wes. My other son, Ty, was great for being independent and completed college during this time. And my husband, Steve, was infinitely patient and supportive, as he's always been of my career. As for my parents, Alan and Julia Fletcher, and my mother-in-law, Ruth Keesing, there certainly are no other octogenarians who—by acting as sounding boards—know more about rehab (without having been there). Thanks to them, as well as to my sister and friend Lois McFall. I cannot write a book without thanking a special person, Larry Lindner, who is always there for me, willing to give great editorial advice, but, more important, as a friend. My friend Christine Kile also offered her ear and tremendous support for the more than four years that it took to write this book.

It almost goes without saying that I am forever grateful for the support and input of Christine Tomasino, whose role always goes way beyond that of being my literary agent. She has a true gift for helping authors shape their visions. Thanks, too, to my editorial cheerleaders at Penguin—Julie Miesionczek, in particular, for her incredibly wise ways and for being so easy to work with, and to Rick Kot for seeing the potential in this project.

A CONSUMER CHECKLIST
FOR CHECKING OUT REHABS

Following are some questions consumers can ask of rehabs, depending on which issues concern them most. More specific questions, according to topic, can be found in various chapters in *Inside Rehab*. (Some of these questions may not apply to outpatient treatment.)

- How soon do you accept people into treatment after they have an assessment and decide they want to come to your program?
- Do you offer inpatient or outpatient treatment—or both?
- What is your overall program philosophy? Some specific questions you might ask include:
  - Do you work more from a disease model or from a cognitive-behavioral standpoint?
  - Is your program based on the twelve steps, and, if so, what does that mean?
- Are clients required to attend twelve-step meetings off-site? If so, how often? Do you hold twelve-step meetings on-site? If so, is attendance required and how often?
- Do you expose clients to or allow them to attend meetings of alternatives to twelve-step groups such as SMART Recovery or Women for Sobriety?
- How are alcohol and drug problems evaluated when a person first arrives—what assessment tools do you use to determine the severity of the substance use disorder, whether or not rehab is appropriate, and, if it is, where clients should be placed?

- Do you offer detox? If so, what determines whether a new client has to go through it and what will it entail?
- When clients arrive, are their belongings searched and are their medications confiscated?
- How long is your program? Or does your program last indefinitely?
- Describe your program's use of the following approaches/strategies:
  — Cognitive-behavioral approaches
  — Motivational enhancement
  — Couples and/or family therapy
  — Contingency management
- What is your staff-to-client ratio?
- How much client time is spent in group counseling?
- How much client time is spent in individual counseling?
- What are the credentials/training of the people who serve as primary counselors?
- Is any of the counseling done by interns or students in training?
- What are the credentials/training of the professionals who administer and supervise your clinical program?
- If medical care is needed, can you provide it? What medical professionals are on staff?
- Do you have any mental health professionals on staff? If so, what are their disciplines (e.g., licensed psychologists or social workers) and the circumstances under which they are available to patients?
- What percentage of the staff consists of recovered people?
- Describe your use of any medications that help people overcome addictions. Do you send people home on these medications?
- Are men and women treated separately for all or part of their time? Is there any gender-specific programming?
- What happens if a patient has a slip or relapse while in the program?
- How do you prepare clients for the possibility of a slip or relapse after they leave the program?
- Do you have a program for people who have been through rehab but then relapse? If so, do they have to start all over again, or is there a separate program for them?

- What proportion of your clients complete your program?
- How do you help people with aftercare or continuing care? If you have such a program, is there an additional fee to participate in it?
- Do you have a "money back" policy for any circumstances?
- How do you monitor the quality and success of your program? Please provide any statistics that are available.
- What percentage of your clients are court ordered to be in your program? What is the percentage who attend voluntarily?
- May I talk with some program graduates?
- What is your smoking policy? If it's not allowed, how do you help smokers manage?
- What is your policy on client drug testing—how often is it conducted and what are the circumstances under which it is carried out?
- What are your house rules—for instance, regarding contact with the outside world, reading material, computer and Internet access, interaction with the opposite sex, food restrictions (such as caffeine), and requirements for doing chores?

SELECTED REFERENCES

Abraham, A., H. Knudsen, and P. Roman, "National Treatment Center Study Summary Report," Athens, GA: University of Georgia, 2010.

Arria, A. and A. Mericle, "Key Elements of Addiction Treatment Effectiveness for Adult Populations: Final Report N01-DA-7-1132," Philadelphia: Treatment Research Institute, 2010.

Atkins, R. and J. Hawdon, "Religiosity and Participation in Mutual-Aid Support Groups for Addiction," *Journal of Substance Abuse Treatment* 33, no. 3 (2007): 321–31.

Brannigan, R., B. Schackman, M. Falco, and R. Millman, "The Quality of Highly Regarded Adolescent Substance Abuse Treatment Programs: Results of an In-Depth National Survey," *Archives of Pediatric and Adolescent Medicine* 158, no. 9 (2004): 904–9.

Calabria, B., L. Degenhardt, C. Briegleb, T. Vos, W. Hall, M. Lynskey, B. Callaghan, U. Rana, and J. McLaren, "Systematic Review of Prospective Studies Investigating 'Remission' from Amphetamine, Cannabis, Cocaine or Opioid Dependence," *Addictive Behaviors* 35, no. 8 (2010): 741–49.

Chi, F., L. Kaskutas, S. Sterling, C. Campbell, and C. Weisner, "Twelve-Step Affiliation and 3-year Substance Use Outcomes Among Adolescents: Social Support and Religious Service Attendance as Potential Mediators," *Addiction* 104, no. 6 (2009): 927–39.

Chorpita, B., E. Daleiden, C. Ebesutani, J. Young, K. Becker, B. Nakamura, L. Phillips, A. Ward, R. Lynch, L. Trent, R. Smith, K. Okamura, and N. Starace, "Evidence-Based Treatments for Children and Adolescents: An Updated Review of Indicators of Efficacy and Effectiveness," *Clinical Psychology: Science and Practice* 18, no. 2 (2011): 154–72.

Clark, D., "Review: The Natural History of Adolescent Alcohol Use Disorders," *Addiction* 99 (Suppl. 2) (2004): 5-22.

Cohen, E., R. Feinn, A. Arias, and H. Kranzler, "Alcohol Treatment Utilization: Findings from the National Epidemiologic Survey on Alcohol and Related Conditions," *Drug and Alcohol Dependence* 86, no. 2–3 (2007): 214–21.

Collins, E., H. Kleber, R. Whittington, and N. Heitler, "Anesthesia-Assisted Vs Buprenorphine- or Clonidine-Assisted Heroin Detoxification and Naltrexone Induction: A Randomized Trial," *Journal of the American Medical Association* 294, no.8 (2005): 903–13.

Dawson, D., R. Goldstein, and B. Grant, "Rates and Correlates of Relapse among Individuals in Remission from DSM-IV Alcohol Dependence: A 3-Year Follow-up," *Alcoholism: Clinical and Experimental Research* 31, no. 12 (2007): 2036–45.

Dawson, D., B. Grant, F. Stinson, and P. Chou, "Estimating the Effect of Help-Seeking on Achieving Recovery from Alcohol Dependence," *Addiction* 101, no. 6 (2006): 824–34.

Dawson, D., B. Grant, F. Stinson, P. Chou, B. Huang, and W. Ruan, "Recovery from DSM-IV Alcohol Dependence: United States, 2001–2002," *Addiction* 100, no. 3 (2005): 281–92.

Dennis, M., S. Godley, G. Diamond, F. Tims, T. Babor, J. Donaldson, H. Liddle et al., "The Cannabis Youth Treatment (CYT) Study: Main Findings from Two Randomized Trials," *Journal of Substance Abuse Treatment* 27, no. 3 (2004): 197–213.

Ducharme, L., H. Mello, P. Roman, H. Knudsen, and A. Johnson, "Service Delivery in Substance Abuse Treatment: Reexamining 'Comprehensive' Care," *Journal of Behavioral Health Services & Research* 34, no. 2 (2007): 121–36.

Ebner, M. and W. Armstrong, "Inside Scientology's Rehab Racket," *The Fix* (March 27, 2011). Posted at http://www.thefix.com/content/narconons-big-con.

Furr-Holden, D., R. Voas, J. Lacey, E. Romano, and K. Jones, "The Prevalence of Alcohol Use Disorders Among Night-Time Weekend Drivers," *Addiction* 106, no. 7 (2011): 1251–60.

Galanter, M. and H. Kleber, *The American Psychiatric Publishing Textbook of Substance Abuse Treatment,* 4th ed. Arlington, VA: American Psychiatric Publishing, 2008.

Gans, J., M. Falco, B. Schackman, and K. Winters, "An In-Depth Survey of the Screening and Assessment Practices of Highly Regarded Adolescent Substance Abuse Treatment Programs," *Journal of Child and Adolescent Substance Abuse* 19, no. (1) (2010): 33–47.

Gerend, M. "How Message Framing Can Inform Clinical Practice," *Clinician's Research Digest Supplemental Bulletin 43* (November 2010): 1–2.

Greenfield, S., S. Black, K. Lawson, and K. Brady, "Substance Abuse in Women," *Psychiatric Clinics of North America* 33, no. 2 (2010): 339–55.

Greenfield, S., E. Trucco, R. McHugh, M. Lincoln, and R. Gallop, "The Women's Recovery Group Study: A Stage I Trial of Women-Focused Group Therapy for Substance Use Disorders versus Mixed-Gender Group Drug Counseling," *Drug and Alcohol Dependence* 90 (2007): 39–47.

Hasin, D., F. Stinson, E. Ogburn, and B. Grant, "Prevalence, Correlates, Disability, and Comorbidity of DSM-IV Alcohol Abuse and Dependence in the United States: Results from the National Epidemiologic Survey on Alcohol and Related Conditions," *Archives of General Psychiatry* 64, no. 7 (2007): 830–42.

Hester, R., D. Squires, and H. Delaney, "The Computer-Based Drinker's Check-Up: 12-Month Outcomes of a Controlled Clinical Trial with Problem Drinkers," *Journal of Substance Abuse Treatment* 28, no. 2 (2005): 159–69.

Humphreys, K., K. Weingardt, D. Horst, A. Joshi, and J. Finney, "Prevalence and Predictors of Research Participant Eligibility Criteria in Alcohol Treatment Outcome Studies, 1970–98," *Addiction* 100, no. 9 (2005): 1249–57.

Humphreys, K., S. Wing, D. McCarty, J. Chappel, L. Gallant, B. Haberle, T. Horvath et al., "Self-Help Organizations for Alcohol and Drug Problems: Toward Evidence-Based Practice and Policy," *Journal of Substance Abuse Treatment* 26, no. 3 (2004): 151–58.

Hussaarts, P., G. Hendrik, H. Roozen, R. Meyers, B. van de Wetering, and B. McCrady, "Problem Areas Reported by Substance Abusing Individuals and Their Concerned Significant Others," *American Journal on Addictions* 21, no. 1 (2012): 38–46.

Imel, Z., B. Wampold, S. Miller, and R. Fleming, "Distinctions without a Difference: Direct Comparisons of Psychotherapies for Alcohol Use Disorders," *Psychology of Addictive Behaviors* 22, no. 4 (2008): 533–43.

Kelly, J., S. Brown, A. Abrantes, C. Kahler, and M. Myers, "Social Recovery Model: An 8-Year Investigation of Adolescent 12-Step Group Involvement Following Inpatient Treatment," *Alcoholism: Clinical and Experimental Research* 32, no. 8 (2008): 1–11.

Kelly, J., S. Dow, J. Yeterian, and M. Meyers, "How Safe Are Adolescents at Alcoholics Anonymous and Narcotics Anonymous Meetings? A Prospective Investigation with Outpatient Youth," *Journal of Substance Abuse Treatment* 40, no. 4 (2011): 419–25.

Kelly, J., M. Magill, and R. Stout, "How Do People Recover from Alcohol Dependence? A Systematic Review of the Research on Mechanisms of Behavior Change in Alcoholics Anonymous," *Addiction Research and Theory* 17, no. 3 (2009): 236–59.

Kelly, J. and J. Yeterian, "The Role of Mutual-Help Groups in Extending the Framework of Treatment," *Alcohol Research & Health* 33, no. 4 (2011): 350–55.

Kimberly, J. and T. McLellan, "The Business of Addiction Treatment: A Research Agenda," *Journal of Substance Abuse Treatment* 31, no. 3 (2006): 213–19.

Klingemann, H., M. Sobell, and L. Sobell, "Continuities and Changes in Self-Change Research," *Addiction* 105, no. 9 (2010): 1510–18.

"Know Your Rights: Rights for Individuals on Medication-Assisted Treatment," HHS Publication No. (SMA) 09-449. Rockville, MD: Center for Substance Abuse Treatment, Substance Abuse and Mental Health Services Administration, 2009. (Authored by center attorneys.)

Knudsen, H., "Adolescent-Only Substance Abuse Treatment: Availability and Adoption of Components of Quality," *Journal of Substance Abuse Treatment* 36, no. 2 (2009): 195–204.

Knudsen, H., P. Roman, and C. Oser, "Facilitating Factors and Barriers to the Use of Medications in Publicly Funded Addiction Treatment Organizations," *Journal of Addiction Medicine* 4, no. 2 (2010): 99–107.

LaVerne, H. and M. White, "Effective Treatment Planning for Substance Abuse and Related Disorders," *Counselor* 9, no. 5 (2008): 10–18.

Lopez-Quintero, C., J. Pérez de los Cobos, D. Hasin, M. Okuda, S. Wang, B. Grant, and C. Blanco, "Probability and Predictors of Transition from First Use to Dependence on Nicotine, Alcohol, Cannabis, and Cocaine: Results of the National Epidemiologic Survey on Alcohol and Related Conditions (NESARC)," *Drug and Alcohol Dependence* 115, nos. 1 and 2 (2011): 120–30.

Mark, T., K. Levit, R. Vandivort-Warren, J. Buck, and R. Coffey, "Changes in U.S. Spending on Mental Health and Substance Abuse Treatment, 1986–2005, and Implications for Policy," *Health Affairs* 30, no. 2 (2011): 284–92.

Mark, T., X. Song, R. Vandivort, S. Duffy, J. Butler, R. Coffey, and V. Schabert, "Characterizing Substance Abuse Programs That Treat Adolescents," *Journal of Substance Abuse Treatment* 31, no. 1 (2006): 59–65.

Martino, S., S. Ball, C. Nich, T. Frankforter, and K. Carroll, "Correspondence of Motivational Enhancement Treatment Integrity Ratings Among Therapists, Supervisors and Observers," *Psychotherapy Research* 19, no. 2 (2009): 181–93.

McCarty, D., J. McConnell, and L. Schmidt, "Priorities for Policy Research on Treatments for Alcohol and Drug Use Disorders," *Journal of Substance Abuse Treatment* 39, no. 2 (2010): 87–95.

McCarty, D. and T. Rieckmann, "The Treatment System for Alcohol and Drug Disorders." In *Mental Health Services: A Public Health Perspective,* 3rd ed. Bruce Levin, Kevin Hennessy, and John Petrila, eds. New York: Oxford University Press, 2010, pp. 284–97.

McKay, J. and S. Hiller-Sturmhöfel, "Treating Alcoholism as a Chronic Disease: Approaches to Long-Term Continuing Care," *Alcohol Research and Health* 33, no. 4 (2011): 356–70.

Meyers, R., H. Rosen, and J. Smith, "The Community Reinforcement Approach: An Update of the Evidence," *Alcohol Research & Health* 33, no. 4 (2011): 380–88.

Miller, W., A. Forcehimes, and A. Zweben, *Treating Addiction: A Guide for Professionals.* New York: Guilford, 2011.

Miller W., J. Sorensen, J. Selzer, and G. Brigham, "Disseminating Evidence-Based Practices in Substance Abuse Treatment: A Review with Suggestions," *Journal of Substance Abuse Treatment* 31, no. 1 (2006): 25–39.

Miller, W. and W. White, "Confrontation in Addiction Treatment," *Counselor* (August 2007): 12–30.

Miller, W., J. Zweben, and W. Johnson, "Evidence-Based Treatment: Why, What, Where, When and How?" *Journal of Substance Abuse Treatment* 29, no. 4 (2005): 267–76.

Moos, R. and B. Moos, "Paths of Entry Into Alcoholics Anonymous: Consequences for Participation and Remission," *Alcoholism: Clinical and Experimental Research* 29, no. 10 (2005): 1858–68.

Morgenstern, J. and J. McKay, "Rethinking the Paradigms That Inform Behavioral Treatment Research for Substance Use Disorders," *Addiction* 102, no. 9 (2007): 1377–89.

National Center on Addiction and Substance Abuse at Columbia University (CASA Columbia). *Addiction Medicine: Closing the Gap Between Science and Practice.* New York: Author, 2012.

National Council on Alcoholism and Drug Dependence, "NCADD's Consumer Guide to Medication-Assisted Recovery," posted at http://www.ncadd.org/index.php/get-help/medication-a-recovery/157-ncadds-consumer-guide-to-medication-assisted-recovery.

National Institute on Drug Abuse, "Principles of Addiction Treatment: A Research-Based Guide," 2nd ed. NIH Publication Number: 09-4180, Bethesda, MD: National Institutes of Health, April 2009.

Nicolaus, M., "Choice of Support Groups: It's the Law!" *Counselor Magazine* 10, no. 5 (2009): 40–47.

Oleson, W., *My Daughter Is Bulimic and the Cat Has Hairballs: The 95-Pound Addict in the Room.* Xlibris, 2009.

Olmstead, T. and J. Sindelar, "To What Extent Are Key Services Offered in Treatment Programs for Special Populations?" *Journal of Substance Abuse Treatment* 27, no. 1 (2004): 9–15.

O'Malley, S. and P. O'Connor, "Medications for Unhealthy Alcohol Use," *Alcohol Research and Health* 33, no. 4 (2011): 300–311.

Parran, T., R. McCormick, and J. Cacciola, "Assessment." In *Principles of Addiction Medicine*, 4th ed. Richard Ries, David Fiellin, Shannon Miler, and Richard Saitz, eds. Philadelphia: Lippincott, Williams & Wilkins, 2009, pp. 305–11.

Pescosolido, B., J. Martin, S. Long, T. Medina, J. Phelan, and B. Link," 'A Disease Like Any Other'? A Decade of Change in Public Reactions to Schizophrenia, Depression, and Alcohol Dependence," *American Journal of Psychiatry* 167, no. 11 (2010): 1321–30.

Santa Ana, E., S. Martino, S. Ball, C. Nich, T. Frankforter, and K. Carroll, "What Is Usual About 'Treatment as Usual'? Data from Two Multisite Effectiveness Trials," *Journal of Substance Abuse Treatment* 35, no. 4 (2008): 369–79.

Schenker, M., *A Clinician's Guide to 12-Step Recovery.* New York: Norton, 2009.

Sellman, D., "The 10 Most Important Things Known About Addiction," *Addiction* 105, no. 1 (2009): 6–13.

Sterling, S., F. Chi, and A. Hinman, "Integrating Care for People with Co-Occurring Alcohol and Other Drug, Medical, and Mental Health Conditions," *Alcohol Research and Health* 33, no. 4 (2011): 338–49.

Stevens, L. and M. Dennis, "Clinical Assessment." In *Lowinson and Ruiz's Substance Abuse: A Comprehensive Textbook*, 5th ed. Pedro Ruiz and Eric Strain, eds. Philadelphia: Lippincott, Williams & Wilkins, 2011, pp. 107–16.

Stinchfield, R. and P. Owen, "Hazelden's Model of Treatment and Its Outcome," *Addictive Behaviors* 23, no. 5 (1998): 669–83.

Substance Abuse and Mental Health Services Administration, *Results from the 2010 National Survey on Drug Use and Health: Mental Health Findings*, NSDUH Series H-42, HHS Publication No. (SMA) 11-4667. Rockville, MD, 2012.

———. *National Survey of Substance Abuse Treatment Services (N-SSATS): 2010. Data on Substance Abuse Treatment Facilities*, DASIS Series: S-59, HHS Publication No. (SMA) 11-4665. Rockville, MD, 2011.

Substance Abuse and Mental Health Services Administration, Center for Behavioral Health Statistics and Quality. *Treatment Episode Data Set (TEDS): 2000-2010. National Admissions to Substance Abuse Treatment Services*. DASIS Series S-61, HHS Publication No. (SMA) 12-4671, Rockville, MD, 2012.

Substance Abuse and Mental Health Services Administration, Center for Behavioral Health Statistics and Quality. *Treatment Episode Data Set (TEDS) 2008: Discharges from Substance Abuse Treatment Services*, DASIS Series: S-56, DHHS Publication No. (SMA) 11-4628. Rockville, MD, 2010.

Substance Abuse and Mental Health Services Administration, Center for Substance Abuse Treatment. *Substance Abuse Treatment: Addressing the Specific Needs of Women*, Treatment Improvement Protocol (TIP) Series 51. HHS Publication No. (SMA) 09-446. Rockville, MD, 2009.

Substance Abuse and Mental Health Services Administration, Office of Applied Studies. *Results from the 2010 National Survey on Drug Use and Health: Summary of National Findings*, NSDUH Series H-41, HHS Publication No. (SMA) 11-4658. Rockville, MD, 2011.

Sussman, S., "A Review of Alcoholics Anonymous/Narcotics Anonymous Programs for Teens," *Evaluation and the Health Professions* 33, no. 1 (2010): 26–55.

Tanner-Smith, E., S. Wilson, and M. Lipsey, "The Comparative Effectiveness of Outpatient Treatment for Adolescent Substance Abuse: A Meta-Analysis," *Journal of Substance Abuse Treatment* (2012), forthcoming.

Tucker, J. and C. Simpson, "The Recovery Spectrum: From Self-Change to Seeking Treatment," *Alcohol Research and Health* 33, no. 4 (2011): 371–76.

United States Department of Transportation, Office of Drug and Alcohol Policy and Compliance, "The Substance Abuse Professional Guidelines," (2009). Available as a PDF file.

United States Department of Veterans Affairs, Department of Defense, "VA/DoD Clinical Practice Guideline for Management of Substance Use Disorders (SUD)," (2009). Available as a PDF file.

Weiss, R., W. Jaffee, V. de Menil, and C. Cogley, "Group Therapy for Substance Use Disorders: What Do We Know?" *Harvard Review of Psychiatry* 12, no. 6 (2004): 339–50.

Weiss, R., J. Potter, D. Fiellin, M. Byrne, H. Connery, W. Dickinson, J. Gardin et al., "Adjunctive Counseling During Brief and Extended Buprenorphine-Naloxone Treatment for Prescription Opioid Dependence: A 2-Phase Randomized Controlled Trial," *Archives of General Psychiatry* 68, no. 12 (2011): 1238–46.

White, W., "Addiction Disease Concept: Advocates and Critics," *Counselor* 2, no. 1 (2001): 42–46.

White, W. "The Future of AA, NA and Other Recovery Mutual Aid Organizations," *Counselor* 11, no. 2 (2010): 10–19.

———. "Interviews with Pioneers: Robert L. DuPont, MD," *Counselor* 11, no. 1 (2010): 38–48.

White, W. *Peer-Based Addiction Recovery Support: History, Theory, Practice, and Scientific Evaluation*. Chicago: Great Lakes Addiction Technology Transfer Center and Philadelphia Department of Behavioral Health and Mental Retardation Services, 2009.

White, W. *Recovery/Remission from Substance Use Disorders: An Analysis of Reported Outcomes in 415 Scientific Studies, 1868–2011*. Chicago: Great Lakes Addiction Technology Transfer Center; Philadelphia: Department of Behavioral Health and Intellectual Disability Services and Northeast Addiction Technology Transfer Center, 2012.

White, W. and S. Ali, "Lapse and Relapse: Is It Time for New Language?" April 2010. Posted at http://www.facesandvoicesofrecovery.org.

White, W. and W. Cloud, "Recovery Capital: A Primer for Addictions Professionals," *Counselor* 95, no. 5 (2008): 22–27.

White, W. and W. Miller, "Confrontation in Addiction Treatment," *Counselor* 8, no. 4 (2007): 12–29.

Wild, T., "Social Control and Coercion in Addiction Treatment: Towards Evidence-Based Policy and Practice," *Addiction* 101, no. 1 (2006): 40–49.

Willenbring, M. "Treatment of Heavy Drinking and Alcohol Use Disorders." In *Principles of Addiction Medicine*, 4th ed. Richard Ries, David Fiellin, Shannon Miller, and Richard Saitz, eds. Philadelphia: Lippincott, Williams & Wilkins, 2009, pp. 335–48.

Winters, K., A. Botzet, and T. Fahnhorst, "Advancements in Adolescent Substance Abuse Treatment," *Current Psychiatry Reports* 13, no. 5 (2011): 416–21.

World Health Organization, *Guidelines for the Psychosocially Assisted Pharmacological Treatment of Opioid Dependence*. Geneva, 2009.

INDEX